GETTING IT WRONG

Fragments from a Cyprus Diary 1964

Martin Packard

GETTING IT WRONG

Fragments from a Cyprus Diary 1964

AuthorHouse™ UK Ltd.
500 Avebury Boulevard
Central Milton Keynes, MK9 2BE
www.authorhouse.co.uk
Phone: 08001974150

First published by AuthorHouse August 5, 2008

ISBN: 978-1-4343-7065-5 (sc)
ISBN: 978-1-4343-7057-0 (e)

Library of Congress Control Number: 2008901357

Printed in the United States of America
Bloomington, Indiana

This book is printed on acid-free paper.

CONTENTS

CONTENTS

LIST OF ILLUSTRATIONS

The contribution of photographs by Christopher Meynell, Mike Gilmore and Lady Davina Gibbs is acknowledged with special thanks.

MAPS

Map and sections on pages X-XVI are Crown copyright material reproduced with the permission of the Controller, HMSO.

The map used is that issued in January 1964 to Joint Patrol officers.

Throughout the text I have used the names that appear on this map. These were the names generally in use in 1964.

Before 1974 most towns and villages had the same name in Greek and Turkish, though they often were pronounced differently. A different name was sometimes used by the British, perhaps deriving from the Lusignan or another prior occupation. (Thus Lefkosia in Greek, Lefkosha in Turkish, Nicosia in English.) Since 1974 most villages and towns in areas controlled by the Turkish army have been given new, wholly Turkish, names.

The sections here reproduced are from my own 1964 map and show annotations, made by me, to indicate population distribution and movements.

Master Map 1 (M1)

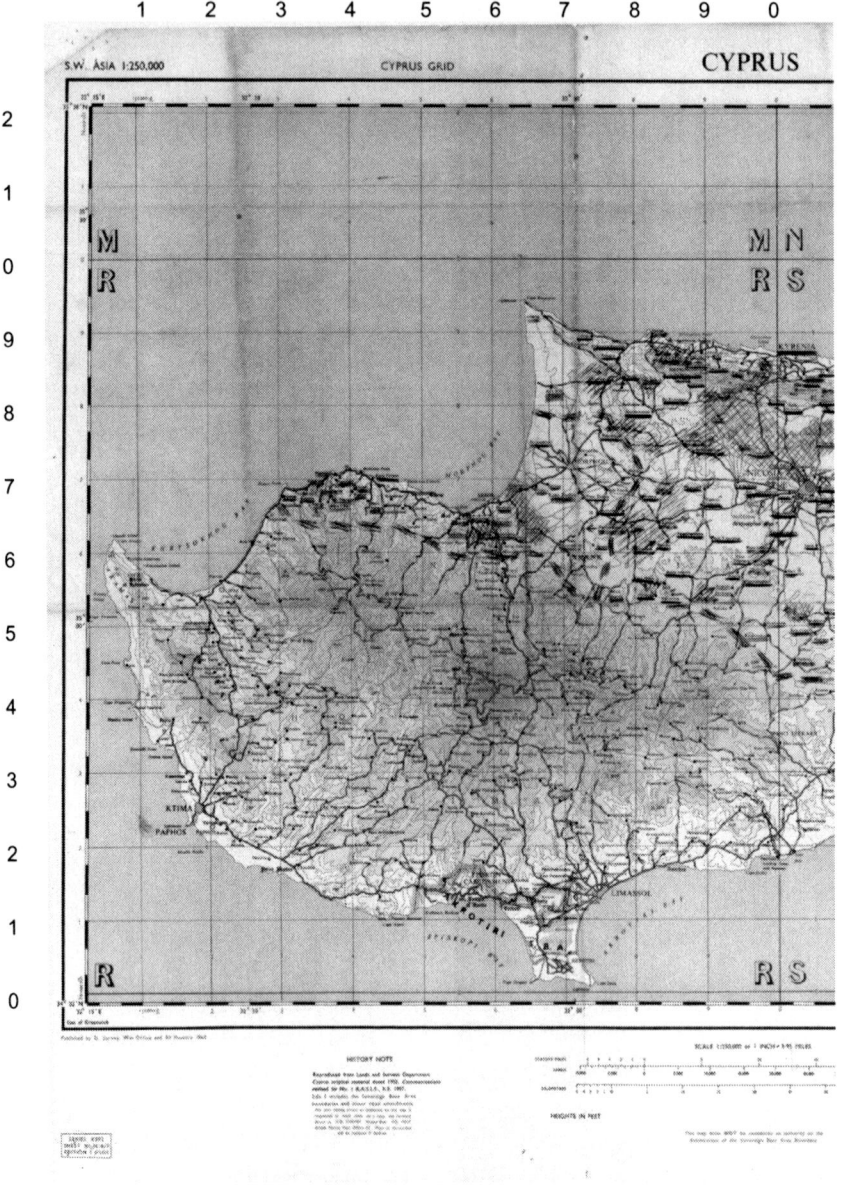

Master Map 2 (M2)

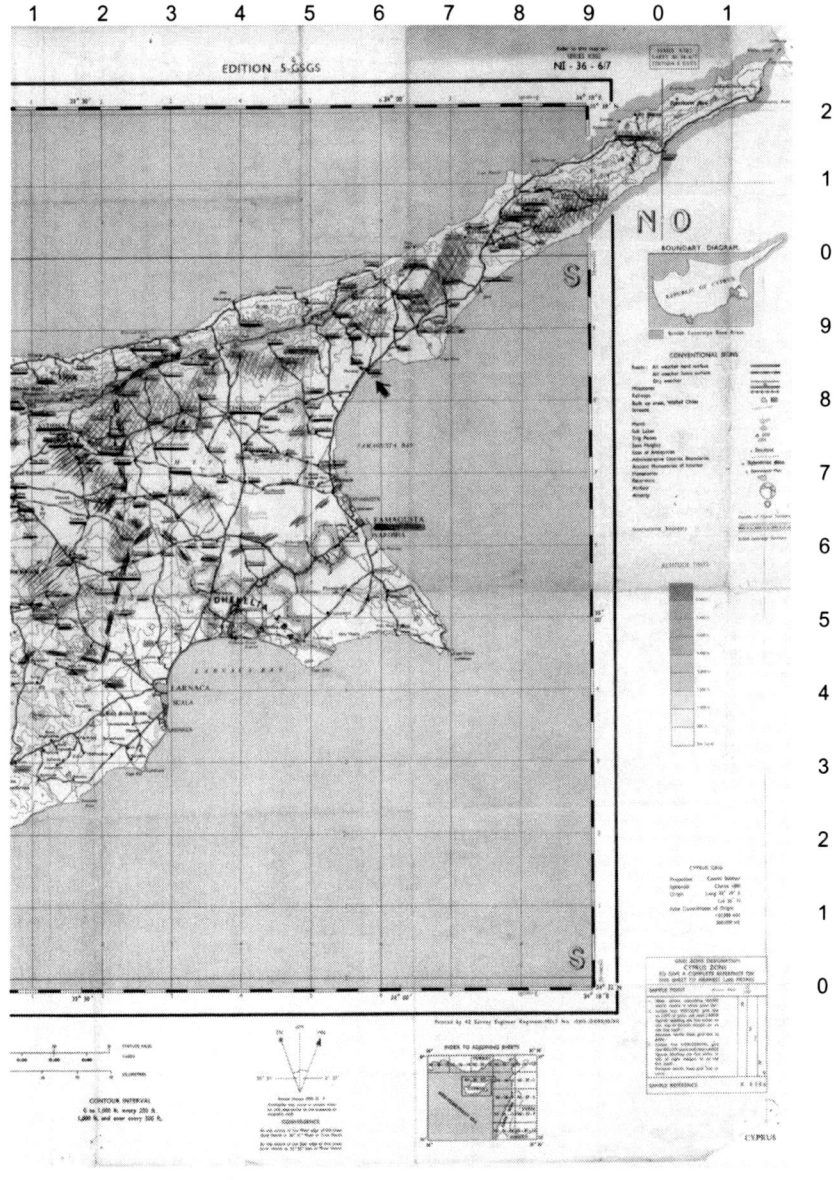

MAPS

Map sections as shown below and following four pages.

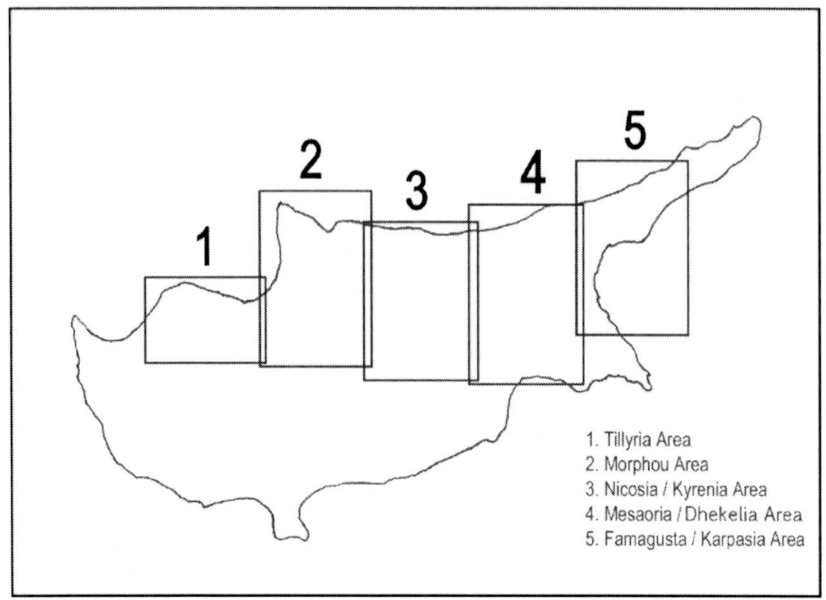

1. Tillyria Area
2. Morphou Area
3. Nicosia / Kyrenia Area
4. Mesaoria / Dhekelia Area
5. Famagusta / Karpasia Area

Map 1.   Tillyria Area.

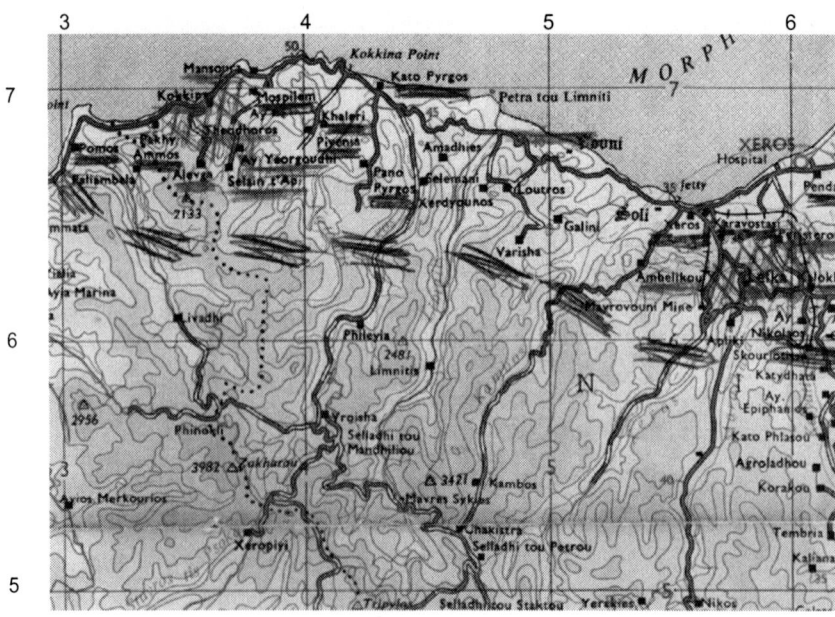

Map 2.   Morphou Area.

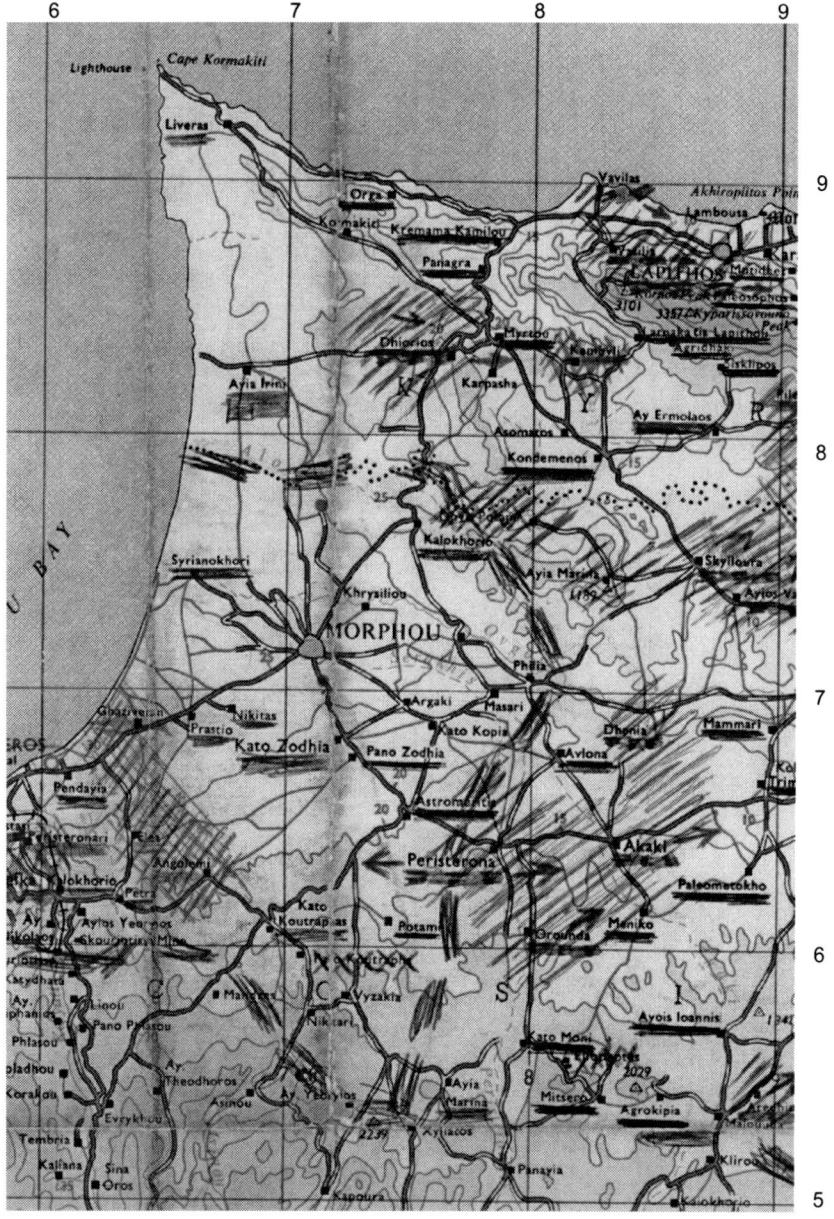

Map 3.   Nicosia / Kyrenia Area.

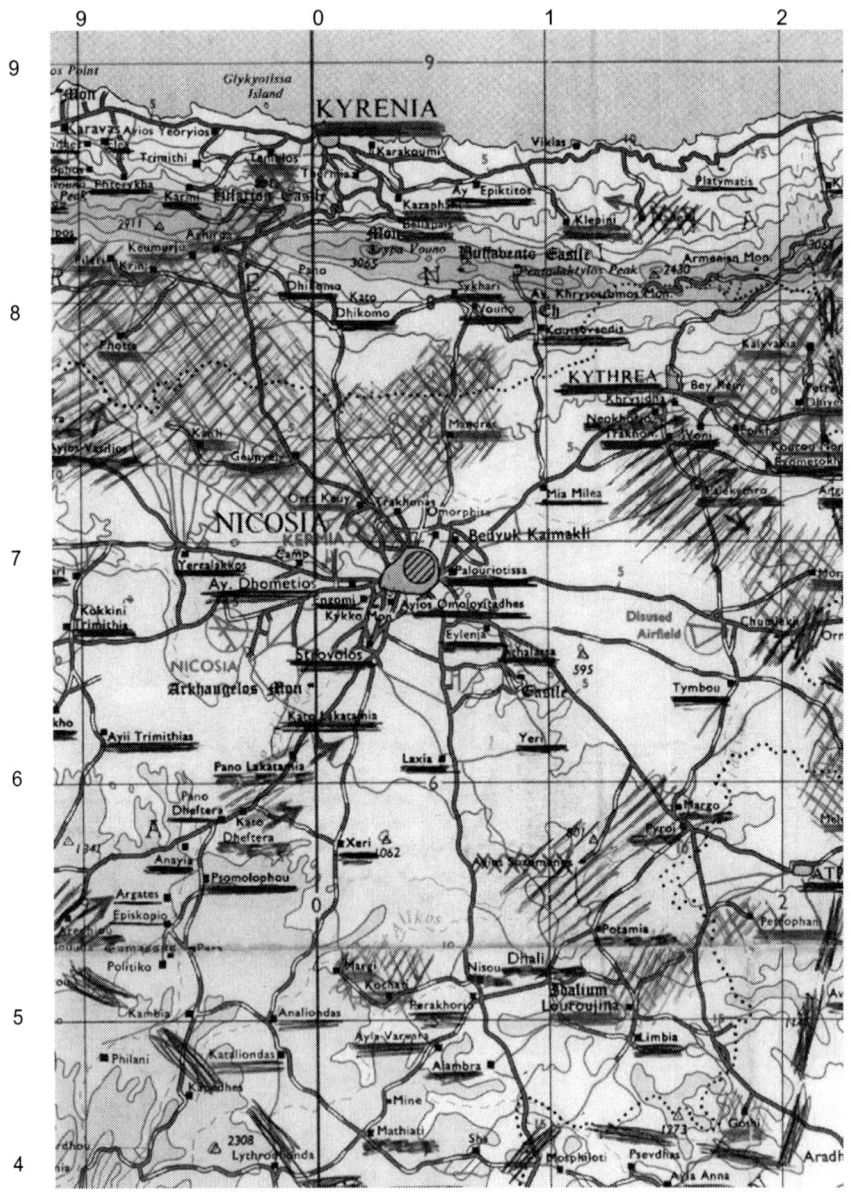

Map 4.   Mesaoria / Dhekelia Area.

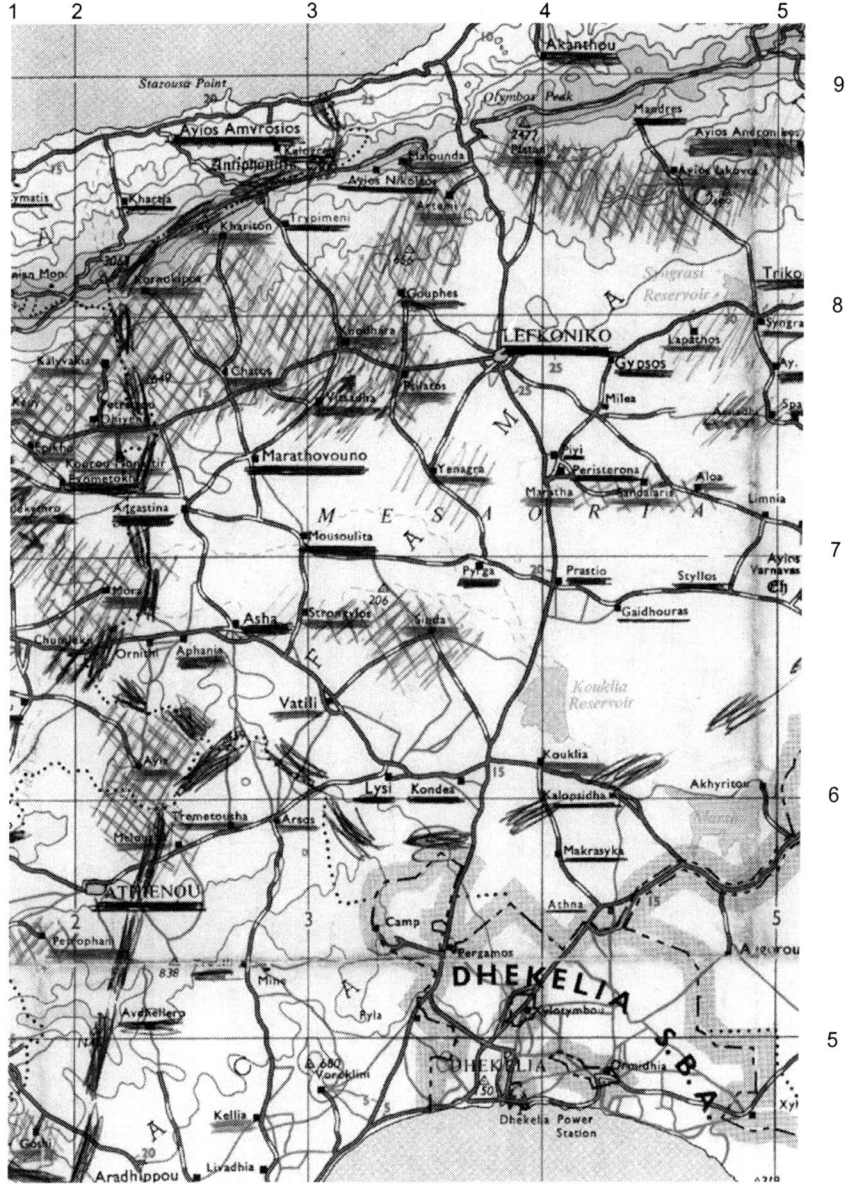

MAPS

Map 5.   Famagusta / Karpasia Area.

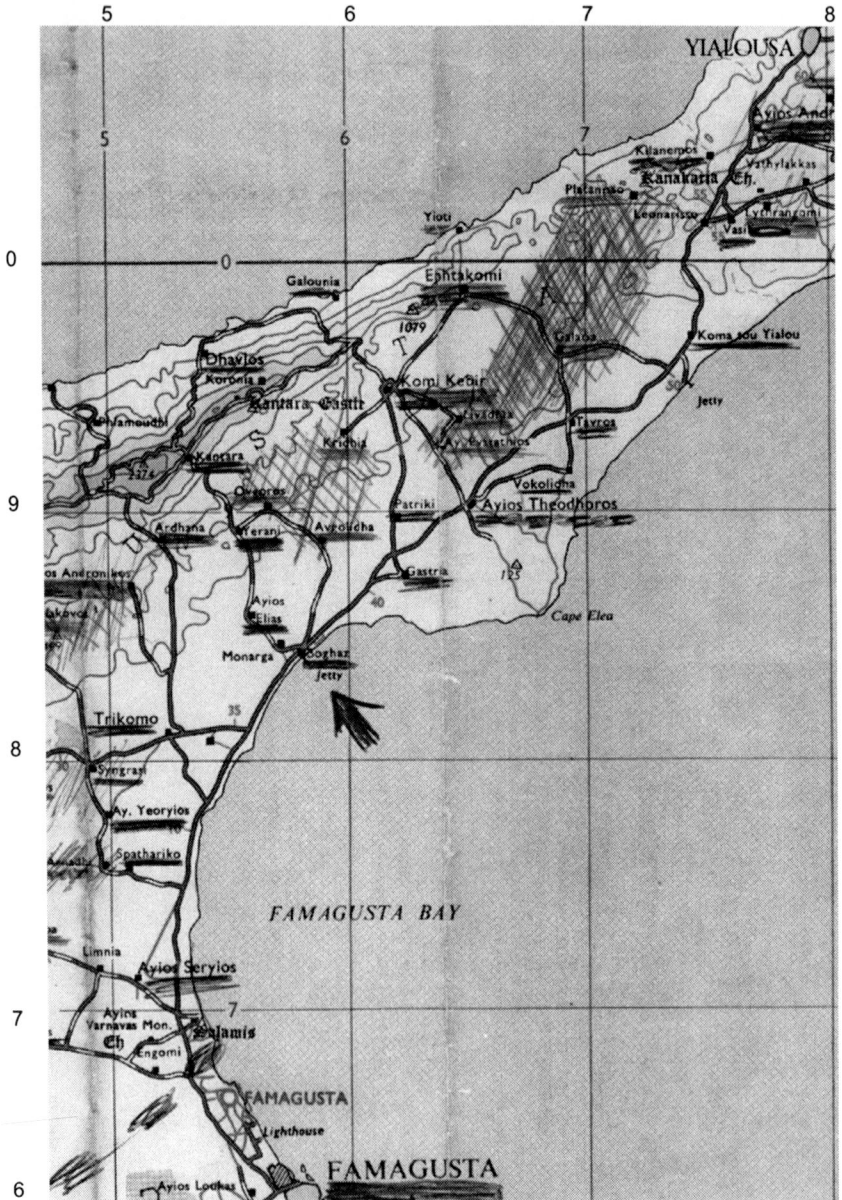

INDEX TO TOWNS AND VILLAGES

FOREWORD

by Peter Murtagh

Those of us fortunate enough to count Martin Packard as a friend know him to be an extraordinary man. He can be intense and infuriating at times because his enthusiasms and commitment are so much stronger than those of others around him. But Martin also is kind, gentle and – above all else in my view – a believer in the innate goodness of ordinary people.

Much of this will become apparent as you read this book. Here is a story told with passion and commitment, with attention to detail and with humour. What comes through is the author's deep conviction that a serious wrong was done to a place and to a people he loves. By his own admission, Cyprus became for Packard an "engagement of passionate intensity". (It is worth adding that Packard brought a similarly passionate commitment to his support for the forces of liberal democracy in Greece during the junta years of 1967 to 1974, when he worked selflessly with the Democratic Defence resistance movement.)

When Martin Packard was thrust into Cyprus in 1964, he was unusually well equipped for the task. An officer with Britain's Royal Navy, he was married to a Greek woman whose family was at home among liberal minded, well educated social democrats from the Athens elite. Martin, who spoke Greek fluently, was moulded, like us all, by his upbringing. His father, he notes in *Getting It Wrong*, was "an ecumenical parson whose acceptance of liberation theology and whose belief in a Quaker approach to inter-personal contact were influential in my formative years".

Packard's approach was thus instinctively conciliatory and in substance non-confrontational – though, as is apparent from several incidents he describes, he can be confrontational in defence of his efforts to bring a measure of peace to communities. His essentially non-violent approach is underscored by his decision, at an early stage of his time in Cyprus, not to arm himself.

Drafting Packard into Cyprus happened because Britain (along with Greece and Turkey) was a guarantor to the 1960 constitutional settlement. Under this, Britain ceded colonial rule to a carefully constructed settlement between the island's Greek- and Turkish-speaking communities, the latter of whom formed about 18 per cent of the population at that time. In handing over control, Britain retained for itself what were designated SBAs (Sovereign Base Areas), two coastal enclaves at Akrotiri and Dhekelia. The settlement was imperfect and communal tensions persisted, erupting into violence in 1963.

In discharging its obligations, the British government and military authorities turned to Major General Peter Young, the then Commander of British army units in the SBAs. Young put together a UK team which would work with Greek and Turkish counterparts to try to restore order. Their efforts were to be based on tripartite patrols, involving British, Greek and

Turkish military personnel working together in harmony, a visible example to the island's two mistrustful communities.

With his background, Packard was a natural choice for Young. And in Young, Packard found a figure of inspiration, a mentor to whom he looked up and for whom he wanted to achieve. Broadly, Young and Packard shared an understanding of the island's main problems and, crucially, they also shared a vision as to what the solutions ought to be. It is not surprising that Packard dedicates this book to the late General, a man for whom the author retains admiration and affection. His feelings are apparent in this description of Young in action, listening and trying to mediate between representatives of the two communities.

"General Young listened to lengthy expositions from those present. They harped back to the constitution and its un-workability. The Greek Cypriots claimed that the authorities of the state were being prevented from carrying out their proper functions. The Turkish Cypriots claimed they were being denied their constitutional rights and exposed to extreme harassment. The General clearly had heard all the arguments before. He was unfailingly polite."

Packard describes himself accurately as "not an academic or a professional historian" but as a participant. This memoir is a participant's book about a personal experience. But the book will be of value to historians nonetheless. In a telling passage he describes how his original records, his contemporary observations and analyses of events, have been "lost" by the British authorities. (They are more than likely filed away somewhere, kept secret by some silly and self-serving rule of non-disclosure.)

"This book therefore has been constructed from surviving fragments of my original notes and from an early draft of my report on field-mediation," writes Packard. "Wherever possible I have checked my accuracy through contacts in Cyprus and through army officers who served alongside me in 1964. Much of the presentation is in the form of an extended diary: at times this may seem banal or repetitive, but it provides archive material for both communities in Cyprus and it is the breadth and detail of my experience that validates the claim that resolution and re-engagement were possible in early 1964."

What follows is a detailed account of one man's mission, with his tripartite patrol colleagues, to intervene at ground level to resolve problems as they arose, seek to prevent them arising again and lay the foundations for trust to grow – classic bottom up mediation, as opposed to top down imposition. Packard eschewed both the Greek Cypriot and Greek penchant for *enosis* (union with Greece) and the Turkish Cypriot and Turkish preference for *taksim* (partition). The idealist in him wanted a third way: a bottom up, cross-community settlement in which the ordinary people of Cyprus could live (and let live) in security with each other. Inevitably, this worthy mission came up against uncomfortable realities.

"Unfortunately there appeared at present not to be any strong popular wish for compromise," Packard notes in a record of his impressions at an early stage of his work. "Each community was fed up with the other: the Turkish Cypriots because they felt bypassed, belittled and insecure; the Greek Cypriots because they felt frustrated and obstructed by a small minority that was abusing powers bestowed on it by an unfair, externally-imposed constitution... The press of both communities had been vitriolic and had helped to turn irritation into hatred. At present there was very little residual trust on which to build."

But Packard could not stop himself from warming to both communities, despite this early gloomy conclusion. People he meets he usually finds to be kind and polite and warm. The work of the tripartite patrol quickly settled down to helping resolve what seem at this remove rather mundane arguments over water, land, field boundaries, missing animals (always presumed stolen – or worse – by the other side), fears of isolation and vulnerability. But behind these, and breaking the fabric of traditional local friendships, lay clashes of nationalistic ideology imported from Greece and Turkey.

The bottom up approach soon showed its worth to Packard. "I came very quickly to appreciate the huge advantages offered by the tripartite formula of the patrol. Not only could we immediately create a bond with each community in its own language, through an officer who was sympathetic to their cause, but we also could present the rural areas with the highly symbolic picture of a Greek and Turkish officer working creatively together, empowered by Makarios and Kutchuk and encouraged by the British."

But successes at village level – indications, surely, for anyone who wanted to see them of what could be achieved – cut little ice in some quarters, where issues were played out on a larger canvas. Packard's judgement is harsh.

"Britain, the supposed bastion of democratic principle, has been a consistent betrayer of that principle in Cyprus, provoking ethnic separatism, sabotaging inter-communal re-engagement and tolerating, or encouraging, Turkish intervention when it was contended that those policies would provide advantage in the retention of British bases and regional influence."

Vested interest critics of this book – there will be no shortage of people pointing out that, because of his marital and friendship ties to Greece, Packard was always "pro-Greek" – should note his attitude towards one of his Turkish army colleagues: "The Turkish officer who served with me longest, Major Sait Sepici, was a man small in size but of huge moral stature. I quickly acquired for him a deep admiration. Despite repeatedly finding himself in situations that were profoundly distressing or difficult for him, I never saw him fail to act with loyalty to the work of the patrol."

To succeed in any deeply divided community the disinterested negotiator, seeking to achieve a good and just outcome, must have a mind as generous and open as this.

Could Packard – or rather Packard's preferred method of ground floor mediation, and escalating confidence-building measures – have worked? Yes, in my view, and it clearly was worth trying. Apparently it was the success of this approach that led to it being wound down and Packard sent packing. Afterwards the situation deteriorated, leading on to the disaster of the Athens' junta *coup* against Makarios, which in turn sparked the 1974 Turkish invasion and subsequent military occupation of northern areas of the island.

True, there has been little or no violence in the past 30 years. But Cyprus remains an apple of discord for almost everyone with a connection to it: for Greece and Turkey certainly; for relations between the region and the US and the rest of Europe also. The problems remain most of all for those who share living space on an island scarred by a crude dividing line that shears across the land and through the capital city, a city arguably now more divided than ever Belfast was. The division imposed by the invasion has made a solution more difficult and remains an enormous impediment to Turkey's European Union membership aspirations.

My own view – and I acknowledge that I am not an expert on Cyprus – is that a huge opportunity was missed when the most recent diplomatic drive to achieve a solution to the Cyprus problem – the so-called Annan Plan – failed to offer a formula that could find overwhelming cross-community acceptance. An *agreed* compromise is the only way communities locked in recrimination can escape their fate, as was shown in Northern Ireland. But that compromise needs to be between the communities in Cyprus, not between Cypriot interests and those of outside powers.

Had an amended Annan Plan won cross-community endorsement and Cyprus entered the EU under common administration, the dynamic (not to say built-up experience) that helped create mature relations between France and Germany, and that played a supporting role in the Northern Ireland peace process, could have been brought to bear on the island. EU policies are blind when it comes to ethnic groups. Legislation emanating from Brussels is increasingly rights-based, as are precedents being established by the European Court. Unfortunately, however, by agreeing to accept certain derogations as part of Annan, the EU, in the eyes of its critics, succeeded only in backing a package that would have resulted in continuing division in Cyprus, irrespective of any settlement achieved under the plan. It must surely be the proper target of EU diplomacy to have a settlement under which all Cypriots have common access to all of the benefits and rights of EU membership.

In the case of Ireland and the EU, the slow burn confidence-builder was the effect of politics occurring removed from the local hothouse context. Away from the poisoned atmosphere of Northern Ireland – where every tiny gesture, every suggestion, irrespective of its intrinsic merits, would be damned by the other side – reality, maturity, common sense got a foothold. People then learnt the benefits of co-operation, learnt that what united the people of Northern Ireland far outweighed anything that divided them. In playing a helpful role, politicians and diplomats from the Republic of Ireland also earned the trust of Northern Ireland unionist (i.e. pro-British) politicians, who came to accept that they could, after all, have mature and mutually beneficial relations with their erstwhile old enemy to the south.

If all that can happen for Northern Ireland, where the religious, historical and cultural divisions were so deep, can it not also happen in Cyprus, where local enmities are of much more recent vintage? It will only happen for sure when there is a confluence of both communities in Cyprus wanting it to happen and all outside powers allowing it to do so. Unitary membership of the European Union could be a critically important context. Ultimately successful compromise rests on all sides recognising their own gains and accepting that the "other side" is also entitled to a gain. There are thus no winners and losers in the conventional sense, only winners. At various stages during the Northern Ireland peace process, one side or the other would pull back, demanding that the other side jump first, as it were. Eventually, all realised that they had to jump together. One day in Cyprus, if a unified state is to be achieved once more, both communities will, after a general framework has been agreed, have to be allowed to trust each other and to jump together.

Getting It Wrong is not a charter for pessimism. On the contrary, as Martin Packard notes in his concluding *Afterthoughts*, his experience "showed that Greek Cypriots and Turkish Cypriots could readily work out effective solutions when provided with an appropriate mechanism through which to do so and with an accurate appraisal of the problems that confronted them". This is what happened eventually in Northern Ireland: the two sponsoring powers (London and Dublin) grew to understand that a pragmatic solution was needed and they began to look beyond their own entrenched positions and assumptions.

The language of the Irish peace process should be applied equally to Cyprus: the pursuit of "confidence building measures", the need for "parity of esteem" between both communities. If the Irish experience is anything to go by (and why isn't it?), the two communities on Cyprus are well capable of working out their differences together, as they did in microcosm so often in 1964 during the time of Packard's tri-partite patrols.

This is an important book. The life-blood of balanced history is the first hand testimony of those who made it, supported where possible by documentary evidence. Martin Packard played a key role at the pit-face of what was happening in Cyprus during a crucial period which helped define the island's current situation. His essential contention – that far from being a disinterested 'honest broker', Britain was a self-interested regional player (and one cannot underestimate the imperatives that flowed from the Cold War) – is supported by his own evidence, backed by contemporary records (his own and others, notably Peter Young's) and the subsequent emergence of private correspondent between more senior players such as Cyril Pickard and Duncan Sandys.

Simply put, it also rings true. True also is Packard's observation that Cyprus has many friends in Britain, real friends (not least Martin Packard himself). Martin has long retired from the fray of direct, high level involvement in events surrounding Cyprus but he has remained in touch through involvement in seminars about what happened, and what should happen in the future; and he works as much as he can with those who share his beliefs.

But in truth, it is for others now, others more centrally involved in the EU and UN– and in Britain, Greece and Turkey – to give what help they can to assist the Cypriots, inhabitants of what Martin Packard describes as "a small country made important by its geographic position and made intensely vulnerable to foreign manipulation by the make-up of its population."

It would be nice to see an honest broker, from the EU, the UN or wherever, giving real assistance to Cypriots towards 'getting it right' for a change. The Irish government intends to use the knowledge it has accumulated from the Northern Ireland peace process to engage in conflict resolution efforts elsewhere. Perhaps Cyprus could be an early target of this initiative.

Those of pure motive who want to assist everyone of the island find a better future, and not manipulate the situation for their own ends, should read this book and take note.

Peter Murtagh
Dublin, December 2007

Peter Murtagh is a Managing Editor at *The Irish Times*. He is author of *The Rape of Greece – the King, the Colonels and the Resistance*, an account of events in Greece from 1967 to 1974.

A mixed village NE of Nicosia in early 1963, with the proximity of church and mosque showing how closely the two communities were interwoven.

INTRODUCTION

On 12 February 1964, US State Department's George Ball, co-author of the Acheson Plan[1] for Cyprus, said to me: "Very impressive, but you've got it all wrong, son. Hasn't anyone told you that our objective here is partition, not re-integration?"

Ball was referring to a tripartite mediating initiative in Cyprus, mandated by Major General Peter Young, the commander of the British-led joint peacekeeping force. Since 6 January I had been a co-ordinator of that initiative in the northern areas of Cyprus. I had spent the day demonstrating to Ball that inter-communal re-engagement was progressing fast, how effectively the two Cypriot communities could work together with proper encouragement and an appropriate framework, and how misplaced was any urging of ethnic separation.

I was unaware at the time of Ball's status and role. I disregarded his comment. I continued with the remit that General Young had given me. By June of that year my unit was providing a conduit between the Greek Cypriot and Turkish Cypriot leaderships, which they were using to move towards an informal, but critical, private accord. On that, I believed, might be built momentum towards a new and workable inter-communal partnership.

When the British authorities became aware of this progress I was precipitately removed from the island, the mediating process in which I had been engaged was neutered and the chance for a Cypriot-led solution receded into the far distance. After returning to London I was told that the Foreign Office was not a supporter of communal re-integration. Later it was reported that Ankara had become alarmed at the degree of communal re-engagement achieved by my unit.

In March 1965 General Young wrote to me: "*I pressed hard for your return last autumn and late summer, as I felt sure that you were the only one who could re-establish contacts which had been completely lost.*" Communal leaders and the UN secretariat also told me they had asked for my return. From the Foreign Office there was a demand that I sever all contact with the island.

This book is a personal account of five months that I spent in Cyprus in early 1964, first under secondment to Joint Force (JF), the original British-led peacekeeping operation formed from military units of Britain, Greece and Turkey, and then under UNFICYP (UN Forces in Cyprus), which took over from the British-led JF late in March 1964. Throughout this time I headed the core unit of the tripartite mediating effort. That meant an intimate involvement in Cypriot affairs, with a unique window into the history of the period and into the realities of inter-communal relationships. My unit became the channel for efforts by the President, Archbishop Makarios, and Vice-President, Dr Faisal Kutchuk, to bypass their extremists and achieve a working co-operation.

To protect our efforts, we sought at the time for a total avoidance of publicity. Subsequently, like other crucial events of that period, the tripartite initiative and its significance seem to have been airbrushed out of recorded history. It rates no mention in the memoirs of General Michael Carver, under whom I worked after he took over command from General Young in February 1964, despite subsequently being described by the UN as the major success under his regime.

This book should have been written immediately after my period of service in Cyprus, but at that time I was constrained by my position as an officer in the Royal Navy. I submitted a lengthy report to the British Government and assumed this would be circulated to those with an interest in the peacemaking process, including officials in the UN. Instead, it 'disappeared'. The UN, which applied for a copy, was denied access.

Ernest Hemingway said that almost any liar writes more convincingly than a man who was there. I accept that in situations of confusion, as in Cyprus in 1964, personal, snapshot observation does not always provide clarity, but personal testimony is needed so that an accurate picture can eventually be constructed.

I write now at the urging of Cypriot friends from both communities, who consider that there are serious gaps in local archives. No previously published account offers an adequate picture of events inside Cyprus in early 1964, of the opportunity that was missed then or of how a mediation process answerable to Cypriots was replaced by an outsider's view of what process would best suit NATO. Particularly missing from published record is the story of the rural areas, which embraced almost three quarters of the population.

It is axiomatic in the game of disinformation that a large lie is as easily dispensed as a small one. Cyprus in 1963/4 was a focus for NATO intelligence activity, with Greece, Turkey, Britain and the US all pursuing their own objectives, none of which envisaged a genuinely independent island. Disinformation was a key weapon in this process, which helps to explain why so much subsequent comment on the period has been inaccurate and how ammunition was given to those with an inclination to demonstrate that an unbridgeable gulf opened at that moment between the two communities in Cyprus. Otherwise excellent academic commentary on the period has been hampered by the absence from public records of any of the history of the tripartite mediation initiative. Added to this, there are potential authors, with knowledge greater than mine of particular aspects of the story, for whom the sensitivity of personal and political relationships appears to have decided them against public exposition.

If truth is the first casualty in war, it is more than ever that of violent civil dispute. For Cyprus, the misrepresentation of the events of 1963/4 has been a major contributor to the prolongation of communal division. Every outside party to the problem, Cypriot, Greek, Turkish, British, American, has at times used a flawed picture of events to justify policies that contributed to inter-communal dispute. The picture of irreconcilability, tailored by those who conceived that their interests would be damaged by a genuine independence, is not one that chimed with any of my own experiences.

No outsider knows better than I what Turkish Cypriots actually went through in the first half of 1964. December 1963 and the following six months did, as they claim, provide a fulcrum to modern Cypriot history, with the balance afterwards tipping towards the events of 1974. But the frictions of

1963-64 did not prove that a bi-communal partnership within a unified state was unworkable: rather, the ease with which they could be resolved by effective mediation proved the opposite.

Misinformed by their politicians and their press, few Greek Cypriots have demonstrated an adequate sympathy for the hardship that events imposed on the Turkish Cypriot community in that period. But the root causes of those hardships were to be found in London, Athens and Ankara, and in the ambitions of the Turkish army, and not only in Cyprus: claims by Turkish Cypriots that their origin lay solely with the Greek Cypriots or that they were seriously threatened with genocide are no more valid than a contention that British attempts to defeat the IRA were genocidal.

Only rarely, on the other hand, have I heard Turkish Cypriots display an understanding of the fear engendered among Greek Cypriots by the proximity of Turkey, the belief that the Turkish army had a determination to impose its own solution on the island and the conviction that TMT[2] and the Turkish army were seeking to prove that a unitary state was not a viable option. It clearly is painful for the Turkish Cypriots to consider the degree to which they became pawns in the British and Turkish pursuit of geopolitical objectives or the degree to which their own interests were compromised in the pursuit of communal separation. Most Greek Cypriots, on the other hand, failed to give credence to Turkish Cypriot fears or to understand the violence that extremists in both communities and rogue elements of their own police forces, acting outside the law and in defiance of Makarios' policy, were sometimes imposing on them. The failure of Greek Cypriot leaders to prevent or condemn these acts enabled proponents of separatism to exaggerate their impact and to condemn the Greek Cypriot community as a whole. The failure stemmed from a wish to avoid internal schism and an unwillingness to be seen as betraying the deep commitment that most Greek Cypriots then had to the concept of union with Greece (*enosis*[3]), but the result was to render unitary *enosis* unachievable.

In my reading of modern Cypriot history I have nowhere found any suggestion of Britain making a serious effort to create a genuine inter-communal unity. I have, on the other hand, read of innumerable occasions in which Britain, in pursuit of its own interests, sought to 'bring the Greeks up against the Turks' or to promote the Turkish Cypriots as an ally against the Greek Cypriots.

Duncan Sandys, as head of the Commonwealth Relations Office (CRO), was the minister at the time responsible for reporting to the British government on affairs in Cyprus. In June 1964, after I had been removed from Cyprus, I was summoned by him to a lengthy private discussion on events in the island. He was enthusiastic and complimentary about the mediating process in which I had been involved, whose genesis had stemmed from his own efforts. He said that my story and views were wholly supported by General Young and the High Commissioner, Sir Arthur Clark, and tallied with his own beliefs, but that they were totally at odds with pictures he had been receiving from the Foreign Office and the intelligence services. Only later did I come to understand that these agencies had created their own, self-serving, version of events.

Cyril Pickard, a rising star in the British diplomatic service, took over from Sir Arthur Clark at the beginning of January 1964 as London's representative in Nicosia. He began his time in Cyprus with a dislike and distrust of Makarios and of the Greek Cypriots which mirrored attitudes that I had seen in British intelligence reports of the time and heard in briefings at the Foreign Office. A 12 January 1964 report from Pickard to London, written soon after his appointment as Acting High Commissioner, notes the Turkish Cypriots, backed by Turkey, as being in process of trying to establish the trappings of a separate state, within the various administrative sectors. The remainder of the report is intemperate, ill informed and virulently critical of President Makarios.* Over the several years that I knew him the views Pickard expressed to me underwent a radical change towards a much more sympathetic understanding of the realities of the island and of its leaders. After his death in 1994 I was contacted by his son, who said his father had asked that I be given his 1964 file of private correspondence with Duncan Sandys. The contents of that correspondence confirmed a profound duplicity in Whitehall's 1964 position on Cyprus.

It is rare in Cyprus for matters of political import to have a simple thread, but the consistent and well-documented British failure there to devote itself to the creation of a common Cypriot identity and, since 1931, its manipulation of matters of inter-communality in an effort to further its own agenda, underlies all recent history. The British agenda in the 1960s, as I was briefed by the Foreign Office in 1963, related to a twin-track policy in which the British military and intelligence presence in Cyprus was seen as critical to the projection of UK regional interests and Britain's special relationship with Turkey, the key regional security-producer for NATO, as having primacy over any consideration of Cypriot independence.

These considerations seem to have meshed with US/UK intelligence thinking in 1963, deriving from the then situation in Iraq, that any genuine independence in the Middle East must be ruthlessly opposed[4].

The special relationship of Britain with Turkey has been a central determinant of modern Cypriot history. Turkey re-involved itself in Cypriot affairs in the 1950s, when Britain encouraged it to do so as a counter to the Greek Cypriot campaign for *enosis*. Subsequently this involvement generated a momentum of its own, which the Foreign Office initially viewed as benign and later as irreversible.

Whitehall's covert policies for Cyprus have generally run in tandem with those of Ankara, with each sometimes taking the lead-position. It was understandable that the Turkish army, anticipating the approaching end of British colonial rule, should wish to counter the possibility of a hostile offshore presence to the south. But NATO, by tolerating, and sometimes contributing to, the covert injection of Turkish and Greek military force into Cyprus, was a betrayer there of fundamental human rights. The security and well-being of the Turkish Cypriots and the building of defences against Soviet influence should, and could, have been realised through other routes.

---

* This report is included in the archives of General Young at King's College, London

The violence in the island over Christmas 1963 was in part an outcome of paramilitary contingency-planning intertwined with the activities of foreign intelligence agencies and in part an eruption of pent-up resentments and frustration. A history of foreign-promoted nationalisms and separatist propaganda, and particularly a clash between, on the one hand, Turkey's determination to replace British colonial rule with its own dominance in Cyprus and, on the other, the irredentist determination of the right wing in Greece, supported at that time by the great majority of Greek Cypriots, to see the island drawn into a single Hellenic unity, had set the scene. Over-arching this was America's conduct of Cold War operations in the area, targeted to counter the twin threats of Soviet incursion and left-wing influence: one aspect of this was the covert promotion of extreme right-wing forces and trends in Turkey and Greece and an implementation of the so-called 'strategy of tension',* Among the recipients of US support was the 'Stay-behind' organisation, which included the Sheepskin and SWD† networks in Greece and Turkey respectively[5], each of which extended its reach into Cyprus.

The pre-eminence of the Turkish army as a contributor to NATO security was a further key factor in determining the UK/US perception of events.

Other tap-lines from the violence went back to the inter-communal clashes of 1958, which had left deep-seated personal antagonisms, and to the inherent divisiveness of both the 1959 Zurich Agreement and the 1960 Constitution. Resentments were turned destructive by armed groups when there was a loss of central political control over the forces of law and order and by the meddling of extremists and of their supporters in foreign intelligence services.

It was assumed in British intelligence analysis that the emergence of an effectively functioning independent unitary state or an advance in the power of the political left would destabilise the south-eastern flank of NATO and lead eventually to pressure for the recovery of territory ceded to the UK under the Zurich Agreement. Low key civil dispute in the island was not viewed in military analysis as necessarily detrimental to British interests: but the threat of a unified leftist campaign and the danger of an escalated armed confrontation between Turkish Cypriots and Greek Cypriots were taken seriously and led to discussion of a possible need for the imposition of NATO control, to be exercised through Athens and Ankara, over the island's affairs.

Inside Cyprus, the clashes of Christmas 1963 produced severe traumata, both communal and personal. There was need for a removal of pressures and for healing. The Christmas turmoil was followed by a recoil from violence, by a hiatus that offered a moment of flexibility: during this period, sympathetic therapy might have gone beyond the curing of recent hurt and led to a genuine

---

* The 'strategy of tension' revolved around the use of acts of violence, which then were falsely ascribed to the left, in order to create justification for anti-leftist political initiatives. Typical of this strategy was the assassination of three Italian police officers in 1972 in Paetano by a right-wing Gladio cell. The murder was publicly ascribed to the left and used to prompt an anti-communist witch-hunt.
† Special War Department.

Cypriot commitment to a workable bi-communal partnership. Help towards that end should have been offered to Cyprus by the international community, but Britain had different priorities. In early 1964 the Foreign Office did everything possible to block the introduction of a UN or Commonwealth mediating presence, on the pretext that the former would lead to involvement by the USSR and the latter to a closer identification with the non-aligned bloc. By March, when the UK grudgingly transferred peacekeeping responsibility to the UN, the process of communal separation would already have been substantially entrenched if not for the efforts of the tripartite mediating initiative, which had acted under an independent remit. For some months after March, while benefiting from an off-loading of international criticism, the UK managed to dominate the UN's operations in Cyprus. During this period, policies established by the British, essentially separative, went unchanged.

At heart this story contributes personal testimony to a record of how the opportunity for a healing in Cyprus was created and then lost.

General Young, the original commander of the joint peacekeeping force, set out to facilitate a healing. He believed that peacekeeping would be counter-productive if it was not led by and coupled to active mediation. He established the Tripartite Patrol Organisation (TPO) to pursue the mediating element of his concept, to run in parallel to the peacekeeping presence.

In February 1964 General Young was unceremoniously replaced, accused in London of being 'too pro-Cypriot'.

The TPO, of which I was a founder-member, lived on. In late March it was converted into the Joint Patrol Organisation (JPO) as an element of UNFICYP. It had notable success. It was acting as a facilitator of major openings towards communal re-engagement, acknowledged by both communal leaderships and by the United Nations, when it was abruptly dismembered by the British in June 1964.

Sir Alec Douglas Home, the British Prime Minister of the time, is reported to have believed, like George Ball, that partition was the proper answer for Cyprus, which tallied with NATO intelligence thinking. This deeply undemocratic stance manifested itself in the manipulation of local weaknesses and helped confer on all of the Cypriots a long saga of suffering.

My own experience in Cyprus made it wholly clear that violence and division there were not inevitable and that their appearance could, with proper help, rapidly be diverted to rational dialogue, mutual sympathy and bi-communal co-operation, even in moments of extreme stress. After five months working on the fault-lines of rural Cyprus, with exposure to almost every inter-communal confrontation there in that period, and of my use as a private conduit between the political leaderships of the two communities, I was left without any doubt that Greek Cypriots and Turkish Cypriots were as capable as any other people in the world of living constructively and harmoniously together. For that, however, each needed insurance against extremism and a real sense of security. Britain and the international community could have helped to provide this, but signally failed to do so.

General Carver, who took over from General Young in February, was later to suggest that I had a naïve belief that solving the problems of rural Cyprus would mean a general solution for the island. In fact I simply believed that one had to start somewhere, and that a bottom-up approach answerable to the Cypriots was the best available route. I took it, probably mistakenly, that London and Ankara would accept this route if it was made apparent that their interests could thus be better served than through an imposed partition or the continuance of a non-solution. Carver's own memoirs refer to peacekeeping solely as a static, blocking process. He accepts that this worked in favour of TMT's drive for communal separation. He rates the success of his brand of peacekeeping by the degree to which British interests were served.

My story is short on details of local participants, whether Cypriot or foreign, because most parastatal leaders with whom I spoke in Cyprus in 1964, fearful of political reaction, did not offer me a name, and I never asked for one. In all other respects I kept copious notes. I forwarded frequent reports and analyses to JF or UNFICYP Headquarters, none of which can now be found in UK archives, and to President Makarios and Vice-President Kutchuk. I wrote a three hundred page report on the mediating process for the CRO which was passed to the Foreign Office and then, they claim, 'lost'. Since handing in my original material to the British authorities I have had no access to it.

This book therefore has been constructed from surviving fragments of my original notes and from an early draft of my report on field-mediation. Wherever possible I have checked my accuracy through contacts in Cyprus and through army officers who served alongside me in 1964. Much of the presentation is in the form of an extended diary: at times this may seem banal or repetitive, but it provides archive material for both communities in Cyprus and it is the breadth and detail of my experience that validates the claim that resolution and re-engagement were possible in early 1964.

In contrast to better-known later efforts at top-down mediation in Cyprus, the process in which I was involved started from the clientele of village coffee-houses and moved upwards through the various layers of leadership. I set out in January with a mandate to deal at individual or village level with the confrontations, disputes, shortages, fears and absences of governmental authority which had reduced much of the rural area assigned to me to a state of near-anarchy. By June that phase was successfully completed and my unit was providing linkage between divided ministries, a back-channel between the political heads of the two communities and help with the groundwork for a series of island-wide bi-communal projects.

Some commentary has claimed that the rescuing of Cyprus from anarchy in 1963-64 was wholly the work of regular British army units and that it was the British military peace-keeping initiative of that period that kept Cyprus from civil war. That the British army deployment throughout Cyprus at the end of December 1963 was very well handled and played a critical short-term role in the curbing of paramilitary excess and the re-establishment of a central authority is not in question. It may also have averted the possibility at that time of a Turkish invasion. But the role that regular army units could play was inevitably circumscribed, in the absence of a common language, in light of the ambiguity of British policy (at least from mid-February onwards) and in face of a quickly intensifying Greek Cypriot hostility to the presence of a British army that up to three years earlier had been the suppressor of their struggle for independence.

In fact, the initial unravelling of inter-communal confrontation outside Nicosia was in large degree made possible by the participation in tripartite mediating units of Turkish and Greek officers and by the active and consistent support that was given to those units by Makarios and Kutchuk and their key ministers. Brigadier 'Roly' Gibbs, later to be a prestigious Chief of the Imperial General Staff, was deputy to General Young. Subsequently he wrote to me: *"We, the soldiery, never could have attempted what you and your team were doing. We could only be peace-keepers and 'Aunt Sallys'."*

With the Turkish Cypriots I dealt in Nicosia directly with the office of Vice-President Fazil Kutchuk or through the estimable Nihat Bey, formerly a District Administration Officer. He was wise, moderate, supportive and provided an excellent link to the Turkish Cypriot leadership. With the Greek Cypriot political sector I worked almost entirely with or through Tassos Papadopoulos[6], then a youthful holder of three separate ministries[6], whose critical commitment to communal re-engagement made the process possible. He was adamant that a failure by the central government to deliver an adequate security to the Turkish Cypriots would be catastrophic for both communities. He provided me with access to Makarios and to other members of the government whenever that was needed; he helped to defuse incidents reported by me that could have led to serious violence; all the patrol's efforts to resolve the needs and problems of the Turkish Cypriots were backed by him. My unit went on to act as executor for secret efforts, spearheaded by him, to channel public works projects towards the Turkish Cypriots, in a specific drive for economic equalisation.

Papadopoulos also gave me introductions to those personalities, usually unapproachable by outsiders, who wielded real power at local level. Although suspicious of his EOKA[7] antecedents, Turkish Cypriot leaders with whom I worked saw him as pragmatic, intelligent and fair. This was a time when the Turkish General Staff was not yet generally seen as a crucial arbiter in Cypriot affairs and when the shutters had not yet come down along lines of communal division. Dr Kutchuk told me that he regarded Papadopoulos as central to hopes for an effective communal re-engagement, and he suggested that his EOKA background would help him in any negotiations. British government officials, on the other hand, clearly have never regarded him as 'one of our people': in every contact that I have had with Foreign Office personnel since 1964 they have always referred to him with a singular venom.

I am not an academic or a professional historian. This is a participant's book about personal experience. I have added notes only because I felt they might sometimes be needed by a reader unfamiliar with the intricacies of Cypriot events or when retrospective comment seemed appropriate.

My father was an ecumenical parson whose acceptance of liberation theology and whose belief in a Quaker approach to inter-personal contact were influential in my formative years. Dom Mintoff, one of the lions of Mediterranean nationalism, was a close friend. The ideas as to prior history that I record are those with which I arrived in Cyprus. I came there with some assumptions that were traditionalist, some that were probably unusual in a serving British officer and some that certainly were contrary to official British policy: I accepted Macmillan's dictum on "the winds of change", opposed any continuance of British imperialism, believed that Britain had more to gain in the eastern Mediterranean through a genuine sympathy and friendship for the area than through the retention of 'sovereign' areas or the subversion of democratically-elected governments.

My exposure in Cyprus in 1964 was inevitably circumscribed. In the exercise of mediating initiatives my time was spent mostly in places where there was friction or violence rather than in those many other areas where inter-communal relationships remained relatively untroubled. The most palpable insecurity was that of the Turkish Cypriots: the Greek Cypriots had less obvious, but equally deep-seated, fears because of the proximity of Turkey, the ambitions in Cyprus of the Turkish army and the belief that Ankara was using the Turkish Cypriot community in pursuit of its own secessionist objectives.

The unravelling of incidents of violence was complicated by the prevalence of deliberate acts of provocation and 'black propaganda' and by the fact that some of the incidents stemmed from intended vengeance for long-past events or from an overlap of criminal activity.

The incidents to which I was summoned were most frequently related to pressures exerted against the Turkish Cypriots and fear engendered as a result. Those pressures sometimes resulted from acts of the Turkish army or extremist Turkish Cypriots aimed at promoting ethnic separation; sometimes they were a rational, even if misguided, response to tactical considerations; sometimes they derived solely from the actions of Greek Cypriot extremists, who tended to claim that the whole Turkish Cypriot community was in a state of insurrection; and sometimes they came from misunderstanding or mistake. The measure of success achieved by the tripartite mediating process lay in the fact that, despite the continuance of centrally-controlled paramilitary initiatives (as in Tillyria and Pentadaktylos) those pressures had by May of 1964 been largely eliminated, leading to a remarkable degree of inter-communal harmony during the harvest period, when outsiders had expected a time of heightened tension and dispute. The early summer of 1964 therefore offered a unique opportunity for the creation of a new inter-communal understanding.

The deep and genuine fear felt by rural Turkish Cypriot communities in the first months of 1964 was sometimes justified, sometimes not. I have reported what I was told by the villagers, and have added a note where I later discovered that elements of the stories told to me were exaggerated or untrue. Until they talked to one of the joint patrols there was little reason for the villagers concerned not to believe that they had justifiable cause for terror, a supposition that was continually being drummed into them by Radio *Bayrak*[8] and by their own extremists. Hostage-taking by both communities was common at the time, although Turkish Cypriots were much more often the victims: the disappearance without trace of relatives or neighbours could be even more unsettling than news of their certain death; and it was often impossible to establish quickly what had actually happened to those reported as missing. In fact, however, contrary to subsequent mythology, the total number of missing showed a sharp reduction over the first five months of 1964, rather than an increase.

In the early months of 1964 Makarios' commitment to inter-communal re-engagement was undermined on the one hand by TMT's violent opposition to that policy and on the other by the obduracy of the leadership of the Greek Cypriot police forces. Nothing did more to damage his policies than the absence in those months of normal law-keeping and the involvement of uniformed gendarmerie officers (mostly 'specials' who had been inducted because of the emergency) in unlawful killings, in hostage-taking and in armed actions against Turkish Cypriot villages.

The regular police had attitudes that sprang from long exposure to the view that Turkish Cypriot militancy was the sharp end of an ambition of Ankara to acquire a controlling position in Cyprus. This belief had been given validation by Britain's encouragement of a Turkish involvement in Cypriot affairs and by Ankara's arming of and support for TMT, as a powerful paramilitary group, which since 1960 had continued to plan for just such a target. The 'Deniz incident' in 1959, when the British navy intercepted a Turkish attempt to deliver arms to TMT, at a time when constitutional arrangements for a unitary state were being finalised, had set the scene for this scenario. A recent BBC documentary has claimed that there was British intelligence complicity in TMT's covert activity[9]. The Greek Cypriot police force saw its over-riding priority as the neutralisation of TMT: it failed to recognise the degree to which even its own aspirations were being damaged by lack of commitment to the upholding of the law or to a defence of human rights.

Events thus combined to produce a remarkable dichotomy between natural and traditional friendships and neighbourliness on the one hand and inculcated fear and suspicion on the other. Villagers were usually comfortable with their local relationships but would regard anyone from beyond their immediate locality as a 'foreigner'. The vulnerability of each community to the exaggerations of a violently partisan and alarmist media was exacerbated by the absence of any easy access to moderate political leadership.

At the time, Cypriots usually referred to each other as 'Greeks' or 'Turks', only using the term 'Cypriot' when they wished to differentiate from those coming from Greece or Turkey. This is reflected in direct quotations used in this account, other than in those of the British military, which normally used the abbreviations 'GC' and 'TC'. Within the text I have for the most part used the terms 'Greek Cypriot' and 'Turkish Cypriot' in full, even though this may sometimes seem cumbersome, except in cases where the meaning is obvious or the passage dictated by direct quotation.

Place-names are now a contentious issue in Cyprus. For simplicity, I have throughout this narrative used the names that appeared on the army issue maps used by the patrols, which were the names then in common usage. Sections of the same map are reprinted in this book. In the same way, I have used the spelling of Turkish Cypriot surnames that was normal in the British reports of the 1960s.

It was hardly surprising that Britain should pursue its own interests in Cyprus. But there were fundamentally different routes for that to be done.

One, which I came to see as that of the Foreign Office, sought above all else to prevent a genuine independence in Cyprus and to preserve a 'special relationship' with Ankara and involved a manipulation of affairs in Cyprus towards this end; the other, which I believed to be that of General Young and of Duncan Sandys, and which clearly was supported by many British political figures, involved attempts to further a just resolution of the island's affairs, with the target of an independent Cyprus which would be a genuine and staunch friend of the United Kingdom. Proponents of the latter route assumed that a sympathetic stance could be elicited from Ankara through the exercise of competent diplomacy by the Foreign Office and the encouragement of a dynamic convergence between Turkey, Greece and Cyprus that would give real benefit to all three nations.

The interplay of communal division in Cyprus had developed during the period of British Colonial administration. No less damaging than the periodic exploitation of that division, was the *laisez faire* abrogation by Britain of its obligations to safeguard the independence of Cyprus: that enabled Turkey to quantify and advance a determination to exercise a control over the island's affairs. The squandering by London of the chance to nurture an orderly evolution of the Cypriot state was to have dire consequences for both Greek and Turkish Cypriots and ultimately to be damaging also to Turkey's long-term interests.

My criticism of Whitehall is not just because key mandarins put their idea of British self-interest ahead of ethics or of human rights but also because the ethical policy which they rejected would in fact have paid much the greater dividend.

For a variety of reasons this account has direct relevance to the later history of Cyprus, up to the present day. The true story of 1964 contradicts all later contentions of communal irreconcilability. The success of the non-public, tripartite, bottom-up, Cypriot-derived approach to conflict-resolution, answerable directly to Makarios and Kutchuk, stands in sharp contrast to subsequent attempts at top-down mediation injected from abroad and answerable to the UN or the UK: it offers a template as to how mediation in Cyprus can best be pursued. The Annan Plan[10] (at least in its later formats) was an attempt by the UN, primarily advised by the UK and the US, to deliver an outsider's concept of how a compromise might be constructed between Cypriot rights and foreign interests: the rejection of Annan 5 suggested that most Cypriots wished solutions to be of their own making.

Any unifying solution in Cyprus needs to stem from an island-wide social consensus: my experience suggests that the basic conditions for that consensus have always existed.

I am very grateful to all those, too numerous to mention by name, whose encouragement and help has made possible the production of this book. Publication is the result of support from both Greek Cypriots and Turkish Cypriots, topped up with grants from charitable trusts.

A percipient commentator on Cyprus has written: "*If Cyprus is to recover from the blows it has been dealt it will have to acquire a common memory, and this will mean less stress on individual or sectarian grievances. If people remember everything they go mad.*

What needs to be remembered, set down and memorised, is the injury done to all Cypriots, to the common home, by distant, uncaring enemies."[11]

'*Getting it Wrong*' describes events that, I believe, have benefit in being remembered. It is dedicated to the much-betrayed people of Cyprus and to the memory of Major General Peter Young, whose commitment to an ethical resolution of communal antagonisms in the island set me off on an engagement of passionate intensity.

Archbishop Makarios, President of Cyprus and George Ball, Under Secretary of the US State Department. February 1964.

1. ARRIVAL. NICOSIA. 5 JANUARY 1964

I pointed out to my driver that there was a body lying by the road. At first glance I had taken it for a bag left there for rubbish collection.

We stopped and my driver, a corporal from the Greenjackets, took a look. He said: "Very dead. Probably killed elsewhere and dumped here. Nothing we can do." As we drove on, he radioed in the details.

It was late evening, 5 January 1964. I had just flown in to Nicosia Airport. Two hours earlier I had been in Athens, still gaudy with the tatters of its New Year celebrations. Here it was sombre and oppressive, the streets deserted.

Skirting the north of Nicosia we stopped at the Ledra Palace Hotel to leave my gear. Then we drove to the Cornaro, a hotel recently requisitioned as temporary headquarters for the British-led peacekeeping force, which had been established on 30 December.

Violence had broken out in the days before Christmas. When the Cypriot authorities failed to bring the fighting under control there had been intense international pressure for the intervention of a peacekeeping force, to stop the bloodshed and to avert the threat of invasion by Turkey.

Just before midnight on 25 December Greek Cypriot and Turkish Cypriot leaders agreed on a cessation of hostilities and issued a joint invitation to Britain to lead a peacekeeping initiative. General Peter Young, commander of British troops in the Sovereign Base Areas (SBAs)[1], was appointed in command. Troops were mainly to be provided by the UK, but Greek and Turkish contingents already in Cyprus under the 1960 constitution were also attached. General Young had asked for additional specialist officers to be seconded to his staff. I, with qualifications as a Greek-speaker, was in Nicosia as a result.

I was taken immediately to report to the General, about whom I noted in my diary that night: "Welcoming; patrician; sympathetic; accessible; compassionate; inspirational; very tired."

He said: "I'm sorry to have hijacked you, but I urgently needed officers with the right skills, particularly Greek- and Turkish-speakers, to act for me outside Nicosia. I need to know what's going on in the country areas. I need engagement with the Cypriot people. I need officers who can identify problems and solve them on the spot. I've decided on a series of tripartite patrols, each with a British, a Greek and a Turkish officer, with special authority from the heads of the two communities. It's going to be an extremely sensitive job, perhaps risky. Major Greenwood will co-ordinate operations. The army will give you whatever back-up is needed."

General Young asked whether I had been in Cyprus before, and I answered 'No'. He said to tell him how much I knew about Cypriot history and the background to the dispute and recent developments, and that he would then give me his own appraisal.

I told him that for the past eight months I had been acting as Fleet Intelligence Adviser on the staffs of Admiral Hamilton, Commander-in-Chief Mediterranean, and of the Commander of NATO's south-eastern sector (COMEDSOUEAST), both of whom were based in Malta. That meant I had been reading diplomatic and intelligence and press reports, but Cyprus had not figured in them very largely. When news reached me of my secondment to his staff I had been on leave in Athens, and members of the British Embassy there had passed on to me their own latest news from Nicosia. In addition the family of my Greek wife had close connections with two senior ministers[2] in the government of George Papandreou, and they and other well-placed friends in Athens had been giving me their views for the past few days.

Before taking up my job in Malta I had been briefed at some length on Cyprus by the Foreign Office, the Commonwealth Relations Office (CRO) and the Ministry of Defence (MOD). What other knowledge I had was sketchy and came from a past reading of history books, of the press and of Durrell's 'Bitter Lemons'.

I had been taught that Greek Cypriots traced their origins to Mycenaean Greeks, who had established themselves throughout the island during the Iron Age of the 2nd Millennium BC, and that the much later and smaller Turkish Cypriot presence originated from the Ottoman occupation of the island in the sixteenth century, when Turks and Janissaries[3] from Anatolia had settled island-wide.

From its earliest history until 1960 Cyprus had been ruled by foreigners: Assyrians, Persians and Egyptians in pre-Christian times: then Romans from AD 30 to the 4th century: then eight hundred years in the Byzantine empire, including a period of joint Romaic and Arabic rule from 691 to 961, ending with conquest by the Crusaders of Richard the Lionheart in 1191: Then Lusignans for three hundred years and Venetians for a hundred, before the period of Ottoman occupation from 1571 to 1878.

Nationality had played no part in the Ottoman's political system. Identity was based on the Islamic faith. Subsequent to the Ottoman invasion in 1571 there had been instances of Christians converting to the Muslim faith and some intermarriage, but the Muslim faith and the millet system[4] had kept the Muslims and Christians as two separate communities, although they sometimes made common cause. Separateness evolved further with the 1821 Greek War of Independence and the disintegration of the Ottoman Empire at the end of the First World War, in which Greek-speaking Christians identified with the rise of Hellenic nationalism and Turkish-speaking Muslims identified with the rise of Kemalist nationalism. Some commentators regarded the two communities as separate occupants of a single homeland; outside pressures had always acted towards such a concept, militating against the development of a common Cypriot identity.

Greek Cypriots had not participated in the Greek War of Independence, but an assumption of their likeliness to do so had led to the execution by the Turks of five hundred of their leading dignitaries. Since that time there had been a strong Greek presumption that Cyprus, like Crete and Rhodes and other islands of the eastern Mediterranean with a Greek-speaking majority, was part of a Hellenic entity and would eventually move to union.

Britain, looking for strategic advantage, had leased Cyprus from Turkey in 1878, then annexed it in 1914. Muslims in the island then lost all of the Islamic privileges bestowed upon them by the millet system: some chose to take Turkish nationality and emigrate to the new Republic of Turkey.

In 1915 Britain had offered Cyprus to Greece in return for Greek participation in the war against Germany, but the offer was withdrawn when Greece decided to remain neutral. Greece did later enter the war, in 1917, but by then the offer of Cyprus was considered by London to have lapsed. After the First World War options for self-determination were discussed but not realised. In 1923 Cyprus became a Crown Colony and Turkey formally relinquished any claim to the island.

In 1931 a period began of Greek Cypriot agitation for *enosis*. This was opposed by the Turkish Cypriots, who made common cause with the British, and met by vigorous suppression and a tightening of the British colonial regime. The British began at that time to encourage the Turkish Cypriots to develop separate political structures as a counterweight to Greek Cypriot organisations.

The 1939-45 war led to new Greek assumptions that Britain would now sanction *enosis*. Instead, London decided on a policy that foresaw the retention of the whole island as the hub of British imperial policies for the region and announced that Cypriot self-determination was barred in perpetuity.

In 1954 Greece appealed to the UN for Cyprus to be granted rights of self-determination. The application was initially supported by the US but in 1955, consequent on British pressure, America withdrew its backing, and the application was shelved. Britain then invited Turkey and Greece to a conference on the future of the island. The motive of this was to obstruct further Greek efforts to raise the issue at the UN.* The Athens' government initially sought to avoid participation, since the 1921 Treaty of Lausanne had stipulated that Turkey had no rights in territories formerly under its jurisdiction. The failure of the conference was followed by attacks in Turkey on non–Turkic ethnic communities, mainly Greeks, and their property.[5] One main result of the conference was to allow both Ankara and Athens to claim grounds for their future involvement in the island's affairs.

Early in 1955 an armed campaign for *enosis* had been launched by EOKA, led by Colonel George Grivas[6] and supported from Athens. The fact that the target was not for straightforward independence, but for a union with Greece that was strongly opposed by Turkey, NATO's key regional ally, gave this a complexity not present in other anti-colonialist struggles.

The British response to the EOKA insurrection leaned heavily on the use of Turkish Cypriots in an anti-terrorist policing role and as informers: this exacerbated communal divisions, which were already defined by language and

---

* Foreign Office documents since released show that the essential motive, as stated by Sir Ivone Kirkpatrick, the Permanent Secretary at the Foreign Office, was "to bring the Greeks up against the Turks."

religion and now also being promoted by militant nationalistic elements in the two communities, which in turn were linked with right-wing forces and irredentist movements in Greece and Turkey. British proposals at this time, including the Macmillan Plan[7], leaned towards an acceptance of communal separation, starting with the municipalities.

By 1958 Grivas was speaking of the Turkish Cypriots as being his third enemy - the other two being the British and the communists. Turkish Cypriot violence against the Greek Cypriots came from TMT, a secret paramilitary force formed in 1957 under Turkish army sponsorship as a counterpart of EOKA: it was as nationalistic and anti-communist as EOKA but not anti-British. TMT received consistent backing from the Turkish army and had a specific remit to project Turkish military power into Cyprus. Meanwhile Ankara would henceforth meet every Athens' demand for *enosis* or self-determination by backing a TMT counter-demand for partition (*taksim*). Unlike EOKA, TMT was allowed by the British to remain legal almost to the end of the insurgency.*

In 1958, an offshoot of the rift between Britain and the Greek Cypriots, and of opportunist urgings from Ankara, was a deterioration of inter-communal relations into serious conflict: the Greek Cypriots were proportionately the greater victims, but both communities were exposed to widespread violence and killings and there were some movements of population. Calm was restored only after an appeal to the Turkish Cypriots by the Turkish Prime Minister, made in response to a conditional offer of US financial aid to Ankara.

The EOKA campaign ended in 1959 when Greece and Turkey, under pressure from Washington, agreed in Zurich to proposals for a form of limited independence for Cyprus, with both *enosis* and *taksim* precluded, with a constitution to be guaranteed jointly by Britain, Greece and Turkey, and with Britain acquiring sovereign ownership of substantial land areas, the SBAs, for military and intelligence use. The 1959 deal was reluctantly accepted by the Greek Cypriots, with deep misgivings and only after intense pressure on them from the Athens' government, which in turn was under pressure from the governments of America and Britain. The arrangement ratified in London was heavily criticised by many observers because it contained clauses that were inherently separatist, because it provided a small proportion of the population with a veto over the functioning of the state, because it gave Ankara and Athens a formal involvement in Cypriot affairs and because its success would be dependent on the doubtful premise of long-lasting goodwill from Athens and Ankara and from all of the key personalities and political elements in both communities.

Since independence in 1960 it had become apparent that some leaders in both communities and in Greece and Turkey saw the London Agreement as no more than a stepping-stone towards their abiding targets of *enosis* or *taksim*. The island's President, Archbishop Makarios, had prevaricated, continuing to talk in public about the inevitability of *enosis* while accepting in private that it

---

* See also note I/9

might not be achievable without unacceptable concessions; former leaders of EOKA had made plain that the struggle for *enosis* continued, albeit by other means; and hard-line Turkish Cypriot leaders had responded that any weakening of the constitution would lead to renewed agitation for *taksim*.

The provenance of the 1959 constitution, the failure to create a common sense of 'Cypriotness' and the continuing activity of *enotists* and of TMT meant that each community felt deeply threatened by the other. From 1962 elements in each community had been secretly organising and arming their own paramilitary units, with help from the Greek and Turkish armies respectively. There was a heavy involvement of former EOKA fighters in covert Greek Cypriot paramilitary groups, whereas Turkish Cypriot units were mainly recruited from men who formerly had served in the British army or in the British-trained Special Police.

At the end of November 1963 Makarios had submitted proposals for a revision of the constitution.[8] Kutchuk had suggested to the British that there might be room for negotiation, but Ankara had rejected any discussion of constitutional change. Tensions rapidly escalated and there were instances of harassment of Turkish Cypriot civil servants. Just before Christmas there was an outbreak of inter-communal clashes in Nicosia. Turkish Cypriot civil servants, claiming that their lives were in danger, withdrew from government, thus initiating a *de facto* administrative separation.

Cyprus now had a population of about six hundred thousand, of whom eighty percent were Greek-speaking Christians, most of whom regarded themselves as Greeks, and eighteen percent Turkish-speaking Muslims, most of whom regarded themselves as Turks.

That much I had culled from the history books and my briefings and the intelligence digests that I had read in Malta. I also knew there were allegations that Makarios' push for constitutional reform had been strongly encouraged, or even orchestrated, by the British High Commissioner in Cyprus, Sir Arthur Clark. A friend in Athens, Costas Kalligas, was the doyen of Greek press commentators on Cyprus; he had spoken at length with the Archbishop at the beginning of December and he told me that Makarios was adamant that he was acting with the strongest possible support from Britain.[9]

General Young said he didn't disagree with any of this. He said that other factors were the Cold War and NATO concerns over the influence of leftist elements in Cyprus. Arthur Clark had been trying to act as an honest broker.[10] He believed a compromise on constitutional reform would have been reached if Ankara had not intervened. He said that he could add to the story of the past twelve months, and that he would do that the next day, when he wanted me with him on a visit to Paphos, on the west coast.

Duncan Sandys, Secretary of State for Commonwealth Relations, on the right. Behind him is, centre, Sir Arthur Clark, British High Commissioner.

Major General Peter Young with his ADC, Captain Christopher Meynell.

2.   6 JANUARY 1964

A helicopter picked us up from the Cornaro Hotel in the early morning and we headed west. On the way to Paphos, General Young told me that ever since 1960 both sides had been making contingency plans against the possibility of a major clash. Each communal leadership believed that it was being plotted against: rather than seek for a bilateral confrontation of extremism, each, perhaps not surprisingly, sought unilateral answers to the perceived threat.

"All through last year," he said, "there was increasingly virulent agitation from both communities, the Greek Cypriots for revision of the constitution and *enosis*, the Turkish Cypriots for separation and *taksim*, and a gathering mutual mistrust was fuelled by extremism in the schools and in the press.

"Then the development of a brawl into a shooting incident on 21 December[1] led to an assumption that wider violence was imminent; both Makarios and Kutchuk authorised the issuance to paramilitary units in their respective communities of arms caches which had been secretly stored by them; 'private' paramilitary groups were let off the leash; the hard guys started to take a poke at each other; the politicians lost control.

"Since then both leaderships have been talking peace, but simultaneously some ministers have been trying to exploit the situation to further their own secret objectives, rather than try to resurrect the constitutional contract."

The General cited the problem of the municipalities as a core element in the dispute. He said he believed, as did other commentators, that the constitutional provision for a separate administration of the communities in each major city was misjudged in concept, unworkable in any practice where there was not real mutual trust and harmony, fundamentally divisive in result and unproductive of any benefit for the local population. He regretted that Britain had supported this proposal. The issue had been used by Turkey and the Turkish Cypriots to advance a process of *de facto* partition. But, he said, the manner of Greek Cypriot attempts to revise or revoke the constitutional provisions for the municipalities had been heavy-handed and provocative. They had heightened people's sense of insecurity and encouraged 'ghetto-isation'.

At Paphos we landed on a football pitch at the edge of the town and were met by the local communal leaders and the police and gendarmerie heads and taken to a nearby coffee-house. My interpreting skills were dispensed with, as it appeared that everyone spoke good English, and I was able to loiter in the background as an uninvolved observer.

Paphos seemed quiet but very tense. The police we saw were all Greek Cypriots and all armed.

General Young led off with an explanation of his role. He said he was not there as a judge. The peacekeeping force under his command was operating with the blessing of the leaderships of both communities to try to prevent further violence and to give the politicians a chance to resolve the situation. He needed help towards that end. Under the agreements of 25 December and onwards between Makarios and Kutchuk, strong-points should have been dismantled, and he was disturbed to learn that had not happened in Paphos. He was authorised to interpose peacekeeping forces between the boundaries of the two communities wherever he thought necessary.

General Young listened to lengthy expositions from those present. They harped back to the constitution and its un-workability. The Greek Cypriots claimed that the authorities of the state were being prevented from carrying out their proper functions. The Turkish Cypriots claimed they were being denied their constitutional rights and exposed to extreme harassment. The General clearly had heard all the arguments before. He was unfailingly polite.

Details of the truce were discussed. Nobody seemed to believe that it would hold.

Watching from the sidelines, and listening to exchanges between the Greek Cypriots, I felt profoundly saddened. All those there were reasonable, pleasant, restrained. There were none of the histrionics that I associated with even the most minor of crises in Greece. These were all nice people caught up in a situation whose implications they seemed not to comprehend.

Later I came to realise that the real, covert, local leadership seldom put in an appearance at meetings of this sort.

On the way back to Nicosia, the General talked about the failures of communal leadership. He said that politicians were covering up for the extremists, rather than challenging them, making it impossible for the originators of violence to be isolated and dealt with. The press of both communities was presenting a wholly distorted picture.

"Everyone has a modicum of right." he said. "Both communities have been led by their press and their politicians to believe they are under attack or threat. The glory boys are trying to carve their own heroic roles in the history books and nobody's calling them to order."

He went on to talk about the role of the Greek Cypriot police. At first the violence had been mainly confined to secret paramilitary units but latterly he had come to see the police as a major factor in the continuance of destabilisation. No longer was it a bi-communal force acting for the common good. Now, in a reverse of the British use of wholly Turkish Cypriot police units against Greek Cypriot insurrectionists in the 1950s, a wholly Greek Cypriot police force was being used against a supposed Turkish Cypriot insurrection. Its officers portrayed the situation in simplistic terms as the response to an armed mutiny against the state, which they were legally empowered to suppress. They repeatedly cited the methodology of British actions against EOKA as the model that they were following.

He said that the police insisted on exercising their right to mount heavily armed patrols into Turkish Cypriot areas and to stop and search Turkish Cypriot traffic on the roads. There had been frequent instances of hostage-taking, claimed as representing the arrest of TMT suspects. The police were confiscating shotguns from Turkish Cypriot villagers but not from the Greek Cypriots. They were making heavy use of reserves and specials, many of whom were known to the Turkish Cypriots as former EOKA gunmen. The manner of this continuing unilateral exercise of force was deeply frightening to the Turkish Cypriots, who had cause enough for alarm already, and was driving them into the arms of TMT and of their own extremists.

On the other side of the coin, he said, TMT appeared to be directly answerable to Turkey and was helping to project Turkish military power into Cyprus. The concomitant to this was an urging of the Turkish Cypriots to deny, or sabotage, opportunities for the development of a unitary stare. TMT had been smuggling in weapons, had access to a considerable pool of men trained in the use of arms by the British colonial police or armed forces, was provoking violence as a spur to communal separation and was receiving direct and substantial support from the Turkish army.*

General Young said: "Up to this point we've had quite an easy ride. The Greek Cypriots so far have been prepared to make concessions when we asked for them, unlike the Turkish Cypriots who have refused to budge an inch from their concept of communal separation. We're surely going to run into trouble soon when our operations clash with the activities of the Greek police. A lot of them already have a chip on their shoulder from EOKA times. They resent us telling them to cool it and they now see us as inhibiting their initiatives. They're probably only waiting for the right moment to test our authority and our resolve. I've talked about it to the Minister of the Interior, Polycarpos Georgadjis[2], and I'll do so again, but he doesn't take kindly to me trying to teach him his business, and our own remit is very shaky."

Back at the Cornaro there was a staff briefing and afterwards I was called into a meeting with General Young, his chief-of-staff Colonel Mike Andrews, Major Paul Greenwood and Brigadier R C 'Roly' Gibbs, the newly-arrived commander of 16 Para Brigade, which was being airlifted from the UK to reinforce units from the SBAs.

General Young said: "I've already spoken to each of you individually. At the risk of being repetitive I'll again run through the background as I see it, and then get to my proposals. It would have been helpful if Arthur Clark could be here, but he and I probably have very much the same view of things."

By the General's account, the 1960 constitution was a bastard, even if no better option was being proposed at the time. It gave Athens and Ankara an excuse for interfering in Cypriot affairs. It was never genuinely accepted by the hard men on either side: the Greek Cypriots, pushed by Athens and the Church and the old EOKA hierarchy, always assumed they would be able to change it in due course and achieve *enosis*. Turkish Cypriot extremists always assumed that a moment would come when events would give them the chance to move towards communal separation, supported by Ankara. For the constitution to have developed a satisfactory basis for statal cohesion there was a parallel need for moderate, mature leadership, with a tight control over the potential sources of extremism and a reasonable level of mutual trust and commitment: but no such experience existed. Instead, key positions in the leadership structure had been taken by men inexperienced in civil

---

* See also note I/9

administration, sometimes with a background rooted in violence or confrontation. Within each community a secret agenda was quickly instituted that ran counter to the constitution, each side claiming to be justified by the threat of attack.

The General said the situation had been blighted by the tendency of Greek Cypriots and Turkish Cypriots to see themselves first as Greeks or Turks rather than as Cypriots. An initial modicum of goodwill in 1960 was soon dissipated through dispute or frustration. The Turkish Cypriots saw the 1959/60 agreements as a victory: to most Greek Cypriots they quickly came to be seen as a trap into which they had been inequitably forced. In consequence, there had been little effort to run the island as a genuine partnership.

In 1960 optimists hoped that trust would develop through the exercise of effective co-operation and that inconsistencies in the constitution could then progressively be eliminated by mutual agreement: instead, relations had steadily deteriorated. Now, even the moderates who wanted to give the constitution a proper shot, were finding that their political lives depended on the paying of lip-service to *enosis* or *taksim* as the long-term target. No one was listening to the proponents of an authentic Cypriot identity within an effective independence.

TMT had remained active since the 1950s and had continued since independence to build up its stock of weaponry and to improve its training. EOKA had disbanded in 1959, but some of its weapon caches had probably remained intact. Since 1962 the Greek Cypriots had been constructing an island wide parastatal network, ostensibly as a response to TMT, and acquiring new weapons. Both communal leaderships therefore were mired in illegality. Serious tension had been mounting since the previous August. Each community had privately been claiming to have evidence of forthcoming attacks against it.

By mid 1963 the major political differences between the two communities, for all of which constitutional change was clearly needed, were seen to be: first, that the separate municipalities arrangement was proving unworkable in practice and the source of profound tension; second, that arrangements for taxation and the Separate Majority Vote had left Cyprus without an effective tax system; third, that a 70:30 ratio throughout the public services was hard to achieve in the immediate term due to the absence of required qualifications; and fourth, that formation of the Cyprus army was blocked by dispute over whether units should be fully integrated or formed in separate Greek Cypriot and Turkish Cypriot platoons.

By mid-December, fighting seemed inevitable. The incident on 21 December, when Greek Cypriot police officers tried to search a Turkish Cypriot car suspected of moving arms, escalated into shooting and Turkish Cypriot deaths. There was inflammatory rhetoric at the subsequent funerals, followed by Turkish Cypriot harassment of Greek Cypriots using the Kyrenia road, where it skirted the barracks of the Turkish army contingent to the north of Nicosia. Paramilitary groups had then been stood to. Widespread fire-fights had started in Nicosia on the 23rd.

The general said that there were fifteen thousand British dependants in Cyprus, in addition to the military. Their protection by use of armed force was authorised under UK treaty rights subject to approval from Whitehall, or from the High Commissioner in the last resort.

At the start of the Christmas troubles, Sir Denis Barnett, Commander-in-Chief Near Eastern Air Force and Administrator of the SBAs, had authorised preparations to be made for military action. The units then available in Cyprus were the 3rd Greenjackets, the Rifle Brigade, the 1st Battalion of the Gloucestershire Regiment and three squadrons of the RAF Regiment.

Early on 25 December, with the situation rapidly deteriorating, the Turkish contingent (TURDYK)[3] had moved out of its barracks, claiming a need to protect Turkish Cypriot villages to the north of Nicosia and to secure lines of communication to Kyrenia. The Greek contingent (ELDYK)[3] then also moved out of its barracks and, reportedly, some of its members became embroiled in an attack on Turkish Cypriot positions in the Omorphita district of Nicosia, bringing imminent danger of Greek-Turkish hostilities.[4] There were reports that the Turkish fleet had sailed. Intense international diplomatic activity was underway. Britain, Greece and Turkey jointly demanded a cessation of hostilities and proposed that a tripartite peacekeeping force, later to be named Joint Force, be constituted from British units together with the Greek and Turkish contingents already stationed in Cyprus.

Turkish and Greek army contingents in Cyprus. Under the constitution, TURDYK and ELDYK units, of 650 and 900 men respectively, were quartered at bases on the outskirts of Nicosia, at Orta Keuy and Plakonas.

At this point, according to the general, Makarios, convinced that there was danger of an early attack from Turkey, became anxious for a ceasefire. At the same time Kutchuk decided that it was vital to secure a respite for the besieged Turkish Cypriots. Just before midnight, the leaders agreed on a cease-fire and that an invitation should be issued for British troops to be deployed throughout the island in a peacekeeping role.

Makarios sought to enforce the ceasefire, but failed to launch an immediate pursuit of the opportunities for rapprochement which were created by it.[5]

Typically ineffectual road block.
Greek Cypriot stands guard in ditch.

Armed irregulars on the move.

It was arranged for further reinforcements to join the British force, the Sherwood Foresters from the UK and the 14th/20th Hussars from Libya, although this would still mean a very thin presence on the ground if serious inter-communal troubles resumed.

What was the British objective at that point? General Young said he had never viewed the situation as one of civil war but rather as a breakdown of civil government leaving a state of near-anarchy. The ordinary Cypriot lacked reasonable security and there was no likelihood that problems could be resolved through existing political mechanisms without risk of further violence. The instruction he had received from London was to "Maintain the cease-fire", but he felt that was insufficiently positive. What was needed was to create an atmosphere sufficiently peaceful for serious negotiation and for normal political mechanisms to be restored. He believed that a British force could not by itself restore law and order: that would need a responsible civil government and a co-operative bi-communal police force.

On 26 December, a first tripartite conference was convened to consider arrangements needed to implement the previous night's cease-fire. Arthur Clark explained the position of the guarantor powers and his understanding of the verbal agreement that had been made. Apparently exhausted by the strain of recent days and deeply affected by the violent murder, at their home in Nicosia, of the wife and children of his regiment's medical officer, the commander of the Turkish contingent had suffered a nervous breakdown and had to be helped out of the conference.[6]

Next day the Greek regiment accepted an instruction from General Young and returned to its barracks, but the new commander of the Turkish contingent, Colonel Saglan, refused to issue a similar order. It was then resolved that the Greek and Turkish contingents would, for the time being, participate actively in JF only through the provision of officers for a number of tripartite patrols under British leadership. Major Paul Greenwood was told to assess how this requirement should be developed.

Duncan Sandys arrived on the 28th with proposals for the convening of a Peace Conference in London. A political liaison committee (The Joint Liaison Committee, or 'JLC') was formed. Present at the first JLC meeting were Duncan Sandys, Sir Denis Barnett, Sir Arthur Clark, General Young, the Ambassadors of Greece and Turkey, the commanders of the Greek and Turkish contingents, and Greek Cypriot and Turkish Cypriot representatives. Cease-fire arrangements and terms for the operation of the joint peacekeeping force were discussed. During the day it was reported that the Turkish fleet had returned to port. Additional reinforcements for JF airlifted from the UK included the 1st Battalion of the Para Regiment and the Guards Independent Para Company.

General Young said that, at a further meeting of the Liaison Committee on 29 December, he had used a green chinagraph pencil to draw onto a map of Nicosia a line which defined a 'border' between the Turkish Cypriot and Greek Cypriot areas of the city. This had become known as 'The Green Line'. With a second blue chinagraph he had hatched in 'Blue-shaded Areas' on either side of the Green Line from which paramilitary fortifications were to be removed and within which the JF would have freedom of action to ensure the maintenance of security.*

The General emphasised to us that the Green Line was intended only to provide a breathing space. We would need to create conditions for its removal as soon as possible. Otherwise, he said, there would be accusations that the measure was furthering partition rather than saving lives.

During the visit by Duncan Sandys the convening of a peace conference in London was approved, but there was difficulty in reaching agreement on its terms. The 12 January start originally scheduled had to be put back to the 15th.

On 30 December the Green Line Agreement was signed.† British troops then occupied positions in the Blue-shaded Areas and along the Green Line and JF Headquarters (JFHQ) were established in the Cornaro Hotel. The following day troop positions were adjusted and consolidated; medical supplies, blankets and food were delivered to areas of Turkish Cypriot destitution; dead bodies were collected, identified when possible and buried.

By the end of December the danger of further large-scale fighting in Nicosia had receded, following the establishment of the JLC, the stationing of

---

* See Appendix A (Addendum)
† See Appendix A and Addendum

peacekeeping troops along the Green Line and agreement on a peace conference. But the fire quenched in the capital had burst into sporadic, though limited, flame elsewhere, particularly in Larnaca and the other main towns, sparked by paramilitary confrontations, deliberate provocations, old enmities re-awakened, rumours of atrocity and hostage-taking and fanned by resentment and fear. The situation reflected the lack of effective leadership from the centre. In the countryside Turkish Cypriot travel was almost at a standstill. In many areas armed men were facing each other across hastily-erected barricades.

General Young said: "That's the situation we now face. We don't have much time and our legal position is tenuous. The Greek Cypriots believe they have exclusive legitimacy of government, that a Turkish Cypriot resort to arms (which the Greek Cypriots claim has long been planned) constitutes a revolt against the national administration, that the police force must have unimpeded rights of action, and that we're here to deal with extremism that's got out of control and to eliminate the possibility of a Turkish invasion. The Turkish Cypriots believe the Greek Cypriots are out to dissolve the constitutional partnership and to eradicate their rights by force and that they now have valid justification for armed resistance and for removing their community from areas where it is threatened, and that we are here to provide a shield behind which they can do so.

"Who's in charge? Normal political management has broken down. Makarios and Kutchuk and all of their senior ministers were probably complicit in, or knew about and tolerated, the creation of illegal paramilitary organisations within their own communities, and therefore are in breach of the constitution. The agenda is now being set not by the government but ad hoc by secret organisations on both sides; by army officers from Greece or Turkey; by the leaders of private armies, including Nicos Sampson[7] and Vassos Lyssarides[7]; and by the heads of the police and the gendarmerie. Additionally the Greek and Turkish intelligence services are pushing things along, the former working through Sampson and other ex-EOKA rightists and the latter linked with TMT."

The General said he had tried to get through to the hard-line paramilitary leaders but they were not willing to meet him. The Minister of the Interior, Polycarpos Georgadjis, probably knew more than anyone about what was going on but he was difficult to approach and he certainly did not seem to be pushing for reconciliation.

Both paramilitary leaderships were clearly ready to use force to the limits of their capacity. The Greek Cypriot target appeared to be an aggressive dismantling of TMT so as to clear the road to *enosis*. The TMT game-plan seemed to be for occasional deliberate provocations against the Greek Cypriots, for pressure on Turkish Cypriots to concentrate in defined enclaves and for the provision to Turkey of adequate excuse for active intervention.

Unfortunately there appeared at present not to be any strong popular wish for compromise. Each community was fed up with the other: the Turkish Cypriots because they felt bypassed, belittled and insecure; the Greek Cypriots because they felt frustrated and obstructed by a small minority that was abusing powers bestowed on it by an unfair, externally-imposed constitution. Neither community had provided the commitment and goodwill that the London formula required. The press of both communities had been vitriolic and had helped to turn irritation into hatred. At present there was very little residual trust on which to build.

Constitutionally, Cyprus was a unitary state that existed on the basis of a partnership between two communities. That partnership was now in a state of breakdown, hopefully not irrevocable. It was the General's view that we had to deal with the rump administration as though it represented the whole island while simultaneously defending the human and constitutional rights of the Turkish Cypriots. Makarios had constitutional power as President and what remained of his government at least carried the electoral empowerment of the vast majority of the population and controlled most of the national infrastructure. Kutchuk remained Vice-President.

The General said: "It's a moot point whether we've been invited here by the President and Vice-President on behalf of the Cypriot government or by Makarios and Kutchuk on behalf of the two communities.

"Most Greek Cypriots are frightened of a Turkish invasion but, in spite of the scare over Christmas, they act as though that threat is not really credible. They genuinely believe that *enosis* is inevitable and somewhere just around the corner. I personally detest the idea of partition: ultimately it would be disastrous for everyone, including the Turks and ourselves. But I don't doubt that there's a real threat of it being imposed by Ankara if the Greek Cypriots don't get their act together and if they fail to gain the trust of the Turkish Cypriots.

"So far Joint Force has not faced any serious difficulty. When it first deployed most of the people greeted it with real warmth, perhaps because they had no sympathy with the violence or because they felt the British presence would increase their life-expectancy."

The General went on: "There are three interconnected levels in this situation. One contains the international players, with Athens and Ankara in the lead. HMG handles that, with Duncan Sandys as our link. Then the politicians here and in the towns, which means most of the principal political activists: they'll be the headache of myself and the High Commissioner. And finally the main population of Cyprus, in the countryside: that effort will be spearheaded by your tripartite patrols."

There was a map of Cyprus on an easel. The General said: "Greenwood will co-ordinate operations. We'll start with two patrols headed by Greenwood and Packard, which will go to wherever the need is greatest. As soon as possible two more patrols will be formed, under Commander Carmichael and Captain Macdonald, which will cover the Larnaca and Paphos Zones. Packard and Greenwood will then have responsibility for Nicosia Zone and Famagusta,[8] although Greenwood's coordinating job may not leave him much time in the field. Patrol commanders will have the support of specific army units, 16 Para for Packard and the Greenjackets for Paul Greenwood and patrols will be able to ask for field back-up from the military and the aid agencies as necessary.

"You will have choppers whenever I can make them available. At other times you can draw Land Rovers from the pool as and when you need, with three drivers and a radio operator attached to each patrol." *

General Young said there was no restriction on whom the patrols could talk to. "You can discuss situations directly with the offices of Makarios and Kutchuk as you feel necessary and with relevant ministers. There's no secret agenda in this, so you can use your discretion on what to tell to whom. In any event your Greek and Turkish officers will be presenting their own interpretation of events to their respective contingents, which will feed on to Athens and Ankara and probably also to the leaders of the Greek Cypriot and Turkish Cypriot communities. It certainly won't hurt for Makarios and Kutchuk to get an objective view from you. And patrols definitely will need to try and establish a dialogue with paramilitary leaderships and with whatever private armies come into play.

"In effect these patrols are being seconded to the Cypriot leadership. I see them as providing a peacemaking thrust at ground level. If the island is not to disintegrate, we have to hold the communities together as best we can, whatever different direction some politicians are driving, until there's a situation calm enough for sensible decisions to be taken and enforced."

The general went on: "Your first job will be to assess what the situation in the countryside really is. There's already been a good deal of movement of Turkish Cypriots in some areas. We don't know whether that's because of genuine fear or intimidation or because of pressure from extremists. We need to create a climate in which that movement can be stopped or reversed.

"Please remember that the Greek and Turkish officers you'll be working with are likely to be both biased and touchy. They've been very close to the violence over the past two weeks and they've been exposed to a lot of tough propaganda. They may try and pursue their own agenda in the villages, so you'll have to keep a tight rein and at the same time be extremely diplomatic."

I asked whether we would be getting a written authority defining our targets and what we could and could not do. The General said he had agreed a brief catch-all instruction with Paul Greenwood: 'To act as necessary to re-establish normal relations between the Greek and Turkish communities in the rural areas.' The aim was to help the communities to recreate a working partnership, not to facilitate their individual concepts of the future.

General Young went on: "I've talked to you at length so that you're clear on my wishes. We're here at Cypriot invitation as a concerned friend. We don't have any powers of search or arrest. We can expect the police to co-operate with us only when they think it's to their benefit or when central government has insisted that they do so. The situation is very fluid and I prefer to rely on your common sense and discretion rather than draft a manual of instructions. On the assumption that you'll avoid dropping us into any serious shit you can simply say that you're acting with my personal authority."

---

* Support staff initially allocated to me were: Cpl K. Jones (QDG); L/Cpl T. Hardiman (R. Sigs); L/Cpl Beaumont (RA); L/Cpl J. Missener (R. Sigs); Gnr Pickwell (RA); Pte S. Causer (Paras); Sig W. Kilgrain (R. Sigs); Sig Spencer (R. Sigs)

I said: "If we're to get people's trust we'll need to deserve it. That means being selective about what we pass on, even to you. We won't get far if we're perceived to be acting as spies for the British or for one or other of the communities. You've confirmed that a lot is going to come down to our discretion. We're to regard ourselves as seconded to the Cypriot political leadership. That suggests to me that our first loyalty is going to have to be to the people for whom we're mediating."

General Young said: "I'll go along with that. If you need further definition you can see me or Roly Gibbs in complete privacy. That applies equally if you need any other confirmation or guidance."

The General ended: "One final and personal word. The situation here has been inherently unstable ever since 1960. Remember it's not just the Cypriots who are to blame for this wretched mess, although obviously they carry the responsibility for stumbling into every trap there was and for failing to control their extremists. In consequence they've brought down on themselves the ceiling of a very rickety building that was designed for them by outsiders. The major onus inevitably falls on the Greek Cypriots because they're by far the majority and it's up to them, whatever the provocation, to stay cool and show some statesmanship. But after the violent background of the EOKA years they started out with a continuing and passionate fixation on *enosis* and an unfortunate blindness to the fact that the future, whatever it is to be, will depend on them gaining the trust of the Turkish Cypriots. I have a strong affection for both communities and a real sympathy for their feelings and I don't want you acting as though we still had some god-given imperial right to dictate their future. In the end it's they who have to find a way forward together. It's our job to help create an atmosphere in which they can do that peaceably."

Heads of British Forces in Cyprus. Major General Peter Young, Air Vice-Marshall Sir Denis Barnett and Major General Michael Carver.

Helicopter view of HQ (Cornaro Hotel). Kyrenia range in background (Pentadaktylos).

Joint Force group photograph outside temporary HQ at Cornaro Hotel. Seated 1st left Major Sait Sepici, 3rd left Major Paul Greenwood and 6th left Lt. Col. Akova, centre Major General Peter Young. Standing 1st right Lt. Constantinides, on his right Capt. Christopher Meynell. Seated 1st right Capt. John Michos, 3rd right Major Edward (Ted) Macey, 4th right me, 7th right (centre) Commander Carmichael.

16 Para Brigade group photograph, taken immediately after the March 27 switch to UN command. Brigadier Roly Gibbs seated centre, Major John Burgess seated extreme left and me seated on extreme right.

Left, Major General Peter Young, during a visit to ELDYK and TURDYK units, which were under his command in the Tripartite Force. Here, 11 January, he is negotiating a reduced level of patrolling activity with the Turkish Field HQ beside the Kyrenia Road at Orta Keuy, where they were dug in. Centre is Capt. Mike Gilmore, Liaison officer with the Turkish army.

Major General Young with Turkish Cypriot leaders outside the residence of Vice-President, Dr Kutchuk.

3.   LEARNING TO WALK.   NICOSIA.
6-7 JANUARY 1964

Later that evening I had a long session with Paul Greenwood, was given the notes he had written on villages and personalities for which I would become responsible, and discussed his own findings. He said that most of Nicosia Zone was in reasonable shape, with the exception of Skylloura, Ayios Vasilios and Mathiati and, to a lesser extent, a couple of villages in the Karpas peninsula*.

Earlier that day, while I was with General Young in Paphos, Paul Greenwood had convened joint meetings in Lapithos and Kyrenia at which police and civic leaders were present. His report noted:

> *"Some progress made in re-establishing a working liaison between the two communities. TC given an opportunity to express their grievances, which mainly concerned abuses of power by some of the GC police special constables. GC stated wish for co-existence and intention to deal with TC complaints. At both meetings GC and TC leaders specifically requested that British troops be stationed in areas north of the Kyrenia Range. I believe such a move would undoubtedly restore confidence, since GC fear TC attack from the south and TC fear the GC police."*

Greenwood said I would have to give special attention to the refugee areas. There were probably five hundred refugees from Skylloura and Ayios Vasilios in Photta; Mandres was overwhelmed with those who had fled from Omorphita; Kochati was crammed with villagers from Mathiati. These refugees were strung between extreme fear and incandescent rage. Some of them had been taken in by relatives but most of them lacked proper shelter or supplies. Military patrols sent to investigate reports of nine dead Turkish Cypriots still in their homes in Ayios Vasilios had been refused entry to the area by heavily armed Greek Cypriot irregulars. Photta, Kochati and Mandres were inevitably turning into centres of extremism, bitterness and militancy, as was Kophinou in Larnaca Zone.

He showed me an end-of-year press report, from the *Guardian* of 31.12.63, that he thought provided reasonable commentary on the situation:

> "A tense and uneasy calm reigns throughout Cyprus but the senseless cruel slaughter of Christmas Eve and morning has so enraged both Turkish and

---

* Also known as Karpasia.

Greek communities that one hot-headed action could set alight the whole island. Cyprus is today in a state of anarchy. Government has virtually ceased to function; roads between the main towns are controlled by armed Greek irregulars; Turkish communities in towns and villages are living ghetto-like existences. The Cypriot police and army have split into national groups and joined their own communities.

"Unhappily a return to normal is not enough. In Cyprus racial hostility and suspicion is normal: the threat of political deadlock is normal: the recent outburst of violence sprang out of what is there the normal state of distrust.

"The most urgent of present tasks is to wrest the initiative from the sinister forces which a few days ago threatened to dominate the situation, and to dissipate the fear of unprovoked attack."

Greenwood said that during the first days of January there had been a big increase in the number of roadblocks set up by armed paramilitaries of both communities and that villagers, spurred on by extremist propaganda, had begun to construct their own local defences, either against neighbouring villages or around communal enclaves.

On the evening of my arrival, 5 January, General Young had extracted from the political leaderships of the two communities a general agreement for the restoration of freedom of movement and communications and for the general lowering of tension: both sides were to dismantle all offensive and defensive positions, remove all roadblocks and barricades, disperse armed bands and end the carrying of arms by civilians. Both leaderships had agreed that there would be no further interference in any way with normal freedom of movement, transport or communications, and that for the time being there would be no requests for proof of identity, search, detention or arrest of persons belonging to the other community.

This key agreement, formerly approved on 6 January, was to be used as a basis for the initial work of the tripartite patrols, which would seek to ensure that its terms were known and observed throughout those areas which lacked regular contact with Nicosia. If they needed support, to emphasise that this was an officially approved line, patrols could for the next few days ask to be accompanied by political leaders of the two communities, so that guidance on the agreement could be given to isolated areas and so that the re-establishment of central political leadership could begin.

This led to my first encounter with Rauf Denktash[1], deputy to Vice-President Kutchuk and reportedly the political leader of TMT, just before his departure via Turkey for the London Conference. I had been sent on 6 January with a Turkish officer, Captain Abdullah Gundes, to the office of Kutchuk to verify that the message going out from there would tally with General Young's dictum on Freedom of Movement. I was directed to discuss the matter with Denktash. I was received with great politeness and affability by a short, shrewd, energetic man who strikingly reminded me of Dom Mintoff, the leader of the Maltese socialists.

Unlike Kutchuk, who looked pasty-faced, tense and unwell, Denktash seemed robust and buoyant, and prepared to talk at great length. He already had been briefed about me and knew that I had a Greek wife. He asked me about my first impressions of Cyprus. He said that terrible things had happened which I would understand better when I met some of the refugees. He disagreed with the latest cease-fire arrangements: the Turkish Cypriots should not be pushed to remove their defences until they were confident that they had genuine security and that it was safe to do so. He did not believe there was any goodwill on the Greek Cypriot side. Nevertheless, he said, he would help me down the road of lessening tension and then assess the result.

Denktash spoke with Captain Gundes and then told me he had instructed the Turkish officer to deliver to the villages the message that I had requested. His support was to prove an effective aid to an initial opening of doors to the covert Turkish Cypriot leadership.[2]

The rest of 6-7 January was devoted to my indoctrination by 16 Para into the ways of the army, meetings with the support that would be available to me and planning with Paul Greenwood for a division of our duties. 16 Para suggested that they arrange for me a parachute jump so that I would feel more at home in their company. Regrettably the subsequent pressures of patrolling prevented me from taking up this invitation.

Leading Turkish Cypriot figures of the post independence administration pictured early 1964.

Dr Fazil Kutchuk (left), Vice President of Cyprus, with Dr S. H. Kiazim and Fazil Plummer, Minister of Agriculture and Natural resources, holding a press conference.

Rauf Denktash (left), President of the Turkish Cypriot Chamber of Commerce with Osman Orek, Minister of Defence, at the Cyprus Conference, Marlborough House, January 1964.

4.   THE MISSION STARTS.   8-10 JANUARY

Against my better judgement I carried a Sten gun on my first patrol.

The Paras, concerned for my safety, had insisted that I should be armed, as was everyone else. They had persuaded me to sign for a standard machine-pistol and ammunition and given me a ten-minute run through on operating procedures.

It was 8 January. Paul Greenwood was in the Morphou and Potamia areas and there was no helicopter available for me, so I opted for other villages to the south west of Nicosia for a trial run. Captain Gundes, from TURDYK, and Lieutenant Constantinides, from ELDYK, were to work with me.

Because General Young's JFHQ was uncertain of the climate in outlying areas, instructions had been issued that for the time being Turkish liaison officers were not to accompany patrols into wholly Greek Cypriot centres, and vice versa. So my Greek officer, Lieutenant Constantinides, and I went on alone to the main Greek Cypriot coffee-house in Nisou, where our arrival was greeted with some suspicion. An introduction from Constantinides and my own exposition in Greek changed the climate to one of interest and considerable warmth. We were joined by the village leaders and plunged into animated discussion on the situation locally and in Cyprus generally. They had no problems, but expressed anxiety over the safety of their grazing lands in the direction of Louroujina.

They undertook to refrain from any provocation. I recorded the local sentiment as 'uneasiness' and 'exasperation' rather than animosity or anger.

I drank several cups of *tourkiko* (Turkish coffee) and was sad to say goodbye.

We had driven a couple of miles out of Nisou when my driver asked me what had happened to my Sten gun. After a moment's mental blockage I realised that I had left it on the table in the coffee-house. We drove back to Nisou. For the second time Captain Gundes was asked to wait in the radio Land Rover outside the village.

The same group was sitting in the coffee-house. There was no sign of the missing gun.

I pleaded in my best and most emotive Greek. I said I was a friend of Cyprus who would be crucified if the gun was not found. I said this was their chance to prove their commitment to peace. I talked myself hoarse.

The coffee-house clientele said they could not imagine how the Sten had disappeared.

Eventually Constantinides asked me for time with them alone. Ten minutes later he returned with the Sten gun. The owner of the coffee-house came out and embraced me warmly, gave me a packet of *loukoumi* (Turkish Delight) and said he hoped I'd be back.

We moved on to Limbia. Before going into the coffee-house there I gave the Sten gun to my driver and told him to guard it with his life until we got back to base. It was the last time I ever carried a weapon in Cyprus, a fact that probably contributed significantly to my survival.

By 9 January, when I ran my first full patrol, foreign press estimates were that, in response to the 6 January agreement, over three quarters of all roadblocks had been removed.

My patrol that day was a helicopter sortie during which we aimed to identify remaining fortifications, roadblocks and gatherings of armed irregulars. When any of these were found we would land as nearby as possible and, with my Greek or Turkish officer as appropriate, I would saunter up to whoever appeared to be in charge and amiably suggest that the new Makarios-Kutchuk agreement meant that there was to be an end to impediments to travel and to the carrying of arms.

I was met everywhere with surprise followed by reluctant compliance. I was left with a naive and erroneous supposition that the road ahead would be relatively easy.

Before leaving Athens an acquaintance there, Panaghis Cavadias, had given me an introduction to his cousin-in-law in Nicosia, Spyros Kyprianou, the Minister of Foreign Affairs. Invited to his home that evening I was offered tea by Mrs Kyprianou, who said that her husband was unable to meet me. She asked what I was doing in Cyprus. The longer we chatted, the more aware did I become of an underlying hostility. Eventually I was told that the British were not welcome back in Cyprus. She questioned British goodwill, suggested that Britain was simply aiming to help the Turks and doubted my ability to be even-handed. She said there probably was no point in my talking to Mr Kyprianou, but added helpfully that a more useful contact might be with Mr Tassos Papadopoulos, whose phone number she gave me and who, she said, was sympathetic to concepts of compromise[1].

On 10 January, I arranged and attended inaugural meetings of joint councils in mixed community villages at Ephtakomi, Komi Kebir, Syngrasi, Arnadhi, Lapathos and Yenagra. The encouragement that had come from the previous day's removal of roadblocks continued, with the day showing how rapidly extreme distrust could give way to goodwill and co-operation. Both communities seemed relieved to get the message of the 6 January agreement, and accepted that tension must be lowered and inter-communal tolerance promoted.

At Ephtakomi the barricades were still up when we arrived. Having been greeted by the Greek Cypriot leaders and explained our programme, we started with a separate meeting with the Turkish Cypriots. I was taken by them to see a small child who had just died. Its parents were deeply distraught. They said that the villagers had been too frightened to travel with it to the nearest hospital for the blood transfusion that it needed and had had no means of communication with which to summon a doctor.

They gave two reasons for their fear. They said that a few days earlier their bus, having set off to collect food, had been waved to a stop at a Greek Cypriot police roadblock outside Trikomo and then shot up with automatic weapons. One villager, who was produced for us to examine, had been hit in the neck. The bus, which we were also taken to inspect, had been riddled with bullet-holes. We were told that only the quick-wittedness of the driver had allowed the bus to escape back to Ephtakomi. After this the Turkish Cypriots had erected barricades between the two sectors of the village and had kept them permanently manned.

Second, both by day and night they had seen frequent comings and goings by armed Greek Cypriot police and auxiliaries, together with men they recognised as former EOKA fighters. None of these had attempted to approach their barricades but they had felt threatened and sure that an attack on them would not be long delayed.

Their only complaint about the Greek Cypriot villagers was that they had declined to give them any help, apparently because they were fearful of 'repercussions from EOKA'. Now they were short of every sort of foodstuff and medicine. They were very reluctant to take part in a joint meeting but agreed to do so after urging from Captain Gundes.

We then met separately with the Greek Cypriot villagers who substantially confirmed the story we had just heard. They were unhappy at the child's death but said that under present circumstances they had thought it 'unwise' to offer help. They were themselves alarmed because their usual source of drinking water was inside the Turkish Cypriot sector of the village.

Neither group felt it proper to enter the other's sector, so the joint meeting was in due course held on open ground outside the village. It was hard to break through the crust of deep suspicion, but eventually there was mutual acknowledgement of their former good relations and agreement on their wish to resume a life of good-neighbourliness and on the need for inter-communal co-operation. This enabled us to establish a joint village committee, upon which we impressed the need to deal with each other's insecurities. We undertook to return every few days and in the meantime to ensure the delivery of essential foodstuffs. The Greek Cypriots said they would help out with urgent supplies and in future get medical help if it was needed. We then witnessed the restoration of the water link and a symbolic removal of one of the barricades. (A follow-up visit six days later confirmed that the committee was functioning effectively. A JF Land Rover had delivered supplies. All remaining barricades had been removed. The Greek Cypriots were helping with telephone and transport facilities.)

In Komi Kebir we heard a similar story. Here, too, the Turkish Cypriots were running short of foodstuffs and felt isolated and under threat. A villager, Halil Mustafa, had left on 31 December with his bus, accompanied by two other Turkish Cypriots, to try to acquire stocks of food. Neither the bus nor any of its occupants had been heard of since.

The lack of real communal integration in Cypriot villages was highlighted by the fact that Turkish Cypriots and Greek Cypriots seldom used the same shops or the same buses. In Komi Kebir, as in most villages in the area, their bus was critical to the survival of the Turkish Cypriots because, as well as being used by them to collect their supplies and deliver their produce, it provided transport for all those who went daily to work at the British base at Dhekelia. The wages they thus earned were the main source of income for the area. Their inability now to get to work had already led to a severe local shortage of cash.

The Turkish Cypriots asked me whether arrangements could be made for Dhekelia or JFHQ to send transport for them. I urged this at headquarters over the next few days, stressing that a restoration of the means and security of travel and a resumption of cash-flow was critical to the stability of the rural areas. My request was refused by JFHQ, not because of technical difficulties but as 'a matter of principle'.[2]

Once the joint meeting that we convened had restored inter-communal communication and upon the mistaken assumption that we would manage to resolve their transport problems, the Turkish Cypriots in Komi Kebir expressed a renewed confidence in the future. Both communities undertook to co-operate, no matter what pressures were put on them.

I was not sure I could share the new-found optimism. Komi Kebir gendarmerie station, isolated between the two sections of the village, looked a monument to insecurity. Its approaches were barricaded, its outer gates festooned with barbed wire, the whole structure extravagantly sandbagged. Inside were four heavily armed Greek Cypriot irregulars, furtive and unshaven for several days, and two regular policemen. The police claimed that they were exempt from Nicosia's instruction for the removal of fortifications, that the specials had been needed to take up the posts of Turkish Cypriot policemen who had left for their homes at Christmas and not returned, and that the station was fully committed to the preservation of law and order in Komi Kebir.

I found the appearance of the fortified police post deeply disturbing and could imagine that it would strike fear into the average Turkish Cypriot villager. I therefore was somewhat surprised when the next patrol visit to Komi Kebir reported that co-operation was holding up well and that inter-communal relations were now good.

The story was repeated in Syngrasi, Lapathos, Arnadhi and Yenagra. In each case the reports that reached them at Christmas had produced a degree of fear that led to a complete separation of the two communities, which had afterwards inched back together through tentative contacts between friends. The Turkish Cypriots were now frightened of the Greek Cypriot paramilitaries and police, had ceased all travelling and were running short of cash and foodstuffs. Their alarm had been increased by radio broadcasts from Nicosia and by stories transmitted between villages by those shepherds who had ventured back to their grazing lands.

Inter-communal meetings in each case started with difficulty and suspicion and ended with goodwill and co-operation. Joint committees were established and given a set of targets. At Lapathos, at the villagers' own suggestion, a local 'Treaty of Friendship' was drawn up and signed by representatives of each community. This particular agreement was honoured for as long as I was in Cyprus, but on numerous occasions in other villages, when a similar proposal was made by the Greek Cypriots, it was rejected by the Turkish Cypriots on the grounds that it was designed to be used for propaganda purposes.

I came very quickly to appreciate the huge advantages offered by the tripartite formula of the patrol. Not only could we immediately create a bond with each community in its own language, through an officer who was sympathetic to their cause, but we also could present the rural areas with the highly symbolic picture of a Greek and Turkish officer working creatively together, empowered by Makarios and Kutchuk and encouraged by the British.

Even though the Greek and Turkish officers tended to be conventionally representative of their country's nationalist viewpoints and prejudices, we were able to fashion around our assignment a modicum of general agreement. We agreed that solutions must come through political or diplomatic process, not through anarchy or an unconstitutional use of force. We agreed that human rights must be defended, that attacks by one community on the persons or property of the other must be prevented, and that there was a paramount need for the rule of law to prevail. We also agreed that dealing with inter-communal stress required the promotion and maintenance of effective links between the leaders of the two communities at all levels: in this, and in seeking to prevent Turkish Cypriot evacuations from mixed areas, my Turkish officers must at times have acted in conflict with the policy of TMT. My Greek officers, on the other hand, were frequently the first to identify, and condemn, instances where Greek Cypriot police or irregulars had used violence against Turkish Cypriots.

However, they seldom agreed on the cause of events. Each officer would usually blame an incident entirely on the faults of the other community. Their reporting of what had happened was usually accurate; their estimate of why it had happened was almost invariably biased.

The Turkish officer who served with me longest, Major Sait Sepici, was a man small in size but of huge moral stature. I quickly acquired for him a deep admiration. Despite repeatedly finding himself in situations that were profoundly distressing or difficult for him, I never saw him fail to act with loyalty to the work of the patrol. Writing to me long after we had both left Cyprus he said: "*That was the hardest time of my life and I saw sights that were terrible for me. But it was also the best time of my life because I was doing something that I felt was absolutely good and working in a team that was only devoted to good.*"

It was advantageous, too, that, in approaching a situation of serious difficulty the patrol members could discuss it among themselves and seek to formulate an agreed approach before engaging in debate with the villagers or paramilitary leaders.

JFHQ was a beneficiary in that it began to receive valid analysis of the climate in the rural areas. Until then regular army patrols had had to communicate in the villages through whatever interpreters they could find there. Usually this meant the local schoolmasters: regrettably they tended to be the most vociferous and militant exponents of the Greek or Turkish nationalist line, and among Greek Cypriots the most dismissive of the British commitment to peacekeeping: so the picture arriving at JFHQ had been consistently skewed.

Tripartite patrols not only carried with them the backing of JFHQ and the imprimatur of the political leadership of each community but, because of their

Greek and Turkish officers, they were able to claim additional authority from Athens and Ankara. We were thus in a position to initiate real political debate, albeit at a parochial level, and did so in innumerable coffee-house gatherings. This served both as an aid to the lowering of tension and as encouragement for the cause of peaceful inter-communal liaison. In many villages we were told that it was the first time they had been exposed to any real debate about inter-communal relationships.

It was, however, quickly obvious that for four patrols to cover the whole of Cyprus, and for a single patrol to cover Nicosia Zone, would place an immense strain on the officers concerned, if effective mediation were to be provided throughout the region. A quick visit might be adequate for problem-free villages, but in most cases the patrols were dealing with a deeply traumatised population. 'Stress-counselling' was not a phrase used in 1964 (nor had post-traumatic stress become a symptom recognised by the British army), but the early efforts of the patrols, when they were trying to stem evacuation and to counter a general alarm among the Turkish Cypriots in mixed areas, incorporated this function. Villagers had no other entity to which they could turn for the exorcising of their fears and for advice and reassurance.

The quality and attitudes of the patrol officers therefore were critical. In these first days I was surprised, moved and impressed by the commitment and performance of the members of my team. Later it emerged that Turkish and Greek officers were sometimes being used by their contingents, under cover of the patrols, to relay instructions to secret paramilitary leaders and that the Turkish officers were sometimes encouraging villages to evacuate. This risk existed in all of the patrols: in mine it was somewhat reduced because the Greek officers who served with me could all speak some Turkish and my Turkish officers some Greek, so that we could keep a watchful eye on each other.

We also could demonstrate effectiveness. Because our requests for supplies and medical help were always fast-tracked by JFHQ and by the aid agencies we gained special kudos. We could take serious problems directly to ministers and in lesser matters we could act on our own initiative. We also had greater expectation than any other group in Cyprus of being able to locate hostages and secure their return.

The damage to stability in the rural areas due to the absence of contact with higher authority was immediately apparent. Communal leaderships in Nicosia benefited by receiving from the patrols an accurate assessment on which to base their decision-taking, and by providing a dependable link to the offices of Makarios and Kutchuk I found that we could act as a shock-absorber when situations were particularly disturbing. We tried to demonstrate, both to the villagers and to central leadership that we were operating with a direct and equal responsibility towards each community.

In giving our primary loyalty to the Cypriots we not infrequently aggravated regular British army units under JFHQ command. Although regrettable, this was not disadvantageous for us. When arguments occurred between villagers and British army units we were able to act either as an advocate for the villagers or as an independent mediator, and our status with the Cypriots was thereby enhanced.

By 10 January regular army patrols were reporting a change in the attitude towards them on the part of the Greek Cypriots. Relations with the police were said to have deteriorated. And instead of the popular welcome that army patrols had received in the villages in the first days of peacekeeping they were now frequently greeted with open hostility.

I used each morning to scan all the main Nicosia papers and in the evening to read those from Athens (and the Turkish officer in my team would report to me on significant items in the Turkish press). For about ten days after Christmas the Athens press had in general been supportive of British efforts and Greek Cypriot papers had tended to follow suit, although even before my secondment to Cyprus I had read in the *Guardian* of 3 January a report which highlighted a growing belief among Greek Cypriots that the British presence was favouring Turkish Cypriot separatism. Early in January, editors in Athens apparently decided that the situation in Cyprus no longer warranted the retention there of their top-line reporters: they reverted to the use of local 'stringers' and the quality of coverage was markedly weakened. On 8 January the Greek Cypriot press delivered a strong broadside against the presence and activities of British troops and against the ulterior motives of the British government, and from there on most Greek and Greek Cypriot newspapers carried an anti-British tenor of varying intensity.

This clearly reflected a view held by some politicians and by senior members of the police force. Although the tripartite patrols were not included in the attack, I was frequently forced into a debate on the subject.

I could agree that past British policies had contributed to inter-communal rupture and had failed to encourage the construction of a common Cypriot persona and I recognised that the Green Line benefited TMT ambitions for communal separation. But I also was by now aware of the blindness of most Greek Cypriots to the degree to which governmental authority had collapsed over Christmas, to the level of persecution to which many Turkish Cypriots had been subjected, to the depth of general Turkish Cypriot fear, and to the reality of the Turkish threat of unilateral intervention.

General Young had convinced me that his sympathies lay with the delivery of security to the Turkish Cypriots within a reformed unitary state and that his own actions had been in good faith towards this aim (as was later to be recognised by Makarios). I did not doubt that the peacekeeping initiative had helped Cypriot moderates to avert a worse calamity for Cyprus. Furthermore, experience was already teaching me that the anti-British vitriol of the Greek and Greek Cypriot press was damaging to their cause.

One frequent element in the debate was allusion to an article that had appeared in *I Makhi*[3] on 8 November, in which the details of a confidential British exercise called 'Roundtable 3' were revealed. This had been mounted in the SBAs, based on a hypothetical situation where rebels trying to overthrow the Cyprus Government had created a likelihood of inter-communal conflict. The High Commission had responded to the leak by saying that 'Roundtable 3' was no more than standard training activity and had vigorously denied that there was any implication of the UK preparing for intervention, but it was hardly surprising that the plans should now be represented as indicative of a sinister British interventionist agenda.

Not only were the tripartite patrols not included in press criticism against the British military presence, but they began to be singled out for commendation. Their effectiveness was boosted by their distancing in the public mind from the regular British military presence.

5.   11 JANUARY 1964

Patrol commanders met as usual at 0800 in the JFHQ operations room at the Cornaro Hotel. They studied the sitreps (Situation Reports) from the previous day and the night's log of incident reports, special force instructions and programmes for short- and long-range patrolling by regular army units. Then they discussed with relevant staff officers the progress that was being made with outstanding requests from the patrols for the delivery of supplies or medical support, for the investigation of missing persons or for other special follow-up. The day's patrol routes were worked out as soon as helicopter availability had been confirmed. Greek and Turkish officers arrived in time for a patrol start at 0900: programmes were never normally passed to them in advance, so as to limit their chances of pursuing any covert mission in outlying regions.

Patrolling so far had not taken me into areas where there had been fighting or evacuations. In the mixed villages which I had visited the Turkish Cypriots had been extremely frightened and all of them had ceased to travel, but in no case had there been serious difficulty in re-establishing inter-communal co-operation. Apart from what I had heard from General Young and Major Greenwood, the violence directly reported to me had all happened either in Nicosia or through the disappearance or shooting up of Turkish Cypriot buses and their occupants somewhere on the roads.

This day's patrol was to take me closer to the core of communal division.

Major Greenwood had taken the only available helicopter for a visit to Tillyria, the mountainous hinterland of the NW Cyprus coast from Pomos to Lefka, so we were obliged again to use Land Rovers from 16 Para. Before we could start there were sensitivities to be resolved, since our Greek officer, Lieutenant Constantinides, complained at having to sit in the back of the Land Rover while the patrol's Turkish officer that day, Colonel Akova, sat in front.

Apart from some police activity around Yerralakos, the roads were empty. As we approached the mixed village of Dhenia, 30 minutes drive from Nicosia, we saw three shepherds and their flocks disappearing at speed. The village itself seemed deserted until we located a small Turkish Cypriot coffee-house in which three very aged men were silently sipping their drinks. They were asked to summon their leaders.

Slowly a small crowd assembled, encouraged by the sight of Colonel Akova's Turkish uniform. Seats and tables were placed in the street. My

Turkish and Greek officers* sat beside me, each of us with a glass of water, a coffee and a notepad in front of us. Opposite me sat the *mukhtar*† and the village schoolmaster. From occasional glances, it was clear that they were deferring to a smart young man in casual slacks and a ribbed sweater, whom we took to be the TMT representative, who stood to one side and said nothing at all. The other villagers, mostly old men soporifically fingering their worry-beads, ranged themselves in a semi-circle behind their leaders.

Colonel Akova explained the nature and objectives of the patrol. The *mukhtar* then spoke at length of the state of fear in which they now lived. Why were they still afraid? Because they had seen strangers moving outside the village boundaries and heard noises in the night. Were they still travelling? No, not any longer: Huseyin Osman had set off for Nicosia on 24 December and Bayron Hasan for Ayios Vasilios and Mustafa Ali for Nicosia on 25 December, and none of them had been heard of since. Now they had no vehicles left. Had anything happened since Christmas? No, but there were rumours of new troubles in Nicosia. Where did they come from? Nobody was sure but they did not doubt they were true. How did they get the news? They had heard it on the radio, and their shepherds had had it confirmed by the Greeks from Philia, who had heard it from other villagers who had special sources of information. How were they off for food? They had nothing left at all. Nothing? Well, almost nothing. What did they need? Flour, sugar, rice, macaroni, beans, potatoes, oil, tinned milk, paraffin, and fodder for their animals. When had they last had a food delivery? Yesterday, but it hadn't been enough. How were their relations with the Greek Cypriots in Dhenia? Not too good: they were very frightened of the Greeks. Why? No real reason, but they all felt frightened because of what was happening elsewhere. How had relations been before Christmas? Good. What had happened since in the village to change things? Nothing, but they felt threatened. Did the *mukhtar* or the schoolmaster ever meet and talk with the Greek leaders? No. Did anyone ever speak to any of the Greeks? Some of the shepherds, sometimes.

I then addressed the assembled Turkish Cypriots, with Colonel Akova translating under the piercing gaze of Lieutenant Constantinides. I talked of the need for peaceful coexistence, of the dangers of even a minor act of provocation, of their need to work for a return to normality, of the fact that they must obey their political leaders but listen to nobody else except the tripartite patrol, of the nature of propaganda and their need to disregard it. I said it was important that they start travelling again and that we would try to ensure that it was safe for them to do so.

Then the leaders were taken aside and encouraged to exercise good and positive control of their people and made to understand that, whatever happened, they must maintain links with the Greek Cypriot village leaders so that the safety of their villagers was never hazarded through misunderstanding. They received all this with apparent understanding and

---

* By then the order, forbidding Greek officers to enter Turkish Cypriot areas and vice versa, had been rescinded.
† In the village the head of each community was known as a *mukhtar*.

agreed to attend a joint meeting with the Greek Cypriots in thirty minutes time. All of the patrol then shook hands with all of the villagers in the vicinity before departing with some solemnity for the Greek Cypriot coffee-house.

The Greek Cypriot villagers were already congregated. A scene similar to that of five minutes before quickly arranged itself, with the addition of the village priest, who joined the front row. Coffee was ordered. The ritual Greek surprise at the discovery of an Englishman speaking their language was expressed. Ritual introductions were exchanged.

Greek Orthodox village priest and me. I am wearing my usual pre-UNFICYP rig, with para jump-jacket with my Fleet Air Arm wings and naval cap.

How were things with them? They were well, thank God. Had they any troubles? Indeed. What was the problem? They were frightened. Of what? Of the Turks. Why? They did not know, but they were certainly frightened. Had the Turks made any move against them? No. Was anyone missing? Nobody, thank God. How had relations been in the past? Good. Had they maintained any contact with the Turks? None. Had they any special complaints? Yes, the Turks had been sent free food yesterday and nothing had been given to them. Were they short of anything? Yes. What of? Well, everything that the Turks were being sent.

I then addressed the crowd in Greek, with Lieutenant Constantinides invited occasionally to emphasise my points and Colonel Akova carefully attentive. I stressed the need for self-discipline and to listen only to the instructions of central government. I said that their history and frustrations and hopes were well understood by me, that the patrol was there with the blessings of their leaders, that the worst thing they could do was to act out of self-interest or provocation, whether real or imagined. The policy of their government was that Greek Cypriots and Turkish Cypriots must discover how to live together in friendship and that problems must be resolved through negotiation. Elsewhere there had been very bad incidents because of anarchy or of violent men taking things into their own hands. We were not in the Middle Ages and violence would not produce solutions, only chaos and disaster. Hellenism was known for its contribution to the world of wisdom and rationality. Greeks were in a big majority in Cyprus, so they had a special obligation to protect the smaller or weaker elements in the community. The Turks had commented on their previous good relationship in Dhenia and that had to be restored.

There was much nodding at all of this and on completion I was embraced by the priest. Then there was more general handshaking before the patrol officers and the Greek Cypriot leaders departed together for the Turkish Cypriot coffee-house and the inaugural meeting of the joint village council.

The leaders of the two communities greeted each other like long-parted relatives unexpectedly reunited. There were general embraces, at first dignified and then warmly repeated, with much mutual backslapping. Then the Greek Cypriot *mukhtar* insisted on paying for the first of several rounds of coffee and Turkish Delight.

The meeting then went into closed private session under my chairmanship. It was agreed that there were no real inter-communal problems in the area and that the two communities needed, and were anxious, to work together as they always had in the past. It was agreed that formal meetings would be held only when the patrol was present but that there would be regular informal meetings between the two *mukhtars* and that they would immediately contact each other if any crisis or problem occurred. I explained that with so much rumour and propaganda in the air, it was natural that the smaller community should feel especially vulnerable and insecure: it was up to the larger community to understand this and to act responsibly.

While more coffee-drinking was in progress I was able to have a private word with the Greek Cypriot *mukhtar*. I said that there clearly was a special sensitivity over policing. Even though it had not come up at the meeting, the Turkish Cypriots were inevitably going to feel particularly insecure so long as the police and gendarmerie patrols were made up entirely of Greek Cypriot officers. I asked him to have a word with the local gendarmerie commander and to try to agree with him on avoiding anything that could be construed as provocative.

Then there was more embracing and handshaking, promises by the patrol to return, a Turkish commending of the patrol to Allah and a Greek wish that it go with God. At the last moment the Greek Cypriot *mukhtar* reappeared with a bunch of flowers for each of the tripartite officers. As the Land Rover moved out of the village, on a rough track towards the north, it passed the abandoned remains of a rusting village bus and the remnants of a totally ineffectual log barricade. Behind us we could see that the Greek Cypriot and Turkish Cypriot villagers were now intermingled and deep in conversation.

A few miles up the road from Dhenia is the village of Philia, with an all-Greek Cypriot population. Here the patrol was told that there were no troubles whatsoever and no requirements and that relations with neighbouring mixed villages had always been good. Since a lorry from Philia went daily to Nicosia, arrangements were made that in future it would call at Dhenia to see if either community there had need of supplies to be collected from the capital.

A little to the north of the Philia-Skylloura road and clamped to the steep side of an isolated hill is the village of Ayia Marina, predominantly Maronite[1] but with a small Turkish Cypriot minority, the approach track from the south swings sharply round an outcrop of volcanic rock and climbs into the village up a one-in-five slope. From the vantage points of this village there is a clear view into Skylloura, which lies in the valley below.

No sooner had the patrol left the Land Rover at the village entrance than it was surrounded by a crowd of hysterical Turkish Cypriots. A young man, violently weeping, flung himself upon Colonel Akova and several women, alternately crying and mumbling, grasped hold of the colonel's clothing. The other two of us were pinned back against the Land Rovers by a surge of Turkish Cypriots anxious to embrace us, much to the alarm of Lieutenant Constantinides. After a little while Colonel Akova succeeded in calming the situation sufficiently for rational conversation to begin. At about the same time we were joined by the Maronite priest and schoolmaster, who mingled without hesitation with the Turkish Cypriots.

This was my first encounter with the Maronites. They were always welcoming to the patrol and claimed that they had no involvement in inter-communal disputes and that they were prepared to help in any way possible. However it later became clear that they were nervous of being seen by the Greek Cypriots as providing comfort to the Turkish Cypriots.

The young man who had been so overwhelmed by the coming of the patrol now did the talking. He was the son of the Turkish Cypriot *mukhtar*, whom he said was a sick and broken man confined to his bed and in urgent need of medical help.

He said that on the evening of 24 December the villagers had heard firing from the direction of Ayios Vasilios and later seen flames rising from the same area. Then they had seen, by the light of torches and car-headlights and the flames, that refugees were straggling into Skylloura. He said they could all clearly hear shouting and screaming. Later, during the night, they had realised that Skylloura too was being evacuated. They had heard more shooting and assumed that Turkish villagers were being massacred. In the following days they had watched Turkish homes in Skylloura being looted and set on fire.

The Maronites had told them that there had been many killings in Ayios Vasilios. They had not heard of any killings in Skylloura, but believed there now were no Turkish Cypriots left there.[2]

The young man said that his community had waited in terror, expecting that their turn for attack would come next. Since then they had lived in a state of profound fear, even though the Maronites had undertaken to make sure they were not harmed.

On 31 December a Greek Cypriot police patrol, including a sergeant whose Christian name they gave me and whom they thought was from Skylloura or Yerralakos, had passed through Ayia Marina. Their schoolmaster had accepted the offer of a lift back to his home village of Geunyely. The Maronites claimed to have seen the schoolmaster being held in Skylloura later that day but nothing had been heard of him since.

Then, he said, two of their men had left for Nicosia in the Maronite bus on 10 January: both of them had been ordered out of the bus in Skylloura and both had failed to return.

The villagers now had urgent need of food but there was no money at all left in their community. The Maronites had done their best to help them but now they too were becoming increasingly scared of the Greek Cypriots and consequently saying that the help could not continue.

The Maronites told us that they considered the display of hysteria exaggerated, but otherwise confirmed the gist of what we had heard. At first they denied any intention to limit their support for the Turkish Cypriots, but later they told us, under our promises of strict secrecy, that the Greek Cypriots in Skylloura had informed them that it would be 'inadvisable' for them to allow the Turkish Cypriots to use their bus again or to provide any other sort of help. Since the Turkish Cypriots could only acquire money by getting back to their jobs in Nicosia, and since the Maronite bus was the only means of doing so, and since the route through Skylloura was the only one passable to the bus, it was clear that we must either make special arrangements for Ayia Marina, or else that the Turkish Cypriot community would evacuate.

The patrol took special note of the details of Mustafa Ali Hodja, who claimed to be a British subject and who asked that Her Majesty's Government make arrangements as a matter of urgency for him and his family to be evacuated to England. Then we held formal meetings with each community and undertook that a substantial supply of foodstuffs would be sent to the Turkish Cypriots within forty-eight hours and arrangements made to convey the *mukhtar* to hospital. We left with the villagers much heartened, although they must still have been as aware as were we of the extent of their isolation.

From Ayia Marina there is a steep two-mile downhill drive into the back end of Skylloura. Lieutenant Constantinides stated that he considered the patrol had no business to do in Skylloura and proposed that it be by-passed. He was over-ruled.

At the first coffee-house the considerable crowd fell silent as the patrol entered. I asked Lieutenant Constantinides to take the lead and to do the talking under my direction. Some words of welcome were spoken but the general air was very hostile. The people appeared acutely traumatised, as though exhausted by recent emotional excess. We were told that all the Turkish Cypriots had left. When we asked why, the response was a shrug of the shoulders and a drooping of the corners of the mouth. Asked if they knew of the policeman named in Ayia Marina there were further shrugs. In the background, some young men started semi-audibly to mutter curses, apparently directed at Colonel Akova and me, which stopped only when Constantinides turned on them in a fury. When I said that we wished to examine the state of abandoned Turkish Cypriot property, the *mukhtar* became surly and uncooperative, then tried to guide the patrol away from the Turkish Cypriot quarter.

In fact the route was easy to determine, sign-posted by a trickle of elderly ladies hurrying towards the Greek sector, each with an item of bric-a-brac clutched to her breast.

All of Skylloura that lies to the north-east of the main road was once Turkish Cypriot. As we approached this sector, we heard shouts in Greek and saw a flock of scavengers take off from the houses like disturbed vultures, old men and women, all in black, dodging away towards their homes, each grasping some object of their looting. The picture was like a stylised excerpt from 'Zorba The Greek', but with overtones that were distinctly more sinister. At the same time we saw that several of the trees around the area had men behind them with guns pointed at the patrol. Lieutenant Constantinides shouted loudly at them, and these men too went scurrying away into the Greek quarter.

All the Turkish Cypriot houses had been fired and their ransacking was nearly complete. Many of them had obscenities scrawled in Greek on what remained of the walls. The Greek Cypriot *mukhtar* was asked who had been responsible and advanced the theory that the Turks must have done it themselves before they departed. His own memory of events, he said, was rather vague. Lieutenant Constantinides suddenly cursed him with a blast of invective beyond my experiences of Greece: the *mukhtar* jumped back as though physically hit and then ran off at speed, ignoring the Lieutenant's orders to stay with us.

Constantinides then said that he felt too sick to continue and departed to wait outside the village in the second Land Rover. Colonel Akova and I continued the tour in silence. Two Turkish national flags were lying by the path side, torn and dirt-spattered. I retrieved and folded them and handed them to Colonel Akova, who carried them inside his tunic for the rest of the day. (I was told later that they were hung for a while in the Turkish contingent's camp and afterwards sent to Ankara.)

Nothing in my earlier patrols had prepared me for what I saw in Skylloura or for the concentrated enmity of the Greek Cypriot community that I felt there. In due course I was to discover that Skylloura and its neighbour, Ayios Vasilios, were in no way representative of the rural areas in Nicosia Zone. They did, however, demonstrate the danger posed when central leadership collapsed and local leadership passed to the hands of violent extremists.* It was clear to the patrol that the events in these two villages would provide the Turkish Cypriots with a powerful argument for communal separation unless they were totally repudiated by Makarios and his ministers and unless steps were taken to eradicate the causes of such enmity.

Such was the impact of Skylloura on my Greek and Turkish officers that it was decided not to stop at Ayios Vasilios, which had been the scene of violence and murder on 24 December, and the patrol drove straight through and on to Yerralakos. There Colonel Akova stayed in the Land Rover, while

---

* Later the local police sergeant told me that, to his indignation, a seventeen year old nominee of Georgadjis had been placed over him in command.

Lieutenant Constantinides and I visited the police station and tried, without any success at all, to elicit some information about local events.

The police were completely uncooperative. The sergeant in charge was surly, evasive and unconvincing. He denied knowledge of a visit to Ayia Marina on 31 December or on any other recent date. He denied that he had any knowledge of the missing schoolmaster or of any other missing Turkish Cypriots or of any stopping of vehicles. He claimed not to know the policeman who had been named to us in Ayia Marina. He denied any awareness of abandoned Turkish Cypriot property in the area or any responsibility for its safeguarding if it did exist.

Lieutenant Constantinides became increasingly exasperated as this catechism continued. Eventually I decided that we were getting nowhere and that Constantinides' interventions were merely increasing the sergeant's hostility. As we left the office Constantinides muttered to me a further string of imprecations.

Not far to the south-west of Yerralakos we stopped in the Greek Cypriot village of Mammari. We were running late and I decided against a full meeting and walked on my own towards the coffee-house, intending merely to check that all was well. A considerable crowd of Greek Cypriots at pavement tables in the village square was engaged in loud and expressive conversation. There was a pause while they glanced at me and the Land Rover, on which only the British flag could be seen.*

It was apparent that they assumed me to be part of a normal British patrol, and their conversation was resumed, with the volume louder than ever.

The ferocity of anti-Turkish expression astounded me. Speaker after speaker regaled his neighbours with racist diatribe, claimed that the Turkish Cypriots were responsible for all of the island's present troubles, passed on stories he had heard of appalling atrocities being committed against Greek Cypriots, explained why agreement with such barbarians was impossible, and boasted of heroic Greek deeds in the killing of TMT terrorists.

I soon learned that this type of highly embellished talk was for the moment common in coffee-houses of both communities. It echoed the extremist language being used in most of the press. But there was virtually no instance where I did not find that an adequacy of engaged discussion would wholly convert the vituperation into conciliatory comment and confirmation of the normality of good relations. At that point it would be explained that all problems could be ascribed to 'foreigners'†. Conversational excesses in the villages were indicative not of local inter-communal hatred but of a failure of politicians to combat extremism and to explain the reality of events and the need for moderation.

Lieutenant Constantinides, trapped in the back of the two-door Land Rover, eventually caught the gist of what was being said and called out urgently to the people to shut up: "The Englishman speaks Greek."

---

* Tripartite units normally displayed the flags of Turkey, Greece and Britain.
† In Greek the word *xenos* means either foreigner or stranger, which was the cause of occasional misunderstanding.

In later days, walking quietly through other villages, I would sometimes hear Greek Cypriot women, seated with their knitting in front of their homes, murmuring an anti-Turkish incantation. This and the sentiment expressed in Mammari increasingly seemed to me like the stylised chanting of the chorus in a Greek tragedy: these same villagers when challenged in conversation would almost invariably attest to the strength of local inter-communal good-neighbourliness.

Such was the weight of extremist propaganda being pushed out by the media and through covert organisations in each community, the encouragement to enmity, the absence of any-self criticism, the placing of total blame on the other community, that the virulence of communal sloganising was hardly surprising. It usually was as shallow as the manifestations of ritualised football-crowd hostility, politically-provoked rather than stemming from any personal experience. It was easily engendered by extremists or demagogues, but equally easy to convert into expressions of regret and sympathy.

We had had a tip-off in Dhenia that one of their missing men had been sighted at the police station in Kokkini Trimithia, and that became our next stop. Several well-armed police auxiliaries were seen by us in the streets but at the police-station we found only some furtive armed civilians. Eventually a sergeant was located at his home. He was told forcefully by Lieutenant Constantinides that unless we had his co-operation he would be reported to Commander Antoniou for having left his station unguarded.

By feigning greater knowledge than in fact we had we were able to get it confirmed that Huseyin Osman had indeed been in the cells from December 25 to 28, as had also Sergeant Ahmet Osman and PC Ozer Emin from Peristerona and one other police constable. It was claimed that they had been held for "self-requested protective custody" and that they had left together in Ozer Emin's car on the 28th. In fact none of them, or the car, was heard of again.

I later was told in private by one Greek Cypriot police officer that an order had been received in late December that all captives 'known' to have TMT connections were to be 'disposed of'. I was unable to discover whether there really had been such an order and if so whether it had originated from police headquarters or from elsewhere. If the report were true, the 28 December specified by the sergeant in Kokkini Trimithia probably indicated the date on which this 'order' was implemented.

Ignoring the fact that Colonel Akova was complaining of severe headaches and Lieutenant Constantinides bemoaning the state of his stomach, the patrol moved on down the Morphou road to Akaki, a large mixed village with a particularly wealthy Turkish Cypriot minority. Here the atmosphere was that of another world, relaxed and normal, with the two communities mingling in what clearly was a genuine friendship.

Our queries as to whether they had any problems were greeted with surprise, as though no-one had heard of the violence in other parts of Cyprus. The Turkish Cypriots said they were travelling regularly without problem. I spoke briefly in private to the leaders of each community and a joint meeting was then convened in a spirit of great cordiality. I commended them on the achievements of their village but warned them of the pressures that were occurring elsewhere. I received from them pledges of their determination to maintain the co-operation and jointly to resist any outside interference in their affairs. Akaki appeared to have an exemplary history of inter-communal relationships and an excellent leadership and I noted that there would be no need for regular visits by the patrol. Nothing gave me an inkling that within a few days the village would be abandoned by all its Turkish Cypriot inhabitants.

It was almost dusk when the patrol reached Peristerona, another large mixed village that seemed rich and well-organised. Unlike Akaki, the atmosphere here was menacing and tense. The Turkish Cypriots took us to their communal office and there immediately burst into a bitter outpouring of their feelings. The source of their fears, and the target of their vituperation, was the Greek Cypriot police. They said that this was not a police force any longer: now, they claimed, it was controlled by 'a bunch of ex-EOKA thugs'. The older policemen, they said, had been decent enough but as soon as the fighting in Nicosia had started the two Turkish Cypriot policemen at the station had been arrested and replaced by a group of aggressive young Greek Cypriot auxiliaries, and the regular police sergeant no longer seemed to wield any authority.

On December 23 they had heard shots from the vicinity of the police station. The *mukhtar* had gone there to investigate. He found that Arif Mustafa had been shot and wounded. There was no sign of their own police officers. Arif Mustafa was later seen being removed by ambulance, but they had had no news of him since. They had discovered that their two Turkish Cypriot policemen had been arrested by the auxiliaries and sent to Kokkini Trimithia and they were worried about what had become of them.

Since 23 December the Turkish Cypriots had been kept on edge by the sound of shooting in and around the village every night. For their own safety the inhabitants of outlying houses had been moving into the Turkish Cypriot quarter each evening. Every morning they found that one or two of the abandoned houses had been broken into and looted. The police had refused to take any notice of their complaints or to offer any sort of protection for them or their property.

Eventually we were joined by the Greek Cypriot *mukhtar* and the Orthodox priest. The priest did most of the talking. He appeared to be a person of sincerity and saintly disposition and the Turks whispered to me that they thought he was a good man. He thought that the Turkish Cypriots were exaggerating but accepted that some people had acted improperly against them and said that his community was keen to accept its responsibilities and to help. He offered to act in future as a go-between, with the *hodja* (the Muslim cleric) as his link-man, and to respond to any misunderstandings or complaints. He asked that we and the Turkish Cypriots trust him.

In the event he failed to act effectively, as he had promised, and the area was to suffer in consequence.

The drive back to headquarters was uneventful. Not a single other vehicle was seen on the road. The armed men had disappeared from Kokkini

Trimithia. There were no roadblocks. Throughout the journey none of us spoke.

When we arrived at the Cornaro Lieutenant Constantinides lodged a complaint with me because Colonel Akova had been allowed to remove the Turkish flags from Skylloura. He withdrew it when I asked what he would have done if we had found a Greek Cypriot village destroyed and Greek ensigns in the mud. Then there were various notes to be compared, that day's Athens' papers to be read, and a review of the day between the three of us.

Akova and Constantinides had both been deeply affected and I had to plead for objectivity. I reminded them that we were inevitably going to be visitors to the trouble-spots rather than to the much larger areas where no trouble had occurred. I said the evidence of violence we had seen was likely to be the outcome of irresponsible racist incitement and local anarchy, and that our mission was precisely to bring matters back into reasoned political control. I asked them to remember that Greek Cypriots had been more largely the victims in the 1958 inter-communal violence, which had erupted during the EOKA struggle. I said that we had to act not judgementally but as counsellors to a disturbed patient with a long background of abuse.

Lieutenant Constantinides then departed for his own contingent, there to eat and make his reports and sleep, while I had further discussion with Colonel Akova. Afterwards I had to make a provisional report to JFHQ Ops Room; instruct on any items that needed JF peacekeeping action next day, including an ambulance for the *mukhtar* of Ayia Marina; fill in detailed reports of missing persons; draw up a rough route-plan for the next day; and grab a sandwich.

Then I gave some time to a discussion of the latest signs and portents with another member of General Young's staff, Major Edward Macey.

Major Edward (Ted) Macey with Dr Kutchuk.

Macey was a major in the Royal Army Ordnance Corps. A short, squat man, fluent in Greek, Turkish and several other languages, he boasted of his prowess as a marksman. During the civil war in Greece he had worked with Greek right wing forces in the defeat of the left and had been decorated in Athens. He had an encyclopaedic knowledge of Cyprus and its history and personalities. He had been introduced to me by General Young as his official liaison with Dr Kutchuk, but he always hinted to me that he had a wider role than this and seemed keen to cloak himself with an air of mystery.

Macey created useful contacts for me with some TMT leaders and was helpful to me in various other more arcane ways. For instance he knew which telephone lines were tapped by whom and instructed me that the fastest way to get a reaction from some key Cypriot quarters was to phone to JFHQ a suitably concocted message on an appropriately tapped line.

Macey's political views on Cyprus appeared to be those of an unreconstructed colonialist but he was a useful sounding-board for matters concerning TMT and Greek Cypriot paramilitary structures and the covert balances of power. He claimed that everyone liked him, and that in any event he was indestructible, and he showed me that he was wearing two shoulder holsters and carrying a throwing-knife concealed in his shoe. Before long I discovered that he was believed by Greek Cypriot paramilitaries to be counselling the Turkish Cypriots on how best to achieve partition.[3]

After my discussion with Macey there was still a full report to be written on the day's patrol activities, a work that invariably took me well into the night.

6.   12 January 1964

Thankfully there was a helicopter available for my patrol. The route away from Nicosia had to be planned with some care as my Greek liaison officer would complain bitterly if his Turkish counterpart were enabled to see the Greek contingent's defensive positions, and vice versa.

After take-off we made rapid sweeps up the main Nicosia approach-roads to see whether any roadblocks were in operation. We spotted armed civilians in the streets of Yerralakos and a barricade in the centre of Skylloura, and a request was passed for both places to be visited by a ground patrol.

Our first landing was at Orounda, close to Peristerona, where a tiny Turkish Cypriot minority lived in considerable poverty within a sizeable Greek Cypriot village. Helicopters were still a novelty and their arrival in the villages was likely to be greeted as a spectator event. At Orounda the entire population hurried out to gather around the landing place, although the two communities managed to avoid any intermingling.

For ten minutes the two liaison officers talked individually with their respective communities, endeavouring to spread the doctrine of political responsibility while competing with the attraction of the helicopter. The two *mukhtars* were then taken aside in turn and given a chance to speak their minds.

This was the typical story of a mixed village in which the Greek Cypriots were in a large majority. Christmas had passed with no more than a sharp increase in tension, with the Turkish Cypriots hiding themselves away in their own homes in fear of what might be about to befall them. Then gradually the Turkish Cypriot shepherds had begun to venture back to the fields and the women to search for food, and tenuous links had been re-established.

Afterwards some militant Greek Cypriots had demanded that the Turkish Cypriots hand over to them all their weapons, which consisted of three or four shotguns, 'for safekeeping', and to this they had reluctantly agreed, although the guns were their most prized possessions. Later still, claiming the need to ensure their own safety, the Greek Cypriots had insisted on searching all the Turkish Cypriot houses to make sure that there were no more weapons concealed there.

These two acts comprised the sum of inter-communal 'incidents' in Orounda, but they were sufficient to have left the Turkish Cypriots feeling humiliated, bitter and insecure, feelings worsened by the fact that the police patrols which passed through the village from Peristerona now lacked Turkish Cypriot participation and were made up of heavily armed men, many of them not in uniform and strangers to the area.

Among the Greek Cypriots the main concern was to avoid being dragged into other people's troubles. Most of them were unclear whether it was supposed to be unpatriotic to consort with the Turkish Cypriots, so they had refrained from doing so for the past two weeks and limited themselves to an occasional stylised salute across the street.

The exception to this distancing, here and everywhere else throughout the region, was the shepherds. They acted as though oblivious to any inter-communal conflict, continued with their friendships as they always had, and disregarded the idea that some of their traditional grazing lands now lay across notional borders. On occasions elsewhere they were killed as a result of this excess of trust.

On being brought together, the village leaders instantly resumed their former friendship, agreed on the need for better co-operation and undertook that in future they would consult each other whenever problems or doubts arose. Then the Greek Cypriots publicly acknowledged that, as the majority, they had the greater responsibility. They promised that there would be no more searches and that they would provide whatever help they could if the Turkish Cypriots faced further difficulties of communication or travel. Then there were a number of rounds of coffee and Turkish Delight to be consumed, and expressions of future commitment exchanged, and commendations to God or Allah pronounced and every villager's hand to be shaken, before helicopter lift-off with all of the now intermingled population waving below.

Kato Koutrapha is a tiny Greek Cypriot village at the junction of the Nicosia-Lefka and Troodos roads. Its gendarmerie station was found to contain a number of amiable and rather somnolent policemen, without the usual leavening of armed irregulars. We had been directed to investigate reports of a police barricade, and the sergeant in charge confirmed that a roadblock had indeed been established, but subsequently removed. It had been erected, he said, to assist them in the checking of driving licences. They had found that almost everyone's licence was out of date, had issued warnings and had decided to take no further action. They did not have in mind to replace the roadblock. They would, as we requested, do everything in their power to be supportive to the Turkish Cypriots in neighbouring villages.

One mile up a minor hill road to the south lies Pano Koutrapha, an all-Turkish village with a total population of sixty. It too had a typical story, this time of the small Turkish Cypriot village surrounded by larger Greek Cypriot ones of a reasonably amiable disposition. The villagers had been alarmed by the news from Nicosia and had kept very much to themselves over Christmas, had refrained from going far from their homes and had had no troubles at all. Then late on 28 December they were visited by four masked and armed young Greek Cypriots, whom they took to be from outside the area. They were told that nothing would happen to them for the moment but that the village would be attacked if the Greek Cypriots failed to get what they wanted out of the forthcoming London Conference.

On 1 January a British army helicopter had come to ask if they needed any help: as soon as it left a party of Greek Cypriot police had arrived from Morphou, interrogated them on the reason for the helicopter's visit and then searched all their homes, claiming a need to check whether the helicopter had left any Turkish soldiers in the village. On the following day they had another visit, this time from a group of armed Greek Cypriot civilians.

In the old days they used to get to Nicosia by walking down to Kato Koutrapha and getting lifts from Turkish Cypriot cars passing through, but from Christmas until 9 January they had been told, by the police there, not to go beyond Kato Koutrapha. However, the day before our visit three of them had travelled to Nicosia and back quite safely. This morning they had heard rumours that the roadblock was to be re-imposed on 13 January: Turkish Cypriot motorists who normally gave them lifts had told them that none of their cars would be on the road that day.

They had no special needs, except that they were running low on oil for their lamps. They said that their relations with the Greek Cypriots in the neighbouring villages were very good, and they expressed no antagonism towards Greeks in general. But they had been deeply frightened by the visits to the village of outsiders and by the way they had been addressed. One family of six had left earlier that day for Lefka, saying they were too scared to stay. The rest of them had not decided yet but if the patrol pledged its support they were prepared not to move for the time being.

The patrol tried in villages like Pano Koutrapha to be as honest as possible. We could hardly say that there was no threat at all of violence against them, but we suggested that the danger was greatly diminished and that through us they now had a regular linkage to a sympathetic authority. We realised that when we encouraged them to stay we were ourselves accepting a burden of responsibility.

We said that the Makarios government was asking for inter-communal reconciliation and making it clear that any attack on the Turkish Cypriots was damaging to the cause of Cyprus, but that there were violent elements in both communities that had a different agenda and which might use force in pursuit of their objectives. They should be very cautious until the situation was clearer. We explained that life as a refugee was one of extreme hardship and deprivation and that, whatever the pressures they now felt, they should try not to be persuaded to evacuate. We would visit them regularly and they could rely on us for an accurate picture of the situation.

We believed that, given adequate time, we could handle the sentiment in the surrounding Greek Cypriot villages, where a traditional good disposition towards their neighbours appeared to have been only superficially dented by the propaganda that was deluging out of Nicosia. What both we and they were scared of was the sudden appearance of a single carload of violent strangers, not under government control, or the misguided actions of a police force which no longer gave even a nod towards impartiality.

Two miles further up the road was the big Greek Cypriot village of Nikitari. Here we were welcomed with unparalleled warmth. The village leaders made declarations of deep and abiding friendship for the Turkish Cypriots at Pano Koutrapha and told us how, at the height of the December troubles, they had sent them a load of essential food supplies and offered to sign a local treaty of cooperation. They said that they wished to offer themselves "as an example to the world" of the ability of Greeks to live in harmony and friendship with Turks, and they added that they would like the press to be informed to this effect. They were thanked and congratulated by the patrol and told that their Turkish Cypriot neighbours had already commended their attitude and good relationship. We discussed the various pressures that might be exerted in the future on Pano Koutrapha and asked them particularly to try to keep strangers out of the area, and this they promised to do.

The next landing was at Eliophotes. This Turkish Cypriot village hangs precariously in the crook of a steep-sided hill, looking out across the big Mitsero ore-quarries. With the wind in the right quarter a small helicopter could get down onto the *mukhtar's* threshing floor but on this occasion a half-gale was blowing and we were forced instead to land on a spur of the hill some way above the village. Wending their way up to us came a hundred near-destitute Turkish Cypriots accompanying their partly-paralysed *mukhtar*.

The story here was not unlike that at Pano Koutrapha. The villagers had kept within their own boundaries over Christmas and had had no trouble. By 5 January their food-stocks were exhausted and some of them set out in their bus for Peristerona, taking with them a quantity of their own grain which they intended to have ground at the Turkish Cypriot mill there. Outside Peristerona they were stopped at a roadblock manned by police and armed civilians and escorted to the police station.

There they were cross-questioned at length about the number of guns within their village and threatened with dire consequences if these were not surrendered. Eventually they revealed the whereabouts of the five shotguns owned by inhabitants of Eliophotes, and a Land Rover with ten police and auxiliaries left immediately for the village. The villagers were mustered in the square and covered with a Bren gun while they and their houses were searched. All their guns were located and confiscated. The bus passengers, who had been held hostage in the meantime, were now re-embarked but were allowed only to visit the Greek Cypriot flourmill in Peristerona before being sent home.

During the night of 7 January, the police Land Rover had returned to Eliophotes, driven by a policeman but otherwise filled with armed civilians, none of whom they had recognised. Two areas had been searched by torchlight and one sheep, three lambs and two goats belonging to Nyazi Naim, the *mukhtar*, had been seized. Then the intruders had demolished the village gypsum machine* before departing.

Next day Nyazi Naim had called on Theodoros Antoni, the *mukhtar* of the neighbouring Greek Cypriot village of Kato Moni, who was believed by the Turkish Cypriots to be the local ex-EOKA strongman, and had asked for his help. Mr Antoni said that his village had not been responsible in any way for the events of the previous night, but he promised to do his best to locate the missing animals. Next day, however, he sent word that there was no chance of their being returned.

The incident sounded to the patrol more like an instance of attempted debt-recovery than an inter-communal attack. Many Turkish Cypriot villagers were heavily in debt to Greek Cypriots and there were later to be a number of occasions when efforts at forceful debt-recovery were

---

* For plaster-making: probably bought with a loan from Greek Cypriots.

misconstrued at JFHQ as political incidents of inter-communal violence. Whatever the intended objective, the manner of such actions, supported by heavily armed gendarmerie auxiliaries, was strongly conducive to rural destabilisation.

The villagers no longer had any special needs. They had been informed by Mr Antoni that they were only to travel with his permission. They had been safely to Nicosia and back the previous day and had been able to acquire as much food as they could afford. However on two previous occasions when Mr Antoni had given his approval they had been stopped by the police outside Peristerona and ordered to return to Eliophotes.

Over coffee the patrol offered what encouragement it could, although it was obvious that this village, too, was so isolated as to be at the mercy of any troublemaker who set out to intimidate it.

After agreeing with the other officers that they would join me later by helicopter and having bid the *mukhtar* an emotional farewell, I set out to walk the two miles to Kato Moni, anxious for exercise and keen to enjoy the scenery. On the outskirts of this all-Greek Cypriot village I found an elaborate set of defensive positions, facing towards the now gun-less Turkish Cypriots in Eliophotes. By-passing these, I reached the coffee-house in the village square, where the customers were so deeply engrossed in conversation that I was able to remain for some time at an outer table without being noticed by any of the villagers. Led by the priest, the usual subject of discussion was being attacked with arm-waving vigour. There was no moderate voice to be heard. Each speaker was trying to outdo the other with a theatrical presentation of stories that he claimed to have heard about the TMT. The mildest of recommended solutions was that all Turkish Cypriots should be transported back to Anatolia.

Eventually I heard the helicopter approaching. I addressed the crowd politely in Greek, described who I was and said that I would like to meet Mr Theodoros Antoni. My presence was greeted with stunned amazement. Finally a young boy announced that Mr Antoni was at home and went off to summon him. Meanwhile, the priest and his fellow coffee-drinkers sat in frozen immobility, gazing into the distance in an apparent effort there to recapture precisely how bad had been the worst of their indiscretions.

After a little while, a magnificently menacing young man came swaggering out of the shadows. Complete with cigarette-holder and pencil moustache, black-suited with a brilliant Edwardian waistcoat, this person stated that Mr Antoni was not at present available, but that he would deal personally with anything that the Patrol Commander might wish to communicate. By this time I had been joined by Lieutenant Constantinides. I said that we were deliverers of their government's policy, which was that all Greek Cypriots must behave with absolute correctness towards the Turkish Cypriots. I said that President Makarios had pledged that there would be complete freedom of movement and this must be applied to the people of Eliophotes: the patrol would return at frequent intervals to ensure this instruction was being complied with. They, as caring neighbours, would be held especially responsible.

The young man accepted all of this in good spirit, saluted me with the tip of his cigarette-holder and departed. (And in fact he was to keep his word, and there was no further pressure put on Eliophotes from Kato Moni.) I then told the priest and his parishioners that I would return soon for a more lengthy discussion on the matters that were concerning them, said my goodbyes and walked off to board the helicopter.

The last visit of the day was to Aredhiou, a mixed village on the road which ran from Nicosia via Klirou and Apliki to the Troodos Mountains. Before Christmas this had been at the end of a string of three mixed villages, but in the last days of December the Turkish Cypriots from both Pano Lakatamia and Kato Dheftera had evacuated, to Nicosia or to other villages to the north, nor were there any Turkish Cypriot officers left at the gendarmerie station at Kato Dheftera. That meant that Aredhiou was now isolated within a militant Greek Cypriot area. It also was on the edge of what we later discovered to be a major training ground for Greek Cypriot paramilitaries.

The Greek Cypriots told their story first. They were obviously apprehensive about being questioned and extremely anxious to make a good impression on the patrol, which quickly concluded they had something to hide. They claimed that inter-communal relations had always been good and that they recently had offered food to the Turks Cypriots, had taken a sick Turkish Cypriot woman to hospital in Nicosia, had helped the Turkish Cypriots to deliver their olives to the oil-presses and in general had repeatedly demonstrated their goodwill.

The Turkish Cypriots, on the other hand, appeared to be in a state of fearful paralysis. They greeted the patrol tearfully, with a sad fervour. After a long and calming speech by Colonel Akova, they said it was true that, in recent days, the Greeks had been trying to help them in various ways and that relations had been good up to 21 December. But in the intervening ten days or so their sense of security had been comprehensively destroyed.

On 17 December Ahmet Musa had left home by bus for his work at Margi: nothing had been heard of him since.*

Fifteen of their children and young men went to schools or colleges in Nicosia: they had had no news of any of them since 21 December and asked me for re-assurance that all were alive and well.†

On 23 December Shafket Cemal had left by motorbike for his work at Akaki: nothing more had been heard of him.

On the afternoon of 23 December, 'several hundred' armed Greek Cypriots, including police, gendarmerie, Cyprus army members, paramilitaries and civilians, most of them from other districts, had gathered near the Turkish Cypriot quarter: all the Turkish Cypriots were ordered into their houses and told that on no account should they come out until told to do so: later they heard several shots.

---

* This was the first time I had been told of a supposed abduction occurring ahead of the Christmas troubles. Some such 'disappearances' may have been actions by TMT against Turkish Cypriot left-wingers, but they contributed equally to the sense of fear.
† Later I was able to give it to them.

On 24 December an even larger number of Greek Cypriots had gathered in the same area. This time the Turkish Cypriots were ordered to hand over their shotguns, and they had done so. Afterwards all of their houses had been thoroughly searched. Since then occasional personal searches of the Turkish Cypriot men had been carried out by the Greek Cypriots, on the pretext that they needed to be sure that the Turks had not obtained any new weapons.

Two hours after midnight on 27 December, a party of armed Greek Cypriots had called at the house of Nyazi Cemal, shouted for him to come out and fired a warning shot when he delayed. Cemal had gone out to them and nothing had been heard of him since. His wife claimed to have recognised the voice of a Greek Cypriot neighbour among the party that abducted her husband, but later I was told that the neighbour concerned was a left-winger who had been trying to intervene on Cemal's behalf.

On 31 December and 1 January armed Greek Cypriots had seized from various of the Turkish Cypriots a number of sheep, goats and chickens and a water pump: this was described by the Turkish Cypriots as theft: it was assumed by us to have been another case of forcible debt-recovery, but none the less intimidating.

During the night of 29 December four uniformed and armed Greek Cypriot police, at least some of whom were said to be from Klirou, had called successively at the houses of Kemal Huseyin, Salih Mehmet and Naim Huseyin: in each case they said that Dr Kutchuk wished to see the man because of an irregularity in his papers: all three men had been removed in a police Land Rover and nothing had been heard of any of them since.*

To all of this, which had happened to a small and isolated Turkish Cypriot community, was added the flood of rumour and propaganda to which the villagers had been subjected. It said much for their determination not to be moved that they had so far refused to evacuate. Out of the sixty remaining Turks only three were able-bodied men; it seemed unlikely that, even if they continued to stay, they could be self-supporting.

The Greek Cypriot villagers of Aredhiou, on the other hand, made it clear that they had no intention of allowing the Turkish Cypriots to evacuate if anything could be done to prevent it. We gathered that this commitment stemmed from a wish to demonstrate the viability of co-existence following severe criticism from Nicosia over the village's earlier record. When a joint meeting was convened by the patrol, the Greek Cypriots undertook to provide any food needed by the Turkish Cypriots, to offer them transport, to search for their lost property and to help them in every other way possible. The Turkish Cypriots, acknowledging that their troubles had come from 'foreigners' agreed to accept all of the offered help. Each community gave the other a pledge of future friendship.

---

* I was later told by my personal contacts in 'The Organisation' (See Appendix D and note 7/3) that these three men were suspected of TMT membership and that they had been killed on local initiative, to the extreme annoyance of the administration and of the central paramilitary leadership in Nicosia.

From the moment we arrived in Aredhiou to the point when we could depart had taken three hours: into that period had been packed the roles of authoritative messenger from central government, confidant, counsellor, interpreter of national events, promoter of unity, purveyor of optimism. We had had to assess what practical help was needed, identify the likely sources and magnitude of potential threat, convince both communities (and ourselves) that we could offer the support necessary for the village to continue to exist, as it had for centuries past, as their common home. These were peoples of long-standing companionship who apparently had never been encouraged to see themselves as other than Greeks and Turks – until our apostolic team descended by helicopter to suggest that they were first and foremost Cypriots.

7.   A PATTERN FORMS

By the middle of January a consistent picture of recent events was beginning to emerge from the rural areas of Nicosia Zone. It was apparent that, despite the creation of an embryonic, centrally controlled defensive network and the receipt from paramilitary sources of some arms, neither rural community had prepared itself either for an attack on the other or for defence against attack. The explosion of violence in Nicosia on 22-25 December had set off shock-waves through the length of Cyprus, triggering local fires where there was particularly volatile material or pent-up resentment, as in the Skylloura-Ayios Vasilios area, stunning other areas with fear, and doing little damage in areas where there had been no encroachment of extremism. During this period central political control had collapsed: in some areas local leadership seized the initiative, with results that were sometimes benign and sometimes destructive. TMT, urging communal separation, had tried to exploit the situation, with mixed success.

An exception to this general picture was that some element of the Greek Cypriot leadership clearly had warned Greek Cypriot contingents within the police forces to be ready for violence, and after the events of 21 and 22 December had immediately pictured the Turkish Cypriots as being in general insurrection against the state and given orders for the national police forces to devote themselves exclusively to the neutralisation of TMT.

We had been told by various gendarmerie officers that they were "temporarily unable to carry out normal policing duties, such as protecting Turkish Cypriot property, because they were now obliged to act as a military vanguard for the Greek Cypriots."

It was apparent that most Turkish Cypriot disappearances on the roads represented either the taking of 'hostages of prestige', the seizure of men who were believed to have connections with TMT or the pursuit of gangland objectives. It also was apparent that some uniformed gendarmerie officers, mainly newly-enrolled specials, had participated in this activity.

We were told that this process had had some central authority up to 28 December, despite the Makarios-Kutchuk agreement for a cease-fire on the night of 25 December. It was reported to us that key Greek Cypriot paramilitary leaders, including Georgadjis, had disagreed with the ceasefire, believed that Turkey's threatened invasion would not materialise and wished to continue until the fighting power of TMT was destroyed by force of arms. This disagreement appears to have had its parallel on the Turkish Cypriot side, where we were told that some paramilitary leaders, including Denktash, had wished to reject the 25 December cease-fire on the grounds that a continuance of hostilities would imminently result in Turkish military intervention.

Instances of the abduction and killing of TMT suspects, probably independent of the official police structure, had apparently continued for a few days after 28 December on local initiative, often followed by severe reprimands for indiscipline.

From 31 December, when Duncan Sandys obtained final agreement from Makarios and Kutchuk for a mid-January London Conference, aimed at a diplomatic resolution of the situation in Cyprus, instructions had gone to the villages that Greek Cypriot policy was now to demonstrate friendship and support for the Turkish Cypriots. But given the events of the previous ten days, the clumsiness of the Greek Cypriot approach, the propaganda to which they had been subjected and the mistrust in which they were now being coached by elements of the Turkish Cypriot leadership in Nicosia, it was hardly surprising that the Turkish Cypriot reaction was of either cynicism or extreme caution. At the same time, exploiting the advantages conferred on it by the violent excesses of Greek Cypriot paramilitary extremists, TMT was endeavouring to maintain the momentum of separation.

In general there had at first been a warm welcome from both rural communities for the arrival of British peacekeeping units. The welcome from Greek Cypriots had now turned to virulent resentment, as the conviction grew that British intervention had prevented the destruction of TMT, that the British-created Green Line was beneficial to the Turkish hard-line target of ethnic separation and that British sympathies were slanted towards the Turkish Cypriots.

The tripartite patrols were therefore now operating within a highly fractured climate. The Greek Cypriots were split between those who sought for restraint and compromise, those who sought for a continuing forceful pursuit of *enosis*, to which end the elimination of TMT was a critical first step, and those who sought to advance their own agendas. For most Turkish Cypriots the overwhelming priority was to hang onto their homes: beyond that they were split between those who believed that a viable compromise could be reached with the Greek Cypriots and those who believed that their future security would be wholly dependent on ethnic separation or intervention from Turkey.

Within both communities the incitement to violence was coming principally from the right wing, while the left was anxious to seek for a cross-community understanding. The right wing in each community was urged forward towards extremism by linkage with extreme right wing intelligence organisations and irredentist sentiment in Greece and Turkey, which in turn drew strength from NATO's anti-communist crusade. Meanwhile, criminal elements were using the situation to cover the pursuit of their own interests. This situation was overlaid by a total absence of any effective policing, with the tripartite patrols providing the only impartial outlet to which villagers could air their complaints and worries.

From the beginning of January, with the London Conference looming, the incidence of ethnic abduction and murder fell off very markedly, but the looting and firing of property in abandoned areas continued and pressure against some isolated Turkish Cypriot communities, from either TMT or

Greek Cypriot extremists, mounted. This was in conflict with central Greek Cypriot policy and despite the formation of joint village councils.

In some cases a decision to evacuate was taken purely on local initiative, in others it followed specific urging by the regional Turkish Cypriot Chamber or by the office of Kutchuk or by TMT: but, in almost every case that came to our notice in this period, the insecurity which prepared the ground for evacuation was mainly attributable to the actions of Greek Cypriots, seldom centrally-directed but usually with an involvement by the police or the gendarmerie. In some cases this was deliberately provoked. None of us seeking to mediate in Nicosia Zone had any doubt that Turkish Cypriot separatists were seeing their aims rapidly advanced through the actions of Greek Cypriot rightists and police.

The process of Turkish Cypriot evacuations might have been halted or reversed in the early days of January if Britain had been able to bolster anti-extremist elements in Nicosia and simultaneously place troops and mediating groups in key areas of rural insecurity and provide a regular escort programme on the main roads. Such moves, which were urged by tripartite patrol officers, would have had widespread co-operation from both communities, particularly in those areas where British intervention had been greeted with relief and warmth: by the time they were first tried, in March, Greek Cypriot sentiment, both in Nicosia and in the rural areas had swung so violently against any further British role that the UK was no longer in a position to act effectively as an 'honest broker'.

In some matters there was fundamental disagreement between patrol commanders and JFHQ staff officers over what tactics should be employed. JFHQ claimed that violence in the rural areas was a natural adjunct to events in Nicosia and that to control events in Nicosia would mean to control the country as a whole. The patrols, on the other hand, believed that the rural areas were not inherently volatile, that good inter-communal relations were sustainable at village level irrespective of events elsewhere, and that an effective stabilisation of the countryside, under the terms already agreed between Makarios and Kutchuk, would help to reverse the general movement towards separation, provide a powerful dampener on the more fissile elements in the cities and lay a foundation from which national agreement for a new partnership formula could emerge. In the event, General Young accepted the arguments of the tripartite patrols, but decided that at this point he had inadequate troops and mediating officers to establish an effective permanent presence in the countryside. Thus an experiment which could have led rapidly towards inter-communal re-engagement was left uncompleted.

JFHQ attention continued to be directed mainly at the prevention of armed conflict in the cities, where paramilitary weaponry had so far been concentrated. The formation of the Joint Political Liaison Committee on 29 December, under the initial chairmanship of Duncan Sandys, had given rise to hopes of a rapid advance towards the re-institution of effective and responsible central government. This hope had so far been dashed by the failure of communal leaderships to establish an effective and general political control over their paramilitary organisations, private armies and individual hotheads. A process followed, only dimly perceived at the time, in which the agenda was effectively hijacked in each community by right wing forces whose prime allegiance was to Athens or Ankara. The JPLC, which lacked the tripartite patrols' access to the structure of parastatal power, became little more than a rather ineffective talk-shop.

I was aware of right-wing thinking in Athens. I had served a short-term assignment with the Greek navy during combined NATO fleet exercises in the autumn of 1963 and had been made uncomfortably conscious of the force of rightist prejudice. My wife had friends with social links to the Potamianos family, who were strong supporters of right-wing irredentism. I had acquaintances in the Greek army.

Also during 1963 I had been briefed at length by US intelligence agencies in Athens over their crusade to neutralise communist and left-wing influence in the eastern Mediterranean. This Cold War mission had led them into unsavoury alliances in both Greece and Turkey. They were now seen as godfathers by those who were the principal foreign subverters of Cypriot stability: the Grey Wolves in Turkey and the Greek intelligence service, KYP[1]. KYP, which was to the forefront in the promotion of action against the Turkish Cypriots, was closely associated with the CIA, which had formed and sponsored it and to which it reported directly. Many KYP officers had a background in Greek fascist organisations: they also were major proponents of the *megali idea*[2], the belief in a 'restoration' of the greater Hellas: as such they were the most energetic activists in the pursuit of *enosis*. Their involvement in Cypriot affairs was to become increasingly baleful and allowed Ankara to claim justification for its own involvement.

The rising level of paramilitary control in rural areas during January 1964 filled a vacuum left by the absence of effective central government.

At the same time there was a substantial movement of Turkish Cypriot village populations away from areas of supposed threat towards what were conceived to be safer enclaves. In the thirty days from 20 December the number of mixed villages in Cyprus halved, from about 135 to 65. This was in comparison to a reduction from 350 to 135 over the previous eighty years, which had generally been gradual and evolutionary but with a sharp temporary escalation in 1958, at the previous high-point of inter-communal violence.

The tripartite patrols attempted to stem this tide, but the impetus for escape from fear was extremely powerful. Members of the Greek Cypriot leadership, misled about events in the countryside by distorted reporting and faulty analysis, grossly underestimated the insecurities created within the Turkish Cypriot community by the events of late December and early January. Their belated directives urging reconciliation were either made counter-productive by the manner of their delivery or negated by local actions of the police or armed extremists. At the same time the insecurities were exploited by TMT and the Turkish Cypriot leadership with increasing vigour. In Nicosia, as in other areas, there was a continuing break-up of inter-communal cohesion.

On 8 January Major Greenwood's patrol had responded to reports of trouble in the Potamia area, where the mixed villages of Dhali, Potamia, Pyroi and Nisou lay among the Turkish Cypriot ones of Goshi, Louroujina, Ayios

Sozomenos, Petrophani, Kochati and Margi, with Greek Cypriot Limbia to the south. No incidents of violence were found but the whole area was very tense, with the usual pattern of inter-communal suspicion and fear. The patrol recorded that the Turkish Cypriots at Louroujina felt both isolated and aggressive; that the Greek Cypriots at Dhali were apprehensive of a supposed threat from the Turks at Louroujina; that the Turkish Cypriot minority in Dhali was extremely frightened of the Greeks in the same village; that the minority Greek Cypriots in Potamia were fearful of the Turks there; that the Turkish Cypriots in Potamia were frightened of the Greeks in Dhali (who had been sending strong fighting patrols through the village); and that the Turkish Cypriots in Pyroi were panicky following the abduction of two of their shepherds the previous day. The small Turkish Cypriot minority in Dhali had secretly asked Major Greenwood that arrangements be made as soon as possible for its evacuation. All of this was without any act of actual aggression by any village against another.

On the following day the Turkish Cypriot minorities at Nisou and Pyroi had begun to evacuate to Louroujina. The move was completed by 12 January without harassment or special notice. Even Kutchuk's office was unaware that it had happened until several days later.

In assessing the cause of these moves the patrol noted that Nisou and Pyroi lie on the main roads from Nicosia to Limassol and Larnaca respectively; that both villages had police stations from which Turkish Cypriot officers had been absent since Christmas; that there had been reports of aggressive police activity on 7 January, including several arrests or abductions of Turkish Cypriots of whom no trace had so far been found.

By Greek Cypriots it was claimed that the evacuations resulted from Turkish political directives. Later it was discovered that during the visit on 8 January Major Greenwood's Turkish officer, Captain Abdullah, had advised the villagers, and those at Dhali, to leave. Some of the refugees later told us they had already been determined to evacuate: they also said that in encouraging them to go Captain Abdullah had used as a final lever a warning that the Turkish air force would bomb the area in the near future and that they must be concentrated in all-Turkish villages before then. From 10 January there also was an intermittent flow of Turkish Cypriot families out of Dhali to Louroujina and Ayios Sozomenos.

On 13 and 14 January two events occurred that heightened apprehension in the villages and placed further strain on inter-communal relations in this and other regions.

First, at Ayios Vasilios, the bodies of twenty-one Turkish Cypriots, who had been killed during the December troubles and buried in two mass graves, were exhumed under British and Red Cross supervision. The condition of the corpses, mostly victims of the December fighting in Omorphita, provided dramatic material for Turkish Cypriot propagandists: the horrors of Christmas, which in many minds had already begun to fade, were stridently recreated. A new frisson of fear permeated the Turkish Cypriot rural community.

Second, the first 'village battle' of 1964 occurred. This was at Goshi, a small, compact Turkish Cypriot village, with a population of about a hundred, which lies at the head of a narrow valley, a hundred yards to the west of the main Nicosia-Larnaca road.

On both 11 and 12 January shots were fired at the village from a car passing slowly up the main road. On the evening of January 13 two Greek Cypriot police Land Rovers arrived from the direction of Larnaca just as the last of the shepherds were bedding down their flocks in byres that lay close to the Nicosia road. The police surrounded one of the shepherds and tried to drag him to their vehicle. The men-folk of the village, who were watching events from the nearest houses, assumed that their man was being abducted and rushed to his assistance, shouting and waving cudgels. Seeing them come, the police released the shepherd, fired in the air over the approaching crowd, retreated to their cars and drove off in the direction of Pyroi. The Turkish Cypriots, fearful of what was to come, armed themselves with their shotguns and stood to on the fringes of the village, facing towards the road.

Half an hour later, with night now falling, four cars or Land Rovers with armed men arrived at the crossroads. A loudhailer was used to address the Turkish Cypriots, but the sound was distorted and they could not make out what was being said. Immediately afterwards heavy automatic fire was directed at the village. Then there was a lull and more unintelligible shouting through the loudhailer and men were seen advancing cautiously down the tree-lined dust-track that connects Goshi to the main road.

Heavy firing then started again from close range, most of it apparently directed at the schoolhouse, which stands just to the north of the village proper and which in fact was unoccupied. When the attackers were seen to be very close to the village outskirts, the Turkish Cypriots began to fire with their shotguns towards the discharge-flashes of the Greek Cypriot weapons. There had been cursing and several shrieks, suggesting that the Greek Cypriots were taking injuries, and then the attackers were seen withdrawing to the main road. Then there was more firing at long range before the cars moved off towards Larnaca.

The Turkish Cypriot villagers had suffered neither casualties nor serious damage. Next morning I persuaded them to put away their guns and to join me for coffee and a smoke. I found them viewing events with remarkable equanimity, despite a natural apprehension as to when there would be further attacks. When I examined the approaches to the village I sighted large numbers of expended cartridge-cases: I also found that some trees were peppered with a mixture of shotgun pellets, blood, flesh and strands of police uniform, to such extent that I wrongly assumed there must have been several fatal casualties.

Taking coffee later with the police who had been involved, I was reassured by them that they had suffered only minor injuries, three constables being said to have received superficial wounds. Their story tallied almost precisely with that of the villagers. They explained, however, that this had been a "normal police operation." They said that their aim had merely been to interview one of the Goshi shepherds in connection with routine enquiries into a recent local case of theft. They disclaimed any knowledge of the shootings at the village on the 11th and 12th, accepted that such an occurrence would have been contrary to the President's undertakings and said they now understood the villagers cause for alarm. We agreed that the absence of Turkish Cypriot police officers created serious problems in the exercise of their duties. I elicited a promise that they would for the time being co-ordinate with me any further need for interviews in Goshi.

The events at Goshi had repercussions in stiffening the resolve of Turkish Cypriot villages against incursions by the Greek Cypriot gendarmerie. They did not attract wide coverage at the time because the attention of the press corps was centred on the macabre revelations at Ayios Vasilios and because the details of what had happened were slow to reach the politicians in Nicosia.

I kept my patrol in this area throughout 14 and 15 January, trying to counter the effects that would stem from uncontested rumours of an armed attack on an isolated Turkish Cypriot village. In all of the nearby mixed villages there were signs of inter-communal fragmentation, a sense that more violence was imminent. A pervasive poisoning of the atmosphere came from the bitterness of those Turkish Cypriots who recently had become refugees. Irrespective of actual circumstances they saw their plight as wholly the product of Greek Cypriot antagonisms and of their lack of any genuine security.

The villagers who had evacuated Pyroi said that the final straw for them had been when some of their number were surrounded and attacked in the fields by a large contingent of Greek Cypriot police, who afterwards had removed their only tractor. The Greek Cypriots in Pyroi said that in fact the Turkish Cypriots had been stealing Greek Cypriots potatoes, that the police had caught them at it and had merely driven them off "in such a way as to teach them a lesson", and that the tractor had been impounded because the Turks had defaulted on their payments for it. They claimed that they had always shown friendship to the Turkish Cypriots and that they would continue to do so.

The Turkish Cypriot abandonment of Pyroi was symptomatic of a general malaise of mistrust and anxiety. Probably it was within some general TMT concept that Turkish Cypriots in the area should be concentrated within wholly Turkish Cypriot enclaves; probably Captain Abdullah, patrolling with Major Greenwood, had urged things in this direction; probably in this instance the police had acted within their rights; probably the Greek Cypriots in Pyroi had endeavoured over the previous ten days to show a real good-neighbourliness; probably there would have been no move if a permanent peacekeeping presence had been established in the area; certainly the Turkish Cypriots had desperately wanted not to abandon their homes: but all of this was outweighed in significance by the fear that was now prevalent.

What the villagers had heard of December's events in Nicosia, Skylloura and Ayios Vasilios, the occasional instances of harassment, the danger that existed for them on the roads and, most of all, their total loss of trust in the national forces of law and order had combined to produce an insecurity that was poured out to the patrols time after time every day with a heartrending plea for help. However much triggered by distorted propaganda or by TMT prompting, these were genuine expressions of deeply-felt insecurity.

Dhali at this point was witnessing a process of gradual Turkish Cypriot evacuation and the Greek Cypriot villagers were uncertain of how they ought to react: on the one hand it was a relief for them to see the Turkish Cypriots going, on the other they had been instructed that their staying would be supportive of the President's policy.

Arriving in Dhali by helicopter on 14 January, my patrol was met by a group of Greek Cypriot officers of the Cyprus army*, Second Lieutenant Olympos immaculately uniformed and the others plain-clothed and unshaven. From their conversation together, before they were warned by Lieutenant Constantinides that I was a Greek-speaker, I was able to gather a good deal about the organisation and command of Greek Cypriot forces in the area.

It appeared that the 'military', comprised of 'The Organisation'[3], the "Secret Army"[4] (which was being created under its aegis), the Greek Cypriot rump of the embryonic Cyprus army, and various 'private' parastatal units, all strongly influenced by regular Greek army officers clandestinely arrived from Athens, was trying to gain a hold on Greek Cypriot loyalties in the district but was having to deal with a reaction from the police and from the left. It was committed to the government's declared policy of amicable co-existence with the Turkish Cypriots: at the same time it had mixed feelings about Turkish Cypriot plans to gather into single-community enclaves. In contrast to official policy, it regarded this as tolerable so long as the enclaves did not overlap or dominate the island's main roads. In cases where a Turkish Cypriot or mixed village already lay astride a major road, the military was happy to see the Turkish Cypriots evacuate.

The Greek Cypriot 'army' officers I was listening to were clearly aggravated by the general intransigence and aggressiveness of the police and particularly irritated by acts of irresponsible provocation which frustrated their efforts to convince the Turkish Cypriots of Greek Cypriot good intentions.

Regret was expressed to me over the 'needless' flow of Turkish Cypriots away from the area's mixed villages: this was said to be provoking pained vexation among the Greek Cypriots, who felt that their friendship was being rejected, and increasing the sense of isolation and alarm among the dwindling numbers of still remaining Turkish Cypriots.

At a fractious joint meeting behind closed doors in the central coffee-house of Dhali, the patrol tried to get the leaders of the two communities to express their real fears and wishes, in the hope that a basis for compromise would emerge. What quickly became apparent was that the sharpest division was not so much between Greek Cypriots and Turkish Cypriots as between moderates and extremists in each community. Ranged on one side were the Greek Cypriot *mukhtar*, thoughtful, middle-aged and responsible, and his

---

* The constitution stipulated an army of 2000 men, 60% Greek Cypriot and 40% Turkish Cypriot. The Greek Cypriots pressed for a wholly integrated force. The Turkish Cypriots demanded that the army be composed of a number of wholly Greek Cypriot and wholly Turkish Cypriot companies. No agreement could be reached and the total strength never exceeded 375 men.

likeable Turkish Cypriot opposite number, a realistic smallholder, together with the local Greek Cypriot paramilitary leader, a tough young man from another region who appeared to have good connections in the government, and Lieutenant Constantinides. All of these were anxious for a formula that would check the slide towards conflict and separation.

Ranged on the other side were a militant young Greek Cypriot (probably a former member of EOKA Youth, who presented himself as a Georgadjis appointee), a local Greek Cypriot policeman, the village's Greek and Turkish schoolmasters and a representative of TMT. These men talked in extremist terms, totally mistrusted the activities and intentions of the other community, maintained that a solution could only be found through separation or through the victory of one or the other side. Discussion was much more articulate than in our usual meetings but it was typical of all those villages where extremism had gained a foothold.

In the case of Dhali the only major local complaint of the Turkish Cypriots was that they had been forced on 31 December to hand over all of their hunting guns to a Greek Cypriot vigilante committee and that some of their houses had then been searched.* Otherwise theirs were the usual stories of rumoured abductions, supposition of impending attack and occasional provocation and humiliation.

The meeting ended with a much-improved atmosphere, mutual demonstrations of cordiality, even from the extremists, and the pledge of all those there to work for the removal of inter-communal tensions. Nevertheless, the patrol departed with considerable pessimism, uncomfortably aware that under the prevailing circumstances in Dhali the good intentions of any number of intending moderates could quickly be neutralised by a single dedicated extremist.

Some days later the patrol talked at length with a number of Turkish Cypriot refugees from Dhali who had moved to Ayios Sozomenos. They all said that some of the Greek Cypriot leaders had strongly urged them to stay and had lectured them on the necessity and benefits of peaceful co-existence: however, another section of the Greek Cypriot community had clearly wished them to go and had exerted continuous pressure on them to do so. Asked to describe this pressure, they could only produce a catalogue of apparently trifling threats and insults. They also claimed that most of the Turkish Cypriots still in Dhali now wished to leave but were being actively prevented from doing so by the Greek Cypriots. After further questioning it was elicited that the villagers who were being so constrained were those of which the head of the family had significant financial debts to the Greek Cypriots.

On the day following this meeting the Greek Cypriots in Dhali reported to me that another five or six Turkish Cypriot families had left during the night, despite their own best efforts to restore confidence in the village. It was alleged that the evacuation had continued on the directions of Colonel Akova. The Greek Cypriot military leader introduced me in private to a Turkish Cypriot who confirmed that the colonel had indeed urged them all to go. This

---

* Unusually, the guns were later returned to them as a gesture of goodwill.

tallied with whisperings in my ear from Lieutenant Constantinides about nefarious statements being made by his Turkish colleague. Another Turkish Cypriot villager told me that the colonel had said that the area was soon to be bombed by the Turkish air force and that any village not flying a Turkish flag would be destroyed.

That night I had a long session alone with Colonel Akova, told him what had been said and asked him for an explanation. He admitted that he had advised people to move into all-Turkish Cypriot villages but denied that he had threatened the consequences of Turkish air attack. He said that he was accompanying the patrol to village after village where he had to listen to reports from the Turkish Cypriots of murders, abductions, searches, humiliations and threats against their community. He accepted that much of this might be exaggerated, or even false, but said it was unquestionably evident that Turkish Cypriots in isolated mixed areas were having acts of violence and intimidation committed against them, that they did lack any real security and that we were the only authority to which they could appeal for help or justice or unbiased advice. In most of the villages that we visited he was the only symbol of government that the villagers could address. Inevitably they asked him for guidance. He felt a deep personal involvement. He knew what deprivation they would suffer as refugees, but he personally believed they would be, and feel, safer in all-Turkish areas. Therefore in Dhali he had told the Turks that he thought it better that they move.

I was grateful for the honesty. I accepted that where security could not otherwise be provided there might be circumstances where evacuation was advisable, even if on a temporary basis. But I said that, so long as we operated as a joint patrol, advice to this effect should only be given with my agreement. He was attached to my patrol but technically not under my command. He must understand that I could not claim to be acting as an impartial mediator if one of my team was privately using the cover of the patrol to promulgate a directive with which I disagreed. Personally I believed that uncalled for evacuations were increasing the risk of violence in the area, not lessening it. The identification and neutralisation of extremists in both communities was the better way to safety.

Colonel Akova was an impressive officer with fine credentials. I respected him and valued the contribution he had made to the mediating process, and I was aware that I might get a replacement who would be far worse. I discussed the position with General Young and said that I wanted a Turkish officer who would be prepared to give his total loyalty to the tripartite patrol. Next day I found that Major Sait Sepici had been appointed to my unit.

I quickly found that Sepici was no less of a patriot and no less moved by the plight of the Turkish Cypriots, but that he accepted that he was assigned to contribute to a tripartite endeavour and that the patrol could only act effectively if it acted as a cohesive unit. So long as he and Lieutenant Constantinides were with me we jointly constituted an exceptionally powerful mediating instrument. However, like all the Turkish officers with whom I worked, Sepici had a profound dislike of Makarios.

Events in Dhali helped to fashion my thinking on key aspects of our operations. Our original remit had been to "re-establish normal relations between the Greek Cypriot and Turkish Cypriot communities in the rural areas" and General Young had expanded on this to say that we must seek to create an atmosphere in which the two communities could work out in peace their own way forward. Neither this nor the patrol's push for a climate in which the two communities could realistically live together in peace and security clashed with the formally expressed policy of either Makarios or Kutchuk.

Our thesis ran counter to the TMT propaganda line that separation was necessary for Turkish Cypriot security, but it accepted that in some areas a limited movement of population would lower tension and enhance inter-communal co-operation: that would apply to localities of extreme friction, to villages whose isolation placed them at special risk so long as travel by road was dangerous, and to communities whose troubles were poisoning relations throughout a larger area.

In certain cases, therefore, I got agreement from both my Greek and Turkish officers that an evacuation protected by the patrol would be preferable to the consequences of one provoked by the extremists of either side. I then explained the situation to the offices of Makarios and Kutchuk, and afterwards to key local leaders, and eventually elicited a general approval. The final evacuations of Turkish Cypriot villagers from Potamia, Vitsadha, Orounda and Aredhiou were arranged in this fashion: these probably were the only evacuations at the time executed as a generally-agreed aid to regional stability.

Later there were to be spheres other than population-movement, such as the reactivation of the village constable system and national passport arrangements, in which initiatives were pursued by my patrol under private understanding with the two leaderships in advance of any sort of formal agreement. To avoid the possibility that media attention would damage the chances of success, these cases could initially appear as initiated on my personal authority and be given political airing only when the results were established. No mishaps occurred, but there were occasions when I had to stand against a wall under threat of execution, with a Sten gun jammed into my guts, while a local leader checked with Nicosia on my claim to be carrying a secret empowerment from his central leadership.

From Dhali on 15 January we moved to the next village, Potamia. Here the Turkish Cypriots were slightly in the majority. Much of what had happened and was to happen here derived from a Greek Cypriot fear that the Turkish Cypriots would try to increase their numbers to the point where they would dominate the village and thus create a line of Turkish Cypriot control running through the villages of Ayios Sozomenos - Potamia - Louroujina. In fact the Potamia Turkish Cypriots had shown no signs of aggressiveness. They did at one point agree to accept some refugees from Dhali but this met with such adverse reaction from their Greek Cypriot co-villagers that the idea was quickly dropped.

By the time of our coming, the Turkish Cypriots in Potamia had convinced themselves that an attack on them was imminent and had begun to prepare for defence by opening up firing slits in the walls of those of their houses that faced towards the Greek Cypriot quarter. Predictably the Greeks claimed that this was proof of an impending Turkish Cypriot attack.

As in many other cases, the Turkish Cypriot sense of insecurity here stemmed from a single incident together with an aggressive Greek Cypriot police and paramilitary presence. On 29 December three of their young men, who were alleged to us by the Greek Cypriot villagers to have been members of TMT, had set off by car for Nicosia: they had disappeared without trace and were assumed to have been seized and killed.

To this was added the sight of frequent patrols in force through the village by armed Greek Cypriot police from Nisou and Pyroi and paramilitaries from Dhali: these never attempted to enter the Turkish Cypriot quarter or search their houses or confiscate their shotguns, but the Turkish Cypriots saw in their activities the threat of future attack. Too scared to return to work and staying isolated in their own section of the village, the Turkish Cypriots became a prey to the virulent propaganda of Radio *Bayrak*: in consequence every ludicrous threat shouted by irresponsible Greek Cypriots, who claimed to believe that the Turks had amassed a large arsenal of weaponry, every noise in the night, every dire warning by their own alarmists heightened their sense of insecurity.

Both communities reacted with relief when prodded by the patrol to renew their former co-operation. A joint meeting produced expressions of strong friendship, although regrettably in this case the healing was wafer-thin and a general climate of fear quickly returned. On subsequent visits Ahmet, the Turkish Cypriot schoolmaster, took to passing me surreptitious notes: "Trust nobody: not even the other Turks." "Do not believe the Greek policemen: this area belongs to Louroujina police station, so why are four armed Greeks wearing police uniforms patrolling the village during the night? Their intention is to create trouble in the village." "We are trying to keep peace, but unfortunately the Greeks are not."

As in certain other villages, the Turkish Cypriots in Potamia declined into an unfortunate dependency on the joint patrol. Rather than address their problems through direct contact with Greek Cypriot neighbours, who were now ready to be co-operative, they would send an urgent request for the patrol's return on every occasion of alarm.

Trying to deal with a region that extended over a hundred miles from Kokkina-Mansoura to Rizokarpaso and from Kyrenia to Louroujina left my patrol stretched very thin and unable to meet every request made of it. Potamia's eventual decision to evacuate, under a composite regional agreement, was approved by me when it became clear that neither the patrol nor the peacekeeping force was in a position to provide the level of support needed to maintain the Turkish Cypriot villagers' confidence.

Another major contributor to the Turkish Cypriot sense of insecurity was the lack of telephone communication. In village after village I was told by the Turkish Cypriots that CYTA, the Cypriot telephone authority, had deprived them of an effective service and that the manual exchanges would connect them only at the occasional whim of a sympathetic operator. I set out to assess the situation by attempting a call from the Turkish Cypriot quarter of each village that I visited.

On those occasions when an operator, usually after a twenty-minute wait, did answer me, a typical conversation would go:

Me: "Nicosia 34011, please."

Operator, immediately: "Unobtainable."

Me: "Why is it unobtainable?"

Operator: "Are you calling from Goshi?"

Me: "Please put me through to your area manager immediately."

Operator: "Who are you?"

Me: "I am Commander Packard, head of a tripartite patrol unit."

Operator: "No you're not. You are a Turk pretending to be an Englishman, and you will not be put through."

After which the line would be closed and no amount of redialling would elicit a response.

CYTA executives explained to me that telephone services for the Turkish Cypriots had been cut because of non-settlement of bills, which I learned to be part of a TMT strategy aimed at communal separation. Apparently CYTA also saw its actions as contributing to the combating of Turkish Cypriot insurrection. CYTA's view mirrored that of the police and gendarmerie. It ignored the fact that the administration's policy since 29 December had been one of encouraging Turkish Cypriots to feel secure by restoring normal facilities and promoting inter-communal reconciliation and re-engagement.

At Potamia there was a more particular complaint. The village had only one telephone, a public call box situated between the two sectors. The Turkish Cypriots, who now kept a permanent watch on their neighbours, reported that the Greek Cypriots had arranged for a visit by CYTA technicians at 2 am during a night in early January. They surmised that the objective was to install a local tap-line on the telephone. This had led to a good deal of animosity.

The Greek Cypriots at first professed total ignorance. Then they claimed that the CYTA visit had been to install an extension so that their *mukhtar* could make calls without needing to go out into the rain. When it was pointed out that the new line did not go anywhere near the *mukhtar*'s house they acknowledged that it was indeed a tap. They justified this by claiming that it was necessary for them to listen to all Turkish Cypriot calls so that they could learn if the Turks were planning an attack.

Eventually the Greek Cypriots agreed that the tap-line breached the code of good neighbourliness and that it should be removed. This was done by CYTA the following night. (We assumed that it was later replaced, less obtrusively, elsewhere. We were to discover that both Greek Cypriots and Turkish Cypriots throughout Cyprus indulged in extensive tapping wherever they had access to the telephone system.)

I obtained the blessing of senior ministers and then spent a considerable time arguing with CYTA executives that they could best contribute by disregarding, for the time being, the financial implications and providing an adequate service to the Turkish Cypriots, whose individual sense of security would thereby be enhanced. Eventually there was a general restoration of services.

Despite concessions of this sort, the government's now more conciliatory stance and the efforts of the four tripartite patrols, the latter half of January saw a continuing seepage of bitterness into this and some other rural areas of Cyprus. The Freedom of Movement agreement of 6 January was increasingly ignored. In the unitary villages, Greek Cypriot and Turkish Cypriot alike, defences were steadily improved, increasingly men stood to in the trenches and by the barricades and those not on guard duty sat in the coffee-houses and talked of atrocities, vengeance and war. To stem the bush-fire of distrust needed constant fire-fighting. It was fanned by virulent press propaganda and fuelled by continuing frictions in the major cities, by the inequity of police operations and by the encouragement of a small minority of extremists and hooligans. Over and again it was proved in the villages that communal re-engagement was eminently viable, only for the process to be sabotaged by a few aggressive individuals. Nor, despite the drive of some ministers for reconciliation, did there seem to be any national comprehension of the dangers of disunity.

So the all-Turkish Cypriot Louroujina and Ayios Sozomenos and Petrophani and Kochati and other villages like them became increasingly isolated. Schoolmasters and young TMT leaders took over effective power from the old *mukhtars*, extremist political jargon became commonplace and compromise became increasingly hard to achieve.

Men from Louroujina had disappeared on the roads over Christmas and local people believed they were still being held hostage, although I could find no trace of them. From Kochati it had more recently been reported that two villagers had been seized while they were driving to Nicosia. At Ayios Sozomenos I was told that a shepherd, Fikret Huseyin, had disappeared with his flocks from nearby fields on 8 January. All of the villages in this area had seen armed Greek Cypriot police units patrolling their boundaries and occasionally had heard sounds of gunfire. Just outside Kochati Greek Cypriot paramilitaries had set up a target range and their daily practising, with Bren guns and small arms, left the Turkish Cypriot villagers feeling exposed and uncomfortable.

In the meantime the Greek Cypriots, urged on by their media, by frequent foreign press reports of the Turkish army's preparations for invasion, and by the eddying currents of alarmist coffee-house gossip, saw themselves increasingly to be the threatened community, faced with an expectation of sudden assault under a Turkish master-plan. No hint had yet been given to the Greek Cypriots by their press or politicians that the Turkish Cypriots in rural areas were exposed to hostage-taking, arbitrary killings, danger on the roads, loss of their vehicles and the destruction of their property, and that Greek Cypriot police forces were not only failing to provide any protection against this, but frequently had members involved in it.*

Instead, Greek Cypriot media portrayed the Turkish Cypriot rural community as a backward peasantry keen to maintain its co-operation with

---

* Those Greek Cypriot villagers who were witnesses to what was happening took it that this was a continuation of EOKA activity and prudently kept their mouths shut.

the Greek Cypriots but misled into revolt by TMT. Only a few Greek Cypriots suggested that intervention from Ankara could best be avoided by providing the Turkish Cypriots with a formula that genuinely satisfied their needs for security, both as individuals and as a partner-community.   Rather than counter the Turkish push for separation with a careful policy that would have isolated Turkish Cypriot extremism, the Greek Cypriots had poured petrol on the fire by allowing free rein to the most extreme elements of their own community.

On 19 January I reported to Nicosia that inter-communal relations had further deteriorated throughout the northern areas of the island. I suggested that in part this was due to a well-intentioned invasion of the remaining mixed villages by Greek newspapermen and welfare agency representatives all seeking evidence that the Turkish Cypriots were anxious for unity with the Greek Cypriots. There was a rush to obtain pictures of Greek Cypriot and Turkish Cypriot villagers smilingly sipping coffee in each other's company. In terms of reconciliation this was wholly counter-productive: Greek Cypriots were misled as to the reality of the rural situation while Turkish Cypriots felt patronised, humiliated and more than ever threatened. Genuinely conciliatory gestures, such as the decision in Dhali to return confiscated hunting guns to their Turkish Cypriot owners, were very rare. Local inter-village agreements elsewhere, sincerely committed to by both communities, wholly lost their effectiveness when they were seized on by the Greek press to illustrate a disparity between the utterances of the Turkish Cypriot leadership and the feelings of 'ordinary' Turkish Cypriots.

In the Dhali-Louroujina area January ended on a discouraging note. A Mr Ismail Ismail, who had set out from Nicosia by taxi to collect his relatives from Louroujina so that they could be sent to London, disappeared en route and no sign of him or his taxi-driver, Mehmet Hasan, (or of the taxi) could be found. There were reports of further drive-by shootings from the main road towards Goshi. The schoolmaster from Petrophani was shot at on the road to Louroujina. Only five Turkish Cypriot families were now left in Dhali. There were indications of a sizeable build-up of weaponry in Louroujina. In Potamia the two communities were again at loggerheads. This whole area was now a highly volatile powder-keg.

8.   MORA AREA.
EARLY JANUARY 1964

Due east of Nicosia was a very different area of Turkish Cypriot concentration, centred on the large the Turkish Cypriot village of Mora and lying beside the old Nicosia-Famagusta road. To the south lay another large Turkish Cypriot village, Ayia, and between them, astride the road, was Chumlekji Chiflik, a large co-operative farm upon which the whole of the local Turkish Cypriot agricultural economy was based. To the north-west of Mora was the mixed village of Palekythro and to the north-east the Greek Cypriot Angastina, which bordered the new Nicosia-Famagusta highway. To the south-east is Aphania and to the south-west Tymbou, the former mixed and the latter Greek Cypriot. Ornithi, the closest neighbour of Mora, had been deserted since the 1958 troubles.

There was no tight grouping among these villages, nor very much co-ordination, although their lands adjoined. There was some sharing of adversity but the pressure was mostly minor and haphazard. The fact that the Turkish Cypriot leaders in Mora were moderate and responsive to compromise, in contrast to those of Louroujina, had a calming effect on the region.

Ayia was never subjected to direct attack and the sum of its untoward experiences was a couple of insignificant shooting incidents in the crescent of hills to the south-west. Ayia's shepherds continued their contacts with those from the neighbouring Greek Cypriot villages and, although its farmers would sometimes rush home in alarm at the approach of strangers, the general agricultural life of the community continued with little disturbance.

Nevertheless, Ayia displayed a sense of isolation more intense than in any other village in Nicosia Zone. This sad distinction derived from a small group of young TMT bravos, Beetles look-alikes, who wore pistols slung low in cheap plastic holsters and who violently harangued the other villagers against the dangers of collaboration with the Greek Cypriots. Village meetings in Ayia were eerie mirror-images of those in Skylloura, with attempts by Major Sepici to preach restraint interrupted by hissings and derision from adolescent extremists.

Neighbouring Aphania was completely different. Here there were no political agitators in either community. Greek Cypriots and Turkish Cypriots maintained their former good relations throughout January and both readily agreed to our proposals for confidence-building co-operation. This was one of the few villages where the Turkish Cypriots bought their food from Greek Cypriot shops, although this fact, which was in defiance of TMT directives, was prudently concealed by the Aphania Turkish Cypriots and strenuously denied by other Turkish Cypriots who slipped in by donkey from Mora and Ayia to replenish their stocks.

Greek Cypriot paramilitaries had been quick to realise that the farm premises at Chumlekji would provide ideal cover for any Turkish Cypriot attempt to mount an ambush on the Nicosia-Famagusta road, and there was pressure against this settlement from 10 January onwards by way of aggressive armed patrols. Turkish Cypriots at the farming complex and the Turkish Cypriot leadership in Mora both pleaded passionately for the stationing of a British army unit at Chumlekji. The idea was accepted by Greek Cypriot village leaders in the area and then strongly supported by the patrol, which believed that such a move would inhibit hostage-taking on the main road, calm the surrounding villages and allow an eye to be kept on the nearby disused airstrip at Tymbou. However the proposal was rejected by JFHQ as contrary to current policy.

On 16 January the Turkish Cypriots evacuated their valuable herd of pedigree cows from Chumlekji to Pergamos and soon afterwards the resident Dutch agricultural adviser also departed, claiming that pressure on the farm was no longer tolerable.

On the afternoon of 21 January a unit of British scout cars passing through Mora was informed by a breathless runner from Chumlekji that parties of armed Greek Cypriots were converging on the farm. The patrol diverted to Chumlekji and on its approach the Greek Cypriot paramilitaries made off at speed towards Tymbou.

After dusk that same evening a number of Greek Cypriot police Land Rovers approached on the main road from both east and west and armed men were deployed to cordon off all of the tracks leading away from the farm. Three Land Rovers were then driven into the main courtyard: police took up firing positions, shouted at the Turkish Cypriots to come out and surrender and simultaneously began to search the outbuildings.

In the meantime one of the Turkish Cypriots had slipped away across the fields to Mora, which now despatched a shotgun-armed party towards Chumlekji. Seeing lights approaching down the tracks from the north, the Greek Cypriots retired towards Tymbou, some of them shooting in the air as they went.

The Turkish Cypriots immediately quit the farm for the fortified safety of Mora, where the entire adult population stood to with their shotguns throughout the night. Next day the inhabitants of Chumlekji returned to the farm for just long enough to collect their moveable possessions.

The Greek Cypriot paramilitaries in Tymbou acknowledged these events when I spoke to them later in the day, but claimed that there had been no intention to dislodge the Turkish Cypriots from Chumlekji. At first they said that the patrolling had been part of a normal training schedule, but eventually they confided that their actions were in response to reports that the farm was being used by the Turkish Cypriots as a prison for Greek Cypriot hostages.[1] They said that all of the firing had been at pigeons. It appeared that the night's action had been co-ordinated between the paramilitaries and the regular police, a rare occurrence at this stage.

Chumlekji Chiflik did not stay empty for long. On 29 and 30 January, refugees staging through Nicosia from evacuated villages to the west were directed by the Turkish Cypriot Communal Chamber to establish themselves in the farm, and a large consignment of Red Crescent supplies was delivered for their support. Structurally the farm was well suited for this role, as its modern sheep-byres and cowsheds were sounder than most of the village homes that had been abandoned, but it was obvious that the Greek Cypriots would see the move as a Turkish Cypriot attempt to establish a Mora-Ayia enclave and to create a strong settlement astride the Nicosia-Famagusta road. I reported that Chumlekji must now be considered a potential flash-point and that the Turkish Cypriot administration had unnecessarily endangered its people by placing them here without any prior consultation.

Visiting the farm on 1 February we learned there were now over a hundred Turkish Cypriot refugees there. By the 5th the number was over a hundred and forty. On the 10th the farm was empty again.

So far as we could discover, the Turkish Cypriots had never moved any weapons into Chumlekji and there had never been a TMT plan to use the farm strategically. The Greek Cypriots at Tymbou had provoked a second departure simply by mounting training exercises, some under cover of darkness, and conducting firing practice along the boundaries of the farm. This time the evacuation was to be permanent.

The Turkish Cypriot abandonment of Palekythro was much more of a mystery. This mixed village had no history of violence or of significant pressure. Tripartite patrol visits on 12 and 13 January reported that inter-communal relations were fairly good and that joint meetings had seemed to defuse potential tensions and to strengthen a Turkish Cypriot resolve to stay. At the first of these meetings it was agreed that defensive positions would be removed and the sandbagged emplacements that faced each other from the two sides of the village were then co-operatively dismantled amid general hilarity.

There was here, as in most other Turkish Cypriot areas, an extreme shortage of cash and some shortage of supplies. There also were difficulties for both communities about a return to work, exacerbated here by the fact that Greek Cypriot workers claimed they had been warned 'by EOKA' that they must not in future work alongside Turkish Cypriots. But none of this would seem to justify the sudden evacuation of the entire Turkish Cypriot community to Mora on 14/15 January. Questioned afterwards, the Turkish Cypriots leaders said that they had no complaints about their Greek Cypriot fellow villagers, but that they had been frightened by a visit of 'foreigners' to the Greek Cypriot sector and had supposed that action was being planned against them.

Shortly after the departure of the tripartite patrol on the 13th a Dutch TV crew had arrived and, having been told by the Greek Cypriots about the successful joint meeting, had set out to do a feature demonstrating the ability of the two communities to coexist successfully. The Turkish Cypriots told me they had been unnerved by this film-making, believing that it was destined to be used as Greek Cypriot propaganda, and that this had been the trigger for their departure.

Alternatively they may have been urged to go either by Captain Abdullah on the 13th, by Colonel Akova on the 14th or by three TMT activists who were reported to have visited Palekythro on the evening of the 13th. Against this, however, was the fact that there appeared no logical reason for this village to be abandoned: rather, we would have expected TMT to have wished the Turkish Cypriot villagers to stay, so as to develop an effective enclave around Mora.

After a protracted meeting with us on the 16th the evacuees resolved to return to Palekythro under the patrol's sponsorship, but they were then harangued by some Mora extremists who claimed that a move back would be damaging to the Turkish Cypriot assertion of the need for separation and who threatened to restrain them by force. A TMT representative seconded this advice and told them that in any case they could soon reclaim their homes since Palekythro "...was to be in the Turkish sector when Cyprus was partitioned..." In the end only one tough and elderly shepherdess refused to be dissuaded, claiming that supplies of fodder in Mora were inadequate and that since arriving some of her possessions had been stolen. She returned with her sheep to Palekythro, where she was warmly welcomed by the Greek Cypriots.

In Mora itself, the course of events was predictable. The village was large and wealthy, the centre of an extensive grain-farming area. It had no natural defensive features, the land sloping in gently from the south-east and stretching away flat to the west and north. At first sight, however, it gave the impression of a fortress under siege, barricaded at every approach and with a network of slit trenches and sandbagged firing positions stretching all around its outer limits. Despite these defences, good leadership and the fact that they had seen no violence whatsoever, the villagers of Mora exhibited a state of constant alarm. Radio *Bayrak*, exaggerated reports from Chumlekji Chiflik and other villages and the frequent sighting of groups of armed Greek Cypriots moving over Mora-owned land had combined to convince them that they were soon to be attacked.

On our first visit I found the leaders in Mora to be thoughtful and moderate men. They were adamant, however, that any attempt by the Greek Cypriot police to enter the village would be met with force. In every other respect they were ready to participate in proposals which the patrol had formulated for inter-communal re-engagement over the local area.

Three days later the climate had radically changed. Arriving for a scheduled meeting we found that the *mukhtar* and his moderate associates had been pushed into the background and that centre stage was now occupied by an aggressive TMT group that had moved in from Nicosia. From that point onwards, discussion ceased to be related so much to the reality of regional problems as to argument about the generalities of inter-communal dispute. Anarchy was now being overlaid by a patchy and apparently haphazard spread of central ideological control, albeit under hard-line direction. Privately the *mukhtar* told us that he would try to do what was best for his people but that it was 'difficult' for him publicly to contradict what Nicosia was saying.

A case in point that immediately arose concerned the distribution of emergency aid. At this point the tripartite patrols were still acting as the main agency for reporting shortages in the villages and for establishing what urgency there was for re-supply. Even for experts specially qualified in such a task, this would have been a difficult assignment in a Cyprus where the reality of need was hard to establish and where genuine deprivation was beginning to be promoted or exploited for political purposes: for the patrols, which had no such qualification, the task was becoming extremely onerous.

On 16 January, the Turkish Cypriots at Mora claimed that their stocks of food were exhausted and that they were too frightened to travel and thus unable to obtain new supplies, even had they the money to do so. We knew this was less than the truth, having just come from Aphania where we had chanced on a Turkish Cypriot from Mora engaged in making bulk purchases from the Greek Cypriot shops, but it was evident that some families were dangerously destitute. I referred to the position in my report that night:

> "It appears that strong political pressure is now being applied by (their own) extremists to the Turks in the villages within the Mora-Ayia area. A considerable problem thus arises as to the recommending of food supplies.
>
> The Turks in these 'fortress-villages' are able to go out and purchase supplies (even at some occasional risk), and are in fact quietly doing so, but are telling both us and their fellow villagers that it is too dangerous to do so. On the other hand it is obvious that some of the villagers are now approaching starvation-point and that they need and expect supplies to be sent by us. What supplies we do send are likely mostly to go into the stockpile. If some of the villagers starve it may be within the framework of a situation politically engineered by TMT. Guidance is now necessary as to whether supplies should be recommended when it is suspected that the 'shortages' are of this nature."

In response, a greater urgency was given to the transfer of responsibility for the recommending of relief supplies to teams from the Red Cross and St John's Ambulance Brigade. In the meantime the patrols used such moral levers as they could find to try and persuade Turkish Cypriot leaders to allocate supplies to the genuinely needy rather than to the underpinning of ethnic separatism.

Genuine fear was also supplemented by political contrivance in the inhibiting of Turkish Cypriot travel in the region. Telephone lines in many Turkish Cypriot areas remained inoperative. Irrigation problems began to assume increasing significance and complaints that in reality were long-standing were now advanced as evidence of a Greek Cypriot campaign of economic pressure. Isolation and inactivity promoted a torpor which gradually consumed even the agitators and extremists.

Most Greek Cypriot villagers in this region displayed towards the Turkish Cypriots an attitude of amicable indifference. It was, however, apparent that a long-standing tolerance of their neighbours had now been overlaid by a fear of their own right-wing extremists (whom they continued to refer to as 'EOKA') and a confusion as to what was Greek Cypriot policy. They were delighted to be told by the patrol that the government's aim was for reconciliation and co-existence: Lieutenant Constantinides and his successor, Captain Michos, became adept in the delivery of this message and in the promoting of a moderation that in fact reflected the genuine instinct of most Greek Cypriots.

During the first visit by my patrol to Greek Cypriot Angastina we were greeted with an outpouring of pro-Turkish Cypriot sentiment. The *mukhtar* and the village priest (reputedly a former regional co-ordinator for EOKA) vied with each other in their expressions of friendship for their neighbours at Mora, proposals were made for local contracts of alliance and there was enthusiastic agreement to our suggestion of a joint meeting of community leaders in the region to discuss measures for the lowering of tension and the building of confidence. Whether these sentiments were politically-inspired or from the heart, inter-communal feeling in this area remained positive for as long as I was in Cyprus. Indeed the reconciliation line was pursued here with unparalleled vigour: visiting on a later occasion I was seized by the villagers of Angastina and threatened with lynching because a police informer had fabricated a story that I had tried in Mora to incite the Turkish Cypriot community against their Greek Cypriot neighbours.

9. VATILI AREA. JANUARY 1964

Not far eastward of the Mora grouping is another complex of villages, having as its hub the gendarmerie station near Vatili and including Greek Cypriot Asha, Mousoulita and Lysi and the Turkish Cypriot Sinda; Strongylos was mixed, as was Vatili itself with eighteen hundred Greek Cypriots and seven hundred Turkish Cypriots. The gendarmerie post, situated midway between Vatili and Asha, at the junction with the Strongylos road, was to acquire a considerable notoriety.

Within this area Strongylos was the problem-village, frequently in need of mediating support. Poorly led in both communities and subject to the usual alarms, it was particularly destabilised by the Turkish Cypriots' well-justified suspicion that one of their leaders, Huseyin Kirmini, was being held hostage in Vatili gendarmerie station. This, coupled with the effects of increasing political indoctrination and occasional acts of provocation, caused a progressive deterioration in communal relations in the village during January.

The Greek Cypriots chose this moment to conduct an ostentatious survey of the Turkish Cypriot population and property. The Turkish Cypriots, after receiving Red Crescent supplies and having had their telephone line restored, declared at a joint meeting that they no longer had need of support from the Greek Cypriots. The Greek Cypriots established on the village border a target range on which they conducted regular rifle practice. On 25 January a grenade being transferred to store in the Greek Cypriot quarter exploded, causing injuries to some Greek Cypriots and extreme agitation among the Turkish Cypriots, who took it as evidence of warlike preparation.

On 26 January, while the patrol was in the village listening to a Turkish Cypriot recounting of recent events, a runner arrived from Vatili searching for Hasan Osman, who had disappeared earlier in the day. He was the rural constable at Vatili and had ridden that morning by bicycle to Strongylos, intending to lodge a complaint with the Greek Cypriot *mukhtar* there. Having arrived, he was persuaded by the Strongylos' Turkish Cypriots not to provoke a confrontation, for fear that bad feeling might be created and their own position jeopardised. He then set off to ride back to Vatili. He had failed to arrive and there was no sign of him along the intervening route.

Leaving Strongylos immediately by helicopter, we did a quick search down the road to Vatili before doubling back to land behind the gendarmerie station. With Lieutenant Constantinides I set off at a run for the main entrance, hoping that if Osman was being held in the station we might get sight of him. Rounding the corner, we collided with several unkempt and agitated policemen dashing in the opposite direction, cocking automatic weapons as they ran. Five loaded Sten guns at close quarters in the hands of

semi-trained men in a state of extreme excitement is something to be
frightened off.

Happily the sight of Lieutenant Constantinides' Greek uniform, and his
furiously shouted order to point the weapons down, cooled the situation. A
lengthy harangue, leaning on the fact that the patrol carried the imprimatur of
both Makarios and Georgadjis, produced assertions of absolute loyalty to the
process of communal reconciliation and a disavowal of any knowledge of
Hasan Osman.

The extremely disreputable appearance of the specials who had been
inducted by Vatili gendarmerie to replace their missing Turkish Cypriot
officers had been a previous cause of acidic comment from Lieutenant
Constantinides and he was further incensed now when his request to inspect
the police buildings was refused. Later we were to discover that Huseyin
Kirmini was indeed still being held there as hostage at the time, and that he
had desperately tried to alert us to his presence.

Next morning, we returned to Vatili after obtaining from Nicosia
gendarmerie headquarters a promise of better police co-operation. The cells
were now empty and there was no sign in the building of Hasan Osman but
on a nearby path which he might have used to try and bypass the station we
found evidence of a scuffle and a great deal of blood.

The results of Osman's disappearance were predictable. Turkish Cypriot
travel, which had begun slowly to resume at the persistent urging of the
patrol, immediately stopped. The Turkish Cypriot community in mixed
villages put up their barriers again and renewed their pleas for aid. It was
claimed that Osman was the first person to have ventured out alone since
Christmas and that his loss was evidence that Greek Cypriot claims of
goodwill and a wish for reconciliation were worthless.

The explanation that we were later given, at a neighbouring gendarmerie
station, was that Huseyin Kirmini, having been held in Vatili for a month, was
moved to Nicosia early on the 27th on central orders, for inclusion in a general
release of hostages scheduled for that day. On local initiative, a decision was
taken to capture Osman as a replacement, but a fight developed and he was
killed accidentally.

The Turkish Cypriots, assuming that the Greek Cypriots were now a
hostage short, decided that in future they would only travel under escort or in
large groups.

The Turkish Cypriots in the area ascribed their troubles to 'EOKA men'
who had come from elsewhere and taken control of the local gendarmerie. In
the same vein the Greek Cypriots spoke fondly of their local Turkish Cypriot
neighbours but claimed that TMT members from Nicosia were now running
the show and that Turkish Cypriots in other regions were 'barbarians'.
Already there was a *de facto* separation which made each community more
vulnerable to the preaching of its extremists and to the perpetual pressure of
media propaganda. In the village of Vatili, and others around it, there was the
usual strong suspicion of 'foreigners' from outside the district but, at this
point in January 1964, as yet no sign of inter-communal animosity. However,
in the coming phase there was to be a steady erosion of mutual tolerance,
helped forward by the designs of TMT, by the errors or omissions of the

Greek Cypriot leadership and by the activities of the police and local roughnecks.

The other settlements in this group kept to themselves. Greek Cypriot Asha and Lysi typified those big, rather sophisticated, economically successful villages that were well run and responsive to governmental directives: their leaders resented any suggestion that they needed guidance from the patrol but were always happy to engage us in abstract discussion of local and world events. Here the attitude to the Turkish Cypriots was one of condescension and impatience.

Mousoulita, on the other hand, was small and poor: its people had a much more tolerant view of their Turkish Cypriot neighbours, at least until one of their teenagers, in Nicosia for a haircut, crossed the Green Line in a gesture of bravado, and failed to return. Lastly the people of all-Turkish Cypriot Sinda, a village which was maligned at JFHQ as a supposed centre of militancy, a 'Louroujina of the east', in fact proved well-led, tough, co-operative and unprovocative.

10.   POLICEMEN AND POWER

I was able to establish good relations with a number of middle-ranking police officers, but never managed to do so with the head of the force, Charalambos Hassapis. He was a tough disciplinarian who impressed me as a competent old-style police chief: he also seemed highly inflexible, and fixated on an extremely narrow view of what was happening in the island. His tunnel-vision target was to eliminate an armed Turkish Cypriot insurrection for which TMT provided the core. He clearly resented the restraints that politicians were placing on him in this task and declined to accept that the underpinning of the state was being eroded by the absence of an impartial delivery of justice and security.

When during January I was seeking to learn how power was dispensed within the Greek Cypriot community, I was almost invariably told that Polycarpos Georgadjis was at the centre of the web. He was Minister of the Interior, to which the police and the gendarmerie,[1] responsible for law and order in the cities and in the rural areas respectively, were answerable. He was claimed to be the author of the 'Akritas Plan', although other Cypriot ministers and Greek officers from ELDYK were supposed also to have contributed to its drafting.[2]

Georgadjis also was responsible for the embryonic Cypriot KYP* and for liaison with its Greek big brother in Athens. Greek Cypriot Intelligence, initially an adjunct of the police, relied heavily on a network of Turkish Cypriot informers. Some of these were presumably double-agents (and perhaps also assets of foreign intelligence agencies): so far as I could determine, much of the information that they supplied was self-serving and inaccurate.

Georgadjis was a consummate power-broker. A former senior EOKA leader under Grivas, with a record of arrest and imprisonment by the British army, he had retained a very strong personal following among ex-EOKA activists, many of whom had been inducted into the police forces, so that he had his own powerful paramilitary and information-gathering networks.[3]

Additionally, I was told at the time that he also was executive head of 'The Organisation',† with Makarios, Tassos Papadopoulos and Glafcos Clerides having equal status on the directorate.‡ 'The Organisation' had been conceived

---

* See note 7/1
† See note 7/3 and Appendix D
‡ Other recent accounts dispute this arrangement and doubt Makarios' involvement. Indeed, he is reported to have viewed the paramilitary initiatives of Georgadjis as a threat to his own position.

in 1961 and from early 1963 had been creating a covert island-wide command structure, through which overall control of Greek Cypriot paramilitary activities was supposed to be exercised, and overseeing the formation of an all-Greek Cypriot paramilitary force. Georgadjis thus was an integral part of almost every branch of his community's power-structure, and he appeared to have the loyalty of most ex-EOKA activists.

Polycarpos Georgadjis, Minister of the Interior, centre.

Of all the acquaintances I made in Cyprus, Georgadjis was the least easy to fathom. He was enigmatic and unapproachable. Generally known as an immensely effective organiser, he also appeared to love conspiracy and power for their own sakes and to revel in the manipulation of those events that fell within his reach. Such personal power did he disseminate, and such was the ferocity of some of his ex-EOKA followers, that the president and other ministers always seemed extremely reluctant to cross him. I came across him occasionally when I was eating with other Ministers in 'The Corner House'. He was always dining alone with his bodyguard.

Only within the realms of the organised left, the communist party and the left-wing trades union (AKEL), did he appear to have no special power, although he claimed that all left wing organisations had been heavily infiltrated by 'his people'.

It was difficult in January 1964 to assess the degree to which 'The Organisation' had effective influence over the paramilitary groups that had been formed under private initiative, by Nicos Sampson, Vassos Lyssarides, George Raftis and others.* These groups were now being assimilated into military command within what JF termed the 'Secret Army' (which in June would emerge as the re-designated National Guard) but, despite the placing with them of army officers infiltrated from Greece in January, they continued during the early months of 1964 to have some degree of autonomy and to be unpredictable in the degree of their adherence to centrally agreed policies.

Despite the centralisation of statal and parastatal power under a single minister, co-ordination, or even co-operation, between the various armed Greek Cypriot groups was at this stage haphazard. In many instances ex-EOKA specials who professed loyalty to Georgadjis appeared to have hijacked the leadership of rural gendarmerie units into which they had been inducted, often to the transparent disgust of the regulars. On the other hand, 'Secret Army' units, also technically under the command of Georgadjis, were often dismissive of, and sometimes antagonistic towards, the gendarmerie and, in particular, to Georgadjis' nominees within it.[4]

Greek Cypriot police forces were particularly resentful that cease-fire arrangements at the end of December had led to an acceptance by the politicians that some predominantly Turkish Cypriot parts of the island must temporarily be regarded as 'no-go areas', with the police barred from entry so as to avoid armed Turkish Cypriot reaction. In mixed areas where no such bar had been imposed, the gendarmerie often patrolled very aggressively and insensitively. No longer did it normally act as a national force with multi-communal responsibilities.

In the villages, the Turkish Cypriots usually saw ex-EOKA fighters and Greek Cypriot police specials as their enemies, but had no animosity for the regular police-force or for the Greek Cypriot community as a whole. Greek Cypriot villagers were themselves often very wary of the old EOKA network, which in some cases was claimed by them to have links with the criminal under-class.

Greek Cypriot propaganda at this point was representing the Turkish Cypriot police (being the 40 per cent rump of the constitutionally combined force) as a reactionary spearhead of TMT, but I saw very little to support this contention. The impression I gained, working at ground level with the Turkish Cypriot community, was that there was an uneasy and rather inchoate splitting of power between, on the one hand, Kutchuk and the various regional Turkish Communal Chambers and, on the other, TMT and the military commanders secretly introduced from Turkey. Uniformed Turkish Cypriot police officers did not appear to be playing the same significant military role as were their Greek Cypriot counterparts.

Arriving for the first time, with some trepidation, at Chatos police station, I found two Turkish Cypriot gendarmerie officers trying to tidy up a rather ineffectual flower garden and three others dozing over their coffee cups. Their sergeant greeted me warmly, but was unable to explain to whom he now

---

* It was suggested that the Lyssarides group was seen by Makarios as a direct counterweight to the concentration of armed power under Georgadjis.

reported or what his mandate was. He said that at present his team was resting 'because there was no crime in their area.'

I found a similar picture elsewhere where the Turkish Cypriots were manning a gendarmerie station in a village to which the Greek Cypriot police no longer had access. Whereas the Greek Cypriot police forces had been brought up to strength by the induction of untrained 'specials', often ex-EOKA, the Turkish police had made up their numbers through the addition of uniformed officers who had evacuated from other regions. At this point the Greek Cypriot police saw themselves as the cutting edge of an armed struggle against Turkish Cypriot insurrection, whereas the Turkish Cypriot police officers that I met appeared not yet to regard themselves as part of a communal paramilitary structure.

Although Turkish Cypriot gendarmes usually carried rifles or side-arms, their participation in fire-fights appeared to be, at most, peripheral. Greek Cypriot gendarmes, on the other hand, were usually at the forefront of such fighting as I saw. For the Turkish Cypriots, fighting outside the cities during this phase was done by TMT, by its paramilitary adjunct (the 'Turkish fighters'), by 'volunteers' infiltrated from Turkey and by untrained villagers with their hunting guns.

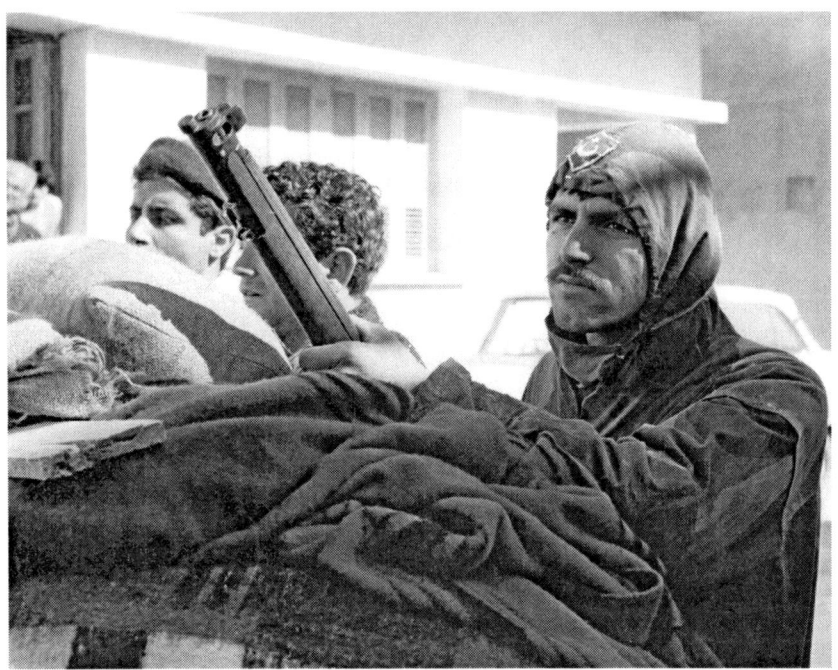

15 February. Turkish badge sewn to the hood of his coat, this fighter stands guard behind a barricade erected in the Turkish Cypriot quarter of Limassol.

11.   THE CHATOS AREA.
JANUARY 1964

North of the Vatili and Mora complexes lay one of the two largest areas of exclusively Turkish Cypriot-owned land in Cyprus. In JFHQ this was referred to as 'the Chatos enclave' and regarded as a single grouping, although the villages in the region are split by the Nicosia-Famagusta district border. The patrol found that there was hardly any co-ordination, or even communication, across the dividing line. A British army proposal that they be administered together for purposes of relief and medical care was not pursued.

The eastern half of the area had the big Greek Cypriot village of Marathovouno to its south and was bounded to the north by the line of the Pentadaktylos range. Jutting into its north-east corner was the Greek Cypriot village of Trypimeni.

Along the Nicosia to Lefkoniko road are the Turkish Cypriot villages of Chatos, Knodhara and Psilatos. For these, peace was to remain relatively undisturbed. They saw no action, suffered no serious shortages, and from Christmas 1963 they were no longer approached by the Greek Cypriot police. The defensive emplacements with which they had surrounded themselves appeared to have been modelled on 1914-1918 trench warfare. Their major complaints concerned the difficulties of travel outside the area, the indignities of being stopped and searched and the fact that their vehicles were occasionally shot at near Lefkoniko or on the Famagusta road at Trakhoni. They had long-running disputes over grazing rights on their borders with Trypimeni and Marathovouno and they were perpetually suspicious of what action the surrounding Greek Cypriots were planning against them.

To the north of Chatos, along the southern foothills of Pentadaktylos, are the villages of Kornokipos, Ayios Khariton and Trypimeni, the latter Greek Cypriot and the other two Turkish Cypriot. All these were poor and dependent on subsistence-farming and sheep-herding, much of which was done illegally on the forested higher slopes of the range.

An excellent east-west dirt-road ran through the pine woods along the crest of the Pentadaktylos range, crossed by north-south tracks above Trypimeni and Kornokipos. Close to the latter junction was the forestry station of Halefka: this had been staffed equally from the two communities until Christmas 1963, when the Turkish Cypriots, on hearing reports of fighting in Nicosia, thought it prudent to leave. Thereafter the Greek Cypriots, appreciating the strategic significance of the position, had built it up into a major military centre, using it both as an operational base for the control of this section of the range and as a mountain training centre. It was inevitable that Turkish Cypriot shepherds and woodcutters from Kornokipos and Ayios Khariton, trespassing along the high forests as they always had, should frequently stumble on covert Greek Cypriot military activity: remarkably none of them was ever harmed as a result. Instead they were driven off with a warning that the area was unhealthy for Turks, a volley of curses or a couple of rifle shots. More tellingly the Greek Cypriots purloined whatever sheep or goats strayed within their reach and used more distant Turkish Cypriot goats for target practice.

These incidents gave rise to frequent reports to JFHQ of armed clashes in the Pentadaktylos. If a shot landed close to a party of four woodcutters each might make off in a different direction, and to whomever he first met describe how they had come under heavy fire from which he alone had escaped. A wide variety of heavily embellished stories would slowly filter back to headquarters. When the woodcutters met again in their own village they would express amazement at the others' escape, deny that they had already made an alarmist report and then jointly concoct a wholly new version of the affair. British military patrols sent to investigate would be left baffled.

The villagers, in the meantime, became convinced that a Greek Cypriot army was assembling in the hills, preparing to sweep down upon them, and devoted themselves to the construction of a line of defensive positions facing towards the heights.

Between Chatos and Trypimeni there was animosity of long standing and a regular exchange of accusations as to the destruction of each other's olive trees and illicit grazing on each other's land. Despite tiring shuttle diplomacy by my patrol, the mutual bitterness increased until, on 23 January, a Greek Cypriot shepherd boy was shot dead in the fields. Turkish Cypriots in the surrounding villages told us it was inevitable there would be a killing in revenge.

Some weeks later we were passing through Knodhara late in the evening and a villager told us that he had just heard gunfire to the north-west. We diverted towards Trypimeni. As we stood watching, we saw three columns of armed villagers coming back across the fields, heads down and sombre, like monks after compline. A fat man from the first column came over and shoved the barrel of a Sten gun into my stomach and said in Greek: "This is our affair. If you try and help in this one, we shall kill you too."

Captain Michos, the Greek member that day of the tripartite patrol, talked for a while to some of the other men and then said to me: "This time it isn't political. It's best that we go home." We never did ask or learn what had happened. Patrolling again through Chatos and Trypimeni two days later we found that the tension was gone from both villages.

The natural route from Trypimeni to Lefkoniko ran through the Turkish Cypriot villages of Knodhara and Psilatos. The Greek Cypriots continued throughout January to take this road without any hindrance or untoward incident, but relentless propaganda from Nicosia eventually convinced them that travel through a Turkish Cypriot-controlled area was dangerous and they switched to a long and difficult diversion along mountain tracks. This imposition left the people of Trypimeni with a deep sense of abandonment, for which they blamed their own government and the British as bitterly as they did the Turks.

Marathovouno, a large Greek Cypriot village, was notable for the intensity of its anti-British feeling. Its leaders expressed friendship and tolerance for the Turkish Cypriots, who were criticised only for their frequent attempts to graze their sheep on Greek Cypriot lands, but were consistently vituperative about past and present British roles in Cyprus.

I had a number of interesting conversations in its coffee-houses, where a natural Greek Cypriot wish to be hospitable and respect for a foreigner who spoke their own language clashed with an apparent deep dislike for the British in general.

It was clear that the intensity of feeling in villages like Marathovouno was being increased by an escalating anti-British sentiment emanating from political and media sources in Nicosia. Britain was portrayed as perfidious in three respects: as an architect of the present troubles; as now letting its military presence be exploited to the benefit of Turkish separatism; and as using its international clout to prevent the adoption by the United Nations General Assembly of Athens-sponsored motions sympathetic to the Greek position over Cyprus.

From mid-January onwards, regular military patrols mounted by the British peacekeeping force, normally constituted by an eight-man unit either in Land Rovers or in Ferret armoured cars, had been meeting real and escalating hostility in many Greek Cypriot villages. It was, however, rare for tripartite mediating units, containing a Greek officer and backed by the communal leadership, to be met with other than interest and warm hospitality.

In Marathovouno, as in other villages with a particularly virulent hatred of either the British or the Turks, the local schoolmaster was an encourager of this venom. I began to make it a habit to take my Greek or Turkish officer for an inconspicuous visit to village classrooms. We would creep unobtrusively into the back row, from where we would sometimes listen to the children being treated to a ferocious exposition of racist diatribe.

On the patrol's second visit to Marathovouno, I told Captain Michos to ride in the rear Land Rover. Arriving first I shouted in Greek to a flock of stone-carrying children who swooped down on us, imagining that this was a regular JF patrol: "The third car!" Michos, emerging with a heart-warming smile that he reserved for the Greek Cypriots, was greeted with a shower of pebbles. He took this in bad humour. Later I was told that a sharp warning, originating from the Greek army contingent, had been circulated to the schools, and in Marathovouno there was a noticeable improvement of behaviour.

Wherever possible thereafter, when we found a particular degree of bias, we tried to talk with the local schoolmaster, emphasising that the future of Cyprus was being badly served by the teaching of ethnic prejudice. There was, however, little we could do about the fact that both communities were using history textbooks whose central theme was that of traditional and inevitable enmity between Greeks and Turks and of disparagement for the other's history, customs and achievements.

The last village in this group, Vitsadha, was two thirds Greek Cypriot and one third Turkish Cypriot. When first visited, each community was found to be in abject fear of the other, with no communication between them and each convinced of imminent attack. We managed to restore relations to a level of cautious neighbourliness, with most barricades being removed, but for the time being the village remained a depressing backwater of suspicion and gloom.*

* See chapter 30 for subsequent events in Vitsadha.

12.   LEFKONIKO AREA.
LATE JANUARY 1964

Since our previous visit, the Greek Cypriot gendarmerie at Lefkoniko had become a target for complaint by Turkish Cypriots over much of the region and the subject of much adverse comment from regular British army patrols. They were, however, now undeserving of this bad reputation. We found them co-operative towards the joint patrols and restrained and tolerant in their dealings with Turkish Cypriots. There was no serious inter-communal trouble anywhere in their area and two of their mixed villages, Yenagra and Lapathos, had the best record for inter-communal relations of any in northern Cyprus. In contrast to the general pattern in other regions, all the more serious charges that were made against them concerned incidents in which they were acting under the direct command of a local lieutenant in 'The Organisation' rather than of one of their own officers.

Early joint meetings in Yenagra were particularly successful. Then in mid-January a TMT representative arrived in the village from Nicosia and the meetings became fractious and difficult. To my surprise, however, the extremist newcomer soon modified his views and turned into a model of moderation (perhaps because of local persuasion, but more probably because of a new directive from Nicosia) and the joint village committee continued thereafter to work with its former harmony. To the patrol's further surprise, there was never any sign of TMT pressure on Lapathos and the two communities, both excellently led, co-operated without apparent stress. It was jointly decided that no outsider should be allowed to come and stay without the full concurrence of each community: this clause was invoked when Arnadhi was evacuated, so as to block the proposal from Nicosia that some of its refugees should move to Lapathos.

Gouphes, the other mixed village in this region, also broke the usual mould. Here there were 250 Turkish Cypriots and 70 Greek Cypriots, most of them extremely poor. After the events in Nicosia at Christmas, the Turkish Cypriots built fortifications around the village, imposed an 1800 to 0400 curfew and mounted guards by night. By day, however, the Turkish Cypriots put away their guns and allowed the Greek Cypriot police from Lefkoniko free access to patrol the village.

Originally these patrols looked menacing, with a single uniformed officer accompanied by four or five heavily armed tin-helmeted auxiliaries. The Turkish Cypriots were increasingly alienated. My patrol discussed the position with the sergeant at Lefkoniko and he thereafter restricted police patrolling in mixed areas to uniformed officers who were already known to the villagers: these, on his instructions, pursued a relaxed and friendly approach to the Turkish Cypriots. The Turkish Cypriots reacted positively to this, with a consequent and palpable lowering of tension right across the area. If this policy had been adopted throughout the countryside it could have had a profound effect on the course of events outside Nicosia. Unfortunately, most other police areas either rejected the concept as unworkable or refused to discuss it with us.

Apparently without outside prompting or financial incitement, and without objection from the Greek Cypriots, the Gouphes' Turkish Cypriots put considerable effort into improving a direct track from their village to Artemi, which allowed Turkish Cypriots from the Platani-Malounda area to enter the 'Chatos enclave' without having to pass through Lefkoniko or any other Greek Cypriot village.

Elsewhere in this region, the pattern was similarly of mutual tolerance. The tiny villages of Maratha, Sandalaris and Aloa in the south were wide open, should anyone have wished to harass or intimidate them, but nobody ever did. In the north-west of the area, the Greek Cypriots in Ayios Nikolaos, a village with the same isolation as Trypimeni but much more moderate in character, maintained excellent relations with Malounda and Artemi and used to pass through those two Turkish Cypriot villages without hesitation, although it was agreed between the villages that there would be no travel between dusk and dawn.

The most isolated Turkish Cypriot village in the area was Platani, hanging on the southern slope of Mount Olymbos. Its inhabitants were also the most embittered. They were suffering real economic hardship and were particularly aggrieved by the frequency with which regular British Army patrols promised to send supplies and then failed to do so. Their shepherds reported to us regularly on the Greek Cypriots' establishment of a new gendarmerie station on the Lefkoniko Pass and on preparations by Greek Cypriot paramilitaries for the demolition of local roads with strategic significance in the event of further conflict. The Greek Cypriots, for their part, just as regularly voiced to us their fears that the Turkish Cypriots from Platani, Malounda and Artemi would one day decide to cut the main north-south road. The two communities continued to co-exist in relative goodwill, but each repeatedly told us that the other was planning military action against it.

13.   TRIKOMO AREA.
LATE JANUARY - EARLY FEBRUARY 1964

During December the Gendarmerie station at Trikomo had acquired an unsavoury reputation with the Turkish Cypriots in the region, mainly because of two incidents at Ayios Andronikos. It was reported to us that at Christmas the Trikomo police sergeant had killed a Turkish Cypriot villager there, an incident which three Turkish Cypriots claimed independently to us to have witnessed. A few days later three Turkish Cypriot villagers had disappeared after setting out to drive to Trikomo in search of food: it was claimed that the same sergeant had organised their seizure as hostages*. The retailing of these events was sufficient to convince Turkish Cypriot villagers in the area that they were in danger of capture or death, and to bring travel to a halt.

In fact, however, the sergeant accused by them had been replaced at the end of December. His successor first came to my attention in mid-January, when my patrol was in Perivolia (east of Trikomo) discussing events with a Turkish Cypriot family. I noticed that I was being observed through binoculars from a range of about fifty yards. I sent Captain Michos to investigate and he returned with a motley band of unarmed Greek Cypriots led by a stout gentleman wearing a bright red sweater and carpet-slippers. We had coffee together and discovered a considerable commonality of views. Thereafter, the patrol had a close and excellent relationship with the Trikomo gendarmerie and the confidence of Turkish Cypriot villages in the area was gradually restored.

Not surprisingly, Ayios Andronikos was the last of the Turkish Cypriot villages in the region to relax, but it suffered no further incidents. Perivolia, a village so small that it did not appear even on our large-scale War Office maps, continued in undisturbed anonymity in the shadow of Trikomo. Ayios Iakovos, with an outstandingly good *mukhtar*, maintained good relations with all its neighbouring villages and on its own initiative activated local inter-communal contacts whenever danger seemed to threaten. Monarga, a tiny hamlet on the coast above Boghaz, at first suffered agonies of fear as the Greek Cypriots worked busily on the construction of their beach defences all around it, but no threatening move was ever made against it and the villagers expressed great relief when the patrol established a linkage for them with the local Greek Cypriot paramilitary leadership.

---

* We later received several reports on the whereabouts of the missing men, but were unable to locate them: up to June they had not been handed over in any exchange of hostages.

June 1964. Greek Cypriot national guardsmen dig anti-invasion trenches in an orange grove at Morphou Bay, on the NW coast of Cyprus.

In the mixed villages of Syngrasi and Arnadhi events unfolded less auspiciously. Syngrasi was one of those badly led villages where a couple of loutish Greek Cypriots were allowed to poison relations and the Turkish Cypriots were thereby provoked into wholly disproportionate alarm. As for a nervous patient with his psychiatrist, a weekly session with the tripartite patrol became essential: even the smallest longer delay and we would arrive to find the Turkish Cypriot villagers packed and ready to evacuate.

In Arnadhi the story was much the same. Again the great majority of the Greek Cypriots maintained their former good neighbourliness, but a small irresponsible element harried the Turkish Cypriots with threats and minor humiliations and abuse and the occasional practical joke. Turkish Cypriot confidence steadily withered. Neither the Greek Cypriot *mukhtar* nor the Trikomo police could impose an effective restraint on the hoodlums. The Turkish Cypriots began to act with an air of frightened secrecy, which further provoked their tormentors. By the end of January the Turkish Cypriot community was in a state of near panic, for which the Greek Cypriots showed neither sympathy nor understanding. On 11 February the Turkish Cypriots decided that they could stand it no longer and the following morning they all left.

The Greek Cypriots, learning at the last moment of the impending move and realising that it would redound to their own discredit, tried to force the Turkish Cypriots to stay, which frightened them all the more. Finally, as the price of their going unhindered, the Turkish Cypriots were persuaded to sign a document stating that they were evacuating solely because of orders from their own extremists and that the conduct of their Greek Cypriot co-villagers had never been other than exemplary.

So precipitate was the Turkish Cypriot departure that they had no time to organise any transport and left behind almost all their household goods and all of their animals. They sent no forewarning whatever to their communal leaders in Famagusta. When most of them tramped into town, the Famagusta Turkish Cypriots, with troubles enough of their own, made some attempt to turn them away. They pleaded that their lives would be in danger if they were made to return to Arnadhi (a contention for which the patrol saw no basis at all) and eventually were allowed to stay. Those villagers, who, more sensibly, did not head for Famagusta, walked over the fields to Aloa and Sandalaris, where they were welcomed as additional strength for those small communities.

The patrol had no news of the evacuation until it was all over. Visiting Arnadhi next day, we received from the Greek Cypriot village leaders their expressions of puzzlement and deep regret at the departure of their neighbours. We inspected the animals and property that had been abandoned and agreed a rough inventory with the Greek Cypriot *mukhtar*, who undertook to ensure that everything was adequately protected. We agreed to try to persuade the Turkish Cypriots to return but when we did so they would only commit to a later consideration of the possibility.

We then separately advised the Greek and Turkish Cypriot communal leaders in Famagusta of our opinion that the Turkish Cypriots would not be in any danger if they could be talked into a return to their homes in Arnadhi, but that if they decided against a return it would be preferable to supervise the collection of their property. We told JFHQ that it would be advisable for a British Army Land Rover crew to keep an eye on any removal, but that a full escort would not be necessary.

We returned to Arnadhi to tell the Greek Cypriot *mukhtar* exactly what we had arranged and we were given his assurance that there would be no attempt to distrain on Turkish Cypriot property in lieu of any debts that were owing. Finally we called on the police sergeant in Trikomo to explain to him what had happened and acquire his promise of co-operation.

Our greatest worry, however, was that the Arnadhi evacuation might further unsettle the Turkish Cypriot villagers in Syngrasi, so that they too would decide to go. To combat this, and despite the existing overload on our schedule, we further increased the frequency of our visits to Syngrasi until the Turkish Cypriots there had overcome their initial inclination to leave.

14. KOMI KEBIR.
LATE JANUARY - EARLY FEBRUARY 1964

When I first visited this area on 10 January I had had time only to assess the situation in the two big mixed villages of Komi Kebir and Ephtakomi. Subsequently I had learned that most extremism in the region originated from Greek Cypriots in Ayios Theodhoros or Turkish Cypriots in Galatia. All the other nearby villages, the Turkish Cypriot Ovgoros, Avgolidha, Kridhia, Livadhia, Ayios Evstathios and Platanisso and the Greek Cypriot Yerani, Patriki, Gastria, Tavros and Koma tou Yialou, took their lead from these larger centres, having at Christmas cut off every link with neighbouring villages of the other community.

The Turkish Cypriots from Ayios Theodhoros claimed that they had never had good relations with the Greek Cypriots. They had evacuated the village on 25 December, fearful that they were about to be attacked.

We arrived in the now wholly Greek Cypriot Ayios Theodhoros by helicopter on 22 January after receiving a report, fictitious as it turned out, that Greek Cypriot villagers were vandalising the mosque. Despite the message that we brought from Nicosia and the presence of Lieutenant Constantinides we were received at first with suspicion, which gave way to open hostility. The crowd that eventually gathered was uncooperative and aggressive. When we said that we intended to inspect recently abandoned Turkish Cypriot property, we were told that would not be wise.

In the space of four weeks every single home had been looted down to the last smallest item. Not only had the contents gone: windows and doors had been removed, tiles stripped off, piping ripped out. Only the shells remained. Only the date on an occasional torn letter or newspaper showed that this was a recent event rather than the aftermath of the 1958 troubles.

Colonel Akova and Lieutenant Constantinides both soon declared themselves too upset by what they were seeing to be able to continue, or to take part in any discussion with the villagers, and they went off to sit in the helicopter.

While I completed my survey, noting that the mosque had so far been left intact, the Greek Cypriots who accompanied me looked here and there with expressions of amazement, professed themselves wholly unaware of how all this had happened and suggested that strangers must have done it during the hours of darkness. When the police sergeant and two of his constables eventually joined me, they examined with professional interest the meagre remains of one half of their village, claimed to be puzzled by the scale of the damage and said that they could not be expected to know everything that went on, since current regulations forbade them to leave their station at night.

In Nicosia I was now talking almost daily with Tassos Papadopoulos, and with other ministers that he thought it useful to introduce. They had convinced me that both Makarios and 'The Organisation' were genuine in their commitment to the publicly-proclaimed policy of re-engagement and reconciliation. As I boarded the helicopter some villagers, apparently now recalling this policy, called out: "The Turks know that we were always their good friends. Tell them that we are looking forward to them coming back to their homes."

At Galatia we summoned the refugees from Ayios Theodhoros and explained the condition of their property. We said that extremist acts almost always stemmed from a tiny section of the community that was vengeful from previous troubles or unbalanced or reacting to racist incitement. The Turkish Cypriots responded stoically: "This is what we expected. It proves we were right to leave."

Effective inter-communal relations in this region had been re-established by tripartite patrol initiatives at the beginning of January and were maintained for a while. Such was the demand from other areas, most of them more conveniently reached from Nicosia, that I was unable to visit here as often as I would have wished. There was, however, no reason to expect that the area would come under outside pressure, since paramilitary leaders in both communities believed that friction here would be contrary to their long-term interests.

Unexpectedly there was a sharp downturn in inter-communal relations at the beginning of February. Apparently this was due to the festering of personal animosities allied to alarmist media reporting of troubles in other parts of the island. The morale of the Turkish Cypriots was further sapped by the sight of widespread coastal-defence building and frequent exercises by the Greek Cypriot 'Secret Army'. At the beginning of February, rumours circulated among the Turkish Cypriots that the Greek Cypriots were preparing to seize additional hostages. By February 8 travel had once more ceased throughout the Karpas peninsula.

15. AYIOS ANDRONIKOS - GALINOPORNI AREA. JANUARY 1964

Around Yialousa, which is the district gendarmerie centre, lies the most northerly and easterly mixed area in Cyprus. Three miles south of Yialousa, astride the only main road, is the mixed village of Ayios Andronikos. Further south are the Greek Cypriot Leonarisso, Vasili and Vathylakkas and to the eastward a line of Turkish Cypriot villages runs parallel to the coast, Neta, Ayios Simeon, Korovia and Galinoporni. Between the two groups is the small mixed village of Lythrangomi. The isolation of this region, which was at the extreme limit of helicopter range from Nicosia, meant that media-engendered fears were inevitably magnified even by the most innocuous of unexplained events.

The Turkish Cypriots at Lythrangomi claimed that it was too dangerous for them to return to work or even to venture outside the village. They rejected offers of help and protection from the Greek Cypriots and resisted the urgings of the tripartite patrol that they resume their former routine. Lythrangomi provided another example of 'refugee complex', which was beginning to become an island-wide problem. Subsistence was eked out on the basis of Red Cross and Red Crescent support: the Turkish Cypriots sat all day in their homes or coffee-houses and waited for the radical developments that their extremists were promising. In this area, when the Greek Cypriots made sympathetic proposals for the creation of local projects that would offer particular benefits to the Turkish Cypriot community, the Turkish Cypriots declined to participate.

The Turkish Cypriot villages around Korovia put up their barricades at Christmas, retired behind them and limited their travelling to an occasional dash to Ayios Andronikos. In early February even this was cut. First a group of Turkish Cypriots was warned off the road by a large Greek fighting patrol. Then on 6 February a Turkish Cypriot goatherd, the father of six children, was killed in the fields to the west of Galinoporni.

Another shepherd who had watched the incident from nearby woodland said that his friend had been knocked down by rifle shots from four or five uniformed men, firing from the edge of the pasture. While he was still on the ground some of the uniformed group had driven off his flock of goats. Then a policeman who had been with the group had come out and finished the man off with a pistol shot through the ear.

A British army reconnaissance patrol later brought in the body, whose wounds were consistent with the shepherd's account. The names of all those involved in the shooting were subsequently reported to me and passed on in confidence to the President's office. Tassos Papadopoulos expressed to me his regret at what had happened, referring to the event as 'an intolerable act of indiscipline'.

Ayios Andronikos was known at the beginning of January as an exemplar of good inter-communal relations. Its Turkish Cypriots continued to travel freely, despite the fact that, contrary to the provisions of the 'Freedom of Movement' agreement of 6 January, they were frequently stopped and searched at police roadblocks near Ayios Theodhoros.

In mid-January the Greek Cypriot press, following government directives, started to publicise the good relations in Ayios Andronikos. Articles appeared in all the Greek Cypriot newspapers extolling the Turkish Cypriot attitude and offering it as proof of a Turkish Cypriot desire to live in harmony with their Greek Cypriot neighbours. As with other similar publicity, the result was a sharp worsening of local inter-communal relations, with the Turkish Cypriots fearful of TMT reaction. At the same time the Turkish Cypriots told me of their increasing concern at what was going on around them, with frequent gunfire and grenade explosions during the course of Greek Cypriot military exercises on the village outskirts. The Greek Cypriots described these activities to me as 'hunting and quarrying'.

On 28 January a Turkish Cypriot car from Ayios Andronikos was badly shot up by automatic weapons while coming northwards through Boghaz. On 1 February there was a similar incident near Ayios Theodhoros.

The Turkish Cypriots told me that they had placed taps on the local telephone system. They showed me a record they had kept of Greek Cypriot discussions on the movement of weapons in the Karpas peninsula and on a possible need for armed action against Turkish Cypriot militants.

At the beginning of February, despite our best efforts, inter-communal relations began to unravel throughout the area. Turkish Cypriot travel stopped, mutual suspicion replaced friendship. My report for 4 February noted:

"*Almost all contact between the GC and TC in the north eastern area of the island has recently been cut again. This is partly due to a TC political directive, partly to clumsy GC attempts to generate 'co-existence propaganda', rather less to isolated incidents or threats of violence on the part of irresponsible elements and less still to deliberate provocation by the GC. Following today's reports from other districts about renewed tension and the arrest of hostages, the whole area appears to be reverting to the state in which it was at the beginning of January, with the difference that the TC are now far less receptive to attempts to get them talking with the GC. In the present atmosphere the most that can be done is to urge patience and restraint on the GC and to counsel wisdom to the TC and calm the worst of their fears.*"

16.   KYTHREA - EPIKHO AREA.
JANUARY - EARLY FEBRUARY 1964

The so-called 'Chatos enclave' was sometimes described by the Greek Cypriots as a dagger aimed at the heart of Nicosia. Within this alarmist analogy Bey Keuy and Voni constituted the dagger's point.

Bey Keuy was represented by the Turkish Cypriots as an embattled outpost set about with dangers. A flicker of vague and indecisive skirmishing in the area at Christmas was followed by a short lull during which tension began to build rapidly in the neighbouring mixed village of Neokhorio and between Greek Cypriot Voni and Turkish Cypriot Epikho. By the end of December the Turkish Cypriots in Neokhorio were suffering agonies of fear due to constant pressure and repeated provocation from a few loutish members of the Greek Cypriot community over whom neither the village leaders nor the local police seemed able to exercise any control. The inhabitants of outlying buildings at Naysan Chiflik, a large farming co-operative on the outskirts of Neokhorio, moved to Bey Keuy for greater safety, returning by day to tend their flocks and work the fields. On the night of 2 January there was an arson attack on one of the deserted farmhouses, which was burnt to the ground.

Epikho's Turkish Cypriots now devoted themselves to the construction of trench defences facing towards Greek Cypriot Exometokhi and the Greek Cypriots at Voni became increasingly belligerent towards the Turkish Cypriots in Bey Keuy, whom they saw as blocking their access to Nicosia. The Turkish Cypriots in Bey Keuy in turn were incensed by the continuing destruction of Naysan Chiflik and by reports of indignities suffered by the Turkish Cypriots in Neokhorio. A group of vigorous young TMT members took over effective control from the ailing *mukhtar* and organised the construction of additional defences and the placing of barricades. Then they sent messages to surrounding Greek Cypriot villages saying that the road was no longer open to Greek Cypriot traffic. At the western approaches to Bey Keuy they erected signs not previously seen in the island and calculated to provoke the Greek Cypriots: "TURKISH FRONTIER. DRIVE WITH CARE."

Meanwhile there was a steady worsening of the situation in Neokhorio itself, induced by lurid propaganda and the abusive behaviour of small groups of loudmouths who now dominated the respective coffee-houses. One wealthy Turkish Cypriot was found to have constructed a sizeable bunker in his backyard: although invisible behind high walls this was taken by the Greek Cypriots as an act of aggression and pressure was sharply increased against the Turkish Cypriots, who responded by confining themselves fearfully to their own homes. On 14 January the Turkish Cypriot community of 230 abandoned the village and moved to Epikho.

So far as we could discover there was no political or TMT urging for this move, although the evacuation on about the same date of nearby Palekythro did have the hallmarks of a departure organised from Nicosia. Thereafter a sense of bitter militancy spread through the Turkish Cypriots in the western section of the 'Chatos enclave', although apprehension among the Greek Cypriots that there would be a reprisal raid on Voni proved groundless.

The 'Freedom of Movement' agreement of 6 January was largely ignored by the Greek Cypriot police in this area. Throughout January every Turkish Cypriot vehicle which ventured through Epikho towards Nicosia was stopped near Trakhoni or Mia Milea, and sometimes there were several roadblocks to be negotiated. Usually the barriers were manned by armed irregulars or police auxiliaries, but regular police officers would also appear (to inspect the validity of road tax licences) if the press or a British army patrol was expected.

The roadblocks probably did little to limit the movement of TMT personnel or weapons, which was their supposed aim. They were not particularly onerous, but they had the effect of reducing Turkish Cypriot road travel to an occasional trickle. This in turn had very adverse effects on the rural economy.

The destruction of abandoned Turkish Cypriot property at Neokhorio and Naysan Chiflik continued, despite the best efforts of Lieutenant Constantinides and myself, and by 2 February all of the buildings at both locations, including the mosque and the school, had been broken into and vandalised or looted. On several occasions Constantinides passionately harangued the villagers on the need for discipline and self-control and on the damage that was being done to the Greek Cypriot cause by their looting of Turkish Cypriot property. Attempts were made to bolster the village leadership. It was agreed between us, the Greek Cypriot *mukhtar* and the gendarmerie that all abandoned property should be re-secured, sealed under the joint supervision of the Greek Cypriot *mukhtar* and a Turkish Cypriot representative, and thereafter given special protection by the local police. Even this proved ineffective.

The Greek Cypriot police at Kythrea were likeable and keen to co-operate with us but wholly unwilling to face up to extremists from their own community*. With their help we got agreement for the removal to safety of the remaining contents of the Turkish Cypriot school and mosque in Neokhorio and for a joint meeting on 6 February with the *mukhtars* and schoolmasters from Voni, Epikho and Neokhorio, with the single aim of deciding how other abandoned property could best be protected.

Arriving at Kythrea on 6 February we found that the police, sipping coffee as usual, were wearing their tin hats. They said that they were on alert because of troubles at Ayios Sozomenos and regretfully would have to give the meeting a miss: they asked that we convey their best wishes and speak on

---

* At one incident at which I was present they arrived in force and sought to take charge but immediately departed for the coffee-house when ordered to do so by an armed civilian who was involved in the altercation.

their behalf. In Neokhorio the Greek Cypriots told us that, as they were in the majority, they were no longer willing to attend a meeting in the Turkish Cypriot school as had been scheduled: as far as they were concerned, we could meet in the Greek Cypriot school or not at all.

Arriving at the Turkish school, to collect the Turkish Cypriots delegates for the meeting, we found that there had been a further break-in during the night. Obscene slogans had been painted in Greek on the walls and the conference table was heaped with the smashed remains of several statuettes of Kemal Ataturk.

We cancelled the meeting and supervised the removal from the mosque and the school of what few useful items remained.

Over the next few weeks the demolition of the Turkish Cypriot sector of Neokhorio continued, to the intense fury of my then Greek officer, Captain Michos. Guided to the village one day by a pall of smoke we found that fire had been set to the looted shells of most of those Turkish Cypriot buildings that were still standing.

Other villages in the area were relatively untroubled during this period. Shepherds from Kalyvakia, like those from Kornokipos and Ayios Khariton, were discouraged by Greek Cypriot paramilitaries at Halefka from using their traditional grazing grounds on the upper slopes of Pentadaktylos. Salahi Abuzek, from Petra tou Dhiyeni, was not seen again after being abducted on the road to Nicosia on 2 January, but his fellow villagers continued with cautious travelling until they had a lorry and a car shot at on the Famagusta road on 25 and 26 January. At Voni, a Greek Cypriot working in the fields was hit by shots from a car passing down the main road. Epikho's Turkish Cypriots were deeply resentful at the failure of British troops to supply all the stores that they had requested. The Greek Cypriot community in Exometokhi, predominantly communist, was restrained and undemanding of our services.

17.   MANDRES AND DHIKOMO-KOUTSOVENDIS AREAS. JANUARY 1964

The main refugee camp for Turkish Cypriots who had fled at Christmas from the Nicosia suburb of Omorphita was at Mandres*. Its normal population of five hundred was now swollen to four thousand, most of them housed in badly pitched tents.

As they had direct access to the Turkish Communal Chamber in Nicosia, which could channel appropriate support to them, the people here were not normally a target of Tripartite Patrol activity. However, to this there were three exceptions. When there was heavy rain, the track from Mandres to Orta Keuy, the only route to Nicosia which did not pass through Omorphita, became impassable and we then had the task of deciding at what point the provision of essential aid should be taken over by British army units. Second,

Children in the refugee camp at Mandres, below the foothills of the Kyrenia Range.

---

* Also referred to as Hamid Mandres.

it was useful for me to have direct contact with the leadership at Mandres so that I could gauge the strength of feeling among the displaced and seek to counter the possibility that bitterness in the camps would hamper the general process of rural reconciliation. And third, we had a constant worry that an expansion of the village's defences might lead to clashes with Mia Milea or with Greek Cypriot villages to the north.

In fact Mia Milea, another Greek Cypriot village in which the leadership was strongly left-wing, and the smaller Greek Cypriot villages of Sykhari, Vouno and Koutsovendis to the north, displayed no animosity to the Turkish Cypriots and placed no demands on the mediating units.

Not so the all-Greek Cypriot Pano Dhikomo and Kato Dhikomo, which came to require a disproportionate amount of our attention. In both, the villagers were bitter because they felt unable to use the direct Kyrenia-Nicosia road through Geunyely, astride which the Turkish army contingent was now established. This route had formerly been taken daily by about five hundred of their number who worked in the capital. Even though the road was theoretically still open to unarmed civilians, any Greek Cypriot travelling it would have been subjected to searches by the Turks and constantly exposed to capture as a hostage. The villagers therefore now used the circuitous track through Koutsovendis and Mia Milea, to their constant irritation.

Others of the villagers of Pano and Kato Dhikomo had depended for a living on marble quarries in the Pentadaktylos Range around St Hilarion Castle. These were now considered inaccessible, having fallen under the control of armed Turkish Cypriot irregulars: the result was a further rise in the level of unemployment and a shortage of income which matched that in many isolated Turkish Cypriot villages.

We tried to arrange for escorts to cover the removal of quarrying machinery from the mines, so that work could be restarted elsewhere, but JFHQ refused on the grounds that this would be a breach of agreed policy.[1] Soon after the denial to the Greek Cypriots of a suitable escort, the Turkish Cypriots removed from the quarries whatever equipment they thought might be useful to them.

By mid-January the Greek Cypriots were regularly reporting activity by armed Turkish Cypriots groups in the heights behind Pano Dhikomo and on 20 January a party of villagers trying to recover a government-owned excavator from the foothills was fired on from the heights above.

The Greeks Cypriots were able from Pano Dhikomo to observe Turkish army and Turkish Cypriot movements on the Kyrenia road, but not to see that Turkish Cypriot paramilitaries were now in unobtrusive occupation of Aghirda Forestry Station.

Although now within easy rifle range of the new forward Turkish Cypriot positions, work at the DEKO cement, lime and asbestos installations and at the big Greek Cypriot co-operative farm at Onishia (north of Pano Dhikomo) continued, for the time being, normally.

18.   PHOTTA AREA.   JANUARY 1964

Between the Myrtou and Kyrenia roads lies a ten-mile stretch of fine undulating cornfields, broken in places by humped-up hillocks and dried-out gullies and criss-crossed by irrigation ditches and deeply indented cart-tracks. Rather above the centre of this stood the large Turkish Cypriot farming village of Photta and along its northern edge, against the foothills of the Kyrenia Range, a line of villages comprising the Greek Cypriot Sisklipos to the west and then the Turkish Cypriot Pileri, Krini, Keumurju and Aghirda. Photta farmlands were bordered by those of Ayios Ermolaos to the west and of Skylloura and Ayios Vasilios to the south-west.

At Christmas, violence in the mixed villages of Ayios Vasilios and Skylloura led to six hundred Turkish Cypriot refugees streaming up across the fields to Photta, bringing with them their flocks and those few small possessions that they could lay their hands on in the panic of their departure. Later, in January, other refugees arrived from Ayia Marina.

Because it had direct access to Nicosia and received regular visits from a unit of TURDYK, it was not until 2 February that I first went to Photta. For the first time in a Turkish Cypriot village, the patrol was given a wholly hostile reception: there was angry and emotional barracking from a crowd of bystanders, one young man had to be restrained from attacking Lieutenant Constantinides and a spokesman declared that they did not need any help from the British and were quite capable of taking care of themselves. I took it that this attitude was imported from Ayios Vasilios, but when we had the same sort of reception in Temblos, later that day, I began to wonder if there had been a new turn in Turkish Cypriot policy. Later, however, I was sent an apology from Photta, with an explanation that the hostility had been provoked solely by the sight of my Greek liaison officer.

Major Sepici and I had a meeting with Kutchuk that evening and received an assurance from him that both his office and TMT command would let it be known that the tripartite patrol was operating with his direct support. Subsequently we returned as a full patrol to Photta and Temblos without provoking any further overt demonstration of hostility but there always was an absence of warmth there when we had a Greek officer with us. Photta and Temblos, like the other main refugee centres of Mandres and Louroujina, were now communities united by an all-pervasive animosity for the Greek Cypriots and for Greece.

Other Turkish Cypriot villagers in the area told us that the Turkish Cypriots in Ayios Ermolaos, a tiny minority of sixteen living among five hundred Greek Cypriots, wished to evacuate but were being prevented from doing so by the Greek Cypriots. It was always difficult to discover the precise truth of a situation where an outside source, perhaps a relative or a villager who had left earlier or a friend in a neighbouring village, alleged that one community was exerting covert pressure on the other and where there was a suspicion that the minority group might be unable or unwilling to speak freely to the patrol, even in private. Investigations into situations like this were usually lengthy, relied heavily on the integrity of Major Sepici and sometimes carried the risk that they would themselves create friction where none had existed before.

In the case of Ayios Ermolaos, we found that the Turkish Cypriots had no wish at all to leave, that they had never been subjected to pressure by either community, but that they were apprehensive about their ability to last out if they were intimidated, either by Greek Cypriots or by TMT, in the future. Our first impression of the village had been that it was well-led and moderate and that the Greek Cypriots would do their best to provide security for their small Turkish Cypriot minority, and this proved to be correct. We had difficulty, however, in convincing Photta and Pileri that the Turkish Cypriots in Ayios Ermolaos were safe and in dissuading them from seeking to provoke an evacuation.

During this period one of the patrol's preoccupations was to see how Turkish Cypriot villages other than Photta and Temblos coped with their influx of refugees. By the end of January the population of Pileri had been doubled by additions from Lapithos, Aredhiou and Kyrenia; Krini had increased by fifty per cent after evacuations from Eliophotes and Peristerona; Keumurju had no additions; Aghirda had fifty evacuees from Skylloura and Lapithos.

To the east of Aghirda, on the site of an old British army camp in the woods beside the Kyrenia road, work was being pushed forward on the construction of a large and well-planned refugee camp: the aim was that two thousand of those currently living under canvas in Mandres and Photta would move into much improved conditions here. It was an added advantage that some of the permanent buildings on this site were already being used as a central depot for relief stores for Kyrenia District. A co-operation which developed between my patrol and the Welfare Officer in charge of the Aghirda camp, Ali Macit, was to prove particularly useful as plans were formulated by us for a general inter-communal re-engagement at village level.

19.   KYRENIA AREA.   JANUARY 1964

Until the end of January the area to the north of the Pentadaktylos Range was handled mainly by the tripartite patrol under Major Greenwood. Each evening I would combine his reports with my own so that a general summary of events in Nicosia Zone was produced for JFHQ consumption.

A party of Turkish Cypriots who left Lapithos on 29 December to seek food had disappeared without trace, but otherwise there had been no major trouble in the area since the arrest of Turkish Cypriot civic and police leaders at Christmas, on the Greek Cypriot pretext that they had discovered a plot in which Superintendent Ali Assad and his associates were going to attempt to seize the Kyrenia armoury.

Tension eased considerably when these captives were released in good health, and on 7 January Major Greenwood managed to convene a JLC and to re-establish a number of links between the two communities: the Greek Cypriots then agreed to several 'concessions', relating to freedom of communication and to the limitation of Greek Cypriot police activities, as part of a conciliation package.

A joint committee was also established in Lapithos, where earlier British army reports had spoken of the Greek Cypriot police 'terrorising' the Turkish Cypriot minority. Meanwhile the two communities were reported to be on good terms and mixing freely at Vasilia and Kazaphani. At Trapeza the Turkish Cypriots were fearful but under no apparent threat. All was well at Temblos and Karmi. The small Turkish Cypriot minority in Klepini had resolved to evacuate but then been persuaded not to by their Greek Cypriot neighbours, who had promised to help them through whatever difficulties might come and had guaranteed their safety. Both communities in all of these villages had strongly requested that British troops be stationed in the area.

However, during the second week of January there was a sharp increase in tension and numerous reports of worsening inter-communal relations. The refusal of the Turkish Cypriots to re-open the direct Kyrenia-Nicosia road, as required by the Freedom of Movement agreement of 6 January, and provocatively aggressive patrolling of Turkish Cypriot villages by the Greek Cypriot police were producing a smouldering rage within both communities and serious friction at leadership level in Kyrenia.

On 17 January large bands of armed Greek Cypriot paramilitaries were reported to be moving into the Karmi Forest and into the hills above Lapithos. Later I was told that this was in furtherance of a plan by the Greek 'Organisation' leader in Kyrenia to capture St Hilarion Castle, take control of all vantage points on the Kyrenia range and reopen the main road through the Kyrenia Pass. After a successful first phase, the plan was vetoed by the overall Greek Cypriot command in Nicosia on the grounds that the moment was inopportune and that success was doubtful. In fact the Turkish Cypriots had not yet established effective defences on the mountain range and if the action had been pressed home in advance of any reaction from TURDYK it probably would have been quickly successful. Later Greek Cypriot attempts to storm St Hilarion were to be frustrated by a combination of tough Turkish Cypriot resistance, further political dithering and a violent reaction from the international community.

That same day the Turkish Cypriots started to evacuate Vavilas and Vasilia. The Greek Cypriots tried to hamper this movement by setting up roadblocks throughout the Lapithos area.

Major Greenwood's patrol managed temporarily to contain the situation to the west of Kyrenia, but when JFHQ declined to sanction the stationing of troops in the area the impetus towards evacuation became irresistible in isolated Turkish Cypriot communities.

Departing from Vasilia, the Turkish Cypriots insisted on handing over their five shotguns to a regular British army patrol that was present. The Greek Cypriot police, determined that events must remain under their own control, demanded that the weapons be given to them. An ugly altercation ensued and the police tried to force off the road the British army Land Rover carrying the shotguns. A serious incident was narrowly averted only by the arrival of senior officers from JF and the gendarmerie.*

In the continuing evacuation, all the Turkish Cypriot families in Lapithos and Vasilia moved either to Temblos or to villages beyond the Kyrenia Range and the inhabitants of Trapeza went to Kazaphani. Almost overnight the population of Temblos increased from 150 to 650.

At this point, TMT leadership decided that there must if possible be no further evacuations from the Kyrenia area. New TMT commanders took over effective control in Temblos and in the Turkish Cypriot sector of Kazaphani: defences were rapidly strengthened in both villages and additional weapons moved in. A permanent Turkish Cypriot garrison was established in St Hilarion Castle and Turkish ensigns raised over its walls. There were more frequent instances of shooting from the hills, albeit ineffectually, towards the Greek Cypriot village of Karmi.

Tension in the area was now very high. On 23 January, the Greek Cypriots sighted considerable movement of Turkish Cypriot paramilitaries and police near the Kyrenia Pass and claimed to Major Greenwood that they had received intelligence that a Turkish landing on the Kyrenia coastline was imminent. Greek Cypriot paramilitary units were brought to a state of readiness all along the north coast. The President issued a call to the Greeks Cypriots to be ready for any sacrifices that the defence of Cyprus might demand.

Then, as quickly as it had boiled up, the situation cooled.[1]

Visiting Karmi on 25 January, my patrol was given a rousing welcome and treated to an excellent meal, with no sign of any resentment at the presence of Major Sepici. The story of the villagers' recent tribulations was recounted

---

* The guns were later delivered by JF to police headquarters in Nicosia.

with some humour and it appeared that they had accustomed themselves to being shot at daily from the direction of St Hilarion. The villagers said their relations with the Turkish Cypriots of Temblos had always been good, but they were anxious about how things would be now that this neighbouring village was a refugee centre. A Mr Tsangarides asked for news of his tourist shop inside St Hilarion Castle and we had to tell him that it had been totally looted.

By the beginning of February, the situation in Kyrenia District again appeared stable, with much better relations in the Kazaphani-Bellapais area and a more relaxed atmosphere in Temblos. Major Greenwood's reports noted that, despite the widespread looting of abandoned Turkish property in the villages to the west, there was a noticeable improvement in inter-communal relations throughout the region.

Turkish Cypriot fighters manning a road block.

20. DHIORIOS AREA. JANUARY 1964.

In contrast to most of Cyprus, the majority of good agricultural land in the Dhiorios area was owned by Turkish Cypriots, and local Greek Cypriots were jealous of this fact. At the same time the Turkish Cypriots were heavily in debt to the Greek Cypriots, who were fearful that the Turkish Cypriots would somehow use the current emergency to evade a settlement of their obligations. The area lies to the north of Morphou and runs up to Cape Kormakiti. It had a populated axis on the village line of Ayia Irini, Dhiorios, Myrtou and Kambyli.

With the direct Kyrenia-Nicosia road via Geunyely now closed by the Turkish army to Greek Cypriot traffic, the best alternative route passed through this region at Myrtou: Greek Cypriot paramilitary leaders were keen to eliminate any Turkish Cypriot ability to disrupt movement on this road. Furthermore, the region's western coastline is low-lying and looked a likely landing-point for an invasion, so that from Christmas onwards there was intense Greek Cypriot activity in the construction of beach defences.

The area had a previous record of good inter-communal relations, and shock-waves from the Christmas fighting in Nicosia had produced only a muted response. The Turkish Cypriots restricted themselves to the immediate vicinity of their villages and the two communities treated each other with an exaggerated wariness.

Before long, however, the local gendarmerie station at Myrtou became the subject of frequent complaint to my patrol. The Turkish Cypriot sergeant there, a benign man well-liked by his Greek Cypriot colleagues, continued after 21 December to report for duty as usual until being told by the Greek Cypriots that his continuing attendance, and that of his Turkish Cypriot constables, would be unwise. From there on, the station, despite its occasional good intentions, exercised a destabilising influence.

At the end of December, the now all-Greek Cypriot gendarmerie suggested to Turkish Cypriot villagers in the area that it would be advisable for them to hand over their shotguns (which were supposedly the only weapons then in their possession) in order to help with the restoration of mutual confidence and to avoid the possibility of untoward incidents. The Turkish Cypriots refused. At about the same time the Turkish Cypriots became aware of widespread Greek Cypriot paramilitary activity in the area, which in fact was geared partly to the preparation of anti-invasion defences and partly to intensive training exercises.

Auxiliaries were now enrolled by the Myrtou gendarmerie. Normal policing activities were neglected. There was a refusal to investigate or follow up Turkish Cypriot reports of acts of hooliganism against them: the Greek Cypriot sergeant claimed to the patrol that this was due to the overriding importance of their new 'military mission'. Turkish Cypriot travel was further cut, then stopped altogether when on 31 December a Turkish Cypriot villager from Ayia Irini disappeared while on his way back from Ghaziveran.

On 14 January Major Greenwood managed to convene a meeting between local *mukhtars*, the Greek Cypriot community leaders of Myrtou and Dhiorios and Superintendent Neophitos Vassiliou, the new chief of gendarmerie for Kyrenia District. The Turkish Cypriots said that they were afraid to travel and increasingly scared by the night-time activities of armed Greek Cypriot paramilitaries. Superintendent Vassiliou was exceptionally conciliatory and an agreement was concluded whereby the Turkish Cypriots would in future be guaranteed freedom of movement throughout Kyrenia District, Greek Cypriots would travel with the Turkish Cypriots when they went to Nicosia so as to assure their safe passage through Greek Cypriot villages on the route, and regular joint inter-communal meetings would be held between local *mukhtars* and community leaders*. Sadly this spirit of co-operation quickly evaporated. As in other mixed areas, in mid-January there was an influx of Greek Cypriot reporters seeking to illustrate the ease and harmony with which the two communities continued to co-exist. Predictably this approach was detested by the Turkish Cypriots and contributed to pushing the communities apart. A similarly unintended result was achieved by the senior 'Organisation' leaders of Kyrenia Zone, Captain Augustis and Sergeant Makrides: genuinely keen to pursue the Makarios policy of reconciliation and aware that hopes of *enosis* would be endangered by a continuing slide towards ethnic separation, these two regularly harangued both local communities on the benefits of co-existence, the senselessness of hatred and the need for mutual understanding.[1] The message was much the same as that of the tripartite patrols, but because it was delivered by Greek Cypriots, and specifically by Greek Cypriots whom the Turkish Cypriots did not trust, and because it was contradicted by the one-sided behaviour of the Myrtou gendarmerie, it did nothing but create a heightened anxiety among the Turkish Cypriots. (Whereas among the Greek Cypriots it was listened to sympathetically by those who were already well-disposed towards the Turkish Cypriots and disregarded by those who were already antagonistic.)

Promoted by separatist propaganda and the misreporting of events elsewhere, imprecise fears built towards a state of panic. On 19/20 January, the same night as the abandonment of Lapithos, the 410 Turkish Cypriots of Dhiorios evacuated to Kambyli. There the enlarged population was kept on edge, convinced of imminent attack, by heavy Greek Cypriot paramilitary patrolling in the area and by broadcasts from Ankara which predicted that extensive fighting was about to erupt in western Cyprus. Nevertheless, with encouragement from the patrol, the Turkish Cypriots made occasional cautious forays to collect stores from Nicosia, including a consignment of Red Crescent tents, and to recover the more valuable items of the property that they had left behind in Dhiorios.

---

* Village and town leaders were also sometimes referred to as 'presidents'.

On 24 January Lieutenant Constantinides complained at breakfast of an ulcer that would prevent him travelling with us that day. This led to the first instance of an Anglo-Turkish patrol through a wholly Greek Cypriot area, an experience that proved distinctly uncomfortable.

Throughout the day we were closely followed by a carload of police auxiliaries with cocked weapons at the ready. At Myrtou, where we had hoped for lunch, the cafes were quickly boarded up at the approach of a fully uniformed Turkish officer. At Dhiorios the Greek Cypriot leaders were effusively anxious to record their sadness at the going of their Turkish Cypriot neighbours and their commitment to the safeguarding of abandoned property, but Major Sepici was balefully glared at throughout the meeting by a hostile crowd of onlookers and at the end of it was physically attacked by a Greek Cypriot, who had to be dragged away by his fellow villagers.

In Ayia Irini, the large majority of the villagers were Turkish Cypriot. They greeted us ecstatically but then poured out the same story that we had heard from the Dhiorios evacuees. Their past relationship with their Greek Cypriot co-villagers, to whom they referred with the same contempt as did many Greek Cypriots when talking of impoverished Turkish Cypriots, had been satisfactory. Then frequent police and paramilitary activity around the village had led to a sense of insecurity, which had been worsened when Captain Augustis and Sergeant Makrides mustered them all for an address on 14 January. They had been particularly disquieted, they told us, by hearing the right things said for what they took to be the wrong reasons. Then on 22 January Sergeant Makrides had phoned them to say that he had heard that pressure was being put on them by some Greek Cypriots to evacuate. He promised to arrest those who were applying the pressure and if necessary to "arrange for a unit of the 'Greek army' to be stationed in the village to protect them."

The Greek Cypriot villagers in Ayia Irini were equally volatile. They cursed the British, blaming them for all Cyprus' current woes. They criticised the patrol for having visited the Turkish Cypriot coffee-house before their own. They claimed that the Turkish Cypriots in the village were now well armed and inherently aggressive. And they claimed never to have heard of Captain Augustis or Sergeant Makrides.

Before leaving the area we paid a courtesy visit to the gendarmerie station at Myrtou. The meeting was entirely cordial. Turkish Cypriot fears were explained. The sergeant acknowledged the recent concentration in the area of units of armed men, explaining that there was "a very large number of men practising for the job of police auxiliary." I was told in private of the positions held by Captain Augustis and Sergeant Makrides, as The Organisation-appointed military and Special Branch commanders in Kyrenia District. Before we left there was a lengthy exchange of mutual compliments and pleasantries.

That evening, a formal complaint was received at JFHQ from Nicosia Police headquarters claiming that the patrol had forced its way into Myrtou gendarmerie station, cross-questioned the resident police officers, attempted to discover what prisoners were held in the cells, tried to view the station armoury and "mounted an attempt to infiltrate into the station toilet." Furthermore that, after leaving the station, the patrol had attempted to spy on the police who were following it and had then made an unsuccessful attempt to force its way back into the gendarmerie building.

Both Augustis and Makrides were later to become friends. They told me that so alarmed had government circles become in January at their apparent pursuit by an English officer* that it had insisted they be permanently accompanied by armed bodyguards, to their considerable irritation.

Returning to the Myrtou area on 25 January, this time accompanied by Constantinides, I tried to repair the previous day's damage. Reconciliation with the gendarmerie was achieved through an acknowledgement that any misunderstandings must have been due to the inadequacy of my Greek or my inability to fathom the Cypriot dialect. A similar explanation to the Greek Cypriots at Ayia Irini so impressed them with my act of self-denigration that a joint meeting was convened in an atmosphere of exceptional goodwill and an inter-communal deal was agreed that was to survive successfully until I left Cyprus in June. Included in this agreement were clauses that there would be regular joint consultations, that all 'foreigners' would be excluded from the village and that there would be no exploitation of village affairs for propaganda purposes.

The Greek Cypriots asked that the patrol arrange for an early visit from their priest, whom they had not seen for several weeks. This worthy and venerable old clergyman was eventually located by me at Liveras, a small village near the tip of Cape Kormakiti. Asked why he had ceased to minister to his parishioners in Ayia Irini, he said that a Turk there had once pointed a shotgun at him, which caused him such great distress that he had not wished to remain in the village. He said that he was able to live in proper peace and quietude in Liveras because there was only one Turkish Cypriot family there.†

On the morning of 26 January, the Turkish Cypriots in Ayia Irini saw large units of paramilitaries to the south and mistakenly assumed that an attack from Morphou was imminent. Sticking by their recent agreement they informed the Greek Cypriot villagers of what they had seen. They then stood to, threw up barricades and took up defensive positions. Much to their alarm, the Greek Cypriot villagers were able to view a much larger array of automatic weapons than they previously had supposed to be in the hands of their co-villagers.

Later that day, after the alarm had been recognised as false and the barricades removed, Captain Augustis and Sergeant Makrides arrived at the village with a large contingent of police but no attempt was made to threaten the Turkish Cypriots. Units of armed gendarmerie similarly visited the Greek Cypriot sector of the village on each day that followed.

On 30 January, a decision of the Lefka Communal Chamber, ratified by the Turkish Cypriot leadership in Nicosia, led to the despatch of a lorry-load of tents to Ayia Irini in preparation for a proposed large-scale movement of refugees northward from the Peristerona area. The lorry was searched by

---

* The 'pursuer' was me, seeking to have an amicable chat with them, at the suggestion of Tassos Papadopoulos.
† See chapter 39 for subsequent events in Liveras.

Greek Cypriot police en route but, surprisingly, was allowed through. The tents were delivered to the Turkish Cypriots in Ayia Irini with a message that evacuees would arrive 'shortly'. The villagers failed to inform Nicosia that such a move would be in conflict with the local agreement they had made.

The Greek Cypriot police now decided that any strengthening of the Turkish Cypriot community in this village would undermine Greek Cypriot control of a key area. Instead of advancing the matter urgently in the Nicosia Liaison Committee, which would have been proper procedure, pressure was brought to bear on Ayia Irini itself. On the evening of 30 January, a party of police and paramilitaries from Myrtou arrived and questioned the Turkish Cypriots about the tents and the refugees that were expected. Later that night Sergeant Makrides phoned the Turkish Cypriots and told them that, as had been specified in their joint agreement, on no account were they to allow any refugees to come. The following morning he phoned again to warn that there would be serious trouble if any evacuees were taken in.

Having pressed JFHQ to try and convince Kutchuk's office that it would be unwise to insist on using Ayia Irini as a refugee destination, I was back in the village on 31 January. The Greek Cypriot villagers there were deeply alarmed at the prospect of an even larger Turkish Cypriot majority, which would be likely to include a number of embittered extremists; the Greek Cypriot police were understandably suspicious of what long-term Turkish Cypriot objectives might be inherent in the proposed move; and the Turkish Cypriots of Ayia Irini were understanding of Greek Cypriot apprehensions, and themselves keen that no refugees should come, but felt that it was their 'duty' to accept whatever decision was made in Nicosia.

While I was talking with the Turkish Cypriots in Ayia Irini, a strong party of police arrived from Lapithos under the command of Inspector Loizos, the senior police officer for the Myrtou/Lapithos area. The lead Land Rover drove into the village with two men in the back pointing cocked Bren guns on quarter bearings and another man, in plain clothes, standing up with a Sten gun at the ready. As soon as the vehicle stopped, all its occupants jumped out and went into an aggressive crouch with their weapons aimed at the nearest Turkish Cypriots.

The Turkish Cypriots whispered to me that this was how they usually had been treated since Christmas: with the gendarmerie from Myrtou, who they knew by name, it was not so scary but with out-of-area police and paramilitaries they felt frightened and humiliated.

Inspector Loizos explained that they were using standard practice, which was copied from British military procedure, to guard against ambush. I took it that this probably was the way the British had trained Turkish Cypriot police to act with them in the fifties during the EOKA struggle. I suggested that rather than imitating an army in hostile territory they ought now to be acting as the forefront of Makarios' policy of inter-communal reconciliation. I used as a lever the fact that they were in default of regulations by having armed civilians with them, which was specifically forbidden by the cease-fire agreement.

If Inspector Loizos was harbouring the usual police resentment of the British, he did not show it. We had a useful discussion and agreed on the nature and complexities of the local situation. He undertook that direct pressure on the Turkish Cypriots in Ayia Irini would be relaxed, that he would stop the obtrusive display of weapons by his police and that in future the patrolling of the village would be limited to occasional visits by the Myrtou gendarmerie.

The Turkish Cypriot *mukhtar* and his village advisers were responsive to positive gestures and anxious to appear conciliatory. Much less so was Ali Cemal, a schoolmaster who fronted for TMT's leadership in this region. He was prickly, usually uncooperative and caustic about the value of mediation. It seemed unlikely that the traditional village leadership would stand up to him in any confrontation and it seemed probable that if refugees did come to the area widespread trouble would follow.

Eventually JFHQ accepted my urging and put pressure on the Turkish Communal Chambers in Nicosia and Lefka to stop them from directing any refugees to Ayia Irini, encouraged Greek Cypriot police headquarters to back up Inspector Loizos' undertakings to moderate police activity in the area, encouraged CYTA to restore a normal telephone service, and agreed to increase the frequency of British patrols to the village. My Greek and Turkish officers undertook to put similar pressure through their respective contingents.

In each case there was a positive reaction. The Turkish Cypriots reversed the decision to direct refugees to Ayia Irini, the Greek Cypriot police presence in the area became conciliatory and the telephone connection was restored. So long as the stock of tents remained Myrtou gendarmerie searched all vehicles approaching the village, in case of concealed refugees: when the tents were returned to Nicosia the searches were stopped. By 3 February I was able to report that tension was down and that inter-communal liaison was working well. The softening of police attitudes was such that the Dhiorios evacuees in Kambyli began to discuss a return to their village.

On 4 February, a vehicle with two Turkish Cypriots from Dhiorios disappeared while en route from Kambyli to Nicosia. The same day there was a sudden increase in tension in other regions after the seizing by Turkish Cypriots of hostages in Ghaziveran. Neither event seemed to damage the new-found spirit of inter-communal cooperation in Myrtou district.

21.   AYIA MARINA AND THE MARONITE VILLAGES

On 11 January the patrol had managed to dissuade the Turkish Cypriots in Ayia Marina from an immediate evacuation, although we had grave doubts as to how long they would stay, given the baleful proximity of Skylloura.

We learned that soon after we had left on the 11th a party of heavily armed Greek Cypriots arrived from Skylloura, demanded that the Turkish Cypriots hand over their weapons, confiscated the two shotguns that were produced and threatened that there would be dire consequences if the Turkish Cypriots failed in any way to comply with their instructions. Thereafter there was aggressive patrolling every day into the Turkish Cypriot quarter by armed Greek Cypriot police and auxiliaries until 15 January, when there was a dramatic change in the pattern of Greek Cypriot activities. That day a Greek Cypriot agency made a sizeable delivery to the Turkish Cypriots of free relief stores and the former patrols by armed auxiliaries were replaced by occasional visits by uniformed police who avoided any excessive display of weapons and consulted the Turkish Cypriots as to what help they needed.

This good work was undone, as elsewhere, by a series of visits from Greek journalists seeking to paint a picture, demonstrative of the government's new policy of conciliation, of co-operative Turkish Cypriots provided for by caring Greek Cypriots. The Turkish Cypriot *mukhtar* endeavoured to play both sides. He made a number of statements to the press describing his satisfaction with Greek Cypriot policy and his earnest desire that the two communities continue to live together in their accustomed harmony. At the same time, he counselled his people to mistrust every Greek Cypriot gesture. To the patrol he gave exaggerated reports of Greek Cypriot oppression, and denied that he had ever said anything complimentary to the press. On being taxed with his failure to mention to us his receipt of government aid, he described the large delivery of 15 January as having been "no more than a few sandwiches."

My report on a visit to Ayia Marina on 22 January noted that it was likely that the Turkish Cypriots would already have left if not for the fact that only that day had the government Grain Commission begun to move the village's accumulated harvest into central storage. The Turkish Cypriots clearly had wished to safeguard their income by seeing their crop safely delivered: as soon as it was gone their thoughts turned to their own departure.*

---

* The same consideration probably applied in the timing of other evacuation plans, as for instance at Palekythro.

On 26 January, the entire Turkish Cypriot population of Ayia Marina abandoned their village. The majority went either to Photta or to Nicosia for redirection to Chumlekji Chiflik and eventual settlement in Mora. Before going, they contracted the sale of most of their flocks to their Maronite co-villagers with a condition that payment was to be made on 1 August if they had not by then returned. As was common practice elsewhere, the *mukhtar* afterwards put it about that all these flocks had been stolen by the Greek Cypriots.

In general, Turkish Cypriot relations with the Maronites in Ayia Marina remained good to the end. The exception was a legacy of strong dislike for the *mukhtar*: In the months to come all his property was destroyed, while that of the other Turkish Cypriot villagers was in every case preserved intact.

After the events of Christmas at Skylloura and the abduction of their schoolmaster, and given their extreme isolation in Ayia Marina, it is unlikely that the Turkish Cypriots could have been persuaded to stay. Even if supported by frequent British patrol visits and by assurances of protection by the Greek Cypriot police against hooliganism, their confidence would have been undermined by reports of violence in other regions. In the event there was general relief, among Greek Cypriots and Turkish Cypriots alike and at JFHQ, that they had relocated without any serious problem.

As has been noted, about two per cent of the population was Maronite. In Nicosia Zone there was a string of villages between Morphou and the northern coast – Ayia Marina, Asomatos, Karpasha, Kormakiti – which, after the Turkish Cypriot evacuation of Ayia Marina, were occupied solely by Maronites. On my first visit to Asomatos, I mistakenly assumed this was a Greek Cypriot village, but was sharply corrected by the villagers that they were "not Greeks but Maronites".

On occasions when other villages flew the Greek or Turkish ensign (the Cyprus ensign being nowhere to be seen), Maronite villages flew the national flag of Lebanon. Apart from bad feelings between the Maronites in Asomatos and the Turkish Cypriots in Kambyli, resulting from incidents in 1958 which had led to an exchange of population and various personal animosities, the Maronites managed in 1964 to preserve a good relationship with both the Greek and Turkish Cypriot communities. Their sharing of Greek language, press and radio led to some measure of alignment with the Greek Cypriots, but in private they expressed sympathy for the Turkish Cypriots, whose treatment by the police and by Greek Cypriot extremists they strongly criticised. They demonstrated their sympathy by providing the Turkish Cypriots with reports and comment on Greek Cypriot activities. For me they were a useful source of relatively objective observation on the affairs of the region.

22. PERISTERONA AREA.
LATE JANUARY 1964

Patrols visiting this area in the first half of January had remarked on the sense of fear and isolation among Turkish Cypriots in the outlying villages and on extremes of bitterness and friction in Peristerona. Inter-communal liaison had been reconstructed with difficulty, in the face of persistent roughneck provocation and police bias. The Greek Orthodox priest in Peristerona had pledged to maintain a supportive contact with the Turkish Cypriot *hodja*, but had failed to do so. Unprepossessing Greek Cypriot police specials, patrolling at night through the Turkish Cypriot sector, frequently let loose a blast of automatic fire: their superiors explained that they had not been properly trained in the use of these weapons and that they were either experimenting with them or firing by mistake. This, they told me, had led to one of the specials accidentally shooting himself. Outlying Turkish Cypriot property was left unprotected by the police and progressively vandalised.

However, the first full-scale evacuation from this area occurred not from Peristerona but from Dhenia and Akaki, the latter a village where the Turkish Cypriots had been firmly established and where inter-communal relations had been exceptionally good.

The Turkish Cypriot community at Dhenia was badly led, lacked supportive contact with neighbouring villages and had continued since Christmas in dread of imminent attack. A slow drift away from the village was followed by encouragement from Nicosia for a general evacuation. On 16 January, a convoy of seven lorries arrived to collect the remaining Turkish Cypriots. The Greek Cypriots at Dhenia seemed delighted to see them go, but were highly critical of a British half-troop of armoured cars which supervised the departure. In fact, not having been cleared with the Greek Cypriot authorities, this was in contravention of current JFHQ policy: it led to increased anti-British feeling among local Greek Cypriots, who saw it as encouragement for Turkish Cypriot separatism.

On the following day, 17 January, Akaki was evacuated. Strongly led and much more sophisticated than the average Turkish Cypriot village community, the Turkish Cypriots here had seemed in relaxed good spirits when I had been there a few days earlier. They appeared to have no disputes with the Greek Cypriots, no-one from the village had been abducted or murdered, they had, unusually, made no complaints about the Greek Cypriot police and their comparative wealth suggested that they would not easily leave. Later we learned that this was a move demanded by the TMT leadership in Nicosia.

The apparent lack of co-ordination among Turkish Cypriot villages in this area probably arose because the zoning of TMT commands differed from the civil district structure. Peristerona, which had seemed likely to be the first to go and which was also in Nicosia District, was subject to orders from TMT commanders in Lefka, rather than from those in Nicosia.

In any event, the Turkish Cypriots were still on good terms with their Greek Cypriot co-villagers when they left Dhenia and Akaki. Behind them, entrusted to Greek Cypriot care, they left most of their wealth: homes and animals and farm equipment and grain stocks. In marked contrast to some areas, the Greek Cypriots set out with great determination to safeguard this abandoned property, tending the flocks and setting guards against the possibility of casual theft or looting. So thorough was this care that when, four months later, a secret agreement was reached for a phased return of the Turkish Cypriots to some of the areas abandoned by them, these two villages were selected to be the first for resettlement.

It bears noting that the Turkish Cypriots in other nearby villages never referred to these evacuations when discussing with me their own worries.

The evacuation of Eliophotes one week later had a much clearer provenance. This was a small, isolated, unitary village. It had never been attacked or subjected to direct harassment, but between 21 December and 15 January the village was twice 'examined' by Greek Cypriot police and irregulars; all hunting guns were impounded; several animals were 'confiscated', in fact as security for debts, although this was not explained to the villagers. Villagers were frequently stopped on the road by armed Greek Cypriots and ordered to return to their homes, and the *mukhtar* of the neighbouring Greek Cypriot village informed them that in future they could only travel with his specific permission. Fear grew, money ran short, food became extremely scarce. Improvements made through joint patrol visits, the delivery of emergency aid and then the Greek Cypriot initiation in mid-January of a policy of active reconciliation were cancelled out by the force of Turkish Cypriot separatist propaganda. A few families slipped away to join relatives in areas of larger Turkish Cypriot concentration. What followed was described in detail to me later by the *mukhtar* and other villagers.

By 22 January there was no money left in the village. Too fearful to travel, those villagers who formerly had worked in Nicosia or Lefka gave up hope of any early return to their jobs. Because he was no longer able to make a living in Eliophotes, the village bus driver departed with his vehicle for Nicosia. The Greek Cypriots at Orounda promised to help with transport, but never did so. Morale seeped away.

On the evening of 23 January, two young former villagers arrived by taxi from Nicosia and in a heated argument urged the *mukhtar* to approve an evacuation. The matter was debated that night by the village council and in the early morning a decision was taken to leave. That message was passed to Peristerona, which relayed it to Nicosia. By mid-morning five lorries had arrived. Each family loaded its most valuable possessions and buried or hid those items for which there was no room. The older people, devastated with grief, had to be helped away from their homes.

Advised by the two young men to go to Peristerona, the lorries set off at noon. The shepherds soon afterwards followed on foot with their flocks.

Meanwhile the Greek Cypriots in Peristerona learned during the morning of the impending move. They quickly informed the Turkish Cypriot *hodja* that no refugees would be accepted and then threw up barricades on every approach to the village and manned them with police and armed civilians.

The Turkish Cypriot *mukhtar* pleaded unsuccessfully for the convoy to be allowed into Peristerona. When this was refused, the convoy moved on to Nicosia where it waited for two hours before being redirected by the Turkish Communal Chamber to Krini, a village close to the north of Photta. Meanwhile the shepherds, having reached Orounda, had been informed that Peristerona was barred to them and had thereupon turned back and retraced their way cross-country to Eliophotes. They were collected by lorry on the morning of 25 January and taken with their flocks directly to Krini. Not included in the evacuation were the village donkeys, which were all turned loose into the hills.

The barring of refugees from Peristerona derived in part from a long-standing Greek Cypriot assumption that the Turkish Cypriots intended to try and build up their community there until it so outnumbered the Greek Cypriots that effective control moved into Turkish Cypriot hands. It also accorded with a determination by commanders of 'The Organisation' that the Turkish Cypriots must not be allowed to build up major concentrations astride the main roads. TMT leaders later told me that they had in fact discussed such an idea for Peristerona, but had rejected it as unfeasible.

The evacuations of Akaki, Dhenia and Eliophotes led to an increase in tension in Peristerona and Orounda. The comparative isolation in which the small Turkish Cypriot community in Orounda now found itself and continuing extremist Turkish propaganda from Nicosia and Ankara made it likely that this village would be abandoned at the next threat of violence.

On 23 January, the Turkish Cypriot *mukhtar* confirmed this position to me. The Greek Cypriots in the village with whom I discussed the situation expressed genuine sympathy for the fears and intentions of their neighbours and undertook to look after their property if they did decide to go.

On 27 January, the Turkish Cypriots informed Kutchuk's office in Nicosia that they were too fearful to stay, and the next day the entire community evacuated. Most household possessions and stocks of potatoes and hay and the donkeys were left behind: the owners had intended to collect these the next day, but the lorry drivers claimed that it was too risky to attempt a second passage through the Greek Cypriot roadblocks. A request for a British escort was refused by JFHQ. On subsequent visits to Orounda I found that abandoned Turkish Cypriot property was being scrupulously cared for by the Greek Cypriot villagers.

By now the situation in Peristerona was unmanageable. Repeated patrol visits had produced a temporary easing of tension which had then invariably been punctured by new instances of Greek Cypriot hooliganism. The Greek Cypriot police failed to provide the Turkish Cypriots with any sense of security. Exchanges at joint meetings became increasingly acrimonious, with the Turkish Cypriots beginning openly to accuse the police of intimidation.

Only the stationing of British troops in the village could have reversed this position, but that was excluded by JFHQ.

When we arrived in Peristerona on 31 January, we found that about a hundred Turkish Cypriots had left earlier in the day and that those still there had been overtaken by collective panic. Throughout the Turkish Cypriot quarter hysterical or wailing women clutched at me begging for reassurance or transport or protection until they could go. Major Sepici, deeply affected, moved among them, radiating calm and cajoling them into making orderly preparations for departure.

Walking towards the police station, we saw several armed Greek Cypriot youths dodging away out of sight. They elicited a volley of curses from my Greek officer.

The Greek Cypriot police sergeant claimed that there were no armed civilians in the village and that his men were fully in control, although he said that they were exhausted after 48 sleepless hours spent "preventing incidents or outside interference." He was delighted to hear that a full evacuation was planned and relieved to concur with my suggestion that, in view of the level of fear among the Turkish Cypriots, it might be as well that this was covered by the informal presence of a British military unit.

During the next two days the Turkish Cypriot quarter was, without further incident, wholly evacuated, apart from four aged villagers who said that they were too old to move and would stay whatever the consequences.

In my report on this evacuation I wrote that Peristerona had been extremely tense since Christmas, largely due to repeated acts of Greek Cypriot provocation, mainly by police irregulars and irresponsible elements from neighbouring villages. During the week immediately before the evacuation there had been numerous incidents of police auxiliaries firing their weapons inside the Turkish Cypriot quarter at night; there had been an escalation in the scale of nightly thefts from unoccupied Turkish Cypriot homes; armed Greek Cypriot civilians had been circulating openly and ostentatiously threatening the Turkish Cypriots; a grenade had been thrown into the Turkish Cypriot sector. As a final example of the situation, I recorded that a Greek Cypriot youth had regularly entered the Turkish Cypriot quarter and fired at dogs in the main street for target practice. The police had explained to me that this young man was the village idiot. Asked why, in that case, he was allowed on the streets with a gun, they said that it had not previously occurred to them that he was doing any real harm.

23. AREDHIOU. LATE JANUARY 1964

Across the hills from Eliophotes to the east was the small, and now totally isolated, Turkish Cypriot community in the mixed village of Aredhiou. Their earlier tribulations have already been described in chapter 6. After a series of abductions (reportedly followed by killings) had left them with hardly any young able-bodied men, there had been instances of intimidation from parties of armed Greek Cypriot civilians. Then, in the middle of the month, there had been a complete volte face by the Greek Cypriot majority: following drastic admonition from Nicosia, they had begun to act with conciliatory support for their Turkish Cypriot neighbours.

Regrettably, the change had come too late. Frequent visits by my patrol delayed evacuation and ensured that adequate relief supplies were delivered, but the breakdown of confidence was beyond repair.

My report of 22 January said that, although there was no new external pressure on the Turkish Cypriots, it was probable that they would already have evacuated if transport had been available; that to keep them in the village would require an inordinate level of outside support; and that it would seem wise to seek general agreement for their relocation.

Initially there were objections to this line from Lieutenant Constantinides. He knew very well the degree to which there had been Greek Cypriot pressure against the Turkish Cypriots in this area and how hard the patrol was working to try to prevent any major movement of population, but he believed it was outside our remit to recommend an evacuation. Eventually he accepted that the core of our mission was to contribute to the general avoidance of conflict and the restoration of a properly functioning bi-communal state, and that there were instances where that process would be made impossible if serious trouble-spots were not eliminated. The proposal was then forwarded, under the joint signatures of myself, Major Sepici and Lieutenant Constantinides, to JFHQ and to the offices of President Makarios and Vice-President Kutchuk.

The Turkish Cypriots were eventually evacuated on 28 January. Although we had obtained support for this move from the Greek Cypriot authorities, and the move went off without incident, the Greek Cypriots in Aredhiou (whose actions at the end of December had destroyed their neighbours' willingness to stay) afterwards complained bitterly that the Turkish Cypriots had gone only because of pressure from TMT. They claimed that TMT had achieved this by forcing the son of the *mukhtar* to support an evacuation. It transpired that in fact the *mukhtar*'s son had gone to Nicosia on 26 January to arrange for transport to collect the remaining Turkish Cypriots. On his return to the village the Greek Cypriots learned of what was planned, obtained from him a 'confession' of TMT responsibility as the price for allowing the Turkish

Cypriots to leave and then confiscated most of the Turkish Cypriot flocks as a forced settlement of those debts that they claimed were still outstanding.

The Turkish Cypriots, now almost destitute, were moved in part to Pileri and in part to Chumlekji. In the latter case Greek Cypriot pressure soon caused them to move on to Mora.

During one of my helicopter sorties I was told to divert to Pyrga to assess why its Turkish Cypriot minority there had evacuated. From the helicopter I noticed armed men in a slit trench to the east of the village, which was a contravention of current cease-fire terms. Landing close beside the trench we were able to see that it was occupied by a number of extremely elderly gentlemen wearing oversized tin hats. They were helping each other out with difficulty when the police sergeant from Pyrga arrived. He explained to me that these were his special auxiliaries: they had been enrolled by him to ensure that abandoned Turkish Cypriot property was not attacked. The patrol was then escorted to Pyrga and given an exceptional welcome. Major Sepici afterwards told me he was convinced there was genuine Greek Cypriot regret at the going of their co-villagers.

In another special assignment during this period I was instructed to act as observer to the routine rotation of units of ELDYK, which was now technically under the command of General Young.

I had been told that the convoy of several hundred troops must proceed direct from Famagusta docks to the contingent's barracks outside Nicosia. The convoy's police escort, on the other hand, was determined that the occasion should be turned into a triumphal procession, with detours through every village along the route. I vetoed the plan for diversions, elicited a promise from the police that they would follow me without fail and then led the way in my Land Rover.

At Angastina the convoy was faced with a large welcoming committee and a crowd with suitably inscribed banners. The Greek Cypriot *mukhtar* of Angastina, who was well known to me, shouted out that he had a speech to make and flourished a thick wad of notes at me. I said that the convoy could slow down but not stop and the *mukhtar* then hurried along beside the road declaiming dramatically as he went, each bus gaining the benefit of one or two sentences.

Soon afterwards a car-load of armed young civilians edged its way past my vehicle and disappeared ahead. The next village was the mainly communist Exometokhi, where there was no welcome at all. A little further on at Trakhoni I saw that another crowd was gathered. As we approached, several armed men ran towards us shouting and firing and two bullets hit my Land Rover, one on the stanchion just behind my ear.

After waving the convoy forwards towards Nicosia, I stopped long enough for a word with the local police. They were anxious to apologise and assured me that the shooting had not been aimed at me but intended as a simple *feu de joie* in honour of the Greek contingent.

24.   TILLYRIA.
JANUARY TO EARLY FEBRUARY 1964

Nicosia Zone extended in the northwest as far as Pomos Point. Eastward of this along the coast as far as Petra tou Limniti and into the hinterland behind is Tillyria, an area of steep mountain foothills with a scatter of Greek Cypriot and Turkish Cypriot villages reputed to have a disregard for the law and an addiction to local feuding. My patrol area ran inland to the mountain villages of Vroisha and Limnitis and eastward into the slopes behind Lefka at Skouriotissa and Apliki and Mavrovouni.

Most of these villages were poor, with a heavy dependence for jobs on the big CMC mining enterprises. During January there were no major incidents, but frequent reports of pending trouble and wild fluctuations of tension.

The Greek Cypriots correctly believed that this stretch of coastline was being used by TMT to smuggle in from Turkey such weaponry and explosives as could not be delivered through the Turkish contingent. In consequence, the Freedom of Movement agreement was largely disregarded. The Turkish Cypriots, isolated in their villages or subjected to rigorous searches if they tried to travel, felt increasingly abandoned and aggrieved. Major Greenwood reported that the Turkish Cypriots of Kokkina and the Greek Cypriots of Pano Pyrgos and Kato Pyrgos were truculent and spoiling for a fight. At the same time friction in the Lefka-Xeros area was spilling westwards into Tillyria. Villages erected defences against each other, dismantled them when local agreements were made, then quickly re-erected them as the agreements collapsed.

Major Greenwood's patrol, handling this area throughout January, found that frequent visits were needed to curb the aggressive inclinations of regional Greek Cypriot paramilitary leaders and to prevent minor irritations from escalating into major violence.

At the beginning of February, the general mood among militant Greek Cypriots was of bitterness and anger. On 3 February there were reports of serious incidents in Paphos Region, with inter-village shooting leading to the seizure of hostages in Ktima and Khrysokhou. Trouble then spread through Tillyria along the northwest coast and there were scattered outbreaks of shooting around Lefka. On the 4th Turkish Cypriot hostages were seized on the roads through Kato Pyrgos and the Turkish Cypriots retaliated by capturing five busloads of Greek Cypriot schoolchildren as they were passing through Ghaziveran. That evening the whole Lefka area was extremely tense, with an expectation that a serious clash was imminent.

Meanwhile, in Nicosia, on 4 February tension was ratcheted up after the seizure by the Turkish Cypriots of four Greek Cypriot policemen in the

Chappas Building, an incident whose misrepresentation in the Greek press led to a sharp increase in anti-British feeling. On 5 February a bomb attack on the US embassy triggered an immediate partial evacuation of American citizens from Cyprus, amid a general foreign supposition that the island was on the edge of widespread inter-communal fighting. There were reports during the day that Greek Cypriot police were again taking hostages on the roads in Nicosia Zone.

5 February saw the police and paramilitaries of both communities stood to throughout the Tillyria region. That night there were scattered exchanges of fire across the valleys which separate Turkish Cypriot mountain villages from the Greek Cypriot ones of Pakhy Ammos, Mospilem, Piyenia and Pano Pyrgos.

5 February 1964. AKEL-backed demonstration, in Nicosia, opposing British proposals for a NATO peacekeeping force. The banner in the foreground reads: "Hands off Cyprus".

25. REVIEW OF DECEMBER/JANUARY

At the beginning of January, when General Young ordered the establishment of a field mediating initiative as a key adjunct to peacekeeping operations, Paul Greenwood and I were given responsibility for Nicosia Zone. Before long the demands placed on the tripartite patrol organisation were so great that Greenwood had to move into the role of general administrator, leaving me responsible for all the field-work in the area.

As designated on British army maps, which dated from the 1950s, Nicosia Zone covered about forty per cent of the island. It included the entire area which TMT leaders were suggesting to me was their target for a self-administering Turkish Cypriot region. Their aim at that time was for about thirty per cent of the island. By the end of January every Turkish Cypriot school and office that I entered was displaying a map showing this area shaded in red.

My patrol therefore found itself as the sole agency seeking at ground level to stem and reverse the process of ethnic separation in northern areas of Cyprus. Simultaneously, we were supervising a limited movement of Turkish Cypriot village populations, promoting a process of inter-communal re-engagement and seeking to aid the re-establishment of a situation of law and order and of central political control. It was for the leaders of the two communities to work out what form of partnership would be appropriate in light of the shortcomings of the 1960 constitution: our task, as we saw it, was to help to construct an atmosphere and framework in which that could be done peaceably by elected leaders rather than through force of arms by shadowy figures of violence.

We had quickly become aware that TMT (and the Turkish army which backed it) was being hugely helped towards its separatist aims by the conduct of some elements of the Greek Cypriot police and by paramilitary extremists, but it took time to convince Makarios and his key ministers of this fact. In the meantime, the cancer of extremism was rotting the underpinnings of the state. At the same time, international opinion, previously for the most part sympathetic to the Greek Cypriots' contention that they had been forced to accept an unjust constitution, which left them subject to the whim of an eighteen percent minority controlled by separatist extremists, had in thirty days swung to a view of the Greek Cypriots as violent oppressors of that same minority. This change appears to have resulted largely from British comment and briefings. Greek Cypriots had failed to realise how significant was this shift in foreign attitudes.

In 1958 there had been a sea-change in the texture of inter-communal relations in Cyprus. British use of Turkish Cypriot police units to counter the EOKA-led Greek Cypriot struggle for *enosis*, British encouragement of a

Turkish involvement in Cypriot affairs, as a counterweight to Greece's international campaign for Cypriot self-determination, and Britain's apparent willingness to accept Turkish demands for separate communal administration in the municipalities, set the stage for an outbreak of serious inter-communal violence, which some Turkish Cypriot leaders described as the first push towards partition. The full force of British counter-insurgency strength was directed against the Greek Cypriot EOKA: TMT, the parallel secret Turkish Cypriot organisation, which was not even proscribed by the colonial authorities until the troubles were almost at an end, was allowed to build up its fighting strength without any serious encumbrance and initially viewed by the British army as an ally.* London's response to the violence was the Macmillan Plan, described by The Times as a proposal for "administrative partition".[1]

The burden of human losses in 1958 fell disproportionately on the Greek Cypriots. Among activist elements of both communities, a sub-stratum of antagonism and distrust was established which the constitutional settlement of 1960 wholly failed to eradicate. Within two years of Cypriot independence, paramilitary forces within both communities were preparing for a renewal of the 1958 struggle. Many of those engaged felt that they had scores to settle.

During December 1963 and January 1964 the fundamental character of Cyprus underwent a further radical change. Before then, except for the violence of 1958, the island had essentially been a place where Greek-speaking and Turkish-speaking Cypriots lived intermixed but separate lives in considerable harmony. They had not greatly trusted each other, seldom intermarried and sporadically been at political odds over the constitutional future of their shared homeland. The great majority had always seen themselves first as Greeks or Turks, rather than as Cypriots, and within each community there was a strong and destructive linkage to the most nationalistic elements in what they saw as their mother countries. But they had fundamentally felt and acted as an integrated citizenry: whereas now it was only in isolated pockets that that sense of oneness was still shakily preserved.

The events of Christmas 1963 had thrown Cyprus into profound trauma, with the agenda temporarily seized by communal extremists. Now the unitary state in its earlier form could be saved only through the defeat of extremism and violence, allied to a real mutual commitment to the process of communal re-engagement. That process required a timescale that was not available. Instead a limited ethnic separation became entrenched during January 1964, planned for and urged by Turkey and TMT as a progression from separation in the municipalities, but fundamentally made possible by the actions of Greek Cypriot nationalist extremists and police units, by the absence of individual security and by a British failure, or disinclination, to counter the onset of division. The number of mixed villages fell by two-thirds. Where inter-communal co-operation continued, it was strained and insecure. The

---

* Turkish army records show that the aim was for an effective, well-armed force of 10.000 men.

old, albeit sometimes uncomfortable, intermixing in the rural areas stuttered towards an end with its chances of restoration largely dependent on a radical intervention by outside powers or on the efforts of the tripartite mediating initiative.

The Greek Cypriots claimed that in virtually every case when the Turkish Cypriots evacuated a village they did so on orders, or under pressure, from the Turkish Cypriot leadership, either TMT or political. The Turkish Cypriots claimed that their communities were evacuating solely because the people feared for their lives or because the Greek Cypriots had so isolated those communities, by hampering their freedom of movement and communication, that normal existence was no longer possible. The Greek Cypriots counter-charged that TMT was pursuing a policy aimed at the maintenance of fear within Turkish Cypriot communities in mixed areas, in order to further the process of ghetto-isation.

These contentions, each containing some partial truth, were duly amplified for propaganda purposes.

Nothing during British colonial rule had encouraged the growth of a common Cypriot identity. Whenever Britain believed that its own objectives would thereby be advanced it had resorted to its traditional tactic of 'divide and rule': this had been particularly damaging to inter-communal cohesion in the use of Turkish Cypriot police units as British surrogates in response to the EOKA insurgency. And British encouragement, or tolerance, of Ankara's interest in the island, aimed to offset Athens' support for *enosis* or independence, had fatally compromised the opportunity for peaceful and equitable change.

In 1963 there was no monolithic view in London as to the island's future. Before taking up an appointment as Intelligence Adviser to C-in-C Mediterranean early that year, I had received very contradictory briefings from desk officers at the Foreign Office, which had responsibility for Greece and Turkey and the CRO, which was responsible for Cyprus. The former advanced to me the view that Cyprus was a potential destabiliser of western regional interests and that it would be in NATO's interests to see Cyprus under the control of a Greek-Turkish condominium: the latter were supportive of an independent unitary state in which there would be a gradual revision of the constitution and an eventual opportunity for *enosis*. This dichotomy was underlined when evidence began to emerge that in late 1963 Sir Arthur Clark, the British High Commissioner in Nicosia and acting for the CRO, had encouraged Makarios to make his proposals for a revision of the constitution and had attempted to broker this issue between the leaders of the two communities, and that his actions had afterwards been vehemently disowned by the Foreign Office.[2]

The sense of ethnic difference in Cyprus was preserved and encouraged in the schools, where children were taught to identify with the history and struggles of Greece or Turkey rather than to see themselves as part of a unitary Cypriot society, and by the Greek Orthodox Church, which saw itself as the inheritor of a heroic role in the creation of a greater Hellenic nation. Greek Cypriots looked on the incorporation of Crete[3] with Greece as a template for their own future: whereas Turkish Cypriots saw the history of Crete's incorporation into Greece as a warning of their own possible fate.

In the 1955-59 period, three strands of violence had permeated Cyprus. EOKA had fought determinedly against the British army; at the same time there had been occasional violence between the two communities, peaking in 1958; also at the same time there was right-wing violence in both communities against the left, reflecting NATO-encouraged Cold War processes in Greece and Turkey.

Circumscribed independence in 1960, fathered by the 1959 Zurich agreement, had ended Britain's direct colonial rule over Nicosia. Two outside states, Greece and Turkey, had formulated for Cyprus the blueprint for a complex future in which their own interests and those of Britain would limit the ability of the island to develop along genuinely independent, democratic lines.

It suited London to maintain that the 1960 constitution was the best achievable under the circumstances. Supposedly, given an absence of outside interference and a general surplus of goodwill, it might have worked until such time as needed adjustments were mutually agreed: but outside pressures were never absent and such local goodwill as did exist was heavily outweighed by a dynamic view among Greek and Greek Cypriot activists that 1960 was only a pause on the road to *enosis* and among Turkish and Turkish Cypriot activists that they must continue to seek for ethnic separation.

The peacemaking process that was injected into Cyprus at the beginning of 1964 found a crucible in which were mixed a multiplicity of ingredients: legacies of the Ottoman empire, of Hellenism, of the Greek struggle for independence, of British imperialism, of unresolved local vendettas; and more currently, reflections of the Cold War, of the replacement of Britain as the dominant regional power, of extreme rightism in Greece and Turkey, of the lack at the time of adequate political control over UK/US intelligence agencies, of the shortcomings of the 1960 constitution, of inter-ministry rivalries in London, of conflicts of personality and disinformation and misconception. The events of 1963/4 were a reflection of all the strands of violence that Cyprus had suffered before 1960. The nation, already conditioned to these elements of strife, to communal insecurities and to an undue parastatal influence on the exercise of power, had not yet matured to a development of those statal mechanisms that are needed to counter extremism.

At the start of the century there were more than 300 mixed villages in Cyprus. That figure was reduced sharply in the 1920s and again during the upheavals of 1958, leaving a total of about 130. Now, in this short period, that figure had suddenly fallen to 65, then to 40. In no area did it seem at this moment that communal intermixing could survive without artificial props.

From January to March 1964 I spent every one of my days in deep and protracted discussion with the villagers of Cyprus and with its politicians and paramilitary leaders. I did so in the company of Greek and Turkish officers who had a sense of intense personal involvement in the events that were unfolding and whose presence engendered a trust enjoyed by no other outsider. The tripartite patrols became accepted as the sole conduit through which shocked and fearful village communities could grope for expression.

Almost everyone talked to me, some seeking affirmation that their actions had a place in an important moment of Greek or Turkish history. TMT leaders made no secret of their efforts to separate the communities. 'The Organisation' leaders made no secret of their belief in *enosis* and of their determination to counter TMT objectives. Greek Cypriot policemen and paramilitaries felt proud of their role as fighters against Turkish Cypriot separatism and against 'TMT terrorists'. Turkish Cypriot villagers, during this short period of anarchy, saw that their rights had no protection from the law, that they could not travel without threat of search and seizure, that members of their community were disappearing and sometimes summarily killed without any judicial repercussion; they were bombarded with propaganda which said that they were targets for genocidal attack: they became genuinely and deeply frightened. Greek Cypriot villagers equally were bombarded with a representation of the Turkish Cypriots as a dangerous and militant spearhead of Ankara's attempts to thwart the will of the Greek Cypriot majority.

It was clear to me that leaders of both communities in Nicosia were being provided by their intelligence services with a grossly distorted picture of events, and had failed to see that those intelligence services, which to a considerable degree were covertly controlled from Athens or Ankara, had themselves become the effective dictators of communal policy. Moderates, fed with the picture of Turkish Cypriot revolt as a possible precursor to Turkish invasion or of violent Greek Cypriot oppression, had no way of knowing what forces were actually contributing to the destruction of the Cypriot state. Later I was to be told that the reports provided by my patrol in those critical days came to be regarded by both President Makarios and Vice-President Kutchuk as their only reliable evaluation of what was then happening in the rural areas of Cyprus.

Officers in the tripartite units recognised that there was no single responsibility for the village evacuations that occurred in 1963/4. TMT pursued an overall concept of the establishment of a Turkish Cypriot-controlled area in the north of Cyprus, as was to be forcibly imposed in 1974. But Turkish Cypriots individually were deeply opposed to the abandonment of their homes, and the plan for ethnic separation depended on a provision by the Greek Cypriots of sufficient harassment for Turkish Cypriot villagers to be persuaded to go, or of sufficient cause for Turkey to invade.

TMT was founded on an assumption that through it Ankara would be enabled to exercise an effective control on the future of the island. TMT envisaged a first phase of concentration by the Turkish Cypriots into a small number of well-defined enclaves, and villagers were told that this would be helpful to the Turkish air force when it mounted attacks against the Greek Cypriots, which TMT claimed would happen before the end of 1964. But even a limited process of population movement by the Turkish Cypriots depended on such actions by the Greek Cypriots as would allow TMT to persuade Turkish Cypriot villagers to go or make them feel too insecure to stay. Actions by Greek Cypriot police specials and paramilitaries, in response to TMT provocations or in an effort to dismantle or neutralise TMT, provided, over the course of a few weeks, much of the justification for fear that TMT sought. On occasions the disproportionality in Greek Cypriot actions was so gross that it was hard not to suppose that some element in the Greek Cypriot community was deliberately seeking to further the process of communal separation.

Greek Cypriot paramilitary planning was explained to me as having two targets: first to isolate TMT or destroy its effective strength; and, second, to create such a deterrent as would prevent a successful invasion from Turkey. TMT was seen as an illegal ethnic paramilitary force whose targets were the blocking of *enosis* and the dissolution of the unitary state. To counter those aims the Greek Cypriots formed their own illegal paramilitary force: originally this was in small 'private' armed militias, which later would be combined into the 'Secret Army'[4]; this, in turn, would become the National Guard. This process fell under a Greek Cypriot command structure, 'The Organisation', which had overall responsibility for the achievement of *enosis* and for the countering of any Turkish Cypriot opposition to constitutional change. With the departure, at the outbreak of inter-communal violence at Christmas 1963, of Turkish Cypriot police officers, the now all-Greek Cypriot force was directed by its commanders to disregard bi-communal policing responsibilities and to act unitarily in an armed anti-TMT role.

The fighting which erupted at Christmas was, with a few minor exceptions, confined to the cities. The villages were unprepared: they reacted as though general civil war was imminent, erected barricades and regarded each other with deep suspicion. In a few instances where prejudices had festered and where leadership was in the hands of nationalistic extremists, the pressure against Turkish Cypriot village communities spilled over into violence, most notably in Ayios Vasilios: elsewhere there were acts of hostage-taking and isolated killings of individuals, but nowhere in the countryside was there a general attack by one community on the other.

What followed was a sustained and unsuccessful attempt by the police, sometimes aided or paralleled by local armed bands, to eliminate TMT strength from the rural areas. At the start of this process the control of regular police forces, which previously had carried the trust of most Turkish Cypriots, was hijacked by ex-EOKA specials, enrolled within a rapid expansion of Greek Cypriot paramilitary strength. Actions against TMT involved extra-legal measures, in violation of agreements that had been signed in Nicosia, and included searches for arms, the taking of hostages and summary killings. This process, of which even some of the leaders of 'The Organisation' were unaware, continued after the cease-fire agreed on 25 December and was a major contributor to the entrenchment of communal division.

On 28 December, with Duncan Sandys arrival in Nicosia and agreement on the London Conference due to be signed, Polycarpos Georgadjis, the Minister of the Interior, executive leader of 'The Organisation' and co-author of the 'Akritas Plan', ordered aggressive action against TMT to be suspended, but some attempts to seize TMT suspects, and occasional killings, continued, apparently on local initiative. Thereafter, the Greek Cypriots endeavoured to re-establish a benign authority in rural areas, working through 'The

Organisation' in cases where the police had become particularly discredited in the eyes of the Turkish Cypriots.

From the second week of January there was a strong initiative on the part of Makarios and his moderate ministers to seek for reconciliation with the Turkish Cypriots and to discourage further evacuations. But by then the residue of trust between the communities had evaporated, to a degree not understood in Nicosia. In any event, extremist elements among the police and local paramilitary gangs continued sporadically to engage in violence, intimidation, hostage-taking and murder, thereby sabotaging the chances for re-engagement. In this period the 'Secret Army'* was heavily engaged in anti-invasion preparations and training. I was told by one of its leaders that he would be 'strategically happy' to see the Turkish Cypriots abandon any villages which lay astride key roads.

Probably the only evacuations in this period in Nicosia Zone that were entirely spontaneous, in direct response to imposed violence, were those at Christmas from the villages of Mathiati, Skylloura and Ayios Vasilios, and from Omorphita and other suburbs of Nicosia. All these particular refugees had stories to tell which, when exploited by the Turkish Cypriot media, were sufficient to give underlying excuse for other evacuations that followed.

In some later cases the Turkish Cypriots evacuated because of Greek Cypriot harassment in instances where TMT would have preferred that they stay and in others Turkish Cypriot villagers insisted on staying despite TMT urging that they should leave. In some cases there was agreement between Turkish Cypriots, Greek Cypriots and the tripartite patrols that an evacuation would be beneficial for inter-communal relations in a particular area. Only in a few instances, Palekythro, Pyroi, Nisou and Eliophotes among them, did villagers tell me that they had abandoned primarily because of a central TMT directive. More often, including the cases of Dhiorios, Peristerona, Ayia Marina, Lapithos and Potamia, evacuation came after the villagers, responding to real or imagined Greek Cypriot pressures, had pleaded with Nicosia to be authorised to go. Villages, from which 'The Organisation' was delighted to see the Turkish Cypriots gone, and to which they embargoed a return when reintegration was being planned, included Nisou, Pyroi, Aredhiou, Dhiorios and Peristerona.

The failure of the Turkish Cypriots in many cases to remove from the villages that they evacuated anything more than a minor proportion of their possessions was sometimes puzzling. Prompted by a desire not to be burdened with the responsibility of having to safeguard abandoned Turkish Cypriot property, most Greek Cypriot village leaders would not, so long as Turkish Cypriot debts had been settled, have put any difficulties in their way. In several cases I was asked to convey messages to departed Turkish Cypriots that they would be welcome to come and collect their belongings. That they seldom did so may often have been due to TMT assurances, or their own wishful thinking, that they would soon be returning home. Time and again I had to inform Turkish Cypriot families that their homes had been looted and

_____

* See notes 7/3 and 7/4

destroyed: to this the usual answer, reflective both of Turkish Cypriot stoicism and of the propaganda of those days, was 'Praise Allah that we escaped with our lives. It proves how right we were to go.' The real moment of evacuation was usually when families realised that there was nothing left for them to go back to in the village which had been their home.

In my report of 31 January I noted:

" . . . *The Turkish evacuation of mixed villages in north-central and western areas of Nicosia Zone continued, in general due to a real sense of fear and isolation among the villagers but spurred on by TMT direction when the tempo flagged.*"

26. PAUSE FOR REFLECTION.
EARLY FEBRUARY 1964

On 7th January, when my first tripartite patrol was mounted, I was only dimly aware of the issues involved. I had arrived in Nicosia as both philhellene and *philotourkos*, but with an assumption that Cyprus would in due course be united with Greece, as had the Ionian and Dodecanese islands in earlier times. My briefings in London had not changed this view, although they had made me more sympathetic to the strategic concerns of Turkey and aware of the priority that London gave to the maintenance of its special relationship with Ankara.

Four weeks later I was at the centre of a maelstrom. I had become uniquely immersed in the affairs of Cyprus, taught by twelve hours a day of intense and emotional converse in the coffee-houses of countless villages, followed by quiet dialogue with key political leaders. I had not seen the earthquake of events at Christmas, but I had lived through the after-shocks. I had become the confidant of great numbers of Cypriots, most of them insecure, many of them seriously traumatised. I could see matters now as a human tragedy in which the old, pervasive nationalisms of Greece and Turkey and the geopolitical ambitions of Britain and Turkey were playing deeply destructive roles. I was acutely aware that the cohesion of the state was being unnecessarily destroyed.

I had come to realise that the communal divide was far more complex than previously suggested to me. DNA profiling now suggests a greater hereditary linkage between Greek Cypriots and Turkish Cypriots than between Greek Cypriots and Greeks or Turkish Cypriots and Turks. During the Ottoman period there had been numerous conversions from the Christian to the Muslim faith. I was told that in some villages, such as Potamia, it was traditional for Turkish Cypriots to have a Greek Cypriot girl as their first love. Where intermarriage did occur it was normal for a son to take the religion of his father and a daughter to take that of her mother, and then to refer to themselves as Greek or Turkish according to the religion they had adopted. Thus a single family might contain both Greek Cypriots and Turkish Cypriots.

January had been a roller-coaster ride of progress and setbacks but with a general advance, as we created a secure channel for inter-communal dialogue.

General Young had warned me to expect anarchy in the countryside, but I was unprepared for the degree to which the normal functioning and controls of government had disappeared. No process of law-keeping existed in the rural areas. The police and gendarmerie had split into their Greek and Turkish components, both of which had then ceased to function as keepers of law and order: instead, by their own description, they had adopted the role of military units fighting on behalf of their own communities.

But fighting against what? No insurrection was discernable in the rural areas and there had been no general attack by one community against the other. There had been instances of deliberate provocation but many others were those of criminal violence inspired by misplaced nationalism, by old grudges or by misdirection. Under normal circumstances state police forces would have been the bulwark against this criminality: but those forces had abandoned the role of law-keeping. Instead, elements of the police now were frequently the instigators of illegality.

The setting of this tragedy was a conditioning to violence, arising from the anti-colonial struggle, from a history of ethnic nationalisms and from the inter-communal troubles of 1957/8. TMT and EOKA intimidated moderate elements within their own communities as well as contributing to inter-communal hostilities. People were already inured to violence; killing was explicable where there was a need for vengeance; the populace accepted that a large degree of power was wielded by secret groups; foreign intelligence agencies were linked with elements of the extreme right and were encouraging them to subvert the process of liberal democracy.

At the core of the problem lay opposed local beliefs, together with an external supposition in NATO that the Cold War or the projection of national interest justified a subversion of the democratic process in Cyprus. The Greek Cypriots felt that their overwhelming numerical majority gave them a democratic right to decide the future of Cyprus, including the option of union with Greece if they so wished. The Turkish Cypriots felt that, although comprising only eighteen per cent of the population, the 1960 constitution had given them an equality in matters of state and that their security was dependant on an ability to veto key governmental decisions of which they disapproved. Turkey believed that its national interests demanded an ability to exercise a covert control over developments in Cyprus. The intelligence services of America, Britain, Turkey and Greece all believed that a unitary, leftward-leaning independent Cyprus would be inimical to their interests.

The Turkish Cypriots were favoured by an externally constructed constitution. The Greek Cypriots saw this constitution as inequitable and needing amendment and considered that they were supported by democratic principle. Each community believed that the other would pursue its perceived objectives through force of arms, and each established illegal paramilitary organisations to counter this possibility or to seek to impose its own will. The situation thus created was acutely vulnerable to the sidelining of democratic process, to a hijacking by nationalistic extremists and to exploitation by foreign agencies.

January 1964 was a month in which I had to deal with the outcome of a variety of killings, each of which had serious political implications. And yet the number of violent deaths that month, in marked contrast to Turkish propaganda, was actually less than the monthly average for the previous year. I also had to report on innumerable acts of theft, looting, intimidation and other instances of illegality, all with an ethnic ingredient. None of this came to the public notice. At the end of January, Gendarmerie headquarters in Nicosia sent out messages to sub-stations congratulating them on the fact that reported crime for the month was at its lowest recorded level since independence. Similarly Kutchuk's office reported to me that "areas controlled by the Turkish Cypriots are now free of crime."

Nor had anything prepared me for the degree to which each community was misinformed about the other and about the reality of events. The populace in the rural areas received its information either through a rabidly propagandist media, through politicised networks or through a process of coffee-house gossip, and central leadership was not much better served. Even the top 'Organisation' leaders were being grossly misinformed by their subordinates and by their own intelligence service, which contributed in large measure to the failure of elected communal leaderships to establish a reasonable discipline. No voice of moderation, either from politicians or press, made itself heard. Elements in each community regarded as traitorous any gainsaying of the nationalistic line.

The average Greek Cypriot, unaware of the killing, hostage-taking and looting that had occurred and continually told by the press and by his leadership that his police forces were struggling to maintain the rule of law in the face of Turkish Cypriot provocation and revolt, was unable to understand the virulence of Turkish Cypriot complaint or why international opinion was now so condemnatory. World opinion, on the other hand, ignored the fact that governance in Cyprus was faced with perpetual threat of subversion by TMT, which acted as a projection of Turkish military strategy. Nor did it realise that Turkish Cypriot fears of domination by the Greek Cypriots were equalled by Greek Cypriot fears that Ankara was determined to establish an effective control over the island.

In general, the Greek Cypriots felt that they had been provoked by the Turkish Cypriots beyond any natural degree of endurance. In almost every case of violence reported to me from the rural areas during January, Turkish Cypriots were the victims and Greek Cypriots the aggressors. Nevertheless, attacks hardly ever reflected a general ethnic animosity: almost all were consistent with the settling of old scores or with an attempt, which the police perceived as legally justified, whether or not formally sanctioned, to eliminate the power of TMT. In a few isolated cases, Turkish Cypriots were subjected to local outbursts of violence, at a moment when normal constraints had collapsed: in no way that I had seen, however, were they ever the victims of genocidal or general attack.

I received numerous reports of involvement by Greek Cypriot policemen in hostage-taking and summary killings. No suggestion that this was happening was given by any Greek source either to the Greek Cypriot public or to their moderate leaders. I was once shown a digest of police reports delivered to Makarios, covering events of which I had personal knowledge, in which every incident had been either whitewashed or reversed so as to show the Turkish Cypriots as the instigators of violence. Similarly, Kutchuk showed me reports he had received from Turkish Cypriot villages for which I had responsibility that gave a wholly exaggerated or distorted picture of events, suggesting a massive persecution by the Greek Cypriots that had never in fact occurred. The realisation of this warping of the intelligence process led to my agreeing with Tassos Papadopoulos that I would in future submit copies of my patrol reports directly and privately to the President and the Vice-President, so that a process of transparency was established.

Some reports that reached me could be seen in retrospect only as part of a process of deliberate misinformation, designed for the effect they were expected to produce. Most puzzling in this respect was an exposition passed to me, and to the British High Commission, by the Minister of the Interior, Georgadjis, which if publicised could only have inflated inter-communal distrust and encouraged communal separation. This particular report was used by the British to denigrate Makarios and to suggest justification for the pursuit of partition, and it may have provided the central prompting for George Ball's denunciation of Makarios in February 1964.[1]

In the early days of January the tripartite patrols had occupied themselves largely with problems of relief requirements and missing persons, with the restoration of inter-communal contact at village level, with the mediation of local disputes, and with learning how influence could best be exercised. The learning process had to cover not only local history and problems and politics, but also key personalities at every level, secret organisations and power-structures, and the limits of tolerance of each side in the process of inter-communal adjustment that was underway.

Some benefits flowed inevitably from patrol activities, irrespective of their competence. Local tensions were lanced because the Turkish Cypriots felt able to express their complaints and fears. Relief supplies could be effectively allocated. Our ombudsman-like presence automatically placed constraints on members of the gendarmerie, who quickly came to recognise (sometimes as beneficial, sometimes with resentment) the fact that we could report on their performance directly to the President and Vice-President.

Some members of the British military were clearly irritated by the tripartite patrols, disliking our exemption from their own chain of command. In fact our independence allowed us to act effectively: it also enabled us to report dispassionately on the Greek Cypriot swing from euphoric approval of the British military presence, when it was felt that Turkish invasion was being prevented and anarchy eliminated, to intense hostility, when it was realised that the freezing of events was supportive of TMT targets and inhibiting Greek Cypriot freedom of action.

The British government had overestimated the level of goodwill built up since 1960. Traditional resentments generated during the colonial administration were now easily being re-ignited by an extremely hostile press, smothering the personal affection that many Cypriots held for Britain. Soldiers in the peacekeeping force failed to comprehend the bitterness felt by many Greek Cypriots at the sight of British troops back on Cypriot soil. Reacting to the slights that they received, being witnesses to acts of injustice and remembering past alliances with the Turkish Cypriots against EOKA, an increasing sympathy for the Turkish Cypriots grew within many British units. The expression of this, which sometimes involved the provision of active assistance to Turkish Cypriot fighters, led to a heightened Greek Cypriot antagonism.

The peacekeeping force and the tripartite patrols should have had similar aims: the isolating of extremism, elimination of violence, promotion of communal reconciliation and re-engagement, restitution of a state of legality and the delivery to political leaderships of a protected forum within which they could negotiate their future. But the more did Green Lines become entrenched the more did tripartite mediators and the peacekeeping force find themselves on divergent courses. The patrols had been directed by General Young to create a situation in which the Green Line could be dismantled: peacekeeping troops increasingly saw their role as the maintenance of Green Lines.

That our opposition to a general communal separation did not generate hostility from Kutchuk or TMT was probably explained by a reality that the Greek Cypriots at that moment failed to recognise, to their profound later cost: that Turkish Cypriot leaders at this point would probably have been prepared to settle for something much less than partition (whatever their long-term partitional aims may have been). It was the denial to Turkish Cypriots of their normal human rights during this phase, in part engineered by TMT, that laid the groundwork for an eventual partition. Safety at that point was the prime target for most Turkish Cypriots, not severance. When I talked with Turkish Cypriots, whether Kutchuk or an obscure villager, I always heard an impassioned plea for personal and communal security. It may have been at the heart of TMT ambitions, but *taksim* was seldom mentioned to me by Turkish Cypriot villagers except as a counter-cry to *enosis*.

Partition became a realisable target only when US and UK intelligence assessments decided that it would fit in with NATO interests and when the excesses of Greek Cypriot extremists allowed Ankara to insist there was no other way that security for the Turkish Cypriots could be achieved. In early 1964 TMT was generally co-operative with my patrol, not because its theoretical lines for partition did not exist, but because it was prepared at that point to settle for a limited relocation of the Turkish Cypriot population and for reformed political and policing arrangements.

The gospel preached by the tripartite patrols was that violence and ethnic isolation were counter-productive, that this was a small island in which the common good must eventually depend, in whatsoever political formula was decided, on mutual tolerance and trust. We did not offer solutions: we did seek to create a climate within which it would be possible for politicians of goodwill to work out compromises. Sadly those who were prepared to compromise, who included the President and Vice-President, found themselves the prisoners of more inflexible forces.

Our mission had a unique advantage because, as a team composed of Greek, Turkish and British representatives working at the behest of both Makarios and Kutchuk, we were ourselves a microcosm of the message that needed to be delivered. We carried the authority of Ankara and Athens and London as well as of Nicosia. We were favourably supported by the press of both communities. We had a simple and ethical target. We spoke to the villagers in their own language, were accessible, were acutely aware of the fear imposed by the collapse of legal authority, were sympathetic to the history and aspirations of both Greek Cypriots and Turkish Cypriots and of Greece and Turkey.

Any community feels secure to the degree that it has trust in the fair administration of an equitable process of law. It accorded with TMT strategy that that trust was lost to the Turkish Cypriots during December 1963. It could have been rebuilt and improved in the first months of 1964. That would have required the Greek Cypriot leadership to obtain international support for the elimination of armed extremism within a sustained effort to restore the rule of law and the observation of human rights. In the climate that existed, and without international help, there was little chance of that happening. Greek Cypriot ministers privately admitted that some of their own extremist elements were out of control. Sadly, the background of key Greek Cypriot leaders made them more inclined to react to events rather than to foresee and pre-empt them.

Some elements in the police and paramilitaries had (as some of them told me, on orders from Nicosia) disregarded the ceasefire agreement made between Makarios and Kutchuk on the night of 25 December and continued until the 28th to try to break down suspected TMT networks in the rural areas.[2] From the arrival of Duncan Sandys on the 28th, orders from 'The Organisation' leaders in Nicosia to the countryside were that further violence should be avoided. But in some areas this order was disregarded.

The leaders of 'The Organisation' also had controlling positions in the government. The assurance of Tassos Papadopoulos that they had instituted an active campaign for communal reconciliation was borne out by what I saw in the countryside. Events there testified to a genuine attempt by elements of the Greek Cypriot leadership to prevent the further destabilisation of mixed areas and to demonstrate to the world that the two communities could live successfully together, despite efforts of TMT to prove otherwise.

'The Organisation's' campaign of moderation gained impetus from the agreements of 6/7 January as to paramilitary disengagement and freedom of movement, and there was a short period when it seemed that, aided by the work of the peacekeeping force and mediating units, this might lead to a substantial communal re-engagement. The rate of abductions and killings fell away; a release of hostages was planned; some families began to return to their homes in Omorphita. Only in the Polis to Lefka area and for a while around Kyrenia was the tension unreduced.

But as the abandonment by the Turkish Cypriots of outlying villages continued, Greek Cypriot paramilitary leaders became alarmed that a *de facto* partition was being achieved by stealth. Failure to recognise the trauma suffered by the Turkish Cypriots, continuing acts of violence by irresponsible extremists and police intransigence combined to blight the good intentions of Makarios. Hopes briefly raised by the announcement of the London Conference were offset by renewed invasion alarms on 15 January, by the impact of the Ayios Vasilios exhumations and by the police attack on Goshi.

At this moment General Grivas issued his invitation to right-wingers to meet him in Athens, forcing Makarios to denounce him for political meddling. This opened new fissures between moderate and right-wing groupings.

On 24 January there was a further invasion scare and reports of skirmishes in the west. Incidents were provoked by impatient extremists in both communities. Barricades began to reappear, searches on the roads were resumed, travel stopped again.

Under the influence of these events, some leaders of 'The Organisation' began to doubt the priority given to the reconciliation process and argued for a policy of greater strength and determination: their aim was simultaneously to build up Greek Cypriot power and to reunite the Greek Cypriot community with a sense of common purpose. Recruiting and training for the Greek Cypriot 'Secret Army' were greatly accelerated and brought more into the open, with a consequent improvement in Greek Cypriot public morale. The main slogan for Greek Cypriots was changed from 'Reconciliation' to 'Unity and strength to meet the common enemy'.

Meanwhile TMT continued its efforts to separate the communities. Turkish Cypriots began to introduce the long-planned trappings of partition. In Turkish Cypriot schools maps showing in red the upper area of Cyprus, above what was later to be known as the 'Attila Line', were increasingly evident. The construction of village defences was resumed; a major redistribution of TMT personnel took place; weapons were moved secretly into those outlying areas which it was decided should be vigorously defended as a matter of policy.

For the Joint Patrols, January had been characterised in the rural areas by the need to deal with isolated and often mindless acts of violence by Greek Cypriot extremists. Frequently there had been involvement or complicity by the gendarmerie. These incidents were totally at odds with the Makarios policy of inter-communal re-engagement. They were deeply damaging for the Greek Cypriots and they provided TMT with a platform from which to intensify pressure for ethnic separation.

From Christmas to mid-January there was some symmetry to the contribution made by extremists, TMT for the Turkish Cypriots and ex-EOKA for the Greek Cypriots, to the process of communal division. TMT bludgeoned the Turkish Cypriot community with the idea that inter-linkage with the Greek Cypriots was traitorous. Greek Cypriot villagers, on the other hand, retreated from their traditional friendships for fear that they might be labelled as traitors by their own extremists.

Cyprus had been destabilised by the events of Christmas 1963. That this was not reversed in January, when the dangers of instability were apparent, was largely due to divergences within the Greek Cypriot leadership. Rather than brace the country against provocation, return the police to a single-minded defence of legality and general human rights and reinforce the consistent pursuit of policies that would have distanced the Turkish Cypriot rural population from the TMT, Greek Cypriot leaders saw the continuing course of events slide into the control of local extremism and foreign manipulation.

27. PRELUDE TO THE 'VILLAGE WARS'. FEBRUARY 1964

At the beginning of February the collapse of the London Conference was followed by reports of troop movements in Turkey. Athens then placed its forces on alert. A renewed sense of emergency became palpable in Nicosia.

Supposedly with the idea of discouraging troublemakers, the Greek Cypriot police now put on a show of strength in all the remaining mixed areas in Nicosia and Famagusta Zones, to the further detriment of inter-communal relations. Such was this new erosion of mutual trust that joint patrols ceased for the time being to convene joint meetings for fear that they might lead to added controversy.

The flare-up of fighting in western Cyprus, starting 3 February has already been described in chapter 24. Trouble had spread through the already tense Tillyria area and along the northwest coast. Reports from Lefka on the night of 4 February suggested that the Greek Cypriots would now attempt to impose their authority across the area and that more extensive conflict was imminent.

Tension had also been raised in and around Nicosia by the Turkish Cypriot capture of four Greek Cypriot police officers at the Chappas Building. Greek Cypriot police were reported to be taking hostages on various roads within Nicosia Zone in retaliation.

The Greek Cypriots were now veering towards a hard-line policy. Their earlier attempt at proactive bridge-building was replaced by a policy of laissez-faire coupled with forceful reaction to all Turkish Cypriot 'acts of insurrection'. TMT, on the other hand, now felt ready to step up the level of calculated provocation. The stage was therefore set for a new phase of conflict and of mediating response.

The fighting that was to erupt at Ayios Sozomenos was not the first since Christmas – Goshi, Timi, Khoulou and Tillyria had all had their firefight incidents – but it was the first time the concerted forces of the Greek Cypriots had pressed home an attack against an isolated Turkish Cypriot village community in an attempt to achieve a specific end by force of arms.

Ayios Sozomenos was a logical outcome of the TMT aim that co-existence must be proved to be impossible; of the Greek Cypriot decision that force must be met with force; and of the failure of British peacekeeping initiatives to achieve an effective removal of the causes of violence or to block paramilitary acts of force.

28. AYIOS SOZOMENOS. FEBRUARY 1964

Few aspects of Cypriot life demanded so much mediating attention as the island's antiquated water system. Water for agricultural use was usually delivered through open conduits controlled by a variety of sluices whose operation was the responsibility of a special village constable. Each landholder would be entitled to have the sluices on to his fields opened for a certain period each day. The water conduits ran haphazardly through Greek Cypriot and Turkish Cypriot property and were vulnerable to blockage or diversion.

Inevitably there were frequent disputes. In areas where there was hostility or a stand-off between the two communities, rows over water sometimes triggered a gunfight.

Domestic water supply to the villages depended on pumping stations that were sometimes remote and to which access was sometimes controlled by a different village or by the other community. The operation of these pumps required a daily visit from representatives of the village responsible.

The village of Pyroi lies ten miles south-west of Nicosia on the road to Larnaca. The supply of water to the village was controlled by a pumping station cross-country to the west, close to the Turkish Cypriot village of Ayios Sozomenos.

On 6 February a party of Greek Cypriot gendarmerie going from Pyroi to supervise the servicing of the pump was ambushed by concealed gunmen. Three policemen were killed. The attackers were seen to withdraw towards Ayios Sozomenos.

Its agreement with the government meant that the peacekeeping force should have been informed before any unilateral use of force was mounted in response. However, Greek Cypriot police headquarters and personnel were in a state of fury over the Chappas building incident, for which public opinion was demanding punitive action. 'The Organisation's' new policy was to respond vigorously to every attack or provocation, and tension in the Nicosia area was already high. What little Greek Cypriot patience there had been was at an end. Strong units of armed police backed by detachments from the Nicosia and Dhali contingents of the 'Secret Army' were immediately moved into the area of Ayios Sozomenos.

The Greek Cypriot police later claimed that an ultimatum was delivered. Villagers from Ayios Sozomenos said there was shouting through loudspeakers but that none of it was intelligible to them and that, in any event, those who had carried out the ambush had never stopped in the village.

The overwhelming feeling among Greek Cypriot militants was that retribution must be had and the Turkish Cypriots taught a lesson.

I was on a visit that day to the north-east of the island, travelling by Land Rover. By the time I heard what was happening, it was too late for me to reach Ayios Sozomenos by nightfall, by which time the fighting had ended. When I got back to JFHQ I was briefed by the commander of a Ferret (armoured car) unit which had been present throughout the engagement and by a contact in the Greek Cypriot police.

I was told that Ayios Sozomenos had failed to respond to a police demand for surrender of the ambushers, and had then been subjected to indiscriminate long-range Bren gun fire followed by an attack against the village as a whole. The Greek Cypriot police attempted to justify this action as a conventional policing operation aimed at the arrest of the perpetrators of the ambush.

Turkish Cypriot families fleeing, with livestock, from Ayios Sozomenos.

Each community accused the British of having acted against it. The Turkish Cypriots charged that Greek Cypriot attacks had been delivered under the cover of British armoured cars. The Greek Cypriots claimed that British troops had opened fire on them, although later it was discovered that no shots at all had been fired by the British. Five Turkish Cypriots and six Greek Cypriots had been killed and a combined total of eighteen wounded. Post mortem examination showed that most of the Greek Cypriot casualties had been caused by shots fired accidentally by members of their own force advancing behind them.

The Turkish Cypriot population was not informed by its media of the ambush and killings that had triggered the battle and was encouraged by its leaders to see this as an unprovoked attack. The failure of the British peacekeeping force to provide any protection to the villagers was noted by Greek Cypriot leaders and vociferously criticised by the Turkish Cypriots. The battle demonstrated that JFHQ lacked a mandate to impose its will and that proactive mediation was likely to be the only effective means of intervention. The Times noted that the British part in the affair was "that of an umpire with no power to enforce his decisions."*

I was never told the identity of those who ambushed the police Land Rover, but there was general agreement that they were not Ayios Sozomenos villagers. From Turkish Cypriot sources I was given three different explanations. One said that this was a vengeance attack carried out on local initiative by refugees from Pyroi who had been forced to abandon their homes. The second, most probable, suggested it was a specific act of provocation, instigated either by TMT or by the Turkish army. The third claimed that 'EOKA' was responsible, seeking to provide justification for a general attack on Ayios Sozomenos. The incident had a suspicious proximity to the visit to Cyprus of Mr Ball and his US fact-finding mission; what was indisputable was that it caused serious damage to the reconciliation process and gave ammunition to those who argued for ethnic separation.

There was a curious coincidence in that a gendarmerie Land Rover had been similarly ambushed in the same area on 22 December. At that point, the gendarmerie force in this region had not yet split and there were two Greek Cypriot and three Turkish Cypriot policemen in the vehicle, all of whom were injured in the attack.

I was in the area early on 7 February, concerned that fighting might spread to other villages. The commander of the Greek contingent had refused Captain Michos permission to accompany the patrol that day on the grounds that there was such unrest that his life might be endangered. This left Major Sepici and me at a distinct disadvantage in Greek Cypriot villages.

We first made a round of leaders in villages near the storm-centre of the trouble, seeking to establish what action was intended that day and to ask them to prevent any further precipitate attacks. Then we shifted to the villages on the fringe of the area, so that we could establish to what range the situation was dangerous and attempt to ring-fence the problem.

In Pyroi we found roadblocks up and a large gathering of heavily armed Greek Cypriots. One of the policemen killed the day before had been a native of this village: now tempers were inflamed and vengeance was being discussed.

To our surprise the gendarmerie was conciliatory. With its help we persuaded the crowd to disperse and we were promised that no further gatherings would be allowed and that a guard would be mounted on abandoned Turkish Cypriot property. JFHQ was requested by me to place a

---

* British Army records note the intercept of a signal from Gendarmerie Head Antoniou to the local police force commander: "Ignore the British. They will not shoot."

standing patrol in Pyroi and to report on any significant movement of Greek Cypriot forces on the Larnaca road.

At Goshi and Petrophani the Turkish Cypriots were standing to in strength, expecting an early attack. All the women and children in Petrophani had been moved to Louroujina as soon as news was received of the fighting at Ayios Sozomenos. Goshi had been fired at from the main road by a Greek Cypriot police patrol on the evening of the 6th, but had suffered no casualties.

Major Sepici spoke in both villages with remarkable effect. The mixture of fear and anger visibly ebbed. He did not minimise the dangers or suggest there would not be sacrifices and suffering ahead, but he said that the right answers would only come through dialogue and if extremism was conquered. He explained about the ambush that had led to the attack on Ayios Sozomenos and said that the circle of violence, of killings for vengeance, had to be stopped. The villagers listened to this in silence and afterwards were persuaded to agree that there must be no further provocation. Outlying posts were then dismantled and guns put away out of sight.

Leaving Goshi, the major and I agreed that further trouble was now unlikely on this key stretch of the Larnaca road unless it was deliberately provoked from Louroujina or by the Greek Cypriot police. We then visited Limbia and Nisou to ensure that tensions were lanced on the southern and western sides of the region. In the latter village we found the Greek Cypriots finalising plans to cut off the water supply to Louroujina: only with great reluctance were they persuaded by us to refrain from this or any other form of reprisal.

The Turkish Cypriot villages of Kochati and Margi were both in a state of great anxiety, with the streets empty and their men standing to in trenches and revetments around the village outskirts. We were told in Kochati that the first rumours of events at Ayios Sozomenos the previous day had been quickly followed by the sight of a strong force of Greek police, Cyprus army and armed civilians deploying to the south of the village, apparently intending to launch an attack. During the night there had been occasional shooting towards the village and that morning they had seen further troop movements in the surrounding hills. As had Petrophani and Goshi, both villages said that they were expecting soon to be told from Nicosia to evacuate and move to a safer area, which they were anxious to do.

Unaware of how ineffectual had been the peacekeeping presence at Ayios Sozomenos, they begged for the permanent stationing in the area of British troops. We said that we would at least arrange for regular surveillance and for frequent patrols to the area and I radioed JFHQ for this and for an urgent delivery of relief stores.

Leaving Major Sepici to continue the counselling, I set off alone cross-country towards Ayia Varvara, and eventually located a gendarmerie patrol. The sergeant in charge assured me that instructions for an attack had already been cancelled and that they were the only unit still in the area, having been told to maintain surveillance on Kochati.

Major Sepici and I then moved on to Dhali. The funeral was in progress of a Greek Cypriot youth who had been killed in the previous day's fighting. The occasion was being turned into a huge and turbulent demonstration of nationalist sentiment. Busloads of children had been brought in from all the surrounding villages and, led by their school-masters, they were efficiently whipping the crowds into a militant, anti-Turkish fury. At one point, when Major Sepici's Turkish uniform was recognised, a shout went up for him to be lynched.

Having established that, despite the intense grief and resentment, it was unlikely that an attack would be mounted from Dhali in the immediate future, we moved on to Potamia. Here too the mood was vengeful and ferocious. The general theme of an agitated discussion was that the ambushing of the gendarmerie Land Rover proved that Turkish Cypriots were still seeking to provoke confrontation and undeserving of common citizenship and friendship.

There were large numbers of armed police in the streets, mostly from other areas: by some of these we were greeted with sullen rudeness, in contrast to the hospitality of the villagers, who knew us well. A British patrol had already told us that only nineteen Turkish Cypriots remained in the village, reportedly of their own free will, the others having evacuated the previous day to Louroujina. We were quickly able to discover, from both Greeks Cypriots and Turkish Cypriots, that in fact most of the nineteen were being detained as hostages, against events in general and in particular against the settlement of local Turkish Cypriot debts.

After eliciting from the police and 'Secret Army' leaders in Potamia a promise that there would be no aggressive action that day, and having arranged that we would return the following morning, we moved on to Louroujina. This was the largest Turkish Cypriot town south of Nicosia and known as a centre of Turkish Cypriot militancy. Here too, not unexpectedly, there was a mood of intense anger.

Before being allowed to speak to the leaders, we were asked to view the bodies that had been brought in from Ayios Sozomenos and which were now laid out on the floor of the mosque. They had been left in the same twisted postures in which they had died, presenting a macabre picture for the press photographers who were busy among them. The body of one seventy-six year old man was riddled with holes, apparently from close-up automatic fire. A ten year old boy had been hit in the throat by a soft-lead (dum-dum) bullet, blowing the top of his head open like a tulip.

I was manhandled into a close examination of the corpses. When the same happened to Major Sepici, he fainted, momentarily overcome by emotion and stress.

The political and TMT leaders of Louroujina, when we met them, were surrounded by survivors from Ayios Sozomenos, all clamouring to have their stories heard. It was not the easiest of moments to preach moderation and restraint, but Major Sepici went to great lengths to impress on them that the initiation of any further act of violence would be seen both by Kutchuk and by Ankara as damaging to the Turkish cause.

The whole town, swollen by refugees to about four thousand, was seething with armed men. At the western road entrance, we found a large posse being formed up for a sortie against Dhali or Potamia. Eventually, Major Sepici persuaded them to call off the planned attack and to disperse: before they did so we had to face a violently abusive crowd which bitterly attacked me for the British failure to defend their villages against attack and Major Sepici for the failure of Turkey to intervene on their behalf.

The army officer in command of the raiding force insisted on speaking in English to me rather than in Turkish to Major Sepici. As we left, and in front of his men, he spat in Major Sepici's face and called him a traitor.[1]

Before returning to Nicosia at nightfall we visited Ayios Sozomenos, but there was nothing of interest to record there except the degree to which the empty houses were pitted with bullet holes. There were several dead donkeys in the streets, contributing a pervasive stench to the atmosphere of desolation.

A veteran American war reporter, Tom Damman, was with my patrol that day. As we drove back to Nicosia he told me he had accompanied the German invasion of Poland and been present at several other second world war battles and acts of atrocity, but that never in his career before had he been so frightened as he was by the intensity of anger that he saw that day in the villages around Ayios Sozomenos. His syndicated column in America and a lengthy article in The Times of 22 February 1964 commented on the degree to which that anger was brought under control and abated through the efforts of the patrol.

The next day, 8 February, we were in Louroujina by early morning. The town was very much calmer. We had a long, closed meeting with the local leaders, for whom Erol Huseyin, a young schoolmaster, acted as spokesman. They did not deny the ambushing of the gendarmerie Land Rover, but claimed it had not been done by people from either Ayios Sozomenos or Louroujina. They poured out to us their bitterness, but then gave us their personal promise that no aggressive action would be initiated from their side. Orders were given on the spot for all armed patrols to be pulled back inside the perimeter defence-line and we were assured that they would be kept there.

We arrived in Potamia to find the village on a war footing. A large 'Secret Army' contingent had been brought in and was establishing itself on the Louroujina road. An assembly of weapons greater than any we had seen in Cyprus before was on view; armed men were everywhere and there were signs that a highly organised military operation was being mounted.

By good fortune, the Greek Cypriot military commander turned out to be a personal friend from Tymbou, who was receptive to rational discussion. Eventually he agreed with us on the need to bring the local confrontation to a close: he then decided that the patrol should be honoured with a display of Cypriot hospitality. The excellent meal that followed lasted for the best part of four hours. During it orders were sent out for forward units to reduce to lookout strength, the carrying of arms in the streets was stopped. I received a firm guarantee that all out-of-area reinforcements would be withdrawn next day and that no attack or other aggressive action would be initiated from the Greek Cypriots. By the end of the meal it appeared that the worst of the Ayios Sozomenos crisis was behind us.

After the meal, sitting on an upstairs balcony sipping coffee, we watched an incident of mishandling by the British army of its relations with the Greek Cypriots. A regular JF unit entered the village, dismounted with guns threateningly at the ready, peremptorily informed the Greek Cypriot *mukhtar* that it was known that a number of Turkish Cypriots were being held against their will and demanded that they be released into British protection forthwith.

In fact I had already arranged, before lunch, for any of the remaining Turkish Cypriots who wished to go to be allowed to leave unmolested, with transportation help from the Greek Cypriots, and they were in the process of packing. The Greek *mukhtar*, incensed at the manner of the British approach, had to be persuaded by me not to withdraw his earlier concessions on the question of Turkish indebtedness. After some delay the last of the Turkish Cypriot villagers departed, with amicable farewells from the Greek Cypriots.

The second-in-command of the 'Secret Army' contingent had been greatly aggravated at being publicly reprimanded by the British officer for carrying a weapon. This was of no deep significance but it provided a graphic illustration of why Greek Cypriots felt that they were being treated with arrogance in their own country by a force, until recently regarded as their oppressor, which was there at their own invitation.

Evacuating Turkish Cypriots from Potamia. To the left an officer of the Cyprus army is being rebuked by a British officer for carrying a gun.

Two days later, on 10 February, I returned to the area after receiving reports that the Greek Cypriots were moving armoured vehicles down the Larnaca road. I had earlier learned that Greek Cypriot police headquarters was claiming to have information that ambushes were planned by the Turkish Cypriots at Goshi.

At Goshi I found the villagers still scrupulously conforming to previous agreements and in total ignorance of the charges that were being laid against them. My assumption that the claim of preparations for an ambush was groundless was quickly verified. It appeared that someone was trying to provoke, or manufacture an excuse for, another full-scale attack on a Turkish Cypriot village.

We warned the villagers to continue in watchful restraint and arranged with JFHQ for a British Ferret patrol to be placed temporarily at the approach to the village. Then I sought out the local 'Secret Army' commander and convinced him that the accusations against Goshi were untrue and that someone was trying to mislead the Greek Cypriot leadership into a wholly unjustified assault. He agreed to make a detailed investigation and later in the day told me that there would be no attack and that the armoured vehicles which had been sent to him were being returned. That ended for the time being the risk of major fighting between Louroujina and its Greek Cypriot neighbours. An atmosphere of comparative peace now spread back through the area.

That day it was the turn of Louroujina, now remarkably relaxed, to offer us lunch. Previously I had found TMT and military leaders there so extreme in the presentation of their separatist views that rational argument was impossible. Now there was a change in climate. I was able establish a linkage that was to prove valuable in the months to come and which enhanced the possibility of real solutions for Nicosia Zone.

Trust in such situations was only gradually developed. The Turkish Cypriots needed to be convinced that I wholly understood their sense of insecurity. TMT leaders needed assurance that I would give an objective hearing to their claims and aspirations.

On 12 February, less than a week after the fighting at Ayios Sozomenos, Major Greenwood reported that the whole area was quiet and calm.

This was another example of tensions rising and falling like a yo-yo. Neither Margi, Kochati or Goshi had evacuated and the Turkish Cypriot women and children had moved back to Petrophani. A gradual return of confidence manifested itself in the region through the rest of February, and there was no further sign of extremist pressure from either community against isolated settlements. Villagers ceased to occupy themselves with thoughts of imminent attack and returned to grumbling over their traditional complaints.

Nevertheless the Greek Cypriots at Ayia Varvara, whose water pump was close to Kochati, decided it would be prudent to end their daily trips to the pump-house and took to drawing their water instead from a long-disused well near the village. An offer by us of sterilising tablets was refused. "Prior to the installation of the pump we always drank this water," they said, "and that led us to produce a particularly healthy race."

29.   GENERAL.   MID-FEBRUARY 1964

The ambush near Ayios Sozomenos and the subsequent attack on the village were a grim milestone on the road to ethnic separation in Cyprus.

In isolation, it was possible for an outsider to see the events of Christmas as a momentary explosion of pent-up frustration, largely confined to Nicosia, in direct line from the violence of 1958. Nationalist extremism had derailed the process of democratic government, but with proper support from external peacekeeping and mediating units the situation could have been restored. Makarios and Kutchuk and moderate ministers had been groping for reconciliation and reengagement, albeit hesitantly.

On 23 December an act of Turkish Cypriot provocation, in blocking the Kyrenia road, had led to a disproportionate reaction by disparate groups of Greek Cypriot paramilitaries, followed by the descent of some areas into anarchy and the threat of Turkish invasion. The events of 6 February had some resonance to this. A deliberate act of provocation, in the well-planned ambushing of the gendarmerie patrol, was followed by a wholly disproportionate Greek Cypriot reaction, this time by organised statal forces. That in turn led to further threats of Turkish invasion.

The incident tallied with extremist propaganda being directed at both communities. The Greek Cypriots were able to say it proved that TMT would continue with violent acts of provocation until its power to do so was destroyed. The Turkish Cypriots could point at an indiscriminate attack on one of their villages as valid excuse for their sense of insecurity. For the moderates, intense damage had been done to their hopes of reconstituting a functional unitary state.

The incident was comparable in communal significance to the Bloody Sunday killing of Roman Catholic civilians in Ireland. The procedure agreed by Makarios with Duncan Sandys and General Young had been totally ignored. Fighting at Christmas had been mostly relevant to Nicosia and the cities: the fighting at Ayios Sozomenos had relevance to every Turkish Cypriot village and mixed area in the island.

When I afterwards discussed with Greek Cypriot ministers what had happened, it was brought home to me again how divorced they were from the reality of events on the ground. No-one had presented options to them or assessed the implications, either local or international, of ways by which the gathering impetus of ethnic separation was to be countered. No-one had explained to them the degree to which some units of their police forces were now heavily canted to the right, through an intake of ex-EOKA activists, and that these were destroying the underpinnings of a unitary state through an involvement in hostage-taking, in the tolerance of summary killings and now in the indiscriminate machine-gunning of a village for whose law-keeping they were responsible.

In a country with a longer-established history of democratic process, key leaders would have based their decision-taking on a variety of sources of information or advice, to each of which they would have ascribed a rating for reliability. Here there was no such availability of guidance. No think-tanks or advisory bodies existed. The press was sensation-seeking and jingoistic, with virtually nothing in it that reflected the reality of what was happening in the countryside. The old EOKA network was fixated on its commitment to *enosis*. 'The Organisation' and the new 'Secret Army' overlapped the other structures, but had not yet developed their own intelligence-processing operations. All formalised reporting came via the police forces to the Minister of the Interior, Polycarpos Georgadjis: what I had seen of this reporting was a self-serving farrago of misrepresentations. The absence of valid analysis left government and each of the communities wholly vulnerable to both miscalculation and manipulation by those opposed to inter-communal cohesion.

After his return from the London Conference, I had begun to develop a much closer liaison with Tassos Papadopoulos, who, since I first arrived in Cyprus, had continued to be commended to me as a pragmatist who was particularly trusted by the President, who provided a rare bridge between left and right-wing forces and who was regarded by key Turkish Cypriots as someone from whom, despite his EOKA background, they believed they would get a fair deal.

I had become convinced that Papadopoulos was willing to support the development of a genuine mediating process. He appeared to be a Cypriot nationalist, rather than a Greek ethnic nationalist. Though still at that time committed to the concept of *enosis* he voiced a real understanding of the insecurities and needs of the Turkish Cypriots. He was willing to discuss the realities of the situation objectively, without needless diversion into the emotional quick-sands of past history. He was clear in his view that British scheming, Greek meddling and the mistakes of Greek Cypriot leadership had equally contributed to the providing to Ankara of an opening to interfere in Cypriot affairs. He sought for Cyprus to have a genuine independence, from which to decide the course of its future.

My own need was clear. I had been given by General Young a remit to work for inter-communal reconciliation in the rural areas of Nicosia and Famagusta Zones. I already had links to the Turkish Cypriot leadership through Kutchuk and Sait Sepici. With the peacekeeping presence now tending to defend separational Green Lines, rather than promote reintegration, and with the Greek Cypriot police and gendarmerie pursuing a no longer realistic ambition to eradicate TMT solely by force of arms, steadily driving the two communities apart, my target would be realisable only if I could obtain genuine engagement from the Greek Cypriot leadership.

From his side, as a pivotal minister who recognised the dangers that an alienated Turkish Cypriot community would pose, Tassos Papadopoulos needed regular and accurate appraisals of events in the rural areas of Cyprus and he needed a conduit through which moderate openings towards the Turkish Cypriots could be pursued.

From the time that we got to know each other, Papadopoulos acted as my link with the Greek Cypriot leadership, seeking support or decisions from other ministers as needed. He acted as my sole channel to Makarios, even after I had got to know Tasos Panayides, the President's personal secretary. Only when Tassos Papadopoulos felt that direct discussion was needed, on a specialised subject that fell within the other's responsibility, would I meet with another minister. This arrangement worked extremely well for me and I invariably felt that I had received whatever support was available.

With Charalambos Hassapis, the overall police commander and a central figure in the problems to which I was exposed, I found no such route to a creative dialogue. He seemed an honourable man, but I never could persuade him to give an inch towards those concessions that were needed if the unitary state was to survive. Nor was he prepared to discuss the degree to which recently enrolled 'specials' were bringing his force into disrepute. He was a devoted opponent of TMT and yet contributed hugely to TMT aims through his inflexibility.

Flanked by Cyprus army commanders. Savvas Antoniou, Head of Gendarmerie, second left and Charalambos Hassapis, Commander of the police second right.

I was urged by Greek Cypriot ministers to be tolerant towards him and to understand the history of the 1950s. Those regular Greek Cypriot police officers who had then continued to work under the colonial administration had been viewed by some extremists as collaborators, which had led to acrimony and resentment. They now felt a need to prove their nationalist credentials. I accepted this, but still found it deeply frustrating to have him scupper conciliatory initiatives which the President had wished to see implemented. Once, when Hassapis countermanded an agreement made by me with the President's office for the return of Turkish Cypriot village buses, I was told that his action had made Makarios "incandescent with rage." Nevertheless, Makarios apparently was unwilling to have an open break with him. From February on I was occasionally told that the President accepted that police rigidity was a major impediment to communal re-engagement and that Hassapis would later be replaced by a more conciliatory figure.

Hassapis reported to Georgadjis, the Minister of the Interior, who was the least approachable figure in the Greek Cypriot leadership. With him I normally communicated through Tassos Papadopoulos.

I sometimes felt that my patrol was wrestling for the future of Nicosia Zone against a multitude of threats, identifying enemies and allies as we progressed. That there were no local repercussions to events at Ayios Sozomenos, other than a general strengthening of village defences, represented a victory for us. But the continuing widespread seizure of Turkish Cypriot hostages represented a failure, though at least those arrested by the uniformed police were now likely to be reasonably treated and eventually released.

The lack of effective mediation at a higher level in Nicosia meant that there was still no real freedom of movement. Coaxed by my patrol, Turkish Cypriot villagers would eventually make a cautious trip, then repeat it if they found that all was well, only to have another man seized. On at least three occasions when I spent several weeks helping a Turkish Cypriot village community to get its bus back that bus was stopped and a man from it seized on the very first journey. By mid-February the level of risk was too high for a continued urging of unescorted travel.

The risk no longer lay with the regular police forces: it was now with local 'vigilante' groups. These groups targeted those whom they suspected of membership of, or association with, TMT. Those seized were unlikely, in fact, to be TMT members, who seldom used the open roads. Those Turkish Cypriots who travelled openly were likely either to have no useful knowledge of TMT affairs (that could be yielded under interrogation) or to be those who believed that their acquaintance with a local 'EOKA strongman' would safeguard them against harm.

The Greek Cypriots cited the continued closure to them of the direct Nicosia-Kyrenia route as a rationale for what was happening on other roads to the Turkish Cypriots. The Greek Cypriots also claimed that the failure to restore freedom of passage on this route showed that the peacekeeping forces were biased against them.

I had only a sketchy awareness, from JFHQ briefings and the international press, of the global response to events in Cyprus. My Greek and Turkish officers told me that Athens and Ankara viewed the situation as acutely dangerous and were debating how anarchic elements in the two communities could be brought under control. I was reporting every day on the increasing virulence of anti-British and anti-NATO sentiment among the Greek Cypriots. From General Young and from discussions at JFHQ I learned of threats of intervention by the Turkish military, warnings from Moscow, increasing concern in Washington, and a decision by the US, following the breakdown of the London Conference, to play a more active role within a new UK/US strategy.

On 12 February I was asked at short notice by General Young to introduce a visiting American official to the mediating effort in Nicosia Zone. I was not told what his status was and when he was introduced to me as George Ball the name meant nothing to me. I took him on a lengthy helicopter tour of the north-east, showed him that the anarchy of Christmas had been almost wholly eliminated, demonstrated the general progress that had been made towards communal re-engagement and the way that joint village councils were operating effectively, explained how radically the performance of the gendarmerie had been improved.

I was able to show him widespread evidence of the fact that a unitary state could be made eminently workable. I described the steps that still needed to be taken. I talked at length about the advantages of a tripartite mediating approach and the opportunity this gave for sources of violence to be identified and isolated, giving realistic hope that a much stronger multi-ethnic society could be created within a bi-communal Cyprus, with genuine security for the Turkish Cypriots. I said that limited movements of population by mutual agreement had been beneficial in areas of particular tension and that in most areas a reintegration of the two rural communities would present no problems once a general political accommodation was reached. I suggested that an extension of the tripartite mediating process was needed, rather than an enlargement of the military peacekeeping effort, and that the lessons we had learned needed to be applied at the upper levels of inter-communal dialogue and co-operation.

When we returned to Nicosia Mr Ball complimented me on what had been achieved. He then said, sympathetically:

"But you've got it all wrong, son. Hasn't anyone told you that our target here is for partition?"

Regrettably I didn't take it seriously at the time. I thought that this was some misguided American politician talking nonsense. I felt relieved that the CRO, rather than the State Department, was responsible for western policy in Cyprus. Nobody had explained to me the key position that George Ball held, in tandem with Dean Acheson, in the formulation of new Washington policies for the island. Nor had I then any understanding of the implications of Washington seeking the leadership of UK/US initiatives for the area.

The visit of George Ball to Cyprus was closely preceded by the violence at Ayios Sozomenos on 6 February*, by the narrow avoidance of violence at Goshi on the 10th† and then on the 11th by acts of provocation that led to heavy exchanges of fire in Polis, Ktima and Limassol, to which the Greek Cypriot response was predictably aggressive. There was a new wave of seizures of suspected TMT members. Serious fighting erupted in Limassol on

---

* See pp. 147-149
† See p. 150

12 February. On the 13th, the day scheduled for talks between Ball and
Makarios, it was reported that a Turkish invasion was imminent: all Greek
Cypriots under arms were brought to a state of immediate alert and
instructions were issued for the heavy sandbagging of all police posts and
vantage points. It was hard, in retrospect, not to assume that these events, of
deliberate provocation followed by disproportionate response, were
orchestrated by opponents, local or foreign, of inter-communal unity.

February 1964. Following a call by President Makarios for 5000 men to join a voluntary
special constabulary force (later to be incorporated into a national guard), a large queue
forms at Nicosia Police HQ of Greek Cypriot volunteers wishing to register.

It was the general supposition at JFHQ, that Turkey had deliberately
raised the temperature in Cyprus to coincide with the Ball visit and to
demonstrate the line, previously advanced to him in London and Ankara, of
communal incompatibility on the island. It also appeared that some Greek
Cypriot element had connived, wittingly or unwittingly, to make the process
effective.

I noted in my comments at the time the oddity that major battles seemed
to reduce tension in the rural areas rather than increase it. Provocation or

provocative response would occur in a particular area; tension in that area and those surrounding it would rise, leading to further and more serious incidents; Nicosia and the press would involve themselves in the situation; major violence would occur, followed by news that a Turkish invasion was imminent; Greek Cypriot security forces would then be put on full alert and move off to anti-invasion positions, with a consequent increase in discipline. With the Greek Cypriots now under proper command and the Turkish Cypriots relaxed in the belief that help was close, incidents would cease. The invasion would then fail to materialise; Greek Cypriots under arms would return to their own areas; the normal cycle of incidents would gradually resume.

On 14 February it was announced that Major General Michael Carver was relieving General Young as head of British peacekeeping forces. A divisional headquarters staff was being flown to Cyprus to bolster the command structure.

At a JFHQ meeting the next day Peter Young gave an emotional farewell to his staff, clearly distressed at leaving a job which was unfinished and to which he had felt a profound emotional commitment.

The manner of General Carver's assumption of command presaged a new and harsher UK approach to Cypriot affairs. General Young was at one point moved to tears while speaking of his sympathy for the Cypriot people. Without waiting for him to finish his sentence Carver strode to the rostrum and said: "That's enough of that. I'll take over now."

This was a definitive changing of the guard. Carver was the man who later, according to Intelligence insiders, was pencilled in for the role of Cromwell by right-wing officers in the UK when they discussed the possible need for a *coup d'etat* against Harold Wilson, whom they supposed to be a Soviet 'asset'.[1] He was considered in the British forces hierarchy to be the most intelligent, tough and decisive military commander of the century. He also was reputed to be arrogant and intolerant of dissent or of any infringement of his authority. His appointment to Cyprus, in the wake of the Ball-Acheson Plan, paralleled that of Cyril Pickard, a CRO high-flyer,[2] who had taken over in January from Sir Arthur Clark as Acting High Commissioner.

General Young was later to be described to me in London as having been "too sympathetic to the Cypriots." However on the day of the hand-over the Ministry MOD took the unusual step of announcing that his removal should not be taken as implying any criticism of his performance.

Whitehall's failure to continue the backing of policies initiated by General Young was matched by its rejection of, and attempts to deny, the position that Sir Arthur Clark had taken on the need for constitutional revision.*

JFHQ now moved from its homely but rather cramped location at the Cornaro Hotel to Nicosia Airport. I established a reasonable relationship with the new Chief-of-Staff, Colonel John Archer, but the old close association that I had had with General Young was lost.

---

* See p. 17 and note 1/8

Probably Carver would have seen me whenever I asked, and third parties later told me that in talking to them he had been complimentary about my efforts. But I was intimidated by him and got the feeling that he had no real interest in or sympathy for the views either of the Cypriots or of General Young or myself.

General Young had always let it be felt that the tripartite patrols were acting as his antennae in the assessment of Cypriot affairs and as the peace-making spearhead of the support that he was trying to provide to Cyprus. General Carver, on the other hand, appeared to attach no great significance to ground-level mediation or to the influence of developments in the rural areas on matters of his own direct involvement. His approach seemed to imply that British troops were there solely as defenders of British interests, rather than as an aid to an independent Cypriot government. I found it hard within the forum of JFHQ staff meetings to counter this with arguments about Cypriot or ethical rights or about the emotional and human ingredients of the situation.

Since my naval uniform was hardly appropriate, I was now dressing comfortably in a parachute jacket, borrowed from 16 Para, a trendy pair of cord trousers and sand-boots, together with my usual Royal Navy cap. In this rig I was easily recognised by Cypriot villagers and by the press corps, but the new general's staff was apparently alarmed at the oddity of my outfit and at my independence of action: they discreetly made sure I appreciated that Carver was going to be running the show in future and that he did not take kindly to anything that he saw as contradicting or diminishing his own authority.

Fortunately there was no move to issue me with a revised mission-statement, probably because General Carver was unaware of Peter Young's original instruction to me. I therefore continued to work on the assumption that I was seconded into the service of the Cypriot state. I saw General Carver as the executive of a now more authoritarian British policy. Paul Greenwood, who had been particularly close to General Young, resigned from the TPO: thereafter I provided appropriate reports to Colonel Archer and in general left him to handle the linkage with JFHQ.

The gulf between the static imposition of military force, which was provided by the peace-keeping initiative and which was now clearly benefiting the process of ethnic separation, and a proactive tripartite peace-making effort, committed to inter-communal re-engagement, was to become progressively more evident. In parallel with this I had an increasing sense of estrangement from the thrust of formal British involvement in Cyprus. With the ending of my contact with General Young, who had launched me on this role, it was as though I had ceased to be part of a British approach to Cyprus and become instead absorbed into an internal Cypriot effort at conflict-resolution, looking out at Britain, as did the Cypriots, as a major element of the island's problems.

Apart from the incidents which preceded the George Ball visit, the mixed sectors of Nicosia and Famagusta Zones had demonstrated a general stability and calm during this first half of February. What little travelling there was by the Turkish Cypriots had led to the occasional seizure of one or two of their people* but this they now accepted stoically as part of the current pattern of life, encouraged by the fact that I could usually offer a reassurance that the disappeared were alive and well.

The destruction of abandoned houses at Neokhorio continued and some minor damage was done to those at Palekythro, but most other incidents were the product of traditional frictions over grazing or water-rights. There was a minor shooting incident between Voni and Epikho. Marathovouno and Trypimeni continued to complain to me that their fields were being trespassed on by sheep from Chatos, and the *mukhtar* of Chatos, a likeable miller who would come to meetings ghostlike with a heavy powdering of flour, continued to plead that he was unable to keep his shepherds under control. Turkish Cypriot villagers from Kornokipos continued regularly to lose goats or sheep when they grazed their flocks too close to the Greek Cypriot mountain post at Halefka. All of the joint committees which we had established in early January had been reactivated and were now working with reasonable success. December's shaking apart of former communal integration had been replaced by an atmosphere of wary co-operation, encouraged by the network of meetings that we convened and by a more relaxed posture in the local gendarmerie.

The *mukhtar* of Chatos, covered in flour, in the centre, and me with notepad next to him. Major Sait Sepici is seated on the left and Captain John Michos on the right.

---

* JF referred to all seizures as 'hostage taking'. The Greek Cypriot authorities referred to these seizures as legal arrests of Turkish Cypriots suspected of complicity with TMT.

30. VITSADHA. FEBRUARY 1964

While I was patrolling in the Chatos enclave on 18 February, a message reached me that there had been a bomb explosion in Vitsadha the previous night.

When we arrived in the village I was told by the Turkish Cypriots that the Greek Cypriots had been manufacturing bombs, one of which had exploded an hour before midnight. The Greek Cypriot villagers flatly contradicted this: they said that at 11 pm Turkish Cypriots had thrown a large bomb at the Greek Cypriot *mukhtar*'s house, without causing any casualties.

After Major Sepici and Captain Michos had cross-questioned the respective communities, it became apparent that in fact two Turkish Cypriot youths had thrown a petard, or large firework, in an effort to provoke a confrontation. A party of gendarmerie had carried out an investigation that morning, questioning both communities without apparent trouble, and had reached a similar conclusion.

A meeting of the village leaderships which we convened went off amicably enough, ending with declarations of mutual affection and promises of future restraint from both Greek Cypriots and Turkish Cypriots. Sepici and I both had doubts about the quality of the Turkish Cypriot *mukhtar*, who had been only recently elected, following the murder of his predecessor at Christmas by one of his own villagers. He seemed weak and evasive. In private he pressed us with the plea that his people had exhausted their stocks of food and were now destitute and in urgent need of support.

I had not been long back at JFHQ that evening when news was received, picked up from the Turkish Cypriot radio link from Chatos to Nicosia, of exchanges of heavy rifle and automatic fire in Vitsadha. A British Ferret (armoured car) patrol was despatched immediately and it reported back that the entire village was shuttered and barred, with desultory, and apparently aimless, shooting still going on. Nobody was in view or so far willing to respond to requests to come out and talk. Units sent to investigate the situation in surrounding villages found that they were on high alert and manning barricades in the direction of Vitsadha but that none of them seemed likely in the short term to intervene.

At 2140 the British patrol reported that all shooting had stopped. Turkish Cypriot women, emerging cautiously from their houses, told the patrol commander that they wanted to leave, and about a third of the Turkish Cypriot population then walked to the nearby village of Knodhara, shepherded on their way, to ease their alarm, by a British armoured car.

While I was en route to the area next morning, 19 February, I was radioed from the armoured car patrol, which had stayed on in Vitsadha overnight, that a large and heavily armed Greek Cypriot police force was moving into the village from the south-east, that a further substantial paramilitary unit was approaching from the south and that another large Greek Cypriot force was assembling in Marathovouno. Greek Cypriot action similar to that at Ayios Sozomenos was clearly planned. The British patrol commander said he had been told by the police that they intended to investigate the previous night's shooting and to ensure that there was no further threat to Greek Cypriot lives. He had persuaded them to postpone any action until the tripartite patrol arrived and he was endeavouring to keep things cool in the meantime by moving constantly between the two sectors of the village.

Arriving at Marathovouno I found the village bristling with armed men and exceptionally tense. I and my Land Rover crews were manhandled, spat at and cursed, and it was some time before Captain Michos and I could calm the situation sufficiently for rational conversation with the *mukhtar* and the paramilitary leadership. It then emerged that the whole village was convinced that the previous night in Vitsadha there had been a concerted attack by the Turkish Cypriots on the Greek Cypriot villagers and that this had been done under the guidance and cover of British troops.

This conviction had been strengthened by the fact that all of that day's Greek Cypriot newspapers carried virulent attacks on British policy and allegations that the peacekeeping force was deliberately encouraging Turkish Cypriot aggression. Furthermore, the villagers said, the matter had been proved to their satisfaction because, while they could still hear heavy firing from Vitsadha, a British armoured car had approached their northern roadblock, fired two shots in the air and then moved off towards the Turkish Cypriot village of Chatos. They had taken this as an act of deliberate provocation with the implied warning that they were not to go to the help of the Greek Cypriots in Vitsadha.

By the laborious and time-consuming process of first convincing the paramilitary leaders and then the *mukhtar* and then arguing the whole situation through with the crowd, Michos and I eventually coaxed the villagers into a calmer frame of mind. We explained how the trouble had started, with Colonel Sepici acknowledging that this was the fault of some Turkish Cypriot 'teddy-boys', that the British patrol had only been trying to keep matters under control until my own arrival, and that the peacekeeping force was only there at the invitation of Makarios. Captain Michos explained that Ferret armoured cars were well-known to occasionally backfire. Michos said he would return to speak with the villagers again when he had investigated matters to his satisfaction.

Approaching Vitsadha we encountered a strong Greek Cypriot paramilitary group moving towards the outskirts of the Turkish Cypriot quarter. Again there was a vigorous exposition of anti-British sentiment, culminating in an attempt to drag me out through the window of my Land Rover. After Michos had calmed the situation, the story we had heard in Marathovouno was repeated to us, with the added refinement that I was assumed personally to have helped provoke the Turkish attack. After more explanations this group was persuaded to return to its base.

Vitsadha was waiting impatiently for battle to commence. A local 'Secret Army' contingent was positioned opposite the Turkish Cypriot quarter. A

Bren gun platoon from the Famagusta unit of the 'Secret Army' was deployed to the south. Large numbers of heavily armed gendarmerie were in evidence. No Turkish Cypriots were visible: we were told that they were concealed in defensive positions in a block of houses in the centre of their sector of the village. The police and paramilitaries, frustrated by the delay in my arrival, were clearly keen on an immediate attack.

I discovered with relief that the police officer in overt command of the Greek Cypriot forces was an old acquaintance for whom I had a high regard. He told me that his units were there because of further Turkish Cypriot provocation the previous evening. The Turkish Cypriots had failed to respond to his shouted request to come out and negotiate. He therefore intended, in accordance with his orders, to move in and arrest those who had been responsible. The attack had only been thus long postponed because he had given his word to wait for my arrival.

I commended him on his patience and on the discipline of his command. I said that at Ayios Sozomenos the police had had every justification for seeking to arrest those responsible for the ambush, but that the way they had pursued this objective had played into the hands of TMT and been disastrous for the government's policy of reconciliation. I suggested that the only cause that would be served by an attack now would be that of the partitionists: if his target was the safety of the villagers in Vitsadha that could best be secured through negotiation. To reassure him that this was not some British trickery I suggested that he verify my comments by phoning jointly with me to the President's office.

I was helped by the fact that the Greek Cypriot *mukhtar* had joined us and embraced me warmly and that other members of my patrol, including Major Sepici, were also being cordially greeted by Greek Cypriot villagers. Recognition of the relationship which we had with the village conferred on us an immediate status.

After lengthy discussion it was agreed that all Greek Cypriot forces would move back from their forward positions and that I would be given a chance to seek a mediated settlement.

Major Sepici and I then went alone into the Turkish Cypriot sector. It appeared to be totally deserted. Walking through empty, shuttered streets Sepici repeatedly called out in Turkish, saying who he was and that there was nothing more to fear.

Eventually voices directed us to an inner courtyard where we found eight very frightened men, armed with shotguns or aged rifles, sheltering behind a barricade. They all greeted Sepici with the relief of men who felt themselves saved from imminent death. After an outpouring of their fears they agreed to pull back their own outposts. A few more haggard, shotgun-armed men then came in and greeted us.

I then brought Captain Michos over and after he had checked on the situation returned with him to the Greek Cypriot sector, leaving Major Sepici with the Turkish Cypriot villagers as a safeguard against any accident or act of idiocy.

With the Greek Cypriots now reassured that the situation was under control, and Michos staying with them to discourage any backsliding, I began to negotiate the terms for a joint meeting, marching to and fro with some solemnity between the two sectors, trailed as I went by a large body of the international press corps which had descended on the village.

As in all such negotiations, this part of the process was inordinately lengthy, since each side needed to preserve its sense of honour and to justify its acceptance of mediation. There was debate as to where the meeting would be held, who was to be present, what precisely was to be the agenda. Agreement was laboriously reached that neither side would initiate any aggressive action nor respond to any unintended provocation, that Sepici and Michos would monitor the cease-fire, that all non-local Greek Cypriot paramilitary units would return to their bases, and that the Turkish Cypriot leaders would join the meeting in the Greek Cypriot sector under the guarantee of British protection.

There was no sign of the Turkish Cypriot *mukhtar*, but the other Turkish Cypriot leaders now walked with me to the Greek school where they were greeted somewhat reservedly by their Greek Cypriot neighbours. Since newspaper reporters were banging on the door it was agreed that statements would be made to the press in advance of a private meeting. I provided a brief introduction to the problems of Vitsadha and spokesmen for each of the communities then gave simple, and moving, expositions of their positions, with Michos and Sepici translating whenever needed.

Before the meeting proper began, Sepici, Michos and I managed to agree on a picture of the events of the previous evening. It appeared that, without the knowledge of the remainder of their community, the same two (probably TMT-connected) Turkish Cypriot youths had again thrown a petard, or large firework or home-made bomb, towards the house of the Greek *mukhtar*. Either this was hooliganism or deliberate provocation. Again it had done no serious damage.

On this occasion, however, some Greek Cypriot members of a local paramilitary unit were keeping watch and they had immediately opened heavy fire with automatic weapons. Each community had then stood to under the impression that it was being attacked by the other. The Turkish Cypriot *mukhtar* and the youths responsible for the 'bomb' had fled the village as soon as the firing began. Firing had ceased only when a British armoured car unit had arrived in the village. Neither community had suffered any casualties.

Despite the restitution of their links with the Greek Cypriots and the logical explanation for what had happened, the Turkish Cypriot leaders made it clear that their community would only stay on in Vitsadha if they were assured that British troops would be stationed permanently in the area. Arrangements of this type were still against JFHQ policy and I did not believe that Vitsadha was sufficiently important to regional security for an exception to be made.

In consequence there was agreement, amicably accepted by all those present, that the Turkish Cypriots would be moved under British army supervision to Chatos and Knodhara and a British unit would stay in the village for the next couple of days to guard against any retaliatory attack, to protect abandoned property, to help an orderly transfer of movable possessions and to allow the completion between the two communities of a formal memorandum of understanding to cover property ownership and future relations.

Agreement had just been reached and the conference delegates were assembled in front of the schoolhouse, exchanging amicable compliments and embraces, to the applause of the press corps, when a British Whirlwind helicopter swept in for a dramatic landing a few yards away. To the astonishment, then hilarity, of the assembled crowd the advance elements of General Carver's newly created Force Alpha[1] leapt out and took up firing positions in approved textbook manner, their weapons menacingly aimed at the village elders and at a number of eminent international reporters.

I assured the Alpha Force commander that all was now well and he ordered his troops to retire. Still keeping the crowd covered, they moved backwards to the helicopter, jumped in and were lifted away back to Nicosia.

At my request, the Greek Cypriot police now left to explain to nearby villages what had happened and to ensure that tempers were calmed. Before leaving, the senior gendarmerie officer confided to me that he had not wished to involve the 'Secret Army' unit from Famagusta, but that the local military leadership had overruled the police view. Nor, he said, had he actually wished to launch an attack, but in this too his own decision had been rejected. This tended to confirm the picture that the patrol now had, of uniformed police units sometimes acting as subsidiary to 'Secret Army' detachments over which command was exercised by leaders of 'The Organisation' through a system of local 'ministerial cabinets'.

With the gendarmerie despatched, the local 'Secret Army' commander arranged for the patrol to be entertained to an excellent three-hour lunch. During the course of this the commander reassured me as reports came in to him of the progress of the evacuation. The only alarm was when information arrived that a small, armed group was approaching Vitsadha from the north. This turned out to be the bedraggled Turkish Cypriot *mukhtar* and a few of his associates returning after an uncomfortable night in the fields, whither they had run when the shooting started.

JFHQ told me that a formal approach had been made that morning to the President's office asking that no attack be launched against the Turkish Cypriots in Vitsadha. The President and the minister concerned had said they were wholly unaware that there were any Greek Cypriot forces in the area, other than the local gendarmerie, or that any attack was intended. They did issue an instruction to defer from further action, but by the time it reached Vitsadha the peace conference had already been completed. Had the attack gone ahead as locally planned, the message would have arrived too late to have any effect.

After lunch the patrol visited all the Turkish Cypriot and mixed villages that were sufficiently close to Vitsadha to have been affected by events there. Chatos and Knodhara were already relaxed, reassured by the evacuees who had arrived from Vitsadha. Psilatos, on the other hand, was very jumpy, fearing an imminent and overwhelming attack from Lefkoniko, where a full 'Secret Army' company had been stood to in case action was needed as a counter to pressures on Vitsadha. Yenagra also was very tense, with the two communities facing each other from behind barricades, but a joint meeting and an explanation of the Vitsadha agreement re-established relations. When the Greek Cypriot force at Lefkoniko was stood down that afternoon, it signalled the end of this particular chapter of confrontation.

That evening I cleared the agreement with Kutchuk and, via Tassos Papadopoulos, with the Greek Cypriot political leadership. In the days that followed my patrol made several more visits to villages in the Vitsadha area.

By 23 February I was able to report that the Chatos enclave was in better mood than at any time since Christmas. Greek and Turkish Cypriot villagers in the region and the Greek Cypriot gendarmerie all declared themselves highly satisfied with the outcome of events at Vitsadha and for the first time in this area there were compliments from all sides for the part played by British troops. Even Cypriot press comment was entirely positive.

The Turkish Cypriot villagers from Vitsadha collected their property in good heart and continued thereafter to stay on excellent terms with their former Greek Cypriot neighbours. The Greek Cypriots, on their side, delighted to have the village to themselves, were extremely conscientious in honouring the undertakings that they had given to the departing Turkish Cypriots.

There had been a successful outcome in Vitsadha because a joint patrol had arrived in time to provide effective mediation, in contrast to what had happened at Ayios Sozomenos, where the Greek Cypriot attack had gone in without waiting for a mediating unit. In my report I highlighted a number of key factors: first, the authoritative presence of my Greek and Turkish officers; then the fact that all the leaders on both sides were known to the patrol, that the patrol knew the village's history, and that the villagers knew and trusted the patrol officers; then that the British army unit in the area had from the beginning asked for the tripartite patrol's presence and after its arrival worked in good cooperation with it; and finally because the close association that the patrol now had with leading political and paramilitary leaders meant that we normally could negotiate with a knowledge of what would be acceptable in Nicosia.

Sadly, these strengths of the tripartite patrol system were soon to be substantially dissipated, when command of the peacekeeping forces was switched to the United Nations.

31. FAMAGUSTA DISTRICT AND MORA AND KYTHREA AREAS. LATE FEBRUARY

By this stage my patrol was going at least once weekly to Famagusta to attend meetings with the district leaders of the two communities. This was particularly constructive in terms of the support that was received from the joint committee and of the added influence that this gave to us in Famagusta Zone. Mr A. Sami (District Officer) for the Turkish Cypriots, Superintendents Georgiades and Constantinides for the Greek Cypriot police and gendarmerie and Pavlos Pavlakis for 'The Organisation' were all men who impressed me as pragmatic, sympathetic, dependable, honourable and moderate. They continued to work constructively together when Joint Liaison Committees in other zones were breaking down, and the relative calm for which their district was known in the early months of 1964 was a reflection of the restraint that they managed to exercise over their own extremists. JFHQ was admirably represented by Colonel Herbert, the peacekeeping force commander for Famagusta District, with whom the tripartite patrol developed a relaxed and constructive relationship.

The odd man out in this committee was a Greek Cypriot assistant district officer, an ill-tempered and virulent little man who claimed a long-standing EOKA background. His uncooperative attitude and the rudeness with which he addressed Sami were totally at odds with the conciliatory spirit that existed between the other committee members. He tried to monopolise all talk concerning inter-communal relations in the villages, on which subject he claimed to be an expert. His obstreperousness continued until one day Captain Michos could stand it no longer. Leaping to his feet he banged the table and shouted in Greek at the man that he was a disgrace to the nation he claimed to represent, an insult to Hellenism, an incompetent and ill-informed meddler who lacked the qualities for the most inferior village committee, let alone for this one. The reaction to this was a pained silence and an unaccustomed restraint that happily persisted through the coming weeks.

It was a benefit of our association with the JLC that we could translate its decisions directly to the villages in the moderate spirit that had been intended and that we could report back objectively to the committee from those villages what were their feelings and concerns and special needs.

From the beginning of this association we never once had a request to the police in Famagusta Zone refused, and this was critical both to the general process of inter-communal reconciliation and to the effective combating of extraneous violence. When the Greek Cypriot administration issued orders that in future no British officer was to be allowed into a police or gendarmerie station without prior permission from headquarters, a specific rider was added that the order did not apply to tripartite patrol officers. Famagusta provided a template for a productive co-operation between statal and communal authorities, peacekeeping force and mediating unit. Regrettably, local leaderships in other areas of Nicosia Zone were unready for this degree of bi-communal co-operation.

While the patrol was on its way to a Liaison Committee meeting in Famagusta in February, news was received by radio from JFHQ that a major incident was developing in the town. We rendezvoused with Colonel Herbert, and then drove directly to Famagusta docks, where we found detachments of armed paramilitaries from each community moving into confrontational positions, the Turkish Cypriots manning the castellated walls of the old city and the Greek Cypriots deploying opposite them along the harbour boundaries.

We discovered that a mixed force of dockers had been unloading the MS Dimitrios, newly arrived from Piraeus. Included in the cargo were nine crates addressed to Nicos Sampson's *I Makhi* Newspapers and labelled "Spares for printing machinery." Six of these crates had been offloaded successfully and despatched to Nicosia under the escort of armed irregulars.

The seventh crate fell out of its sling, broke open and was seen to contain ammunition. The Turkish Cypriot dockers immediately seized this and the remaining two *I Makhi* crates and drove off with them into the old walled city. Alarms were then sounded through both sectors of Famagusta and 'Secret Army', TMT and paramilitary groups stood to. Scattered rifle-fire between the front lines was beginning as we arrived.

Tension was somewhat lowered when a gentleman in a blazer and peaked cap emerged from cover waving a large banner in the style of an old-time herald. Behind him came a winding procession of strangely dressed people, some with white shirts tied to umbrellas, all the others waving handkerchiefs. My first thought was that this was a political demonstration against violence but when I approached the group its leader told me: "We are Yugoslav old people tourists, but we do not like the climate here and we are going to ask the captain of our ship to take us home."

Through a series of meetings, led by Colonel Herbert, tension was further lowered. The Turkish Cypriots complained about the illegal import of arms. A request by Mr Sami that the tripartite patrol be allowed to inspect the Dimitrios was refused by the Greek Cypriots.

I was taken to examine the captured hardware. The ammunition was obviously new, but the rifles were apparently from deliveries of British .303s parachuted to Greek resistance groups during the German occupation in the 1940s: carved on the stocks were a variety of stylised inscriptions – 'Long live Churchill'; 'EDES' (the acronym of the British-supported non-communist resistance organisation); 'Death to Hitler'.

Both communities reported to Nicosia for further orders, the Greek Cypriots meanwhile claiming that only their own 'legal forces of the state' had any right to investigate the matter. While discussions were continuing, the MS Dimitrios suddenly slipped her moorings and sailed: so precipitate was her departure that her captain was left behind. He had to be sent out to international waters later in a pilot boat.

In the evening, it was resolved that the matter would be followed up by the JLC in Nicosia. All paramilitary and police units were then stood down.

Freedom of movement was now the only serious remaining problem in the north-eastern sector of Famagusta Zone. Joint village committees had been reactivated by me in all mixed areas and these were working well, after some initial friction in Ephtakomi and Komi Kebir. At Ephtakomi the main cause of trouble was 'Secret Army' activity in the vicinity of Yioti, where a major beach defence point was under construction. Turkish Cypriot villagers approaching too close to these beach-works found themselves warned off with a few rifle shots.

Ephtakomi was also one of several villages in which Greek Cypriots were killed or injured during February by accidental pistol shots or premature bomb explosions. Turkish Cypriot villagers enquiring about a bang they had heard in the Greek Cypriot sector and the absence of one of their neighbours were told that the man had been struck by lightning.

In Komi Kebir, the Greek Cypriot *mukhtar* was a touchy man who made no secret of his dislike for the British. Regrettably his feelings had been exacerbated by a number of instances of rudeness that he felt had been directed at him by regular British army patrols. He claimed to see these as proof of British alliance with the Turkish Cypriots: he passed on his thoughts to the local press, which added further acid to the vicious circle.

British troops, many of them already pre-disposed towards prejudices of the 1950s, were in some areas now being greeted with great warmth and hospitality by Turkish Cypriot villagers, but with extreme hostility by the Greek Cypriots, with abuse and whistling and spitting and an occasional volley of stones from the children. The inevitable result was that the soldiers would spend as little time as possible in the Greek Cypriot sector and as much as possible with the Turkish Cypriots.

The Greek Cypriots, encouraged by a rabid press and apparently unable to appreciate that this cycle was likely to redound to their disadvantage, became increasingly bitter at what they labelled as British collusion with the Turkish Cypriots. The Greek Cypriot leadership allowed this process to fester in the belief that the Greek campaign for UN intervention would thereby be advanced. Occasional acts that came to light of genuine bias by a few British soldiers, including the smuggling of arms and other provisions of help to TMT, further inflamed the situation.[1]

More pernicious than most, but in tone and intention typical of much that was being purveyed, was an article that appeared in I *Makhi* on 21 February. Run under a front-page banner headline, this claimed to give details of how British army vehicles had stopped a Greek Cypriot bus near Tavros the previous day and tried to force it to go through the Turkish Cypriot village of Galatia. This was represented as a deliberate British attempt to repeat the notorious 'Geunyely incident' of 1958.[2] It was an allegation which struck powerfully at the Greek Cypriots' collective psyche. Greek Cypriots in north-east Cyprus, already primed to believe the worst, took the article at face value.

Normally I ignored press comment, but I was concerned at the likely impact of this particular article. I first discovered that the report was a total fabrication: the sum reality was that while the Greek Cypriot bus had been stopped by the road with a boiling radiator, two British scout cars which were passing had paused and the patrol commander had asked if they could help. Superintendent Constantinides, head of Famagusta Zone gendarmerie, confirmed to me that this was the correct story and said he had already contacted all major papers and got agreement from them to carry a prominent retraction in their next edition.

Nicos Sampson, the proprietor of I Makhi, was such a hate-figure for the British that both the High Commission and JFHQ had issued instructions that no British officer was ever to approach him.

I consulted with Tassos Papadopoulos. He greatly doubted that I would get a helpful response, but at my insistence undertook to try to fix a meeting. Later I received from him a message that Sampson would be expecting me at the Greek Officers Club at 1300 next day. I was told to go alone and unarmed.

When I arrived at the Officers' Club I was frisked for a hidden weapon or a concealed recorder, then ushered into Sampson's presence. He was talking to two Greek army officers, one of whom he afterwards told me was Brigadier Dimitrios Ioannides[3], the head of security for ELDYK. Ioannides stared at me piercingly for several minutes as though wishing to convince me of my insignificance. Sampson then said: "Since I was in gaol, you are the first Englishman who has ever asked to speak to me."

Speaking in Greek I said: "Forget the other Englishmen. I've been looking forward to talking with you. You have an important role in shaping the future of Cyprus. I've been asked to do a job for President Makarios and I want you working with me, not against me."

From their comments and attitudes it became clear that the two officers were part of an element of the Greek army on which I had been instructed at length by Costas Kalligas. These were middle-ranking officers, usually of peasant background and often coming from families which had been refugees from Asia Minor after the catastrophic Greek defeat by Turkey in 1922. Of all Greeks they were the most passionate believers in the megali idea, the concept that a greater Greece must be created from the gathering in not only of Cyprus but also of the lost territories of Anatolia and Constantinople.

The Greek civil war and subsequent American training programmes had welded this element of the officer corps into a ferociously anti-leftist phalanx, which US intelligence agencies regarded as their prime asset in Greece.

Additionally the group harboured a collective sense of resentment: it felt that it was invariably passed over for promotion to higher rank in favour of elitist officers who came from a more cultured background or who had better political connections. This was a key ingredient in the political plotting in which the group frequently indulged.[4]

Recognising the whiff of this background I did some name-dropping, mentioning my family connections with Stavros Kostopoulos and Admiral Toumbas, two of the most powerful ministers in the Athens government of George Papandreou, and with the Potamianos family, who were known right-wing funders of irredentist causes. I then rattled on about my understanding of the dreams of Hellenism and of the *megali idea*. Bored by the absence of a proposition with which they could disagree and satisfied that Sampson was safe in my company, the two officers eventually departed.

After a little while, Sampson proposed that we move on to his home and continue our discussions there. We talked all through the afternoon and evening. He told me how he had felt as a schoolboy demonstrating against the British and then when he was in the front line of the EOKA struggle. He reminisced about his time under British arrest and about the deeply influential bond that had developed between him and his warder. He repeatedly reverted to his commitment to *enosis*.

I told him he should have been one of the heroic figures of 1821, when the fight for a free Greece was a simpler process. I suggested that violence was now usually the end result of someone else's stratagem – Turkish partitionists, Greek fascists, the British – and that it was likely to be damaging to the causes to which he was committed.

I said: "Every Turkish Cypriot who is killed or alienated here makes genuine *enosis* less easily attainable and partition more probable. The only secure route to unfettered independence or to union with Greece is to prove that Turkish Cypriots are in every respect more secure and better off within a unitary state than in a partitioned one: not just in terms of physical and economic security but also in the preservation of their own Turkish Cypriot persona and traditions."

As the day progressed I began to realise that Sampson had a profound need to lean on someone else's guidance or inspiration. He kept referring to figures who had, in the fulfilling times of his life, told him what to do. At first it had been his schoolmaster; then Grivas; then his warder; then Ioannides and the other Greek officers who were now his friends. Later, talking about his actions in 1963, he once said to me: "I only ever did what Ioannides asked me to."[5]

Sampson said he couldn't understand why nobody had ever before talked to him as I had that day. He would now be supportive of the mediating effort, he told me, but that didn't mean he would soften his campaign against the British.

Late in the evening we gave up talking. Sampson's brother-in-law, George Fessas, a superb guitarist, was there and with Sampson's wife and her mother sang 'Varka sto Yialo' and other plaintive Greek ballads. Tassos Papadopoulos also joined us, although it was soon apparent that neither he nor Sampson had musical talents to rival those of the Fessas family.

Late in February I handed over responsibility for the villages of the extreme north-east Karpas peninsula, to a newly constituted patrol under Major Oldnall. It was a wrench to lose contact but the weight of non-patrol activity in Nicosia and Famagusta was making it impossible to spend as much time in the field as I previously had. The main loss was of contact with the covert leaders of secret paramilitary units in the north east region. Trust had to be earned from a new beginning. Sometimes the linkage was impossible to re-create.

Typical village conference with *mukhtars* and villagers, Turkish coffee and loukoumi. Seated from left are Major Oldnall (shortly to form a new patrol with responsibility for the Karpas Peninsula), me and, half hidden by my cap, Captain Michos.

Armed now with the support of *I Makhi*, I made a series of visits to those Greek Cypriot villages which had become notorious for their rudeness to regular British patrols. Faced with a Greek-speaking Englishman who had a better knowledge of Greece than they did, who was prepared to argue about the problems of *enosis*, who was happy to acknowledge past imperial mistakes, and who carried the approval of both President Makarios and Nicos Sampson, most of the villagers were soon assuring me of their traditional affection for London. I reminded them that Greeks were universally known as the most hospitable of people and suggested that politics should not be allowed to damage this reputation. Peace was usually made with me by way of a big embrace from the *mukhtar* and a bunch of flowers delivered, as I left, by one of the children.

Regional calm was disturbed by a new spate of seizures of Turkish Cypriot villagers by the Greek Cypriot gendarmerie, followed by an announcement from police headquarters that various Turkish Cypriot 'malefactors' had been 'arrested and interned'. I was told privately that in fact the arrests were intended to increase pressure for the release of the four Greek Cypriot policemen who were still being held after their capture in the Chappas building. Immediate British protests in Nicosia caused a rescinding of the order and tripartite patrols were able to inform the villages that their people were being released, as happened later that day.

The Turkish Cypriots were further mollified when the High Commission provided an immediate refund to all of those whose money had been 'confiscated' during the incident. In the same spirit we secured the return to Sinda of its village bus, which we had located at Vatili. The Turkish Cypriots had claimed that the vehicle had been 'captured': the gendarmerie said that it had merely been impounded for non-payment of its road tax licence and that they were happy to let it go on my personal undertaking that settlement would in due course be made to them.

During this period there were occasional claims from Turkish Cypriot leaders in Nicosia and Famagusta that trouble was somewhere about to erupt within the region, but I was confident that my unit now had a better knowledge of what was afoot than did any of the politicians. Mora and Sinda and Ayia all had occasional alarms because of Greek Cypriot paramilitary patrolling on their borders but, following the resolution at Vitsadha, Strongylos was the only village that still gave me cause for concern. Here Greek Cypriot leadership was poor and undertakings given by it at joint meetings tended to be quickly forgotten.

In all other mixed villages and mixed areas, the signs were encouraging. Inter-communal linkage, with access to the patrol in times of stress, was working well and the co-operation of the gendarmerie was now impressive.

At this point, at the very end of February, there was an unfortunate clash between the twin British roles of peacekeeper and peacemaker. Mishandling by JFHQ turned what should have been a quantum advance in the process of communal reintegration into a further worsening in Greek-British relations.

Since the beginning of January, the tripartite patrols had been advocating that a regular British peacekeeping presence should be established at certain trouble-spots where that would contribute to inter-communal re-engagement. We saw the move as one short-term part of a programme to restore a sense of security to Turkish Cypriot villagers and as a first step towards the recreation of a joint Greek Cypriot-Turkish Cypriot police presence. Central and critical to this project, we had stressed, was that it must only be used as back-up for a mediating process and that it must only be implemented with the full agreement and support of the central and regional leaderships of both communities. We had already identified the areas where that approval would be available.

Instead JFHQ resolved to move ahead with the scheme, in the decisive manner that had been the norm since General Carver's assumption of command, without any genuine consultation either with the mediating teams or with the Greek Cypriots. The experiment was first tried in Famagusta Zone, the area that had least need of it. The manner of its implementation was arrogant towards Greek Cypriot sensitivities and undermined the success being achieved by the tripartite patrols in tandem with Famagusta JLC. By alienating the most co-operative of gendarmerie forces, it was counter-productive, even in terms of its own declared intention, by leading to a further diminishing of Turkish Cypriot security.*

JFHQ's attitude was that it had received a general mandate for peacekeeping duties and that no suggestion must be given that Cypriots or mediators had any rights of veto over the specific disposition or conduct of British forces. This view (which I heard repeated by a subsequent British force commander at a 1995 UN conference) went to the heart of the periodic contradiction between peacekeeping and peacemaking. It rested on a supposition that the mandate's aim was to impose a barrier to violence, rather than to assist local leaders in the restoration of political control to a properly functioning state.

Peacekeeping units were often successful in obtaining an end to momentary violence but seldom contributed to long term solutions. Neither the British, nor subsequently the UN, military force in its early presence in Cyprus was in itself an instrument of mediation, other than through the independent joint patrol units. Standard army units performed only a limited policing role, and were unable to address the roots of communal disagreement, or on their own to provide such degree of security as would allow the normal political process to resume. Peacekeeping should have been an adjunct of international mediation, but after the removal of General Young in February 1964 it was seen by its commanders as an end in itself. By converting their short-term role into a permanent bureaucratised function, they became the preservers of an unsatisfactory status quo rather than part of an impetus for progress. That was to make them an element of the problem rather than of its solution.

In late December, the peacekeeping force had helped to prevent the outburst of inter-communal violence at Christmas from descending into civil war, and during January and early February, under General Young's leadership, it had played a positive role while the process of mediation was being put in place. Now was the time for it to provide focused backing wherever mediation opened up an opportunity for inter-communal re-engagement. The loss of this opportunity in Famagusta Zone and elsewhere was a further step towards the peacekeeping role ossifying into a defence of lines of separation rather than be an agency working for their progressive elimination.

In implementing its decision on troop disposals, JFHQ ignored the successful JLC in Famagusta and needlessly aggravated Greek Cypriot sensitivities. It did arrange for Georgiades and Constantinides to be told what had been decided, but this was done so insultingly late that, while the meeting was taking place, they learned from various gendarmerie stations that British officers were already there discussing the implementation of deployment. The Greek Cypriot leadership in Famagusta asked for time to

---

* The abduction and killing of 32 Turkish Cypriots in May would later provide tragic testimony to worsened regional relationships.

consult with Nicosia, but the deployment of troops started before this could happen.

If Cyprus had been some primitive area of central Africa, isolated from effective political control, or if these had been the days of December when the channels of political communication and control had temporarily disintegrated, JFHQ's approach might possibly have been justified. But these villages had now moved beyond December. Police, politicians, 'The Organisation', TMT and the 'Secret Army' all had their own networks through which control could be exercised. From the moment that the Greek Cypriot leadership was alienated and turned against the scheme, its main potential benefits were lost. Worse, the manner of JFHQ's action could be represented by an already antagonistic media as that of an arrogant and insensitive occupying army. The process of inter-communal rapprochement was in no way advanced and in some respects seriously damaged.

I tried to restore the old good relations that had existed in this area, but the Famagusta leaders told me, apologetically, that the matter was now out of their hands. In some villages I was invited to introduce the newly stationed British officer to local leaders. The Turkish Cypriots, happy with the new arrangement, invariably felt that joint village meetings were now no longer necessary. The Greek Cypriots viewed the development with deep antagonism. 'Secret Army' and 'Organisation' representatives declined to be introduced. Greek Cypriot *mukhtars* and gendarmerie members invariably said that the move was unwelcome and opposed by them, and that the sooner the British departed from Cyprus, the better.

32. KYRENIA AREA. FEBRUARY 1964

A relative stability in inter-communal relations in Kyrenia and the villages adjacent to it at the start of February drained away as the month progressed. The Greek Cypriots became increasingly irritated at the continuing closure to them of the direct road to Nicosia and at the sight of Turkish ensigns flying on the battlements of St Hilarion Castle. The large Turkish Cypriot minority in the city, fearful at the absence of their own officers from the police force, was cowed and un-cooperative, with old friendships replaced by an awkward wariness. As their frustration grew, the Greek Cypriots became less and less willing to offer the compromises that the situation required.

With the Green Line in Nicosia protected by peacekeeping troops, TMT had found itself able to move additional fighters onto the Pentadaktylos Range. Turkish Cypriot paramilitary strength at St Hilarion was now such that when its leaders talked to me they referred, for the first time, to the possibilities of aggressive action. Automatic weapons and fighters were infiltrated into Temblos and Kazaphani and Turkish Cypriot communities north of the Kyrenia Range were given assurances that they would be supported in case of attack. This served on the one hand to encourage the Turkish Cypriots in Kyrenia itself and on the other to create among the Greek Cypriots the myth of a powerful and resolute force preparing to attack them from the hills.

On 22 February the tripartite patrol reported that Kyrenia was very tense, with Turkish Cypriot complaints of police harassment. The next day British troops moved into the city to establish a permanent presence.

This time I was able to give advance warning of the new policy and the troops were greeted politely by the Greek Cypriot leadership, although I doubted that the welcome would last for long. Within a few days the Greek Cypriots were claiming that the British presence was encouraging the Turkish Cypriots to become more aggressive, with the Turkish Cypriots claiming that it had led to increased Greek Cypriot harassment. Fortunately both communities developed a genuine respect for the Parachute Brigade troops that were quartered on the town and an affection for the unit's commanding officer, who handled the assignment with exceptional sensitivity.

Meanwhile, the Turkish Cypriots in the mixed village of Kazaphani began, under TMT direction, to construct a strong complex of concealed defences.

33. Dhiorios Area. February 1964

On 4 February it seemed that Ayia Irini and Kambyli had been saved from crisis, when a proposal of the Turkish Cypriot leaders in Nicosia to direct large numbers of refugees into the area was dropped. Police pressure immediately eased, limited travel resumed and I was encouraged to believe that the position was now stable.

However, on that same day, Greek Cypriot roadblocks were again thrown up in all the villages along the Nicosia-Myrtou road. This was ostensibly in response to disturbances around Lefka and to the previous day's heavy toll of hostage-taking at Pyrgos and Ghaziveran: it also reflected a more aggressive police attitude in light of the Chappas Building affair.

Two Turkish Cypriot farmers, Shefket Mustafa and Jamal Mehmet, who were unfortunate enough to have chosen this particular morning to drive from Kambyli to Nicosia with a load of thirty-two young lambs, were passed from one roadblock to the next before being seized at Ayios Dhometios.

Within two days we had managed to secure their release. Their safe return to Kambyli was greeted with delighted amazement by the other villagers. Neither their van nor the lambs were returned, however.

Turkish Cypriot communities in the Kormakiti peninsula lacked any direct links with Nicosia or with other Turkish Cypriot centres. Despite the agreement I had obtained from CYTA, their telephones were only rarely connected, at the whim of sympathetic operators, and, unlike other isolated areas, they lacked a two-way radio. This, together with the satisfactory state of local inter-communal relationships, explains why the bus from Ayia Irini set out for Nicosia on 8 February, a day on which Turkish Cypriot travel had totally ceased in all other areas around the capital.

The bus, having already negotiated various roadblocks, was stopped at Ayios Dhometios and the driver and all the passengers were seized by the Greek Cypriot police as hostages. At about the same time, a Turkish Cypriot lorry on its way to Ayia Irini was stopped at Myrtou and its driver and passengers were questioned for two hours concerning the number of weapons held by Turkish Cypriots in the area. Before being released and sent on their way they were told to let it be known that if any of the Greek Cypriots in Ayia Irini was harmed, all of the Turkish Cypriots there would be killed.

In Nicosia that day Greek Cypriot sources confirmed to me that a Turkish Cypriot villager from Ayia Irini who had disappeared on the roads in December had been killed. Kutchuk's office told me that Lefka communal chamber and TMT command had the previous day renewed its advice that Ayia Irini should be evacuated.

I arrived in Ayia Irini early on 9 February. At Greek Cypriot insistence a joint committee meeting was held before any private discussions: at this the

Turkish Cypriots said they had no complaints as to village affairs, but that they were very short of supplies and that they were distressed that Greek Cypriot paramilitaries from Myrtou and Morphou were continuing to exercise near the village borders. The Greek Cypriots, not to be outdone, complained of the conduct of British troops: in particular, they said that several women had been made hysterical by a night patrol into the village on the 7th.

Afterwards we had a private session with the Turkish Cypriot leaders. The *mukhtar* said: "Out of respect we did not speak of it at the joint meeting because the Greeks here were not responsible, but we have lost our bus and many of our men. You say they will return safely, but we fear it won't be so. This trip was arranged only so that we could collect Red Crescent supplies from Nicosia and without those our situation is now very bad."

While we were talking, a lady entered the schoolroom and started to scream at the *mukhtar* and his committee. The *mukhtar* told her to calm down and to leave. When she continued screaming he walked across to her and felled her with a blow to the jaw. After she had been helped out of the room Sepici translated for me. He said: "The boy lost in December who you now say is dead was her brother. The men who were lost in the bus yesterday included her father, her husband, another brother and her son. She was saying to the *mukhtar* that if he and the Turks were men, they would go out and kill Greeks in revenge. The *mukhtar* told her not to behave like that in front of you and not to interfere in the discussions of the men."

On 10 February, the patrol located the Ayia Irini bus and the missing van parked out of sight behind the gendarmerie post at Koutrapha. The sergeant in charge was straightforward and helpful. He admitted that the occupants had been arrested for use as hostages on orders from senior police officers in Nicosia. He said, expressively, that he himself deplored the taking of hostages but what was he to do when his superiors decided that this was the proper policy. He would be happy to release the vehicles to us, but this too would require the approval of his superiors. In the meantime, he said, there was a problem with the lambs: they were dying off regularly and it obviously was stupid to waste them. He assumed we would understand.

On 13 February, with fighting in progress in Limassol (apparently another instance of deliberate provocation followed by disproportionate Greek Cypriot reaction), George Ball in Nicosia and new rumours circulating that invasion was imminent, the Turks at Ayia Irini began to receive threatening telephone calls warning that they were soon to be attacked. I myself was handed the phone to listen to one of these calls when I visited the village briefly on the 14th: a Greek voice, having completed a string of imprecations, said: "After Limassol, your turn is next."

At my subsequent request, JFHQ increased the frequency of regular Ferret patrols into the village, although the Turkish Cypriots continued to complain that they were not adequately protected and the Greek Cypriots that they were distressed by the frequent British presence.

Within the senior hierarchy of each community there were now diametrically opposed views as to whether or not it was advantageous that certain further villages, or areas, be evacuated by the Turkish Cypriots.

Nowhere was this more apparent than in the Dhiorios region. The Turkish Cypriot council in Lefka believed that if it could not be strengthened by the addition of refugees then the whole area should be evacuated; the council in Nicosia believed there should be no further move out of the area; TMT wavered between the two views, accepting that it was unable to provide effective support against attack, but believing that any Greek Cypriot attack would redound to Turkish Cypriot benefit. Makarios and his moderate ministers were urgently seeking to discourage any movement and to promote inter-communal re-engagement at local level. At the same time, some 'Organisation' and 'Secret Army' leaders were anxious that no Turkish Cypriot settlements should be left astride the main roads or in such position as to inhibit the anti-invasion defences that they were constructing: since the Kormakiti peninsula was regarded as a likely landing place in the event of a Turkish invasion, they would in general have preferred to see it entirely cleared of Turkish Cypriots.

The police were impatient to see Turkish Cypriot villagers disarmed and an end to no-go areas, but they were aware that any attempt on their part to pursue such an outcome in this area would almost certainly trigger an evacuation. The Turkish Cypriot villagers themselves seesawed between a horror of leaving their homes and a feeling that to stay longer might be intolerably dangerous. The Greek Cypriot villagers would have preferred to see the Turkish Cypriots go, but were under orders from Nicosia to act as good neighbours and restrain them.

The situation had strange twists. The Greek Cypriots in Dhiorios, responding to a pronouncement by Makarios on 4 February concerning the need for reconciliation and understanding, urgently sought to persuade their Turkish Cypriot evacuees to return, sometimes offering them monetary inducements to do so. Some Turkish Cypriots were inclined to accept. They were then warned by the Greek Cypriot police, acting on instructions from 'The Organisation', that under no circumstances should they try to go back.

By 21 February the mood of the Turkish Cypriots in Kambyli was bitter and aggressive. No one had travelled from the village since the loss of their van two weeks before and they were now short of supplies. They had asked a British Ferret patrol for urgent medical help to be sent for a sick young boy: no help had come; now the boy had died and they had had themselves to cremate the body.

They also were alarmed by Greek Cypriot paramilitary patrols which they frequently saw on the move in the surrounding hills. Refugees from Dhiorios were saying that their homes had all been looted and that when they tried to go out of Kambyli they were stopped by Greek Cypriot policemen who shouted at them: "Go back or we shall shoot you." The men were all sitting about without work or cash and their sense of frustration was growing. When they talked to the patrol their previous stoic acceptance of fate seemed to have gone. "We are stranded here like animals," they said. "We have nothing to live for. Here it is impossible even to exist like human beings. Better to go out and die like men than to go on living here like rats."

Major Sepici sat with them and talked at great length and was able to dispel the tension. I radioed JFHQ for an immediate delivery of relief stores and managed to persuade two of the villagers that, following the representations I had made to the police after the recent hostage-taking, it was safe for them to set off to deliver produce to the market in Nicosia.

While we were there on the 21st, a British ambulance arrived in the village and provided treatment for a number of minor complaints. I was perturbed to find that among three patients in the ambulance, being transferred to Nicosia for 'hospital treatment', was Ali Cemal, the schoolmaster of Ayia Irini and regional TMT co-ordinator. He had been fine when I spoke to him a couple of days earlier in Ayia Irini and still looked in excellent health, but he claimed to have had a sudden bout of stomach pains. That night I tried to convince JFHQ how justifiably incensed the Greek Cypriots would be if they learned that British vehicles were being covertly used to help with TMT's travel arrangements.[1]

To verify the state of abandoned Turkish Cypriot property in Dhiorios, I arranged for a full inspection later that day. Accompanied by the former Turkish Cypriot *mukhtar* and another Turkish Cypriot villager and by a Greek Cypriot police corporal from Myrtou, Major Sepici, Captain Michos and I tramped around the Turkish Cypriot sector examining every house.

Their condition was appalling. None had been spared. Some houses had been broken into, looted and subjected to minor acts of vandalism. The others were all being progressively dismantled, stripped of their electrical fittings and wiring, metalwork, window-frames and doors.

The Greek Cypriot villagers professed to great shame at what had happened, but denied any knowledge of how it had occurred. The Greek Cypriot *mukhtar* received the standard harangue from Captain Michos for his failure to exercise adequate control. This was repeated by the corporal of police, whom we asked to make daily inspections in future and to ensure that no further damage was done.

Back at Myrtou police station, we were met by the local sub-area commander of the 'Secret Army'. He had prepared a speech for me, which he delivered rather dramatically, standing in front of his men. He wished me to know that his army was committed to friendship with the Turkish Cypriot people. Whoever helped with that would be his friend. He believed that I was devoted to the good of his country and therefore we would work together. He would be happy also to co-operate with the British army, but first it must demonstrate its goodwill by helping to re-open the Kyrenia road: he proposed that this be done by a joint British-Greek attack on the pass at St Hilarion.

Meanwhile there were ominous portents again in Ayia Irini. On three successive nights, the Turkish Cypriots had been wakened by explosions on the boundary of their sector, with the Greek Cypriots later explaining these away as 'accidental'. One Greek Cypriot villager told Captain Michos that they were uneasy at the weaponry held by the Turkish Cypriots and aimed to provoke them into some action sufficiently serious to justify a response from the 'security forces'. We were pleased to find that the Turkish Cypriots had heeded Major Sepici's warnings and declined to be provoked.

On Sunday 23 February Ali Cemal* and Huseyin Saro were abducted while returning from Nicosia to Ayia Irini in a Land Rover belonging to the *mukhtar* of Kambyli.

Cemal's significance to the region quickly became apparent. The news of his disappearance caused consternation not only in Ayia Irini but also in Kambyli and in all the villages in the Photta-Aghirda area. Seeking for his immediate return, the Ayia Irini Turks threatened to attack the Greek Cypriot sector of the village; Kambyli threatened to attack Myrtou; Photta threatened to attack Ayios Ermolaos.

The supposition among the Turkish Cypriots was that the missing pair were either already executed or else being held as hostages in Ayios Ermolaos. For some reason JFHQ, which had sent out a search party not accompanied by either a Greek or Turkish interpreter, had come to the same view.

My patrol disagreed. I contacted Tassos Papadopoulos, explained that Ali Cemal's survival was critical to the peacemaking effort and asked him to discover through 'Organisation' channels what had occurred. Then we drove to Kambyli and argued that any militancy on their part would seriously reduce the chance of our getting Ali Cemal back alive.

The same plea was made in Ayia Irini, whose evacuation was now clearly the unofficial aim of some elements of the Greek Cypriot police and 'Secret Army'. With seven men lost since Christmas, their real leader now gone, their bus missing, their communications with Nicosia tenuous, food extremely short, frequent alarms from the patrolling of Greek Cypriot paramilitary units close around their borders and with rumours that an attack on them was intended, it was remarkable that the Turkish Cypriot villagers were not yet gone. I reported to JFHQ that they could only be dissuaded from departure if a British unit was deployed permanently to the area in the near future.

I received a provisional assurance from headquarters that troops would be made available, and immediately set about securing acceptance for their stationing from key leaders in the area. The Turkish Cypriots were predictably delighted. The Greek Cypriots villagers seemed glad to be convinced that the move could be to their advantage. The local 'Secret Army' commander received the news sympathetically, as an event necessary in the light of government policy that had to be fitted into his plans. The police sergeants in Morphou and Myrtou were much harder to convince, but in the end grudgingly accepted that there was no other way for the President's current policy of active encouragement for inter-communal re-engagement to be achieved.

Despite these acceptances, there was continued harassment of Turkish Cypriot shepherds from Ayia Irini on grazing lands towards Morphou. During the night of 27/28 February, after a long and stormy village meeting, the Turkish Cypriots again decided that they would evacuate. When we arrived next morning most of the transport was already loaded. The women sat passively on the lorries while we argued with the *mukhtar*. They and the

---

* See previous page.

children then climbed back down into the square when departure was postponed.

Another village meeting was convened and Major Sepici and I made emotional speeches, assuring them that they would have our help if real danger threatened, saying that the tide was turning in favour of communal re-engagement and asking them to fight with us against the anarchy that still existed. Visibly moved, they agreed to stay on at least until one of their communal leaders from Nicosia could come and speak with them and in any event not to evacuate without further discussion with my patrol.

I was beginning myself to have doubts as to whether this level of effort was justified in light of the danger that undisciplined extremists could still provoke a violent clash, but I arranged by radio with JFHQ for a Turkish Cypriot political leader to be sent by helicopter. The Turkish Cypriot villagers talked with him and then decided to stay on, but said to him that they were doing so "only because Commander Packard had asked them to do so and in any event only for a little while."

Despite their good neighbourliness, the Greek Cypriot villagers had been elated by news of the Turkish Cypriots' impending departure: now they were plunged back into gloom by the news that the decision had been reversed. The supposition that they would irritate the Greek Cypriots by staying may well have influenced the Turkish Cypriots towards that decision. Nevertheless, inter-communal relations in the village continued to hold up well.

With the situation in Ayia Irini temporarily stabilised, I concentrated on an attempt to locate Ali Cemal, whose fate was clearly of high significance to the course of inter-communal affairs in this part of Nicosia Zone. Within a few days I managed to discover how the abduction had been arranged, and where and by whom and on whose orders it had been carried out. I discussed what had happened, and what would be the implications of Cemal's death, with the local 'Secret Army' commander and with Tassos Papadopoulos and asked them to use their own contacts to ensure that he was kept alive.

I had not yet established effective contacts with the overall TMT leadership for the Aghirda - St Hilarion area, nor with the leaders of Photta, who fell under their control. This worked to my disadvantage. When we reached Photta, its leaders refused to budge from their belief that Ali Cemal and Huseyin Saro were being held as hostages in Ayios Ermolaos, if not already dead. They were derisive of our arguing that Cemal's life could best be saved through negotiation. They said we were naive: "These Greeks only understand the use of force."

On 28 February, a group of armed Turkish Cypriots from Photta seized two Greek Cypriots from Ayios Ermolaos while they were working in the fields to the east of the village. The following day, a Greek Cypriot shepherd and his son, who unwisely had ventured into the same area, stumbled onto another group of armed Turkish Cypriots from Photta who were hiding in ambush. The Turkish Cypriots opened fire and hit the shepherd, then continued to fire at the boy as he tried to support his dying father.

The activities of my patrol that day were complicated by urgent and separate demands on it from Pano Dhikomo, Ayia Irini and Photta. At Dhikomo, the trouble lay with the increasingly aggressive disposition of

Turkish Cypriot fighters on the Kyrenia Range. The presence during daylight hours of a British patrol had allowed the Greek Cypriots to continue working at the DEKO Cement and Lime works and at the big Onishia co-operative farm on the Pentadaktylos foothills near Pano Dhikomo. Now the Turkish Cypriots were harassing the workers with occasional rifle shots and were progressively looting the cement works during those hours of the night when they had control of the area.

The Greek Cypriot authorities had asked that a permanent British post be established near the cement works. Local circumstances obviously justified this and it would have needed no more troops than were already being deployed to the area on a day-by-day basis. Furthermore, it would have had useful publicity value: this was one of the few areas where the British had so far retained the general goodwill of the Greek Cypriot community and it was significant that there had been a specific Greek Cypriot request for a British presence. I therefore strongly backed the Greek Cypriot application and argued at JFHQ for an early response.

It seemed to me that for JFHQ to turn down the Greek Cypriot request would show an unfortunate bias, but the request was summarily rejected. The Greek Cypriots never again asked the British for military assistance in Nicosia Zone. TMT responded by ratcheting up pressure in the region.

Having viewed the further damage that had been done by the Turkish Cypriots to the DEKO works the patrol dashed westward to Ayia Irini, where the Turkish Cypriot villagers were once more threatening to evacuate. At a communal meeting in their coffee-house, the Turkish Cypriot villagers told me that a visit the previous day by a representative of Dr Kutchuk had been a farce. The person who had come, they said, had shown no understanding of their problems or any real sympathy for them and before they had finished explaining to him their fears and difficulties he had announced that he had to return urgently to Nicosia for other business. Now, they said, they would like to leave with the help of the patrol and on good terms with their Greek Cypriot neighbours.

After a long, intense and emotional discussion, the Turkish Cypriots first wavered and then agreed to delay a final decision until we could arrange to bring either Dr Kutchuk or his deputy, Dr Kiazim, to speak with them. Sepici, Michos and I then flew by helicopter to Photta after first sending off the patrol's two Land Rovers to rendezvous with us later in Ayios Ermolaos.

While we were en route, it was reported to me by radio that a serious firefight was developing on the western approaches to Photta.

We landed to find that we were under heavy incoming fire and that the Greek Cypriots were in process of launching an attack. I sent the helicopter back to land Captain Michos in rear of the Greek Cypriot forces and went off at a run with Colonel Sepici, taking what cover we could, to locate the Turkish Cypriot leaders.

Within thirty minutes all firing had stopped. Michos had persuaded the Greeks Cypriots to pull back into defensive positions and Sepici was holding back the Turkish Cypriots from any retaliatory fire.

At this point I had an urgent message of further trouble. Our Land Rovers had been driven into Ayios Ermolaos exactly at the moment when the body of the dead shepherd was being brought back into the village and paraded through the main square. The Land Rover drivers, Lance Corporal Pickwell and Gunner Beaumont, were immediately surrounded by an angry mob and were ordered by armed men to leave their cars and surrender their weapons. They refused to do so and, despite being told to close down their radio, managed to get off a guarded message to headquarters explaining the situation.

JFHQ had rapidly moved British units to positions south-west of Ayios Ermolaos and northeast of Photta but, at my request, no attempt was made to interpose troops between the two villages.

The *mukhtar* and TMT leader in Photta confirmed to me that the two men missing from Ayios Ermolaos were being held by them as hostages and said that they would be killed unless the Turkish Cypriots received proof that Ali Cemal was alive and well. I radioed this information to Captain Michos. Ten minutes later he got back to me. He said that the ultimatum had caused some hilarity. The Greek Cypriot commanders had told him: "We wouldn't give ten shillings to get that pair back."

However little value they might place on the two missing men, the fact of their seizure and the killing of the shepherd was considered by the Greek Cypriots to give sufficient justification for a full-scale attack on Photta. When I had reassembled my patrol in Ayios Ermolaos we found a situation of great excitement, with more and more armed units moving into the village, including an extremely well-organised 'Secret Army' Bren gun platoon. When eventually we managed to convene a meeting, the talk from the Greek Cypriot side was very aggressive, with violent harangues that the time had come to break the Turkish Cypriot insurrection. At one point, the young shepherd whose father had been killed broke into the meeting and started to scream hysterically that Major Sepici should be shot in retaliation.

The new aggressiveness of the Turkish Cypriots in the Aghirda-Photta area, engendered partly by an influx of trained fighters and better weapons, partly by the proximity of TURDYK and partly by the sense, however inaccurate, that they were backed by a well-armed force in St Hilarion Castle, gave me some sympathy for the Greek Cypriots' frustration. However, I was acutely aware that the stability of Nicosia Zone would be threatened by serious fighting here.

All through the afternoon, I argued that an attack would be catastrophically damaging to Makarios' current policy; that, unlike Ayios Sozomenos, the Turkish Cypriots in Photta were well armed, in good defensive positions, and spoiling for a fight, so that in no way could this be a straightforward police action; and that a serious battle here could trigger an attack by the Turkish air force. In the end I got undertakings from the 'Secret Army' and police commanders that no attack would be launched unless there were further acts of violent provocation by the Turkish Cypriots. It was agreed that no British troops would be moved into Photta, since that might result in a further hardening of the Turkish Cypriot attitude, and that it would be left to me to try to negotiate the release of the hostages.

Despite these arrangements, there remained a clear danger that independent extremist paramilitaries from one community or the other would attempt some spoiling action. I had already sent one of the Land Rovers back to base for a change of crew and with instructions to meet me later in Photta. The other Land Rover stayed with Captain Michos in Ayios Ermolaos. Major Sepici and I then walked with the 'Secret Army' commander up to his forward position and verified that they had been warned against any more firing unless directly attacked. Sepici then shouted to the Turkish Cypriots that he and I were coming over and received in return a shouted "Go ahead", after which we had an uncomfortable moonlit walk across to the front line of the Turkish Cypriot positions.

The Turkish Cypriot leaders in Photta had calmed down during the afternoon and they now had a better idea of the forces ranged against them. We persuaded them that their cause would best be served by transferring the hostages into our care and, with some reluctance, they agreed to do so. However, while the two Ayios Ermolaos villagers were being produced, so that we could verify their wellbeing, a section of the TMT area command arrived, countermanded the release order and renewed the demand that Ali Cemal be released from Ayios Ermolaos before their own hostages were set free.

I explained yet again that Cemal was alive, but that he was not held in Ayios Ermolaos and never had been. The TMT area commander said he could prove I was wrong and produced a certain Mehmet Kanara, who claimed he had been with Cemal when he was captured and that he had been imprisoned with him for three days in Ayios Ermolaos. I was given a copy of a report on the incident written by Kanara which had been delivered by Kutchuk's office to JFHQ.

Sepici and I were allowed to cross-examine Kanara in private. He soon began to contradict himself, then broke down and confessed that his story was an entire fabrication which he had been instructed to tell by the Turkish special police in Nicosia.

It was apparent that TMT leaders were still intent on confrontation and that they thought they were in a position to inflict a serious military setback on the Greek Cypriots, but Kanara's exposure threw them off balance. They reluctantly approved that the hostages be released, but said the handover could not take place until ratified by Dr Kutchuk.

I had kept in touch by radio with Captain Michos. We agreed that the situation now seemed sufficiently stable for both paramilitary leaderships to be advised to stand down their forward positions but that, to safeguard against any rogue attack, he would remain in Ayios Ermolaos for the night and Sepici and I in Photta.

The *mukhtar* hospitably insisted that Sepici and I use his home. In the bedroom I found a wall-long couch, which normally accommodated an entire family of eight. Major Sepici took one end of this, and lay throughout the night apparently sleepless and rigidly at attention, still wearing his boots and cap, while I slept, bootless and relaxed, at the other end.

JFHQ maintained an observation post in the area for the next few days, but there was to be no further trouble between Photta and Ayios Ermolaos. Three days later, the Turkish Cypriots released their two hostages, one to my patrol and the other to the Red Cross. Four days later Ali Cemal was included in a general release of hostages by the Greek Cypriots.

The avoidance of a major clash at Photta came, as at Vitsadha, from an effective use of the tripartite patrol in conjunction with sensitive support from a peacekeeping unit. The positioning of Captain Michos with the Greek Cypriot paramilitaries and of Major Sepici with the Turkish Cypriots imposed a discipline on the situation that left me free to concentrate on active mediation. The knowledge that peacekeeping troops were in the close vicinity, but not interposed as an artificial barrier, created a positive influence. Both Greek Cypriot and Turkish Cypriot reports on the incident were complimentary about the British role. Follow-up work by my unit enabled both Photta and Ayios Ermolaos to feel that their honour had been satisfied. With the confrontation past, in the months to come these two villages provided a model for neighbourly good relations.

To bring a closure to the killing of their shepherd, Michos and I talked at length to the villagers of Ayios Ermolaos. I said that what I read in their newspapers did not have much to do with reality: that there were elements in both communities who believed passionately in their objectives, but who were in fact destroying their own cause. I told them of what had happened at Ayios Vasilios, of the many Turkish Cypriot villagers who had been lost while travelling on the roads and of the truth about Ayios Sozomenos. I said this was a critical moment in Cypriot history: if we failed to break the circle of violence, then foreigners would find an excuse for dismembering the country. Captain Michos backed me in all this. The villagers asked why none of their politicians had ever come and talked with them like this. I said: "This is a time of passionate causes. Even good politicians are afraid that one day they could be accused of betrayal."

I could speak with some authority, because I was becoming increasingly aware of the problems faced by moderate leaders in each community. To help with the mediating process, Tassos Papadopoulos had earlier given me a complete structural explanation of 'The Organisation'* and an outline of the Akritas Plan. He had been explicit about the difficulty of stamping out anarchic violence when that was being represented by the press and extremist politicians as part of a heroic struggle for the realisation of people's dreams of union with Greece. He thought it disastrous that the Greek Cypriots had been drawn into inter-communal conflict at Christmas, instead of letting events gradually evolve. He believed they had been provoked, by some of their own people as well as by foreigners and by TMT, into unleashing a tiger and that now they had no option but to try and ride it.

What led to the near-attack on Photta, as to other previous crises, was a combination of blurred targets, faulty intelligence, inadequate leadership and undeveloped command structures. I gathered that Makarios, Clerides and Papadopoulos were all unaware of the continuance of hostage-taking by Greek Cypriot special police or of the implications of the seizure of Ali Cemal: none of them had been presented with an analysis of what would result from

---

* See Appendix D

the planned general attack on Photta; all of them were wrong in supposing that 'The Organisation' was now in a position of effective control over those who believed their objectives were obtainable by force.

34. PERSONALITIES

The leaders of 'The Organisation', holders of all the key ministries, had come to positions of political power by way of a lengthy liberation struggle against Britain. They now clearly found it difficult to deal with the consequences of factional extremism and of residual violence within their own community.

Those that I met all seemed ambitious and competent, but ambivalent as to whether their futures lay in an independent Cyprus or in a new united Hellenic state. None of them would for a moment publicly condone violence against the Turkish Cypriots: they were all aware that such violence played directly into the hands of Turkish Cypriot separatists. But none appeared at that time to feel that he had the political strength to push publicly for a policy that would put an inclusive multi-ethnic society ahead of the old dream of *enosis*. So instances of criminal violence were tolerated for the sake of communal unity and chances to re-engage with the Turkish Cypriot community were lost. Events progressively overwhelmed the capacity of these leaders to control or contain them.

Kutchuk and Makarios both lamented lost opportunities, first in the approach to constitutional adjustments, then in the failure over Christmas to grasp the chance for a joint campaign against extremism and violence.

Key Turkish Cypriots, members of the judiciary and the civil service, told me that the absence of any rule of law, the lack of understanding of their insecurities and the premature severance of their (central government) employment had driven them against their will into the arms of Ankara.

In these first months of 1964, it puzzled me that the drive from the Greek Cypriots to develop an effective new partnership with the Turkish Cypriots was so fractured and so weak. The sources of Greek Cypriot frustration were clear enough but, apart from a few ultra-rigid police officers, I was talking to no Greek Cypriot who was not prepared to be persuaded that a sympathetic re-engagement with the Turkish Cypriots was the best way forward.

Nicos Sampson, a case in point, was popularly selected by foreigners for vilification as an arch *enotist*, but I came to see him as a simplistic patriot who was being manipulated by foreigners in the cause of Greek nationalism. The Greek intelligence agency, KYP, to some of whose members Sampson deferred, was the repository of extreme right-wing thinking in Athens and a prime schemer for *enosis*. It reported directly to the CIA, which had set it up after the Greek civil war, had subsequently been its mentor, and which used it as a surrogate in its secret war against leftism in Greece and Cyprus and in its attempts to establish an armed 'Stay-behind' network for activation in the event of Soviet invasion.*

From my time as an adviser to the NATO area command responsible for this region (COMEDSOUEAST), I had been acutely aware of the degree to which US intelligence agencies viewed the left in Greece and Cyprus as a potential threat to their regional interests. When Sampson talked to me about the persuasion used on him, it suggested a duality of foreign purpose: the dangers of confrontation between NATO members Greece and Turkey demanded a NATO ability to influence the island's affairs, even if towards communal separation; and support for the Cypriot right would assist the CIA's campaign to hamstring the Cypriot left.

It was because he acted as a proxy for the Greek intelligence services, and sometimes as the alter ego of Ioannides, that Sampson's role had particular significance for me. Critically, however, he appeared willing to be weaned away from his KYP mentors and converted to support for communal re-engagement.

Sadly the same could not be said of Charalambos Hassapis, the police commander, who was a more intractable figure and, in reality more threatening to the process of mediation.

In my several meetings with him, Hassapis was invariably stiff and uncommunicative. It was apparent that he felt that tripartite patrol activities were intruding on his own fiefdom. He declined to be drawn into any discussion about routes to the retrieval of Turkish Cypriot trust, implying that such a process could only start when the Turkish Cypriots were totally disarmed, but saying only: "I have my orders." The impression he gave was of a rigid, honest disciplinarian, contemptuous of politicians, intellectually blinkered. He appeared to be deeply resentful of the use made of him by the British colonial administration in the years before independence and determined now to establish his nationalist credentials. Equally, he was now resentful when his force was told to take orders from the 'Secret Army'. He maintained that the Turkish Cypriots were in a general state of insurrection which must be totally crushed. He was incensed that there were Turkish Cypriot-controlled no-go areas from which his police forces were currently excluded by decision of the politicians.

Hassapis stated forcefully to me that the police must have the right to re-establish their remit throughout the island. I suggested that the island- wide remit had, rightly or wrongly, been based on provisions in the 1960 constitution for a bi-communal police force. I said that I was wholly sympathetic to his commitment to the rule of law, but that it was my impression that his government was seeking to re-establish a general situation of legality through reconciliation and peaceful re-engagement, rather than through a unilateral use of force. He refused to countenance any suggestion by me of wrongdoing by police specials.

I was never able to establish with Hassapis such private rapport as would have allowed a quiet co-operation in shaping police attitudes towards an

---

* See note I/5

encouragement for reconciliation, as had been urged by Makarios and as had proved successful in Famagusta Zone. I therefore had to seek for a modification of police attitudes through discussion with Tassos Papadopoulos, rather than with Hassapis, as I would have preferred.

I did not see Hassapis as in any way an evil man, but my patrol kept running up against his inflexibility and his narrowness of view, which clearly were contributing to the failure of the Greek Cypriots to isolate their own and Turkish Cypriot extremists or to secure the negotiated settlement that mediation could have made available in early 1964.

To police intransigence, the machinations of KYP and its proxies and the leaning of foreign powers towards a separatist solution, were added weaknesses of government leadership. This was a young nation, saddled by outsiders with a complex and non-democratic constitution, inheritor of the foreign-promoted inter-communal violence of the late 1950s', stretched between moderate leftism and right-wing nationalist extremism, hammered by a multitude of internal and external pressures, faced with deliberate efforts by some elements to make the unitary state unworkable.

Despite the intellectual excellence and drive of many of its key ministers, the administration as a whole was characterised by political immaturity. Poorly served by its intelligence services, it reacted yo-yo-like to extremist provocations and failed to generate proactive long-term strategies in support of Makarios' more conciliatory policies. It continued to act as though the Akritas Plan remained a viable blueprint for national development, even after events at the end of December had proved that Turkish Cypriot paramilitary power was too deeply entrenched to be eliminated by Greek Cypriot force alone without provoking intervention from Ankara. That the Greek Cypriot administration was unable adequately to deal with extremists in its own community was soon to provide cause for the return of Grivas to Cyprus, which in turn would lead to an even more profound left-right splitting of Greek Cypriot society.

Although I received from him such specific help as I asked for, I never established an effective relationship with the enigmatic Polycarpos Georgadjis*, the 'playmaker' at the heart of the Greek Cypriot administration. A former deputy to Grivas in EOKA, he had a powerful 'clientele' following and he was a consummate plotter. As Minister of the Interior, he played the pivotal role between police, 'Secret Army', intelligence services and politicians. He was both a prime drafter of the Akritas Plan and the key commander of 'The Organisation', which had been set up to oversee its implementation. Makarios, Clerides and Papadopoulos may have had equal status at the head of the Organization, but Georgadjis seemed usually to be working outside their control. I was told later that Makarios had said of Georgadjis that he was 'the true Machiavelli of Cyprus.'

Georgadjis was viewed by JFHQ as a saboteur in December of the inter-communal peace agreements made between Makarios and Kutchuk and as a prime motivator of ex-EOKA and nationalist extremists.

---

* See note 2/2

My first contact with him suggested a complex division of his loyalties. I approached him after, in my early patrols in January, being asked by various Turkish Cypriot villagers to seek news of relatives who had been at Nicosia General Hospital.

Two days after my query was passed to him I received from Georgadjis a confidential response. He said that he deeply regretted having to tell me that twenty-one Turkish Cypriot patients at the hospital had been killed in their beds by a member of the hospital staff, loyal to Nicos Sampson, who had run amok. The bodies, he went on to say, had been removed by night in two trucks and delivered to the area of Skylloura/Ayios Vasilios where they had been dismembered, incinerated, ground up in farm dicing machines and then seeded into arable farmland.

I had no reason at the time to doubt the validity of the report, since it had come from the best informed of Cypriot ministers. Deeming that the moment had not yet come when a truth of this nature could be helpful to the peace process, I kept the story entirely to myself, although I later learned from Cyril Pickard and from archive material that it had also been delivered by Georgadjis to the British High Commission and used there to support their contention of inter-communal incompatibility.[1]

It was thirty-six years before it was suggested to me that the story had in fact been an elaborate piece of disinformation. First I was told that UN investigations had determined that only three Turkish Cypriots, suspected TMT members, had been killed in the General Hospital (and in the matron's quarters rather than in their beds). Then I learned from the 1963 director of International Red Cross operations in Cyprus, Shelagh Folke, that after the Christmas fighting, she herself had collected twenty-one Turkish Cypriot bodies from the streets of Omorphita, using RAF ambulances, and deposited them in the morgue of the General Hospital. She had been told that the bodies, together with those from the matron's flat, had later been removed to Ayios Vasilios so that the morgue could be cleared.

Why should Georgadjis have disseminated so detailed and horrendous a story, particularly if it was untrue? At the time, I naively assumed that it had been decided that, if I were to mediate effectively, it was better that I have private knowledge of the worst that had happened, upon which basis I saw the minister's confiding in me as a commendable act of trust. In retrospect, it was clear that I had been used.

Alternative explanations were either that he had been misinformed, which seems unlikely in a matter of such import; or that he was seeking, by putting the blame on a deranged member of the medical staff, to cover up another equally damaging story, possibly involving the police force, for which he was directly responsible; or that he was assuming the story would be circulated and that some political target, presumably by way of increasing inter-communal tension or provoking communal separation, would thereby be achieved; or that, as a consummate player of power-politics, he was seeking to pre-empt a belief that Britain and the US would in any case prevail in imposing a partitional solution. Such was the general picture of violence over Christmas and such the provenance of the story that I failed at the time to suppose that it might be a contrived fabrication. The story would have been highly supportive of a UK/US push for communal separation, either through the condominium route or by way of the Ball/Acheson Plan.*

There were clear parallels between the positions and *modus operandi* of Georgadjis within the Greek Cypriot community and of Rauf Denktash in that of the Turkish Cypriots. Both men were consummate organisers and plotters, both used disinformation to pursue their aims, both were deeply feared, both (as it later emerged) were heavily promoted by foreign intelligence agencies in their campaign against leftists and leftist influence.

The inevitable response by the Turkish Cypriot community to any story of Greek Cypriot atrocity against them was a heightening of their sense of insecurity, a reduction of their travel on Greek Cypriot-controlled roads and an added urgency in their relocation into predominantly Turkish Cypriot enclaves. The continued occasional taking of hostages by police specials or ex-EOKA extremists had this same effect, making it unnecessary for TMT to exert much pressure to maintain the process of demographic re-adjustment.

In late February, with the Greek Cypriot administration in urgent need of added revenue, a decision was taken that there could be no further leniency in the collection of Road Fund taxes. Rather than receive a clear statement of intent, the Turkish Cypriots were issued with vague threats that they were likely to be arrested and their vehicles confiscated if they were caught without a licence. The Greek Cypriot police, who had seen the continued flouting of licensing regulations by the Turkish Cypriots as an insult to their authority, received the order for a clampdown with enthusiasm. On 26 February a number of Turkish Cypriot buses were seized, on the pretext that their tax discs were out of date: one of them was the bus which had only recently been restored by us to Sinda.

It was important for the Turkish Cypriots that their buses and cars continue running, but funds in Turkish Cypriot areas were now so short that meeting the licence charge was frequently beyond the villagers' means. The tripartite patrols worked with the gendarmerie to try to clarify the position with the Turkish Cypriots and to help them make arrangements to pay where that was possible. We also persuaded the gendarmerie to be more forbearing in their approach to the licensing problem, and the Sinda bus was rapidly returned, but there was a still further drying up of the already meagre flow of Turkish Cypriot travel.

During the second half of February, beyond the continuing process of upgrading their weaponry and training, the efforts of the 'Secret Army' were concentrated on those three areas where it was considered most likely that the Turkish army might attempt a landing, Morphou Bay (Kormakiti), Famagusta Bay and the coastal strips to the east and west of Kyrenia. In the first two cases defence was envisaged in terms of fighting on the beaches, and the construction of a great number of fixed defensive positions was consequently put in hand: in the latter case it was assumed that the major line of defence would be along the Kyrenia Range, so the passes were prepared for

* See note I/1

mining and covering defences were constructed along those sections of the crest that were under Greek Cypriot control.

Although the 'Secret Army' leadership was fairly open with me about these activities, my patrol had some awkward moments when it stumbled unexpectedly on centres of construction activity. Once on Lefkoniko Pass we were held at twitchy gunpoint for half an hour while the local commander sought for central guidance as to whether we were to be shot or to be offered a share of their wine and *mezzedes*.

The leaders of both communities continued during this period to be hampered by deficiencies in their gathering and interpretation of field-intelligence, but in other respects the mechanisms of central administrative control were being markedly improved. Except for fire-fights, I was becoming confident that we could now usually find solutions by dealing with central communal institutions rather than, as had been the case early in January, by having to work with local strong-men or through newly-created local joint committees.

The combination of absolutist propaganda with this improvement in communal organisation led to the emergence of a hard-line political tendency which was markedly different from the conciliatory, mainstream position that had been presented to me as that of President Makarios. In a summary that I wrote in early March, to cover the events of February, I noted that during the last ten days of the month I had gathered from leaders of 'The Organisation' and other Greek Cypriot advisers to Makarios that they were leaning towards an acceptance of certain population adjustments, implying some form of federal or cantonal arrangement. However, these pointers towards a moderate inter-communal settlement were soon counter-balanced by the appearance in the Secret Army and in some non-'Organisation' political circles of a new spirit of self-confident belligerence and a belief that no further concessions need be made to the Turkish Cypriots.

Shortcomings in the Greek Cypriot leadership were seldom criticised in the Greek press, which instead concentrated on a vituperative and prolonged attack on British policies and actions, which it blamed for every aspect of the island's problems. Its virulence found a ready response in the Greek Cypriot rural community. Hostility towards British peacekeeping troops led to a heightening of international criticism of the Greek Cypriots.

JFHQ made little attempt to seek an improved relationship with the local press, which it regarded as too biased to be worth cultivating. Tripartite patrols, on the other hand, maintained reasonably good relations with the leading papers, sometimes directly and sometimes via the Greek or Turkish liaison officer or well-disposed members of the police. Because of this I never found it particularly difficult to get a denial printed or to elicit a sympathetic clarification.

By the end of February, the Turkish Cypriots had come to regard the British as generally helpful but ineffectual in times of crisis. The Turkish Cypriots were looking for international sympathy, and often using the British to achieve it: the success of their tactics could be judged from the fact that even in those instances where confrontations arose because of deliberate

Turkish Cypriot provocation, it was almost always the Greek Cypriot reaction that made the international headlines.

Having been several times disappointed when an expected Turkish military intervention failed to materialise, Turkish Cypriots were now, at the beginning of March, beginning to take a long-term view. Turkish Cypriot friends told me that Prime Minister Inonu was a fox who pretended to strike many times to lull his opponents into a sense of security, then actually struck when they least expected it.

In January, my patrol had been pitched into a situation of anarchy in the rural areas of Cyprus and had struggled to reduce the fear and isolation that it found, to re-establish central political control, to restore inter-communal linkages and to identify and isolate the sources of violence. During February, with central authorities now much more involved in the development of events in rural areas, we had moved closer to political leaders in Nicosia and at the same time had become adept in the resolution of village confrontations. Around us throughout this period was taking place a major adjustment in the demographic profile of Cyprus, like an ice-shelf shifting after a sudden storm: in part this process was a reaction to violence or pressure, in which case it militated against a general reconciliation, and in part it was accomplished with mutual sympathy and agreement, in which case inter-communal relations were the beneficiary.

The paramilitary situation in the countryside also had changed radically during the past two months. The Greek Cypriot 'Secret Army' had been rapidly expanded, its weaponry had been upgraded, training had produced a new discipline and self-confidence: now discussions were under way for its formal conversion to a National Guard, into which it was intended to absorb Greek Cypriot members of the embryonic Cyprus army and those police and constabulary 'specials' who had been recruited since Christmas.

The 'private' paramilitary groups of Vassos Lyssarides, Nicos Sampson and George Raftis, totalling several hundred well-armed men, had since early January been placed under the operational command of Greek Army officers sent secretly from Athens.[2] Nevertheless, elements of these units continued to have an independent influence in Nicosia Zone, for which reason they were now viewed with concern by the heads of 'The Organisation', who would have liked to see them fully incorporated into the proposed National Guard or disbanded, but believed this was not the moment to provoke a public row.

At the same time Athens was beginning to build its own clandestine force in Cyprus, aiming for a total of twelve to fifteen thousand men by the end of 1964: two members of George Papandreou's government, Admiral Toumbas and John Sossidis, were to tell me in November 1964 that this build-up was intended to impose a discipline on the Cypriots, to avert a situation whereby Makarios could trigger an unwanted war with Turkey and to satisfy assurances given to Washington that Athens would be able to impose its will on the island if necessary.

Within the Turkish Cypriot community, TMT was now much better organised and armed: by early March it had expanded its armed presence from Nicosia and the other major cities to all those rural areas where there was a significant Turkish Cypriot presence. At the same time, the core area along

the southern stretch of the Nicosia-Kyrenia road remained under the control
of TURDYK. Disregarding agreements made in December, TURDYK had
refused to accept orders from General Young to confine itself to its barracks
and to clear the Kyrenia road.

To complement TMT and as a counter to the 'Secret Army' the Turkish
Cypriots had created a tough paramilitary fighting force, originally recruited
from British-trained former soldiers or special police. 'Volunteers' from
Turkey were also now often in evidence, adding to the professional military
command structure that had been secretly infiltrated during 1963.

The third military grouping in Cyprus was the peacekeeping force (JF),
now with about 6,000 British troops, which since February had been
commanded by General Carver. JF theoretically also included TURDYK and
ELDYK, the Turkish and Greek army contingents in Cyprus, with 650 and
900 men respectively, but the only active involvement of these units in JF was
by way of those of their officers who were attached to the tripartite mediating
patrols. However, this contribution had significance vastly greater than the
small numbers would imply.

For all practical purposes, therefore, the peacekeeping element of JF was
wholly composed of British troops. This body judged its success by the
absence of major fighting. Its presence, and the Green Lines which it
established and patrolled, were now generally seen as formalising the
communal divide: it created a shield behind which Turkish Cypriot
separatists were building an effective military capability and creating the
mechanisms of independent political control, albeit within a progressively
more impoverished community.

Greece and the Greek Cypriots had begun in January to lobby
energetically for the United Nations to take over peacekeeping responsibility.
For some weeks this was strongly opposed by the UK and the US, on the
assumption that such a move would open the way to a Russian,
Commonwealth or Third World involvement in Cypriot affairs, but in early
March this opposition was dropped, under the pressure of world opinion, and
an appropriate Security Council resolution was approved.* The assumption
voiced to me at JFHQ was that Britain would continue to exercise effective
control over the peacekeeping process by virtue of its established
infrastructure, its control of the intelligence process and the preponderance of
its military contribution.

No international diplomacy of this period seemed aimed at an equitable
solution for the Cypriots. Turkey and Greece, fractious neighbours with an
inter-twined history, had failed to build on the understanding of common
interests which produced the 1959 Zurich Agreement: they, Britain and
America were all now looking at Cyprus solely from the viewpoint of their
own interests, and of the danger to those interests that might be posed by a
genuinely independent Cyprus. Inside Cyprus, ministers, conscious of the
electoral sway of jingoist oratory, had little scope for bridge-building with
their former colleagues of the other community. Joint Liaison Committees

---

* Resolution 186 of 4 March 1964: UN security Doc. S/5575.

between Greek Cypriot and Turkish Cypriot administrators, with a British chairman where appropriate, in the major cities provided a formal structure for inter-communal problem-solving, but they were seldom effective. Despite a few successes, most notably in Famagusta, they tended towards sterile political debate and a static bureaucracy: they were vulnerable to media pressures and failed to create significant momentum towards re-unification.

The independent tripartite mediating organisation, backed by JF and answerable jointly to Makarios and Kutchuk, therefore remained the only entity which permanently and actively was seeking to drive forward a process of communal re-engagement.

I was so submerged in the day-to-day pressures of patrol affairs that I failed to realise the opportunities for mediation that were being lost in the townships. Sucked into whatever crisis occurred in the rural areas of Nicosia Zone, and for the most part confined to meetings with parastatal activists, I had little chance of contact with the mainstreams of the Greek Cypriot and Turkish Cypriot left and centre. These were the sections of society which tended towards compromise and the vision of an inclusive society, and their support would have helped to underpin my efforts. Only later, when I read the writings of T. C. Lanitis, did I realise that the militant views to which I had been for the most part exposed represented only one limited strand of Cypriot thinking.

The advent of General Carver was followed by one change in the constitution of the patrol. That I was a fluent Greek-speaker and married into a politically-connected Greek family had led initially to a Turkish Cypriot supposition that I must be biased against them. This view was largely dissipated by the trust that Kutchuk and Major Sepici gave me and later by the achievements of the patrol, but there were occasional moments in January when I thought I would be shot on suspicion of spying for the Greeks. Similarly there were times when the Greek Cypriots, having heard of my previous job in Malta as a naval intelligence analyst and not understanding the meaning of that title, took it that I was in Cyprus as an agent of British intelligence with a covert pro-Turkish agenda.

In reality, during my secondment to Cyprus I never knowingly had any connection with the Intelligence world, other than through casual chats with Major Macey. From my time in Malta and my briefings in London I had arrived in Cyprus already convinced that British intelligence agencies were seriously prejudiced in their analyses of Cypriot affairs: listening now to briefings at JFHQ meetings, it was hard to discern attitudes that offered much encouragement for the reconciliation process.

Having seen the strength of anti-British feeling among Greek Cypriots, it was easy to assume that in a unitary Cyprus there would be pressure for a reversion of the SBAs to Cypriot sovereignty. The British army and intelligence services, contrary to most political commentators in London, continued to claim that the SBAs were essential to the fulfilment of the country's regional mission. Their argument for this was strengthened by a magnification of the threats posed by the strength of the left and by inter-communal frictions.

When Greek Cypriot paramilitaries first began to use home-made tanks, usually converted and armoured bulldozers, Tassos Papadopoulos discussed the matter with me.

He said: "A lot of us are getting fed up because your intelligence sergeants are poking all over the island trying to discover where these tanks are located. They keep trampling on our flower-beds at night trying to see through our garage windows. It's upsetting our wives. There's no reason we shouldn't build tanks and we don't have any objection to General Young knowing about them." He then handed me a list of every Greek Cypriot tank currently in existence or under construction and said: "That's on condition that no more of our roses get destroyed."

Home-made tank, converted from a commercial bulldozer, crashes into a building during fighting in Ktima, 11 March 1964.

Locally constructed armoured car in 1 April parade.

Tanks aside, I was singularly unobservant of military hardware. It therefore must have strengthened the British army's insight into the build-up of weaponry in the rural areas of Nicosia Zone when Major John Burgess was attached to my patrol in early March, designated as a MILO (Military Liaison Officer). I was told that this was to remove some of the burden from my shoulders, to enhance my position with the Turkish Cypriots and to increase my personal security, since I continued to refuse to carry a weapon of any sort. I assumed that its probable true aims were to compensate for my unwillingness to act as a reporter on the military dispositions of the two communities and to enable General Carver to suppose that he was keeping an eye on me.

I was put in something of a quandary. I was determined that the patrol should merit the trust of the Cypriots, on whose behalf it was operating, and I thought that mediation and military-intelligence-gathering were fundamentally incompatible. On the other hand, as Tassos Papadopoulos had demonstrated, it was better to have an accurate picture of the military scene openly acquired than one that relied on the assessments of a Whitehall-serving spook.

Whether or not he was reporting privately to Carver, I came to see Burgess as a tower of common-sense and a real asset. I believe his main loyalty was transferred to the mediating process, but I never gave him access to my relationships with the politicians or the secret military leaders of the two communities, except when these were openly conducted.

On one or two occasions I passed out from exhaustion while on distant field patrols. Burgess would then pick me up, dump me into the Land Rover and drive me back to Nicosia. He and I jointly rented in Nicosia a house that lay plumb in the middle of the Green Line, equidistant between Greek Cypriot and Turkish Cypriot firing positions. We were never ourselves disturbed, but one or other group after nightfall would occasionally hoist a machine gun onto our roof and from there fire across the Green Line. Outsiders wishing to visit us for an evening drink had sometimes to run the gauntlet of a blast of automatic fire in order to reach our door.

Photograph taken of members of the Cypriot administration after the Turkish Cypriots had withdrawn from the government.
From the left front row: Glafcos Clerides, President of the House of Representatives, Dr. Spyridakis, Minister of Education and Culture, Antreas Araouzos, Minister of Commerce and Industry, Renos Solomides, Minister of Finance, Tassos Papadopoulos, Minister of Labour and Social Security. From the left back row: Stella Souliotou, Minister of Justice and Efstathios Lagagos, Greek Ambassador.

35. WAITING FOR UNO. MARCH 1964

'The resolution recommends the creation with the consent of the Government of Cyprus of a UN peacekeeping force. The composition and size of the force shall be established by the Secretary-General in consultation with the Governments of Cyprus, Greece, Turkey and Britain. The commander of the force shall be appointed by the Secretary-General and report to him. The force would contribute to the maintenance and restoration of law and order.'
(Excerpt from Security Council resolution 186)

UN resolution 186 of 4 March was greeted rapturously by most Greek Cypriots, who saw it as a major diplomatic victory over Britain and America, and with resignation by most Turkish Cypriots, who believed that only Ankara could produce a solution to their liking.

For a while conversation in the coffee-houses centred on the likely implications of a direct UN involvement in the island's affairs. The general Greek Cypriot view was that the change would lead to a straightforward enforcement of the principle that the majority had an absolute right to rule, so long as human rights were properly respected.

Regional leaders in Cyprus, assuming that they would soon be extending their authority to those areas currently under Turkish Cypriot control, began to increase pressure at key spots, with the British military presence increasingly ignored, except where it was believed to provide insurance against the threat of intervention from Turkey.

Irrespective of performance, the British had, in fact, exhausted their acceptability as exclusive peacekeepers. London could hardly claim to be a disinterested intermediary, when there was such a profound national involvement in the SBAs, with intelligence analysis deeming they would be threatened by an independent unitary state. The *de facto* separation imposed by the Green Line may have been the only obvious option at Christmas, but its continuance had locked the British into a divide-and-rule policy that was promoting sectarian division.

The Greek Cypriot leadership had succeeded in convincing its people that a NATO peacekeeping force would be no more than an extension of the British one, and that the British role was motivated not by goodwill but purely by imperial self-interest. The reality was that the imposition of any military force answerable to an outside authority, rather than to a mediating mechanism answerable to the Greek Cypriot and Turkish Cypriots leaderships, was almost bound to have a separatist effect. General Carver was later to write to me complaining that I appeared to think that he was responsible for all the woes of Cyprus and that I was the only one who could have solved its problems. In reply I suggested that there surely was no comparison between our roles: he had been an effective executor of a self-interested British policy, whereas I had merely been one component of a tripartite mediating initiative seconded into the service of the Cypriot people and answerable directly to the president and vice-president.

That tripartite mediating patrols should have peacekeeping troops working under their direction, rather than vice versa, was a concept probably unacceptable at the time to General Carver, and later to other members of the UN military command. This was despite clear evidence of the success achieved by the patrols when they led peacemaking efforts with support from sympathetic military peacekeeping units, both in the defusing of battle situations and in the achievement of political advance. Through pro-active tripartite mediating at ground level it was possible, for instance, to identify and neutralise extremist tendencies, whereas a purely military peacekeeping presence created barriers behind which extremism could develop and flourish in both communities.

From the beginning of March, with the apparatus of communal control now operating with reasonable effectiveness out of Nicosia, the tripartite patrols were increasingly called on by JFHQ to perform a trouble-shooting function rather than to act as general promoters and monitors of regional inter-communal relationships.

Also at the beginning of March, Major Greenwood was re-appointed to other duties. He had felt a special loyalty to General Young and was uncomfortable with the Carver take-over; he had been an original architect of the patrols, then had acted as their co-ordinator, while continuing in tandem with me to have a joint patrolling responsibility in the Kyrenia and Tillyria districts. Major McIntyre was a competent replacement, but Greenwood's intimate personal knowledge of and contacts in these two critical areas could not be easily or fully reconstituted.

Furthermore, it was now proving difficult to maintain internal cohesion in the patrols. At the beginning there had been a simple common thesis that anarchy and violence in the rural areas needed to be replaced by discipline and dialogue. Discipline was still a common target, but whereas Greek policies favoured reconciliation and reintegration, Turkish policies specifically advocated communal separation. This did not greatly matter in areas where questions of Turkish Cypriot evacuation did not arise, but elsewhere it began to lead to friction within the patrols and increasing distrust between the Greek and Turkish officers. Most of the problems centred on Captain Abdullah Gundes, a member of the Turkish Intelligence Corps who made little attempt to conceal his extremist sentiments or to conform to the concept of objective tripartite mediation.

The psychological pressures on patrol officers were intense. The patrols were continuously exposed to the worst and most violent aspects of inter-communal dispute and misunderstanding, which was harrowing for men whose emotions were deeply engaged. For the Greek and Turkish officers there was a three-way pull for their loyalties, between Athens or Ankara and their national contingents, the Cypriot communities on whose behalf they were involved, and a tripartite patrol which asked them to act as objective conciliators. Greek officers were often distraught at the violence they identified in Greek Cypriot extremists; Turkish officers were distraught at their inability to respond to what they saw as the intimidation of the Turkish Cypriot community.

There was a need for the villagers to be encouraged to release their pent-up tensions through discussion with the patrols and this meant that the officers had regularly to listen to virulent abuse directed at the governments that they were seen to represent: the Turkish officer would be condemned for the failure of Ankara to intervene; the Greek officer for the failure of Athens to achieve a constitutional formula which allowed the majority to manage the island's affairs; and the patrol commander for Britain's contribution to the problems and its failure to act as an affective guarantor of individual and collective Cypriot rights. Paradoxically, the more that patrol officers were trusted by the villagers, the more were they subjected to these complaints.

I was never once aware of being let down by Major Sepici, whose even-handed excellence provided powerful testimony to the ability of a regular Turkish army officer to act ethically and objectively in mediating situations of great intensity. Similarly, the two Greek officers who served with me, Captain Michos and Lieutenant Constantinides, were outstandingly good at the tasks that were given to them. Other patrol commanders were not always so fortunate: it was sometimes as difficult for them to produce a consensus within the group as it was to mediate difficult inter-communal disputes.

On the evening of 2 March, a British Land Rover taking Turkish liaison officers from JFHQ back to their contingent's barracks at Orta Keuy, as was normal routine, was hit by a Greek Cypriot truck. Major Sepici was severely injured.

Sepici was a man of simple faith, with a passionate hatred for the needless infliction of fear and suffering and violence. He had been a superb mediator whose efforts had provided hope for eventual reconciliation between the two rural communities in Nicosia and Famagusta Zones. As he lay injured in the road, Greek Cypriot bystanders stole his revolver and made notes for next day's news story, which charged that his presence in a British vehicle was "blatant evidence of Anglo-Turkish collusion."

36.   KYRENIA AREA.   MARCH 1964

Each eruption of violence in Cyprus, volcano-like, threw out incendiary fragments into the regions round about. Days of careful attention from a joint patrol were often then needed to ensure that none of these ignited a further blaze.

On 3 March, my unit circled the Photta-Ayios Ermolaos area to check that nothing explosive lingered from the confrontation there three days earlier.

One of the villages visited was the Greek Cypriot Sisklipos, small and isolated a few miles to the north of Ayios Ermolaos. There had been reports that Turkish Cypriot fighters on the Pentadaktylos range were advancing their forward posts in this direction so that they could, when appropriate, exert pressure against a Greek Cypriot village to the south of the Kyrenia hills.

By chance Sisklipos had never before been visited either by a tripartite patrol or by a regular British unit. All that its inhabitants knew of the course of current events had come by way of second-hand reports or by perusal of the Greek press.

When we drove into the village there was no sign of life anywhere: battens were up on the door to the coffee-house, the school was empty, nothing moved in the streets. I had an unpleasant feeling that the village might already have been attacked and evacuated. My Greek and Turkish liaison officers both declined to leave their Land Rovers, fearing that we might have stumbled into an ambush.

Eventually I located two small children hiding behind a farm building. When they had been calmed to the point where they could speak coherently, they told me that the villagers had seen "the British army" approaching, had been terrified and had run away to hide.

The children were despatched to inform the village's men-folk that, rather than the British army, we were one Greek, one Turk and one Englishman, and that we were waiting at the coffee-house to have a drink and a cigarette with them.

The owner of the coffee-house arrived first, followed somewhat cautiously by a stream of villagers. Hesitation was quickly replaced by warm hospitality. Our explanation of recent events as seen by an independent observer was greeted with surprise and great interest and with the request that in future we should visit the village regularly to keep them better informed. However, when at the end of the meeting we mentioned that it was intended that a regular British patrol should in future be stationed near Prophitis Elias, on the heights to the north of the village so that it could observe the whole area and forestall any Turkish Cypriot attempt to attack Sisklipos, the villagers were unanimous in saying this would be unacceptable. They would, they said, rather be attacked by the Turks than have British troops located so close to them.

Next day, 4 March, my patrol returned to the area to complete the handing back of the last of the Photta hostages. With us that day was an American film crew from CBS compiling a programme on the work of my unit. After successful filming in Photta, to record the Turkish Cypriot point of view, a meeting was convened in the village square at Ayios Ermolaos. Every one of the inhabitants attended. I explained the object of the filming, congratulated the villagers on their restraint and co-operation during the Photta 'battle' and then made a brief speech to camera about recent events and the general situation.

One of the more weighty members of the audience said he would like to make a reply and after combing his hair and preparing himself for some minutes he launched into an earnest and demonstrative discourse on the rights of the Greek Cypriot cause.

After solemnly filming this for fifteen minutes, the camera crew ran out of film and started to put away their equipment. At this the speaker became outraged. At his urging, the uncomprehending Americans were seized and manhandled by the crowd. Requested by me to behave more civilly and to explain themselves the villagers told me that the Americans were, as they had been warned by their press, obviously biased against them: the crew had filmed my speech in its entirety, they said, but had cut off the filming of their own representative before he had finished expounding his views.

We restored good relations and rescued the CBS crew, who then pointed empty cameras at the Greek Cypriot spokesman for the lengthy remainder of his discourse. Then we returned to Photta, where we were told by the Greek Cypriot hostage that he had been treated so well by the Turkish Cypriots that he had decided not to return to Ayios Ermolaos. I explained to the TMT leader that it would not be in Photta's best interest if the man stayed on: when this was reluctantly accepted the patrol set off to deliver him back to Ayios Ermolaos.

However, en route we stopped with the aim of consuming a large chicken and champagne hamper that had been sent out to us from Nicosia by Mr Ernie Birnbaum of CBS in recognition of our services to his crew. We had hardly started on this meal when a message was received from JFHQ directing that we were urgently required elsewhere. Fighting had broken out around Kazaphani.

Kazaphani was a large mixed village, predominantly Turkish Cypriot, lying a few miles south-east of Kyrenia: close above it, on the north-facing slopes of the Pentadaktylos Range, was the all-Greek Cypriot village of Bellapais. Lawrence Durrell had written movingly about this village in 'Bitter Lemons', a book that I re-read regularly to remind myself how things had been in Cyprus at the start of the EOKA campaign for *enosis* in the 1950s.

We arrived at Kazaphani, having returned the now much-confused hostage to Photta as we sped through, to find that the Turkish Cypriot quarter was under desultory siege. This had been one of Major Greenwood's villages and I had no contacts there and only a sketchy knowledge of the local

'Secret Army' and TMT command-structures. On neither side would anyone confess to being in charge.

Eventually, we persuaded a Greek Cypriot police detachment, which had been firing into the Turkish Cypriot sector from the direction of the approach roads from Kyrenia, to pull back and to refrain from further shooting unless directly attacked. Then we set off to press a similar arrangement on the Turkish Cypriots facing Bellapais, but ourselves came under heavy Greek Cypriot fire from the south. Captain Michos, having several times been narrowly missed, was despatched by me to locate and restrain the Greek Cypriots who were firing at us: while he was doing so, the Greek Cypriot police to the west and a group to the north opened up again, apparently convinced that 'overs' and ricochets from their compatriots to the south constituted an attack on them.

Leaving Colonel Akova in Kazaphani to keep the Turkish Cypriots there under control, I collected Captain Michos and drove with him up through orange and lemon groves towards Bellapais. We left the Land Rover outside the village and walked up to the commanding crest-line from the rear. It was a day of mixed rain and sunshine and the glimpses we had across Kazaphani to the sea were breathtaking.

Over a hundred members of the 'Secret Army' were stretched along the ridge in firing positions. The commander of the most advanced flank we discovered to be a pleasant young Athens University undergraduate. We persuaded him to withdraw his men and to guide us to whomever was in overall command.

There we came upon a furious confrontation. A small unit of the 1st Parachute Regiment, which had been in Kazaphani when fire was opened from the direction of Bellapais, had moved straight out and up the hill towards the Greek Cypriots in an effort to stop the battle. During the climb they had themselves come under well-directed fire. Now the Greek Cypriot and British units were facing up to each other, each in a state of blazing anger.

Captain Michos and I were in the process of trying to resolve this situation, when a number of Land Rovers arrived at speed from Kyrenia and thirty or so policemen leapt out with their weapons at the ready, clearly spoiling for a fight. They were led by a senior gendarmerie officer who waved his revolver with such impatient menace that Michos hurried off in search of cover. The officer shouted to be told where 'they' were and added a hair-raising description of the fate that he intended to inflict on 'them'. He calmed down abruptly when told by Michos, from a safe distance, that there was a Greek-speaking Englishman present.

The officer said that the police station in Kyrenia had been informed that British troops were attempting to disarm members of the Greek Cypriot security forces. He had come specifically to prevent such a development. He intended to arrest the British troops and he would use whatever force was needed to do so.

Eventually the conversation was steered into calmer channels and the officer was convinced by me that the six British soldiers had had no intention of trying to disarm a force of over a hundred Greek Cypriots, but were simply seeking to persuade them to cease firing.

I despatched the Paras back to their HQ in one of my Land Rovers and Michos and I treated the Greek Cypriot police and army commanders to coffee and cigarettes in Bellapais square. It was then amicably agreed that the time had come for a Kazaphani peace conference.

Just as talks were beginning in one of the schools in Kazaphani there was a flurry of shooting from the eastern edge of the village. Discussions were interrupted. I went out and discovered that a Greek Cypriot policeman had accidentally shot himself. Other posts had then opened up under the impression that his shooting signalled a new attack.

Talks were resumed in unexpected good humour. Attitudes were surprisingly moderate and agreement was quickly reached on preliminary terms for a long-term cease-fire. Both sides said, however, that they would need to get approval from higher authority before any terms could be ratified. It was agreed that the meeting would reconvene at 1000 next day and that there would be no militant action of any sort in the meantime. The conference then broke up in a spirit of general cordiality.

By now I had been able to get a clearer picture of how these hostilities had started. They had been preceded by a heightening of tension during the last week of February: in part this was due to an increasingly belligerent attitude from the Greek Cypriot police and in part to claims by a newly robust TMT, broadcast through Radio *Bayrak*, that it was now prepared to 'guarantee' protection for Turkish Cypriot communities to the north of the Kyrenia range. The announcement had been preceded by the transfer of additional TMT weapons and fighters into Temblos and Kazaphani.

The Greek Cypriots, who already ascribed to TMT a greater strength in this region than in fact it possessed, noted these movements and concluded that the Turkish Cypriots might attempt to cut the coastal roads out of Kyrenia, westwards towards Lapithos and eastwards towards Ayios Amvrosios. TMT leaders later told me that they had indeed pondered such a move but had concluded that it was impracticable. In purely local terms this was a logical decision, seeing that Temblos and Kazaphani would have been impossible to defend against determined Greek Cypriot attack, but in terms of seeking to provoke an intervention from Turkey, the concept was not so far-fetched.

Late in February, the Greek Cypriot leadership decided that TMT's reinforcement of the villages was creating a potentially explosive situation and that an attempt to re-impose police authority throughout the region, which had already been planned, should be pressed forward without further delay.

Before the arrival of TMT reinforcements, Greek Cypriot police units had patrolled into the Turkish Cypriot sector of Kazaphani and occasionally also into that of Kyrenia. When British troops established a permanent presence in Kyrenia, they tried to persuade the Greek Cypriots to limit these patrols or to carry them out in units composed jointly of British soldiers and unarmed Greek Cypriot police, but this proposal was firmly rejected by senior Greek Cypriot authorities. I could find no indication that the British had similarly tried to persuade TMT to withdraw its armed units from the villages.

The Greek Cypriots now tried to re-establish their former pattern of patrols and began also to send heavily armed units ranging close to known Turkish Cypriot defensive positions. Turkish Cypriot fighters became increasingly jumpy and the other villagers more and more frightened. On 4 March, a Turkish Cypriot position on the western edge of Kazaphani opened fire in nervous reaction when a police Land Rover approached on a track not normally used by the Greek Cypriots. The police took to the ditch and returned fire. Shortly afterwards, two large detachments of police and auxiliaries moved into the area from Kyrenia and 'Secret Army' units took up positions to the north of Bellapais. Firing soon afterwards became general.

When the peace conference in Kazaphani was concluded, my patrol drove to Kyrenia police headquarters and spent some time there establishing a relationship with the Greek Cypriot police leaders. Then Colonel Akova pleaded an urgent need to return to his contingent for consultations and Captain Michos and I moved on to Clio's for a three-hour working dinner with Captain Augustis, a key regional leader of 'The Organisation', to whom Tassos Papadopoulos had provided me with an introduction.

Cyprus police in action. March 1964.

37. KAZAPHANI AND KARMI.
5 MARCH 1964

The day started badly. At JFHQ I was told by Colonel Akova that it had been decided that Captain Abdullah Gundes would in future be the Turkish member of my patrol, since he was "the expert on the Kyrenia villages." I had a nasty feeling in my stomach, knowing that Captain Gundes had been the cause of friction and complaint in every tripartite unit of which he had been a part. The only reason that a formal request had not been made by JFHQ to the Turkish contingent for his replacement was that it was feared such a move might trigger a general Turkish withdrawal from the patrol organisation.

When we reached Kazaphani, Captain Gundes launched into an abusive outburst against me for speaking to the villagers in Greek rather than through my interpreters. He then disappeared alone into the Turkish Cypriot sector, despite my request not to do so. When eventually he returned, he told me that he regarded the situation as critical and that he must return immediately to his unit so that the Turkish contingent could "itself take such steps as were necessary to defend Kazaphani." There were further acrimonious exchanges when I refused to accede to this demand or to accept that the patrol should in any way divert from its normal style of operation. In the end I told him that either he could conform with our normal procedures or I would immediately request that his service with the mediating patrol be terminated.

It quickly became obvious that the continuation of the Kazaphani peace talks was going to be very difficult. In part this was because there was no longer a consensus in my own team and in part because the Greek Cypriots and Turkish Cypriots had both received directives from above as to the implications of the discussions and the limits to which they could negotiate. Instead of the previous day's negotiators, Superintendent Neophitos Vassiliou was acting for the Greek Cypriot police, Captain Augustis for 'The Organisation' and the 'Secret Army' and Superintendent Ali Assad for the Turkish Cypriots, these being joined by the *mukhtars*, a TMT representative and village constables from the Greek and Turkish Cypriot sectors of Kazaphani.

The previous evening's meeting had established "on a realistic basis" the need for the final agreement to be signed on behalf of the Turkish Cypriots by representatives of whatever bodies exercised power within their community. This wording was now rejected by Superintendent Vassiliou who said that it was a Greek Cypriot precondition that there could be no continuance of negotiation with representatives of an organisation that the Cypriot State did not recognise (i.e. the Turkish Cypriot police) or of one that it considered to be illegal (i.e. TMT). Vassiliou was unimpressed by assertions that the men were not there as representatives of any organisation, but simply as those members of the Turkish Cypriot community who were able to bind the Turkish Cypriots in Kazaphani to an agreement.

Superintendent Vassiliou then said that he was rescinding all undertakings given by his deputy the previous evening. From this moment, the hope of a constructive outcome from the meeting was dead. Members of the Greek and international press were now present in force and under their gaze, Ali Assad and two other Turkish Cypriots were forced embarrassingly to leave the room. The session then continued with the Turkish Cypriots represented solely by the now totally silent Captain Gundes and by the village *mukhtar*, who was too overawed and nervous to speak coherently. Superintendent Vassiliou made it clear that the police would refuse to enter into any undertaking that might be construed as compromise on their part. Captain Augustis spoke constructively and with moderation but was not prepared to have a public disagreement with Vassiliou. After an hour, the meeting was again recessed to allow the participants to have discussion with their superiors over a proposal for disarmament of the Turkish Cypriots to be followed by joint British/Greek Cypriot patrolling of Turkish Cypriot areas.

Captain Gundes now rediscovered his voice. He reiterated that the situation required immediate action by the Turkish contingent and demanded that he be taken back to Nicosia forthwith. His request was again refused. He declined my offer to pass to JFHQ whatever message he wished to send so that it could be relayed to his regiment.

At this point I was told by Superintendent Vassiliou that he had been informed that Karmi was under attack. It was agreed that I would seek to verify the position there before any movement of Greek Cypriot forces was authorised.

Karmi was a Greek Cypriot village a few miles to the south west of Kyrenia. It was reached either by a direct road that passed through the Turkish Cypriot village of Temblos or by a more roundabout route through Ayios Yeoryios and Trimithi. It lay on the upper reaches of the Pentadaktylos foothills. It was highly exposed to crags below St Hilarion Castle which had been developed as forward positions by Turkish Cypriot fighters.

As my Land Rovers came out of fruit orchards into a patch of open ground on the eastern edge of Karmi, they were hit by automatic fire from the hills above. My own driver accelerated into the cover of the first houses in the village. Looking back, I saw the second Land Rover skid off the road and Captain Gundes dive out of it into the ditch.

There was nobody out of doors in the village but somebody shouted at us from behind shutters that the *mukhtar* was in the coffee-house on the left near the top of the main street.

The main street of Karmi runs steeply upwards in the direction of St Hilarion. The Turkish Cypriots on the heights above were sporadically directing heavy Bren gun fire down this road, with ricochets zinging off the houses on both sides. Major Burgess, Captain Michos and I worked our way cautiously up the right hand side of the road, dodging from cover to cover, until we were opposite the coffee-house. I then was the first to go, sprinting across the road and diving from bright sunshine into the semi-darkness inside the coffee-house.

As my eyes adjusted to the half-light I made out a handsome moustachioed Greek Cypriot sitting in the depths of the room. Without getting up he said: "Commander Packard, I presume."

This was the legendary Sergeant Makrides. He had figured prominently in the stories of Turkish Cypriot villagers throughout the Kyrenia and Ayia Irini areas as a strongman who would appear from time to time to lecture them on the need for peaceful co-existence (which invariably had had the effect of increasing their sense of insecurity). I had for some time been seeking a meeting with him, but he had been warned by Hassapis to beware of me.

Burgess and Michos joined us after making their own runs when there was a lull in the Turkish Cypriot firing. We were treated to coffee and toasted halloumi cheese and then exchanged toasts with Makrides in a fine local brandy.

On the opposite side of the road from the coffee-house was an antiquated telephone kiosk. Every once in a while the phone would ring. The owner of the coffee-house would then curse, grit his teeth, cross himself, sprint across the road and answer the phone, speak briefly, cross himself again, run back and collapse puffing into a chair. At each of these appearances the Turkish Cypriot Bren gun fire would intensify, spattering around him as he made the crossing.

Makrides explained to me that this was the only telephone in the village and that the coffee-house owner had a duty to answer incoming calls. The shop was the purveyor of an excellent local wine and most of the calls, apparently, were from neighbouring villages wishing to place an order.

The village schoolhouse was in a highly visible position downhill from the coffee-house. Its windows had all been shot out and its only door, already shredded with bullet holes, was directly exposed to incoming fire. I was told that all the schoolchildren were still inside the building and that they had been lying, frightened, on the floor since the Turkish Cypriot attack started five hours earlier.

Since my radio Land Rover was out of sight at the bottom of the village, I was obliged to emulate the coffee-house owner and sprint across to the village phone. From there I got through to JFHQ, explained the situation and asked for military support.

An hour later a patrol of British scout cars entered the village. Captain Morgan Jones, nonchalantly smoking a large cigar, led this unit in on foot. Since it was impossible to get the armoured cars into covering positions close to the school, the crews formed a protective barrier in front of the door and the children were then led out behind them to safety.

The Turkish Cypriots chose this moment to resume firing towards the school. Considering that the children were endangered, I signalled to Morgan-Jones that he had my authority to fire in return. British troops then fired a series of heavy bursts towards the hills. I was unaware until later in the day that this was the first time since the peacekeeping mission was agreed on 28 December that British troops had opened fire.

There was a pause in the Turkish Cypriot firing and the children were all quickly ushered to security to the rear of the village.

After a wholly amicable exchange of views and having agreed that we would soon meet again, Sergeant Makrides saw me off with an expansive hug. On the way out of the village we located Captain Gundes crouched on all fours for protection behind a horse-trough. I sent him on ahead to St Hilarion Castle to tell the TMT leaders to call off the attack on Karmi and to expect me there for a meeting later. The ferret patrol stayed on in the village as a safeguard against any renewal of the attack.*

The Turkish Cypriot attack on Karmi was delivered in an attempt to relieve Greek Cypriot pressure against Kazaphani. Outside Tillyria it was the only occasion of my experience where the Turkish Cypriots in Nicosia Zone initiated a major and sustained attack against a Greek Cypriot community. The attack killed no-one and did not in fact have any effect on the course of events elsewhere: in any case its objective did not become apparent until after the cease-fire at Kazaphani had been achieved. A subsequent TMT demand that the Greek Cypriots were to pull back all armed units from around Temblos and Kazaphani before the Turkish Cypriot fighters would withdraw from above Karmi was flatly rejected by the Greek Cypriot command.

At nightfall, cease-fires were effective in all areas throughout Kyrenia District, but no progress had been made towards a lasting regional settlement.

While Captain Gundes conferred with TMT leaders in St Hilarion Castle, Captain Michos and I went to police headquarters in Kyrenia and discussed the events of the day with Superintendent Vassiliou and his senior officers. The effect on them of what had happened at Karmi was startling. They claimed it was the first concrete example of a British initiative supportive of the Greek Cypriots. They phoned through to all the main Greek newspapers and asked them to publish tributes to British peacekeeping efforts in Kyrenia Region; they issued instructions that anti-British demonstrations which had been planned for the next day were now to be banned; most importantly they finally agreed to discuss what practical compromises could be made towards a general settlement for the region.

Dinner was brought up from the police canteen, so that there need be no break in the discussions, and we concluded on a mutual high. As we were leaving, Superintendent Vassiliou pointed out to us a monitor that was being run from his office on the operating frequency of the Para unit in Kyrenia. At that moment a transmission opened up and the clear voice of an English officer launched into a tirade of imprecations against the Greek Cypriots, claiming that the police had broken their word and re-opened fire against Temblos.

Vassiliou, Mamas, Michos and I stood in embarrassed silence. It became clear that the report was coming from a British unit stationed at the approaches to Temblos. Vassiliou said to me mournfully: "I gave you my word

---

* It provided fair comment on the situation in Cyprus that Karmi remained passionately pro-British for about a week. Two weeks after the fighting, a regular British patrol entering the village was stoned by schoolchildren, with their teacher urging them on.

that all action against Temblos would be suspended. I can't believe the report is true."

Michos and I drove back to Temblos, where we located the British section commander bubbling with rage against the Greek Cypriots. We investigated the shooting and were able fairly quickly to establish that it was in fact only the Turkish Cypriots who had fired. The British lieutenant, duly chastened, admitted his error and was advised both to verify his facts in future and to watch his language on open radio lines.

Vassiliou accepted my explanation and my apology for what had happened, but it was clear that his earlier general goodwill towards the British had evaporated. He told me: "Things start to go better and there is hope of co-operation and then something like this occurs and proves that the English are indeed prejudiced against us."

I said: "No. It just confirms that some individuals have prejudices and that people make mistakes", but I knew the incident would continue to rankle with him and that it would be harder in future to get his agreement on any proposal that involved the use of British forces.

At St Hilarion Castle, I had a few words with the TMT leaders about the wisdom of avoiding a confrontation over Kazaphani or Karmi. Then I drove Captain Gundes back to Nicosia. On the way I told him, as diplomatically as I could manage at that late hour, that it was clear he did not fit into my team or accept my concept of how the patrol should operate, and that I therefore would be requesting the attachment of a different officer for the future.

When we arrived at JFHQ I was presented by Captain Michos with a note which said that he would refuse to accompany any further patrols in which Captain Gundes was a participant.

I located Colonel Akova, explained the position and pressed on him how vital it was that the patrols work as integrated and harmonious units. I then asked the JFHQ duty officer to explain to General Carver that there might be a storm coming.

38. KYRENIA AREA.
7-11 MARCH 1964

No Turkish officer appeared for the morning briefing on 7 March, so Captain Michos and I had to operate alone. In the evening I was told by Colonel Akova, to my considerable relief that he had appointed Captain Oust Pamir to work with me in the future. At the same time JFHQ provided me with a copy of a letter which it had received from the commander of the Turkish Regiment:

> "Subject: The Work of Liaison Officers.
>
> 1. According to what has been learnt from the people, when Commander Martin Packard went to Temblos with the Turkish Liaison Officer, Captain Abdullah Gundes and a Greek officer, he took no notice of the fire, threats and advanced preparations for war made by the Greek Cypriots who surrounded the village. He said to the villagers, in a threatening manner, "Have you received reinforcements from St Hilarion? I want to go there and see. If you try to stop me I will go there by armoured car and if necessary I will open fire." Later on in Karmi village, without any good reason, he put his threats to open fire into action. Attention is drawn to the fact that the aforementioned officer, who is a representative of the peacekeeping force, instead of lowering the high state of tension which existed, had recourse to fire, which was contrary to the procedure of British units up to now and which was provocation to one side.
>
> 2. Liaison officers who are with your headquarters are posted by the Regiment because of the special situation in the area. Our liaison officer is not under the command of Commander Packard, but has been detached to work jointly in accordance with military administrative customs. Commander Packard's request to change the Turkish liaison officer who works with him when he desires is not met favourably by us. I submit that the aforementioned officer be kept from behaving in such a way which damages the spirit of joint work."

JFHQ had responded to this with a brief note pointing out that on an extremely difficult day, cease-fires had been achieved throughout the region. It suggested this was an adequate refutation of the Turkish charges and said that, since the aim of the appointments was to establish effective teams, it was fortunate that Captain Gundes could now return to his regular position with Major McIntyre's patrol.

It was symptomatic of a growing distancing between the tripartite units and regular peacekeeping troops that on 7 and 8 March, when the situation in Kyrenia Region was clearly building towards further inter-communal trouble, the JF unit in the region declined the offer of tripartite mediating support. Instead, we undertook missions in the Kythrea and Myrtou areas, where serious problems also seemed to be impending.

At the same time we received reports from Kazaphani that the situation was steadily deteriorating. On 6 March, the Greek Cypriots had advanced their forward positions towards the Turkish Cypriot sector and on the following afternoon there had been a prolonged exchange of fire, apparently triggered by an accidental discharge. Sergeant Makrides had then moved 'Secret Army' reinforcements into positions to the south, but had been persuaded to keep them under cover, although they had gone on to alarm the Turkish Cypriots with a vociferous singing of the Greek battle hymn. At a cease-fire meeting which followed further firing, the Greek Cypriots claimed that the incident had been started when four Turkish Cypriots tried to approach Bellapais behind a flock of sheep.

On the afternoon of 8 March, Greek Cypriot automatic fire directed at the Turkish Cypriot quarter had led to more general shooting. There were no casualties, but the Turkish Cypriot villagers, now extremely frightened, sent word that they wished for help in arranging to evacuate.

That night urgent discussions in Kyrenia and in Nicosia, involving JFHQ, the Greek Cypriot police and the JLC, but not the mediating unit, covered two options: first that there should be a jointly agreed evacuation; or, second, that the Turkish Cypriots would give up all their weapons and that the responsibility for their protection would then be taken over by the British.

The same night, of 8/9 March, the entire force of Turkish Cypriot fighters and TMT left Kazaphani and moved with their weapons up through Greek Cypriot and British lines to rejoin the main body of TMT paramilitaries at St Hilarion. Their departure was known immediately to leaders of 'The Organisation', who told me what had happened but who declined to pass on the same information to the Greek Cypriot police authorities.

On the morning of 9 March, the Para unit in Kyrenia reported that there was a further worsening of the situation at Kazaphani and asked that I get there without delay. On the western approach road, I found Greek Cypriot and British troops confronting each other, the Greek Cypriots apparently having stated that they would resist with force any British attempt to move troops into the village.

I got to Kyrenia police headquarters as fast as possible. There Superintendent Vassiliou told me it had been decided that the Greek Cypriots would re-impose their authority over the whole of Kazaphani, in the course of which they would disarm the Turkish Cypriots, using whatever force was necessary. Until this was completed, no British troops were to be allowed into the village, nor would any further Turkish Cypriot movement in or out of Kazaphani be permitted.

Meanwhile, he said, discussions were proceeding in Nicosia to finalise the terms for a settlement. He refused to accept my suggestion that there probably were now no TMT units left in the village. I said that with the

Turkish Cypriot villagers cut off from all links with higher authority and lacking any independent advice there could soon be a collapse into chaos and that any armed attack on them could lead to a heavy and wholly unnecessary loss of life.

Vassiliou claimed that the British military presence had exacerbated the situation. He refused permission for the whole patrol to move into Kazaphani but said he was happy to accept that I go in alone.

Leaving Captain Pamir and Captain Michos for a long wait at police headquarters, I took off with both Land Rovers for Kazaphani, being saluted by the Greek Cypriot police as I passed through their roadblocks.

The Turkish Cypriot sector of the village was in a state of turmoil. It was immediately apparent that all the fighting men had gone. The women and children and old men who were left were all terrified, convinced that a holocaust was about to burst upon them. They had crowded into a small square at the top of the village, dragging with them whatever they hoped to save. At the side of the square were two aged buses apparently about to topple over, so loaded were their roofs with an assortment of furniture, bedding, baskets, animals, plastic containers, boxes, kitchenware and sacks. The approach roads were littered with a sad trail of other items discarded as untransportable. Three old men were laid out in a corner, apparently too incapacitated to stand. Scattered clusters of women, surrounded by screaming children, were producing an awful cacophony of wailing.

The three soldiers in my Land Rover crews applied themselves with a natural skill to the calming of this scene. Having parked their vehicles at the entrances to the square, so as to provide a suggestion of physical defence, they circulated among the villagers, patting backs, cooing at babies, tidying up the square and conveying a general sense of competence and good order. We had taken to carrying with us on patrol a large stock of chocolate and cigarettes, precisely for situations such as this, and these were an additional aid to the ending of collective hysteria.

When some measure of calm had returned, I addressed the crowd in Greek,* apologising for my lack of Turkish and explaining what was being negotiated in Nicosia. The people told me that it was not so much the firing into the village that had frightened them but that they had twice tried to evacuate and had each time been driven back by the Greek Cypriot police, who had told them that the village would be attacked if they did not hand over their weapons. They had said that all that was left were a few hunting shotguns, but the police had refused to believe them. They told me that none of them would stay if control of the village were to pass into the hands of the Greek Cypriot police.

As decisions were taken at the negotiating table in Nicosia – and they were taken, contradicted, reworded and rejected with rapidity throughout the day – they were relayed to me by radio from the Para unit transmitter in Kyrenia. The discussions revolved around the implications and *modus operandi*

---

* Most Turkish Cypriots could speak reasonable Greek. On the other hand very few Greek Cypriots could speak any Turkish.

of a proposal that the British take full responsibility for the physical safety of the Turkish Cypriots in Kazaphani in return for full and total Turkish Cypriot disarmament.

Eventually I obtained permission from Kutchuk's office to try and prevent an evacuation on the basis of these terms. The wording of the clause relating to British rights of defence, as it was dictated to me over the radio, made it clear that the intention was for protection to be continued for as long as a need existed. This enabled me to say to the villagers that, for the first time since the fighting at Christmas, a Turkish Cypriot community was being offered an open-ended guarantee of armed protection by the peacekeeping force.

I found it hard to believe that this was what was really intended by the British and Greek Cypriot authorities. Both had previously gone to great lengths to avoid anything that even hinted at such an arrangement, which had always been a target of the Turkish Cypriots. However I was told by JFHQ to stop querying the text.

On that basis I persuaded the Turkish Cypriots to stay, although they lodged a proviso that they must be free to evacuate later if they felt that circumstances justified it.

Those villagers, who had been sitting in the buses since dawn, fearing that they would lose their seats if they left them even for a moment, were now coaxed out. A slow movement began to recover belongings and move back into abandoned homes.

Early in the afternoon, British troops were allowed to move into the village and the commanding officer of 1 Para arrived with Mr Berberoglu, who was acting on behalf of Kutchuk. Meanwhile Vassiliou and Mamas moved into the Greek Cypriot sector to await the Turkish Cypriot 'surrender'. The local and international press were also there in force, having been advised by the Greek Cypriot authorities that this was to be a decisive moment in Cypriot history.

Then something went wrong. The effect of Mr Berberoglu's talks with the Turkish Cypriot villagers was the reverse of what he intended. They decided that they wished after all to evacuate and not to hand over their few remaining shotguns. Women and children began to hurry off to recapture their seats in the buses.

Kutchuk's office, when contacted by radio link, announced that the negotiated terms were now deemed, on reconsideration, to be unacceptable. The Greeks Cypriots issued a two-hour ultimatum.

This pattern continued throughout the afternoon, with the Turkish Cypriots dithering, changing their position again and again, but now refusing to accept any arrangement that could be represented, even indirectly, as one of ignominy or surrender.

A stream of messages went from me and the Paras to JFHQ urging that pressure be applied at top level to get a clear and final agreement. The Greek Cypriots continued to build up their forces, clearly now intent on military victory. The Para Brigade troops in Kazaphani began to build defensive positions in preparation for a firefight with the Greek Cypriots. I shadowed Superintendent Vassiliou, urging on him that Greek Cypriot paramilitary units must be held in check and fighting avoided so long as an opportunity still existed for negotiated settlement. Vassiliou still refused to accept that there were now no TMT or Turkish Cypriot fighting units in Kazaphani. Berberoglu became increasingly frustrated with the difficulty of making contact with Kutchuk by way of my Land Rover radio. One Greek Cypriot ultimatum after another was cancelled. Each time, a new and shorter one was imposed.

As evening fell, it became obvious that Mamas and the younger Greek Cypriot police leaders would not be restrained for much longer: they were convinced that the Turkish Cypriots still had automatic weapons in Kazaphani and that some sort of treachery was being cooked up between the Turkish Cypriots and British forces. Vassiliou's refusal to give the go-ahead was the only bar to a general attack, and I was concerned that he was close to physical breakdown.

In the event it was a very close-run thing. Acceptance of the final terms reached us from Nicosia only minutes before the expiry of what even I had taken to be the ultimate deadline. Vassiliou afterwards let it be known that it was only because of his personal undertaking to me that he had refused to allow the attack to begin. Captain Augustis and Sergeant Makrides, with either of whom I would have found it easier to deal, both kept well out of my way until the final decision had been taken.

The last of ten shotguns still in the village was sorrowfully handed over to the police just before nightfall. A few minutes later, Superintendent Vassiliou collapsed, from a mixture of exhaustion and nervous stress, and Sub-Inspector Mamas took over command of the Kyrenia gendarmerie forces.

In his report of the day's events, the commanding officer of 1st Para, after describing the actual hand-over of the shotguns, wrote:

"*After further delay I accompanied Inspector Mamas to Kyrenia police station to have the receipt typed. On the way he stalled over moving the police roadblock outside the village, claiming that he must get orders from above.*

'*A' Troop of RHA were held up there. I ordered them to by-pass the block on foot. This was achieved in the dark without detection and they had control of the 'Green Line' (i.e. the inter-communal dividing line in Kazaphani) by 2030, with a troop also controlling the high ground to the south of the village. 'A' troop of Life Guards was also in position. Inspector Mamas stated that he was to control the village as the Turks had not handed over their automatic weapons. He was furious when I told him that British troops were already in control and would protect the disarmed Turks, with fire if necessary. He eventually calmed down and agreed to a joint search the following morning and to withdraw his police and roadblocks once they were satisfied there were no arms in the village. He appeared to get his orders by telephone from Augustis.*"

In fact, Captain Augustis was dining with my patrol at Clio's, occasionally excusing himself to receive reports from and issue instructions to Mamas by telephone.

The agreement hammered out for Kazaphani was taken as applying also to the town of Kyrenia, where there had been great tension but no shooting. From here, too, the entire Turkish Cypriot fighting strength had surreptitiously withdrawn to St Hilarion under cover of darkness, leaving Temblos as the only Turkish Cypriot community to the north of the Pentadaktylos Range which contained a TMT fighting unit.

Unfortunately there had been a failure in Nicosia to append any signatures to the Kazaphani-Kyrenia agreement and the interpretation of its terms was soon in serious dispute. The Greek Cypriots claimed that no formal text had ever been drawn up and they denied that any special rights had been conferred on the peacekeeping forces with regard to the provision of permanent security for the Turkish Cypriots.

On 10 March, the climate around Kyrenia was fairly relaxed. On this day there was a thorough search of the Turkish Cypriot quarter of Kazaphani by joint patrols made up of Greek Cypriot gendarmerie and British soldiers. Some explosives, detonators and Molotov Cocktails were discovered but none of the rifles, automatics or mortars expected by the Greek Cypriot police. A few Turkish Cypriot families packed up and left Kazaphani and Kyrenia, telling us that they thought they would feel safer in Turkish Cypriot villages to the south of the Pentadaktylos Range.

On 11 March, however, we found that things had again sharply deteriorated. The Greek Cypriots had now come to realise the interpretation that the British and Turkish Cypriots were putting on the agreement of the 9th, and they claimed that they had been tricked. Roadblocks were set up throughout the region, strong paramilitary forces moved out to surround Temblos and police headquarters formally notified the local Para commander that British troop movements must be restricted to those agreed in advance in writing and that the British post must immediately be withdrawn from Kazaphani.

Arriving at Temblos to rendezvous with me, Major Burgess was stopped at a gendarmerie roadblock and refused permission to pass. He and the gendarmerie sergeant both became increasingly pugnacious and, summoned by Burgess' radio operator, I got there to find them glaring eyeball-to-eyeball, each with a Sten gun stuck into the other's ample stomach.

An explanation in Greek and a phone-call to the now-recovered Vassiliou resulted in general embraces and good humour. Burgess and I then moved into Temblos to find a strong group of fighters standing to in expectation of imminent attack, repeatedly talking by radio-link to St Hilarion Castle in the belief that they could co-ordinate their defence.

Captain Pamir and I persuaded them that there would be no Greek Cypriot attack unless they themselves provoked it and I arranged with JFHQ for regular air surveillance to be mounted so that we could monitor any aggressive movement by paramilitary units.

At this point I was radioed from JFHQ that the Greek Cypriots had issued an ultimatum that British troops would be attacked throughout Kyrenia District unless the British garrison was withdrawn from Kazaphani by 1500. I was asked to resolve the position without delay.

I found 1 Para headquarters preparing for siege and was shown the ultimatum they had received.

I spent the remainder of the afternoon with Superintendent Vassiliou searching for an amicable resolution. A copy of the British proposal for the Kazaphani-Kyrenia Agreement, drawn up from notes taken at the original Nicosia conference, was produced and advanced by me as being the only valid text of the Agreement itself. I was able to convince Vassiliou that the Turkish Cypriots would undoubtedly evacuate both Kyrenia and Kazaphani if the Agreement were not implemented in the sense that had been intended when the Turkish Cypriots agreed to disarm.

Eventually, after a long and intensely emotional debate, Vassiliou agreed that he would personally accept the British interpretation of the Agreement, so long as there was no question of a formal signature, and with the reservation that he could not guarantee that his superiors would approve his decision. In effect this was the end of the crisis, since I already knew that the arrangement would be acceptable both to Captain Augustis and to 'The Organisation' leaders in Nicosia, so long as I could obtain gendarmerie approval. Orders were then sent out by Vassiliou that freedom of movement was to be restored to British forces. As I was leaving his office, Vassiliou said he hoped I understood that he had never really meant his warning to be taken as a genuine ultimatum.

On 11 March there was a further considerable exodus of Turkish Cypriot families from Kyrenia, but from there on the situation became generally stabilised throughout the region. The Turkish Cypriots around St Hilarion continued occasionally to fire a few rounds into Karmi or to shoot at the tires of the school bus as it wended its way down to Kyrenia, but this was apparently intended, and taken, to be no more than a reminder of the Turkish presence. The Greek Cypriot gendarmerie established permanent positions around the northern and eastern boundaries of Temblos and there were occasional exchanges of fire between these and the advanced Turkish Cypriot emplacements, without any damage being done.

The remaining Turkish Cypriots in Kyrenia and Kazaphani sank into an attitude of mournful discontent. They felt permanently insecure and seldom ventured far outside their own sectors. Their traditional fellowship with their Greek Cypriot neighbours was not much dented – it being the police, not the neighbours, who were blamed – and they were frequently encouraged into the Greek Cypriot coffee-houses when the Greek Cypriots wished to prove to visitors that co-existence remained a reality. Nevertheless, lacking any judicial authority to which they could relate, they felt themselves now to be living as hostages in an alien land.

The police maintained a permanent roadblock between Kyrenia and Temblos, but in fact no Turkish Cypriot ever travelled by that route, preferring the hazards of a circuitous track via the St Hilarion foothills. There was occasional further friction between the Greek Cypriot gendarmerie and British troops, but it never again approached the level of confrontation. On 20 March, TMT units astride the pass, anxious again to ease Greek Cypriot pressure against Temblos, asked me to inform Kyrenia that they were planning to obliterate Karmi by triggering an avalanche above it. This was not taken seriously by the Greek Cypriot authorities, and nothing more was heard of the threat.

39. AYIA IRINI - KAMBYLI AREA. MARCH 1964

The visit to Ayia Irini of Kutchuk's representative on 28 February had made an unfortunate impression there and evacuation had only been prevented by the persuasion of Major Sepici and a promise from me of an early visit from a more senior member of the Turkish Cypriot communal leadership. On the 29th, the Turkish Cypriots again informed the resident British garrison that they wished to leave. The next day, after our night in Photta, Major Sepici and I went back to Ayia Irini.

This time we were accompanied by Dr Kiazim, the leader of the Turkish Communal Chamber and generally supposed, in the absence of Rauf Denktash, to be the strongman of the Turkish Cypriot leadership. During the helicopter journey, I explained to him the recent history of the village and its present problems and suggested that it would not be easy to persuade the people to stay.

"Don't worry", Dr Kiazim told me, "as soon as I tell them to stay there will be no more problems."

The meeting was held in the Turkish Cypriot school. The villagers were invited by Dr Kiazim to explain their troubles to him and did so at considerable length. Then he explained to them the feelings of Dr Kutchuk and the way their leaders viewed the inter-communal troubles and the desire that no more Turkish Cypriot communities should be evacuated unless it was absolutely necessary. He stressed the indignities being suffered by those who had already been forced to leave their homes and the difficulties that central leadership was having in catering for their needs. He ended with a stirring call to the villagers to stay where they were.

The villagers heard him out to the end and then one by one protested that he had failed to understand their problems or to appreciate the degree of fear and insecurity with which they had to live. It was clear that no-one had been convinced by him.

Then Major Sepici asked the villagers whether they felt that he knew them and understood their difficulties and they all nodded, and the *mukhtar* said that they trusted him and believed that he shared their thoughts. So the major talked to them for half an hour, quietly and without histrionics, as though he were addressing parents at a school meeting, and the younger men sniffed meditatively at the flowers that they usually wore behind their ears and the older men fingered their worry-beads less angrily.

He said: "We are not talking here today about politics or about whether Makarios or Dr Kutchuk or Ankara or Athens or London want to change the shape of Cyprus. We are talking about you and your children and how you should live, when all around you there is so much reporting of violence and fear and pressure. Each day since I first came here you have had this difficult decision of whether to stay on in your own homes or whether to move. Each time I have spoken to you I have said that I thought you should stay, but that only you should make the decision. Often it is difficult for me to tell you to stay, because I know the dangers. Perhaps in the future I shall advise you to move. But if you do move it should be for the right reason, because that is the best way to build your future: it should not be because some extremists and thugs have decided to press you into going."

As he spoke there was a draining away of the atmosphere of frustration and bitterness that Dr Kiazim had failed to dissipate. Sepici's talking was low key and very personal. He described his own experiences of suffering and his view of the sacrifices that people sometimes must make because of whom they are and what they believe in. He said that he and the Commander and Captain Michos came from different countries and different backgrounds but they all had the same belief that the Cypriot people deserved a chance to live together in peace and to work out answers for themselves without the threatenings of a few men of violence.

When he finished speaking he was solemnly embraced by the *mukhtar*, who said that for the time being they would stay.

Michos and I were both very moved. We realised that Sepici had put down a significant marker for moderation that could have a resonance beyond the borders of Kormakiti.

There were to be more and worse troubles in the future and this was not to be the last time that the Ayia Irini villagers would debate whether or not to evacuate but it was a particular watershed in the village's affairs.

Sepici had not, however, changed Turkish Cypriot attitudes over co-operation with the Greek Cypriot authorities. On 5 March, a battle was narrowly averted in the village. A party of workers from CYTA, the state-owned Cyprus Telephone Authority, arrived under heavy police escort and, without any prior advice to the patrol organisation or arrangement with the Turkish Cypriot *mukhtar*, demanded access to Turkish Cypriot property. The Turkish Cypriots refused, claiming that they no longer recognised the rights of any central Greek Cypriot authority. The Greek Cypriots responded by calling in heavy paramilitary reinforcements, surrounding the Turkish Cypriot quarter and preparing for a general attack. There was intervention by the resident British garrison and consultation with Nicosia. Eventually the Greek Cypriots decided to postpone the CYTA works until a later, unspecified, date.

In the early morning of 7 March, a wounded girl was found on the outskirts of Ayia Irini. She had spent the whole night crawling from Kolya Chiflik, an isolated Turkish Cypriot farm three miles to the north. She said that the previous evening some Greek Cypriots from the nearby village of Liveras had come to the farm after dusk and called to her family to come out and then abused them and shouted threats. They had all tried to run away and the Greek Cypriots had shot at them from behind. Her father had been killed in the fields and she had been hit, but she and her mother and grandmother had managed to get into the woods and hide and eventually the Greek Cypriots had given up searching and gone away.

When I reached Ayia Irini later that day, British soldiers there were talking with great anger about the incident, having brought in the two missing women and the body of the girl's father. I told them to keep their emotions out of it and to take nothing for granted, as this might be a dispute over property or debt rather than a killing for ethnic reasons. That evening I asked Tassos Papadopoulos to use 'Organisation' channels to try and get at the truth.[1]

All through March there was increased activity along the coastline, with the 'Secret Army' stepping up its programme to construct beach defences so as to create a viable anti-invasion capability. Attempts by Turkish Cypriot shepherds, upon whose regular grazing grounds much of this went on, to get a close look at these activities sometimes resulted in their being shot at, although so far as I knew never with intent to kill. The shepherds concocted highly embellished stories about these incidents, which contributed to the villagers' sense of general unease.

A more valid source of alarm was the large 'Secret Army' training camp which had been established in the wooded area to the north of the Ayia Irini - Dhiorios road. Although discipline here was usually excellent, there were regular disappearances of sheep or goats from outlying Turkish Cypriot byres and from time to time a Turkish Cypriot shepherd would report that he had been seized and interrogated.

On 7 March forty-nine Turkish Cypriot hostages were released in Nicosia by the Greek Cypriots. Among them were six of the seven villagers missing from Ayia Irini. Their homecoming was greeted with amazement and rapturous delight. The patrol, probably undeservedly, was given credit for their survival, which further enhanced its influence.

On 11 March, the Turkish Cypriots in Ayia Irini again summoned us to discuss the possibility of evacuation. Those released from custody had brought back with them stories of their seizure and incarceration which had added to the villagers' general sense of unease. They had been further unsettled by the frightening of their shepherds, by the CYTA affair, by gendarmerie patrols from Morphou and by the story of the girl from Kolya Chiflik. Also the Greek Cypriot police had failed to return their village bus, so that travel and the trading of their produce remained an impossibility. Food supplies in the village were again running short.

When I visited Morphou gendarmerie headquarters to discuss the situation, I was given a pledge that there would be less aggressive patrolling and closer co-operation with the British garrison in Ayia Irini. I also was told, as justification for police action against them, that the Ayia Irini Turkish Cypriots were suspected of poaching in Kalokhorio Forest and of stealing antiquities.

From the relief organisations in Nicosia I obtained an undertaking that regular deliveries of food would be resumed. Reporting on this to the *mukhtar*, I impressed on him that he should talk more to the resident British unit commander, rather than asking for a visit from my patrol whenever he felt the need for reassurance.

A similar message was being delivered to Kambyli on 20 March, when I was asked to speak privately to a Maronite shepherd. I was told by him that a

Turkish Cypriot family of seven in Liveras, a village to the north of Ayia Irini close to Kolya Chiflik, had been murdered a couple of weeks earlier. He said that the father had been shot, the mother and the five children strangled and the bodies thrown down a well. The story was not unlike others that had been reported to me in the past and then proved groundless, but in this case there was a nasty echo of the 7 March killing at nearby Kolya Chiflik.

When we reached Liveras, we found it to be a depressing huddle of houses, with none of the colour and vibrancy that characterised other Greek Cypriot villages. We had it confirmed that this was a wholly Greek Cypriot community with the exception of a single Turkish Cypriot family of seven.

Despite the best efforts of Captain Michos, the villagers were extremely reluctant to talk to us. Eventually we coaxed out of them a story that three TMT members had come in the night of 6 March and ordered the Turkish Cypriots to leave with them immediately. They said that the family had loaded all of their belongings onto the truck of one of the visitors and left with him.

They claimed that the Turkish Cypriots had been forced into going by TMT threats: "Why else should they leave? They were happy and safe here."

Something didn't smell right about the story. I radioed for JFHQ to run a check with Kutchuk's office and with the Turkish Cypriot leadership in Kyrenia. A quick swing through nearby Turkish Cypriot villages failed to produce any news. The TMT leader in Kambyli denied that there had been any contact with the family.

We went back to Liveras. The more we cross-examined the Greek Cypriot villagers, the more unlikely did their story seem. When we asked to visit the Turkish Cypriots' home, they took us there with extreme reluctance.

Wherever else I had seen recently abandoned Turkish Cypriot homes, there had been a few items of furniture or bric-a-brac left behind, as though the owners had wanted to convince themselves that they would soon be back. The inside of this house was entirely bare.

We came out of the house into bright sunshine. Captain Michos took my arm and said; "Let's go."

As we were walking away towards our Land Rovers he said: "Don't look back. I don't want the villagers to think we are suspicious. The Turkish Cypriots must have been killed. There were seven pairs of shoes out of sight under the stairs to the porch, two of adults and five of children. Nobody in a poor family in this country has more than a single pair of shoes. Even if they did, it would be the last item they would ever leave behind."

The gendarmerie at Myrtou declined to take an interest, just as they had over the killing at Kolya Chiflik: crimes against Turkish Cypriots were no longer regarded by them as being within their area of competence. I therefore asked Captain Michos to find out what more he could through his own channels, passed a private note to Sergeant Makrides and gave a detailed report to Tassos Papadopoulos.

One week later I was told that our suspicions had been confirmed. The names that I had hazarded as probably responsible were also verified. Michos told me that the affair had been the subject of urgent discussion by the commander of his regiment with Athens.

At Tassos Papadopoulos' request, I attended a meeting with him and two other ministers. He said: "We're grateful to you for bringing this matter directly to us rather than letting it be handled through JFHQ. The President is deeply upset. We thought we were sufficiently in control for these incidents to have been ended and we are shocked to find we were wrong. We want you to understand the difficulty in which we now find ourselves. We have got ourselves into a position from which we are unable to do what should be done. You know and we know who's responsible for an appalling crime. They ought to be brought to justice, but that isn't going to happen."

Papadopoulos said that since Christmas the situation had been, to say the least, 'anomalous'. "We needed to revise the constitution so as to allow a normal democratic working of the state. We were encouraged in this by Arthur Clark, which we took to mean that we had British backing. The Turks were arming to oppose the revision by force. We created a force to defend ourselves against an armed Turkish reaction. There was provocation, followed by violence. Makarios and Kutchuk agreed that normal order must be re-established, but that wasn't achieved. In legal terms, we now regard the paramilitary Turkish Cypriot leadership and TMT as being in insurrection against the state."

"As you know, we are now committed to a policy of re-engagement and a new approach to communal relations. Privately the President has accepted that it will be better to agree together on a movement by the Turkish Cypriots out of mixed areas where there is friction into areas where they will feel more secure. You have a part to play in that because we need objective assessments and a channel of communication that we can trust.

"We agreed after Christmas with Duncan Sandys and Peter Young on ways to avoid further bloodshed, but these have been exploited by Kutchuk and the Denktash people to start a process of partition, using the 'Green Line' and British troops as cover. It's intensely galling for our police that they cannot now enter some areas controlled by the Turks without running the risk of serious armed clashes.

"At Christmas, groups emerged which wanted to fight for the Greek cause, and particularly for our right not to be blocked from *enosis*. These fighters have acquired the status of heroes and a position stronger than we have as politicians. We've tried to incorporate all of these fighting groups into what will become a National Guard, but some units and some individuals are still determined to pursue their own agenda, irrespective of national policy. This has created a very dangerous situation for us.[2]

"Now let's discuss what happened at Liveras and Kolya Chiflik. This was entirely against our wishes and very damaging to our aims. Properly those who did it should be arrested and tried for murder. But we're talking about men who a lot of our people, particularly the right wing, regard as heroes. Trying to bring them to public trial now could lead to civil war and a much worse situation than we already have.

"The only alternative we can see is for a secret drumhead court-martial with powers of capital punishment. That's how it would have been dealt with during the EOKA struggle. But now all of us here, whether or not we used to be part of EOKA, are politicians, with hopes to lead the country in the future.

No politician could survive who was found to have been involved in the summary execution of someone who could later be presented to half the nation as a hero. So we find ourselves trapped by circumstances that are deeply repugnant to us."

I said: "You have a heavily armed police force that's already been involved in plenty of shooting against Turkish Cypriots. Can't they handle it?"

I was told: "No they can't, or won't, and you surely know why."

Later that evening, Tassos Papadopoulos took me to dinner at Lemonias and we talked more about the problems of controlling violence and how deeply it was rooted in some elements of Greek society. I told him that since I first went there, I had been aware in Greece of the rifts created by the civil war. I repeated to him what Dom Mintoff had told me about Ben Bella's difficulty in dealing with political violence after the Algerians' underground war against the French, and of my understanding that the violence inherent in an anti-colonial struggle could not easily or rapidly be expunged from the new nation that emerged. In particular I talked about the way that western intelligence agencies, which saw the eastern Mediterranean as a special battleground in their Cold War against the supposed threats of communism, were encouraging nationalist factions to use violence against the left.

I told him about an incident in 1963 when I had visited Athens as an official observer for NATO exercises and, as Intelligence Adviser to COMEDSOUEAST, had been looked after for one day by resident US intelligence agencies. To demonstrate one facet of their undercover mission, I had been taken to a training camp to the north of the city where American instructors were indoctrinating Greek gendarmes in covert techniques for counter-insurgency, including instruction in modern methods of interrogation, torture and killing. They were teaching that communists were sub-human, that they had forfeited their civil rights and that they should be exterminated like vermin. The pupils were being schooled in the use of extreme violence against communists as a weapon against the spread of left-wing dogma. I was shown some pigs with KKE* emblems on their backs and told with some pride by the instructor that his trainees would be told to kill these as viciously as possible, visualising them as 'commies who had raped their sisters'.

I said that, from what Nicos Sampson and others had told me, there appeared to be a deep involvement by Greek intelligence agencies in the encouragement of violent action against Turkish Cypriot militants and I asked to what degree this was a cover for action against the Cypriot left.

Rather than respond directly, Papadopoulos asked me what impressions I had gained of the left in Cyprus. I said that left-wingers I had met seemed to be first of all nationalists and anti-colonialists, like left-wingers that I knew in Malta and militant socialists in the UK. But that was not how they were being portrayed by NATO. They clearly were much more committed than the right to the creation of a multi-ethnic society, and consequently more helpful to the process of communal re-engagement. Obviously, also, they were a prime

---

* Communist Party of Greece

target for subversion and disinformation by western intelligence agencies, and particularly by the Greek and Turkish Cypriot surrogates of those agencies.

I realised that the party expressed general allegiance to Moscow, but I had not yet met a communist in Cyprus who had seemed other than primarily a Cypriot. It obviously simplified things for NATO to label them as dangerous men who were threatening the stability of the Mediterranean. I supposed that a left-leaning Cyprus would be just as intolerable for the establishment in Athens as it would for Ankara and for the British and Americans.

I was asked to keep entirely private what I was to be told. It was explained that political polarisation meant huge problems for the President and for other moderate leaders (among whose number the speaker clearly felt himself to be included): it forced them into a constant balancing act. Then there was a reversion to what had happened at Liveras. I was told that the only solution they could see was to accept a return to Cyprus by Grivas and give him the job of clearing up the whole problem of uncontrolled violence from Greek Cypriot extremism.

Grivas, he said, was a 'disciplinarian par excellence. He would without any compunction court-martial and execute anyone who was betraying what he saw as the cause of Hellenism. The problems were that he was now so fanatically anti-leftist as to be frequently irrational on political issues and that it was doubtful how loyal he would be to Makarios. Nevertheless they were confident that if Grivas was brought back, Makarios and the moderates would be able to control him and that he would not pose a threat to the process of inter-communal re-engagement.

He said that Georgadjis therefore had been authorised to arrange for Grivas to return covertly to Cyprus.[3]

The significance for me of what had happened at Liveras and Kolya Chiflik was not just that isolated and unprotected Turkish Cypriots had been murdered without provocation at a time when there was a significant peacekeeping presence in the immediate area: that could have been the act of a homicidal maniac triggered by something other than ethnic prejudice. More disturbing was that no mechanism existed that would undertake to investigate and act upon the crime, that there was no element of the police force that felt it had responsibility for the Turkish Cypriots, even when urged by Makarios to act without discrimination. In the eyes of many of the police, the Turkish Cypriots had at Christmas become non-people, excluded from any recourse to the processes of justice or the safeguarding of their human rights. Only now were we beginning to get an acceptance from some gendarmerie units that the future was likely to depend on their regaining the trust of the Turkish Cypriots. Where this concept had been adopted, there had been very rapid progress towards inter-communal re-engagement.

By the time I had confirmation of what had happened at Liveras, it was already twenty days after the killings. I discussed the position with Kutchuk, told him of Makarios' distress and got his agreement that the event was entirely contrary to the general trend in the area and ought to be treated as a one-off aberration. Kutchuk appeared determined that the Turkish Cypriots should not abandon Ayia Irini. In general he had been strongly supportive of the patrol's efforts and of the process, urged by Tassos Papadopoulos, to establish through me an unofficial, wholly private and conciliatory back-channel to the President. I took it to be because of this that the Turkish press, which could have been expected to use the incident in the most inflammatory manner possible, carried only a minor report that the family had disappeared.

In the following weeks, I used the stories of Liveras and Kolya Chiflik as leverage with Greek Cypriot leaders when I was arguing with them about the dangers of complacency and the need to provide the Turkish Cypriots with a genuine security that would justify their trust.

As part of the effort to restore normal order, President of Cyprus, Archbishop Makarios. and Vice-President, Dr. Fazil Kutchuk, chatting to village *mukhtar* in the coffee shop of a village outside Nicosia.

40. KYTHREA - EPIKHO AREA. MARCH 1964

On 6 March a Greek Cypriot shepherd from Voni was shot and left dying in the fields. His flock of sheep was afterwards impounded inside the boundaries of Epikho by Turkish Cypriot villagers. Within a few minutes of the shooting, firing became general all along the border areas between Epikho and Bey Keuy and Voni and Kythrea.

The shooting of the shepherd was probably the act of embittered Turkish Cypriot refugees from Neokhorio, but the wider incident that it triggered reflected the intricacies of a complex land dispute.

This was not the first time that I had been drawn into the unravelling of Cypriot laws governing land ownership and transfer, village jurisdictions and the special rights of Rural Constables. In this case it appeared that the land where the shooting had occurred was within Voni village boundaries but was owned by a Turkish Cypriot in Epikho who had leased it to an absentee landlord in London who in turn had sub-let it to a Greek Cypriot in Voni who had last year failed to pay his rent: to whom the field had reverted because of this failure was in dispute but it seemed certain that Greek Cypriot sheep were being grazed on it illegally that day.

Rural Constables normally had no power to impound livestock not found within their own boundaries, but in certain instances this did not apply where the trespass was obvious and no other party was within view, as was here claimed by the Turkish Cypriots to be the case.

I did a good deal of shuttling between Epikho and Voni trying to make sense of the differing Greek Cypriot and Turkish Cypriot assertions.

A Greek Cypriot threat to launch a general attack on Epikho was followed by a movement of British peacekeeping units into the area. Late that evening I persuaded the Turkish Cypriots to return the sheep to Voni "purely as a gesture of goodwill." However, Greek Cypriot paramilitaries now felt that they had justification for a show of strength and there was intermittent shooting in the region for the next five days, mostly by the Greek Cypriots against Bey Keuy. Total casualties, from a huge expenditure of ammunition, amounted to one Greek Cypriot paramilitary fatally wounded.

On two occasions, the firing against Bey Keuy was carried out by well-organised 'Secret Army' units which told us they had come out from Nicosia in order to "exercise under battle conditions". Mostly, however, shooting originated on the Greek Cypriot side from local youths who appeared to be under no control whatever.

Major Burgess' report on 11 March covered a typical incident:

"Visiting Bey Keuy I found the villagers very worried and distressed, having been under fire on 8 March from Kythrea with LMG and rifles and again, on the morning and night of the 10th, from Voni. While I was attempting to reassure the Turkish villagers, fire was opened again from the direction of Voni, some fifteen shots hitting a wall above and around the patrol vehicles. The Turks did not return the fire.

I moved towards Voni and discovered a group of seven young Greek irregulars armed with rifles and shotguns. They admitted they had fired, but described it as having been an 'accidental discharge'. When I pointed out that it was hard to believe that fifteen shots had been discharged accidentally in such a short time, they said they were very sorry and it was all a mistake.

I despatched the youths to their villages and went to Kythrea police station. There I reported the full facts to Inspector Lemis, who promised that he would investigate the whole incident."

In fact this incident proved to be the last of the confrontation.

We were now usually achieving results not by working through JFHQ, but by dealing directly and privately with the police at local level and with senior authorities through Tassos Papadopoulos and Doctor Kutchuk.

Wherever we could achieve close co-operation with the gendarmerie forces and have this authenticated by Tassos Papadopoulos there were great benefits for the peacemaking process. With increasing frequency we began to be asked by the police in this region to help them in areas where their contacts with the Turkish Cypriots had been severed. The fact that this was followed up through personal channels and without any publicity, and without reference to the Joint Liaison Committees in Nicosia and Famagusta, allowed a process to develop that gave a real boost to the restoration of effective inter-communal dialogue.

Meanwhile we were seeking, with mixed results, to remove the more obvious of local irritants. When Epikho returned the impounded flock to Voni, the episode had seemed over. However, two days later, the Greek Cypriot owner of the sheep decided that he was one lamb short. He began to create considerably more fuss over the loss of this one animal than he previously had over the loss of his shepherd.

The Turkish Cypriots in Epikho denied absolutely that they had purloined the lamb, but Captain Michos refused to lunch with them for fear that he might be consuming vital evidence. The patrol tried to buy a replacement lamb from the Turkish Cypriots but they refused to sell in case that was taken to imply a reflection on their honour. Eventually, I provided the price of a lamb to the Kythrea police for them to deliver to Voni, and the matter was then taken by all sides to be settled.

We also were finally successful in clearing up a long-standing dispute over water between Epikho and its adjacent Greek Cypriot villages. Again this was typical of matters that were now being allocated to my patrol, on the grounds that it provided the only effective link between rural communities.

Epikho owned the rights to a certain proportion, in hours of full-flow, of the water from a spring that lay several miles away in Kythrea. The main flow of the open channel ran through Neokhorio and the now abandoned Turkish Cypriot farming co-operative of Naysan Chiflik and thence to Palekythro. Epikho's water was tapped at midway stage by a one-third sluice and the Epikho channel afterwards led on to Exometokhi. Each village through which the water flowed provided a Water Guard who was responsible for maintaining the flow and operating the various sluices within his section according to rights of ownership. Each village was responsible for paying a contribution to the wages of every Water Guard who operated between it and the original source, such contribution being in proportion to the hours of flow going to the village. This was the only source of irrigation water for the villages in the area and as such was of life-and-death significance for them.

Inevitably, the position was further complicated by the current inter-communal dispute. The allocation of water from the Epikho-Exometokhi duct was made by hours or minutes to individual land-owners rather than on a block basis to each village. Now the Exometokhi Water Guards could no longer pass through Epikho to alter sluice settings, as they needed to do several times each day and night if the proper amounts of water were to be delivered. It appeared that Neokhorio had always had a bad reputation for harbouring 'water-thieves': now it was stealing water that should by right have belonged to the Turkish Cypriots at Naysan Chiflik.

Central control for these matters was vested in the Nicosia District Water Board. This had always been a bi-communal body but now its senior Greek Cypriot officials were denied access to administrative records, which were held in offices in the Turkish Cypriot sector of Nicosia. The local administrative committee was based at Palekythro and was supposed to contain a member from every village on the network. It had not met since early December and I was told that, in any event, its chairman did not get on with the Neokhorio member, who therefore refused to attend, and that Exometokhi, a Greek Cypriot village which was predominantly communist, had for some time been refusing to pay its dues on account of some obscure matter of principle.

At Christmas, someone had blocked the channel before it reached Epikho, which therefore had been without irrigation water for over two months. The problems that needed now to be resolved were how much water was Epikho entitled to, where should Naysan Chiflik's water go, who owed what in rates and to whom, and how were the channels in future to be kept open and managed.

Little by little we untangled the threads of the issue, as we were having to do in a raft of similar problems in other areas of Nicosia Zone. The gendarmerie was now being helpful, and the joint village and area committees that we had set up in the early days of January provided a basis from which to work. Furthermore, the involvement of villagers from both communities in the resolution of these problems provided a powerful tool for the rebuilding of fractured relationships. The Epikho water channel was re-opened with something of a fanfare, closed again when there was a renewal of tension, then opened again when the crisis had passed. As these arrangements became more secure, so the feeling grew that normality was now returning.

In other parts of the region there were alarms but no serious incidents. The Turkish Cypriots in Mandres and Greek Cypriots villages to the north and east, Sykhari, Vouno and Mia Milea, fired occasionally at each other's shepherds, but no-one was hurt. A Greek Cypriot attack on Mandres was threatened on 7 March after reports that the Turkish Cypriots had captured a large flock of sheep from Koutsovendis together with two attendant shepherdesses, but Captain Michos and I managed to prove that the story was pure fabrication: in fact the shepherdesses had glimpsed Greek Cypriot paramilitaries moving in the woods, assumed them to be Turkish Cypriot and run off in panic, then concocted a story to explain the loss of their flocks.

There was more substance in a land dispute at Ayia, which led to the impounding of a flock of Turkish Cypriot sheep by the Greek Cypriot gendarmerie and exchanges of fire on 3 and 6 March. Here, patrol co-ordination with the police led to a quick return of the sheep, an ending to the shooting and the beginning of direct and amicable co-operation between the Turkish Cypriots in Ayia and the neighbouring Greek Cypriot villages. Our encouragement of inter-communal meetings and co-operation also led to the ending of some irritating acts of vandalism, by Greek Cypriots in the destruction of abandoned property in Neokhorio and by Turkish Cypriots in the felling of valuable Greek Cypriot olive trees near Bey Keuy.

The core problem remained that of freedom of movement and Turkish Cypriot access to Nicosia. After a number of postponements, the process of vehicle re-licensing had gone ahead, but with an unprovocative approach from the gendarmerie and with my patrol, as elsewhere, acting as agents in the acquisition by the Turkish Cypriots of those few licenses that they were able to afford. More disturbing, although understandable in light of Greek Cypriot intelligence about the movement of TMT arms, was the imposition by the police on 16 March of positive control on all access to the capital, involving the thorough searching of all Turkish Cypriot vehicles entering and leaving Nicosia, even though this was contrary to the January Freedom of Movement Agreement.

Initially these searches were conducted by armed police auxiliaries, with no indication given of their objective, and this led to intense Turkish Cypriot resentment and international press condemnation. After pressure from JFHQ, the Ministry of the Interior issued a list of prohibited items and announced that in future all searches would be conducted by uniformed regular officers: from there on the Turkish Cypriots grudgingly accepted the process as a necessary part of any visit to Nicosia.

British patrols were normally stationed to keep an eye on the search-points: it was noticeable that where these patrols created a relaxed rapport with the police, the searches were usually fair and good-humoured, whereas they were often rough and aggressive when the police and the resident British unit were on hostile terms. In the case of the most aggressive and demeaning searches, often conducted in front of a crowd of sightseeing Greek Cypriots, the police used to explain that they were merely using the same methods as had the British, with Turkish Cypriot help, during the 1950s EOKA crisis.

For the Turkish Cypriots, the most upsetting aspect of the early searches was the seizure of any cigarettes found in their possession. Shops in the Turkish Cypriot sector of Nicosia were selling these at full standard price, but the cigarettes were regarded by the police as contraband because they did not carry the government's taxation seal. Between 16 March, when the searches started, and the 18th, when the Turkish Cypriots made special arrangements for the settlement of excise duties, the volume of confiscations was substantial. The police gave no receipts for the items they seized and refused to return them even after the duty had been fully paid. The Turkish Cypriots were deeply angered by this and I had to waste a day dissuading them from attempting to lay an ambush on the Famagusta road for a Greek Cypriot cigarette delivery en route to the capital.

One other incident gave further confirmation of a change in police attitudes. On the evening of 16 March, a Turkish Cypriot bus returning from Nicosia to Platani was stopped at gunpoint soon after passing through an official police roadblock. The passengers were searched and robbed, but the hold-up was aborted when a police detachment arrived on the scene. With a number of guns still pointing at them, the Turkish Cypriot passengers were too scared to make any statement to the police about what had happened, but later to me and to Captain Pamir they gave a very detailed report.

I passed these details on to Tassos Papadopoulos and asked that he handle it with the police, and I soon afterwards learned that all of the perpetrators had been arrested and gaoled, despite the fact that they were all 'Secret Army' members. I also was given a promise, sadly never kept, that financial restitution would be made to those who had been robbed.

News of the consequences of the hold-up was circulated among Greek Cypriot police and paramilitary forces with a tough warning that 'criminal' acts against Turkish Cypriots in future would be treated with severity, and we used this news to help persuade the Turkish Cypriots, who had feared that acts of banditry might become common, that they could in fact travel safely. No other similar act of attempted highway robbery within Nicosia Zone was reported to me in the months to come.

41. Other Areas of Nicosia and Famagusta Districts. March 1964

As March progressed, a feeling began to grow in most of the northern areas of Cyprus that the worst of the storm was past and that a gradual, but real, process of inter-communal re-engagement was underway. Turkish Cypriot evacuations had led to a lowering of tensions in mixed areas which previously had been vulnerable to extremist trouble-makers. The misuse of police power had been drastically curbed. Most paramilitaries had been welded into an increasingly disciplined force under central control. The development of private conduits between Makarios and Kutchuk and between key regional leaders was allowing potentially explosive issues to be addressed pro-actively without the political baggage associated with formal liaison committees in Nicosia. The participation of Greek and Turkish officers placed a special cachet on the negotiations of the tripartite patrols, and our links with the 'Secret Army' and TMT meant that we could now play an unobtrusive role in support of the two communities in their search for a new format for partnership.

The danger remained of events being derailed, which might be by accident, by misunderstanding, by the rigidity or wounded pride of the police, or by deliberate design. Nationalist extremists, those addicted to violence, and outsiders who believed that their ends would best be served by a divided Cyprus, were all potential saboteurs of the re-engagement process.

The fact, that we could now devote adequate time to the resolution of disputes over grazing and water rights, attested to the degree to which the risk of armed clashes had been reduced. The network of joint village committees that we had created was holding up well, and by working together to resolve their own problems the Greek and Turkish Cypriots began to develop a real sense of shared responsibility.

Various reasons were given to me by Turkish Cypriots as to why TMT did not try and counter this re-association. One was that TMT was still too weak to do other than concentrate its efforts in the cities. Other TMT leaders felt they had advanced as far as was possible in this phase, and that now was a time for consolidation. Clearly, also, Kutchuk and his advisers were surprised at their inability to persuade many Turkish Cypriots in rural Cyprus to abandon their homes, in favour of Turkish Cypriot cantonments, so long as a reasonable chance remained that a *modus vivendi* with the their Greek Cypriot neighbours could be found. The nub of the problem was whether genuine security could be constructed. No Turkish Cypriot believed that this could be achieved until there was a full Turkish Cypriot participation in the policing process.

In most areas, the Greek Cypriot gendarmerie was now using a much more sympathetic approach to the Turkish Cypriots, and this was paying dividends in the lowering of tension, but there were occasional backslidings. An 'Organisation' officer was appointed to the command of a gendarmerie unit in Lefkoniko area, and between 7 and 10 March he disturbed the balance of the region through a series of aggressive and extremely provocative patrols. On the 7th, a passenger in a Turkish Cypriot car which failed to stop at a roadblock near Trikomo was shot dead. On the 8th, there were repeated Turkish Cypriot reports of harassment on the roads between Vatili and Trikomo. On the 9th, several Turkish Cypriots in Yenagra were subjected to humiliating searches.

Having been assured by senior 'Organisation' leaders that there was no change of policy and that the problem stemmed wholly from a local initiative, I tracked down the gendarmerie patrol to Lefkoniko, explained the damage that was being done and obtained a pledge of new tactics and future co-operation. Afterwards we heard of no further complaints.

In the Photta-Aghirda-Ayios Ermolaos area, the relaxation of friction which had followed the release of Ali Cemal on 7 March continued. Interest in the region now became centred on major Turkish Cypriot construction work to the south of Aghirda: initially the Turkish Cypriots claimed to us that this was a new motor-road from Photta to Geunyely; then that it was the basis for a new refugee township; finally we were told in confidence that it was an airstrip (which we had not doubted in the first place) and that it was being built by Turkish Cypriots under instructions from the Turkish Regiment. As this work progressed, so did the build-up of 'Secret Army' emplacements on the boundaries of the Turkish Cypriot enclave, around Ayios Ermolaos to the west and Pano Dhikomo to the east.

The Louroujina-Kochati area was also quiet during the early weeks of the month. Travel from this region by the Turkish Cypriots ranged from very limited to non-existent, one deterrent being that the police searches at Athalassa (western Nicosia) were exceptionally rigorous. British units sometimes agreed to accompany Turkish Cypriot vehicles until they were past Athalassa, even though this was contrary to JFHQ orders.

A minor incident on 17 March, when a Greek Cypriot guard-post fired a few shots at a Turkish Cypriot shepherd, failed to cause much excitement. However on the 23rd, the area came to the brink of another serious confrontation.

Two Turkish Cypriots had gone by car from Louroujina to work in their fields near the main Larnaca road. A detachment of armed gendarmerie passing down the road spotted these men among their crops and, claiming that they suspected an ambush, stopped to investigate. They surrounded the Turkish Cypriots, who tried to escape, shouting for help, but were finally captured. The police then searched the Turkish Cypriots' car and when they found a hunting rifle and ammunition informed the owners that they were under arrest for illegal possession of arms and set off with them and their car for Larnaca.

A couple of Turkish Cypriot shepherds who had been nearby returned in haste to Louroujina with an alarmist account of the arrest, and soon afterwards a strong party of Turkish Cypriot fighters moved out and laid an ambush on the main road. Several passing vehicles were shot up, with two or three Greek Cypriots slightly wounded, and three vehicles were stopped and seized. When the site of the ambush was approached by a police patrol, which had been alerted by the first of the cars to be shot at, the Turkish Cypriots retired to Louroujina, taking with them a captured bus containing eight people, a Greek Cypriot lorry and its driver and the driver of another lorry which was left abandoned. Heavy Greek Cypriot gendarmerie and paramilitary forces now began to move into the area and the whole fighting strength of Louroujina manned its defences.

My patrol was in Epikho when the episode started, but we got by helicopter to Louroujina within thirty minutes. Before landing, we were able to make a quick aerial survey of the forces confronting each other. The Turkish Cypriots at Louroujina, presumably under the direction of their resident Turkish army officer, had constructed a patchwork of deep interlocking trenches along the crests of the hills that surrounded the town: these were now fully manned and would have posed a daunting prospect for any attacking force.

JFHQ's Force Alpha arrived soon after us, followed by a large contingent of international journalists. I had by then learned that the total of ten hostages included two women and a small child.

The Turkish Cypriot leaders in Louroujina, led at the negotiating table by Erol Huseyin, were well known to us and welcoming. The Greek Cypriot police and paramilitary commanders, on the other hand, were all from Larnaca and none of them had previously met us: it took some time to convince them of our credentials: I then managed to obtain from them an undertaking that they would not advance their positions without prior warning to me, so that we could seek an agreement from Louroujina without the pressure of ultimatums or deadlines. For the rest of the afternoon some of the policemen occupied themselves in leaping aggressively over a low wall, so that the Greek press could obtain action pictures (of an attack against Louroujina) for the next day's editions.

An hour's argument, during which I harped on about the damage that would be done to their image if they acted like barbarians, resulted in a decision by the Turkish Cypriots to release the child and the two women. This was done in style, with a press presentation and a ceremonial handing-over to me.

Then it took another two or three hours for agreement to be elicited that hostage-holding in general was undesirable and that an exchange of prisoners should take place. After another hour of shuttling to and fro, pursued by the press corps, approval was acquired from both sides as to how the exchange was to be conducted.

At this point, the local Greek Cypriot police commanders said they had received orders from Nicosia that the whole arrangement was to be cancelled.

A different scheme for the exchange was then negotiated and the senior police commander authorised me to tell the Turkish Cypriots that their men were being brought up from Larnaca.

Then this new arrangement also was cancelled on orders from Nicosia police headquarters. The Greek Cypriot inspector with whom I was negotiating was by now cursing his superiors with considerable venom. The 'Secret Army' officer in local charge told me that he had repeatedly contacted his superiors asking them to put pressure on the police to provide their commanders on the spot with adequate authority. None of my own senior 'Organisation' contacts was reachable.

The waiting reporters began to shout out as each deadline approached: "Hurry up and get a deal or you won't be on the six o'clock news" and so on through the evening. Yet another agreement was reached and yet again word came from Nicosia that it was unacceptable.

Finally, with our patience wearing thin after eight hours of continuous talk, Captain Michos and I drove to Larnaca, got through on a direct line to Commander Antoniou, the national head of the gendarmerie, and hammered away at him in turns until he reluctantly agreed to accept the latest terms of settlement.

There was still a final lap to run. The Greek Cypriots declared that they would release the Turkish Cypriots only after their own people were brought to Larnaca. The Turkish Cypriots, professing now to suspect a Greek trap, refused to free their hostages until their people had been returned to Louroujina.

We wearily devised a scheme that was generally acceptable. I went with the father of one of the arrested Turkish Cypriots to Larnaca. There a British armoured one-tonner was driven into the courtyard of the police station, the gates secured behind it and the two men transferred from their cell and locked with the crew inside the armoured vehicle. The Turkish Cypriot father then returned with me to Louroujina where he confirmed that the missing men were safely transferred to British control. The seven Greek Cypriot hostages were then placed in another British armoured one-tonner, with Captain Michos taking their place as a symbolic hostage, and driven to Larnaca, where the exchange took place at 1 am.

The many hours of intensive talk that it had taken to solve what should have been a relatively simple problem were a reflection of the danger that senior police officers in Nicosia saw in making any gesture that the Turkish Cypriots could view as a concession.

The two Turkish Cypriot prisoners complained on their return that they had not been given any food all day. The Greek Cypriot hostages, on the other hand, had been given an excellent lunch, despite the extreme shortage of supplies in Louroujina at the time, and on leaving were each handed a packet of halloumi cheese as a souvenir of their visit.

As I was helping the last of the Greek Cypriot hostages out of the armoured car in Larnaca a Greek Cypriot woman came up to me and said: "Why don't you British go away and mind your own business. We have no use for you here."

42. GHAZIVERAN AND KALOKHORIO AREA. MARCH 1964

On 12 March, I was in Morphou for discussions with the gendarmerie commander, Superintendent Rigas, about how pressures against Ayia Irini could be eased. Having accepted my argument, the Superintendent asked whether, as a quid pro quo, I would try and persuade the Turkish Cypriots in Ghaziveran to reopen the road through the village to Greek Cypriot traffic.

Ghaziveran was normally covered by Major Mcintyre's patrol and he had told me that the roadblock was being maintained on orders from TMT in Lefka, either as a symbolic response to Greek Cypriot restrictions on Turkish Cypriot travel elsewhere or in an attempt to provoke a Greek Cypriot attack. Arriving there, I was shown a Turkish Cypriot car which had been badly shot up the previous day while on its way to Elea. Afterwards I was told by the villagers that they would be delighted to see the road reopened, but that they were scared of the consequences. After an amiable chat they undertook that all barriers would be removed so long as there was no Greek Cypriot action against them during the next twenty-four hours.

Five minutes later, while we were drinking a celebratory coffee, heavy automatic fire was directed into the village from a Greek Cypriot car driving past to the north. The Turkish Cypriots dashed off to their defensive positions, calling back to me over their shoulders that now I would understand their situation. A few minutes later there was more firing into the village, this time from the south.

We set off to investigate the first shooting. We spotted a number of Greek Cypriot paramilitaries working on beach defences close to the source of the attack and Burgess and I walked over to ask them what they had seen. When we were a couple of hundred metres away they grabbed their rifles. Ignoring my shouts, and presumably taking us for Turkish Cypriots, they started to fire at us and continued until we had retreated out of range.

We were preparing to return to Morphou, when a new group of 'Secret Army' soldiers arrived and took up firing positions opposite us, blocking our route. This time I despatched Captain Michos to talk to them. He too was told, to his extreme aggravation, that he would be shot unless we left the area immediately. Returning to Morphou, we explained to Superintendent Rigas that the Turkish Cypriots in Ghaziveran seemed disposed to dismantle their roadblocks but that it would help if the Greek Cypriots would desist from shooting at them.

Later, Kutchuk's office confirmed to me that they favoured the re-opening of the road, but other sources told me that Lefka TMT had ordered that the blocks must remain.

On 13 March, the Greek Cypriots began to build up substantial forces in the area, and by the 18th the village was surrounded. That evening Major Macey delivered to Ghaziveran instructions from the overall Turkish Cypriot leadership in Nicosia that the road was to be re-opened unconditionally. This was accepted by the village. News of the acceptance was relayed immediately to Nicosia, and Turkish Cypriot fighters then moved out of Ghaziveran to other locations.

Early in the morning of 19 March, the Greek Cypriots launched a full-scale attack against Ghaziveran, now weaponless except for hunting guns. The battle-toll was six killed and seven wounded.

When I talked afterward to commanders of the 'Secret Army', they told me that the Turkish Cypriot agreement to remove the roadblocks was reported to a full meeting of the army command on the evening of 18 March and that an order was then sent to all their units in the area for the cancellation of the planned attack. They claimed that this instruction was rescinded on orders that purported to be personally from President Makarios, and that the attack therefore went ahead.

The Archbishop's secretary said that no such instruction had been issued from the Presidential palace. Such an initiative would have been wholly out of character with what I had seen of the President's position and intentions over the past three months. I took it as most likely that there had been a deliberate subversion of the chain of command, or that the attack had been initiated by some element of the police and that the 'Secret Army' had then felt obliged to intervene.

The end result of the attack was that a British military post was established in the village, which was exactly what the Turkish Cypriots there had always wanted. Major Mcintyre's report of 23 March stated that the Turkish Cypriots in Ghaziveran were now "all in a thoroughly cheerful mood."

On the day of the fighting in Ghaziveran, 19 March, I was inspecting abandoned Turkish Cypriot property in villages along the Nicosia-Morphou road. Major Mcintyre's patrol was sent to Ghaziveran and reports on the fighting were relayed to me by him and also by the police in Aredhiou and Peristerona.

JFHQ asked me to divert and investigate the situation in the abandoned Turkish Cypriot village of Pano Koutrapha, following a report from a recce aircraft that houses there were on fire. The press corps, probably alerted by JFHQ, got there before we did. That evening, British television channels carried dramatic footage of Captain Michos and me walking into the burning village. The walls ahead of us were shown to be covered in Greek graffiti, which was virulently anti-Turkish and couched in highly explicit sexual terminology. Michos was seen in the footage to dodge sideways into a narrow alley. I was left with half a dozen microphones thrust in my face: "Commander Packard, would you translate the Greek for us?"

Unfortunately we did not hear at the time that fighting had also started that day at nearby Kalokhorio. Two days later, on the 21st, we learned that the village was still very tense, with further armed incidents expected, and we were asked to try and ease the situation.

In Kalokhorio, we found the two communities facing each other across barricades a few dozen yards apart. Each community had had a man killed and each bitterly accused the other of having started the fighting.

By now we had a well-drilled routine for addressing violent stand-offs. Captain Pamir and Captain Michos identified the Turkish Cypriot and Greek Cypriot leaders, explained our credentials, demanded their help and persuaded them to move their units back from their forward positions. Then we held a first joint meeting at which agreement was reached that all outside reinforcements would be sent away and firing positions evacuated and at which we identified the main sources of dispute (which, not unexpectedly, were related to water, abandoned property and debts). Next day we returned to examine these issues in greater depth and suggested solutions. Then in the evening we explained in Nicosia to the two communal leaderships what were the village's problems and what had been decided. We asked that there be continuing help for both communities to maintain the good relationship that had been re-established and that in future we are given early warning of any likely causes for dispute.

That my patrol had come under fire several times during March was probably explained by the fact that we and the occasional shepherd were the only people now likely to venture into contested areas of no-man's-land. We had a worse experience on 20 March in Kondomenos, a Greek Cypriot village which had lost several of its number in a 1958 massacre by the Turkish Cypriots for which the British were held by the Greek Cypriots to be responsible.*

On a previous visit, during what I had taken to be an animated but friendly conversation, the Greek Cypriot *mukhtar* had taken down from the wall a picture of the murdered men and tried to smash it over my head. On this occasion Major Burgess and Captain Pamir, who were escorting a carload of seriously ill Turks from Kambyli to Nicosia, were incautious enough to stop in Kondomenos to wait for me and Captain Michos. Burgess and Pamir and their Land Rover crews, together with the Turkish Cypriots, were surrounded by fifty heavily armed Greek Cypriot paramilitaries, searched, jostled, threatened and generally roughed up. When Michos and I arrived we found the two groups set to shoot it out. A lot of acrimonious shouting about British collaboration with the Turks followed before we were sullenly waved on our way.

---

* See note 31/2 re Geunyeli incident.

43.   SEASON OF CHANGE.
END OF MARCH 1964

The events of late-March were strongly influenced by the imminence of the United Nations take-over of peacekeeping responsibilities. The authorities in London and Ankara had fought against this development, claiming that it would afford an opening for Soviet and Third World interference in the island's affairs: Greece and the Greek Cypriots, on the other hand, had invested great hopes in it, believing that it would favour the general imposition of unitary democratic rule by the country's eighty per cent ethnic majority.

In anticipation of the take-over, the Greek Cypriots attempted to extend their authority, through a strong military response in instances where it could be suggested that this was justified by TMT provocations. This led, after paramilitary confrontations, to a restoration of Greek Cypriot police access to the Turkish Cypriot areas of Ktima, Kyrenia, Kazaphani, Ayios Andronikos and Mallia, albeit in joint patrolling with British troops. It also led to a tighter control of Turkish Cypriot movements in and out of Nicosia and to a stricter police attitude in other areas. The intention, so I was told, was that pressure for extended control should be applied up to somewhere below the level at which a real threat of intervention from Ankara would be provoked. In the case of Ktima this level was overstepped and on 13/14 March there was a real fear among 'Secret Army' commanders that Ankara might feel it had justification to invade.

Events at Ghaziveran seemed to fall outside this pattern, strengthening the supposition that the attack was mounted in an attempt to sabotage the re-engagement process.

At the same time, there was a genuine effort from the Greek Cypriot authorities to improve some aspects of their relationship with the Turkish Cypriots. Makarios, albeit belatedly, was now speaking out very strongly against the practice of hostage-taking, and gendarmerie attitudes towards the Turkish Cypriots were progressively improving. Sadly, though, the damage already done had lowered the appetite for compromise. When there was a general release of officially held hostages (forty-nine by the Greek Cypriots on 7 March and the four Chappas policemen by the Turkish Cypriots on the 12th), the reaction was not one of relief so much as of fury at the number of those who had disappeared and not been returned.

Whatever improvements of performance there were from the Greek Cypriot authorities, the Turkish Cypriots still felt a deep sense of insecurity: this was hardly surprising in view of the absence for them of any process of constitutional justice and of the occasional armed attacks that for two months had been made on them with participation by statal police forces. Furthermore, the undermining of unity and cultivation of distrust had been specific targets of TMT.

Although they acted with passivity in mixed areas and continued to have amicable relations with their traditional Greek Cypriot neighbours, a belief was now taking hold among many Turkish Cypriot villagers that only in their own enclaves and under their own police could they establish a satisfactory life. The process of alienation could now be reversed only through a confluence of Greek Cypriot political determination, US/UK pressure on Ankara and a comprehensive and sustained extension of mediating initiatives. A need to identify and counter the causes and instigators of extremism (often genuinely conceived by those locally involved as being in the communal or national interest and by foreigners as being justified by their own national interests) was central to any hope of reconciliation. Given the events of the past three months and the external pressures on Cyprus, a cantonal arrangement was now likely to be the least divisive option.

The British peacekeeping presence was now generally recognised, both in Cyprus and abroad, to have been a two-edged sword. On the one side it had helped put an end to serious inter-communal fighting and averted the threat of Turkish invasion: on the other it had established barriers behind which TMT had been able to advance its encouragement of ethnic separation, to the rising anger of the Greek Cypriots and the consequent creating of other tensions. The general view at JFHQ was that US and UK intelligence assessments were now supporting the thesis that communal separation was the outcome that would best suit NATO interests.

When General Young created the tripartite patrol organisation, there had been a very real belief that the British army would act as an extension of the mediating process, rather than as an arbitrary blocking force. This concept was lost when the Acheson-Ball plan was formulated, with the concurrent replacement of General Young by General Carver. From that time on, the tripartite units and the peacekeeping force were on divergent tracks, even if neither realised it clearly at the time.

Although the rumblings of dispute continued, February/March 1964, with the violence of the previous Christmas having led to a chastening of right-wing nationalist fervour, was a point in Cypriot history at which a resolution of the root problems of the inter-communal relationship was within reach.

The route of compromise would have included some further, mutually agreed, movements of the Turkish Cypriot population and the establishment of some enclaves into which there would be such measured devolution of local authority as would enable the Turkish Cypriots to develop a real sense of security. In reality, much of the needed demographic re-adjustment had already happened by the end of March. Key leaders with whom I spoke recognised this and saw it as a process that could go forward by quiet and private initiative, to be formalised later when its shape and benefits were clear.

Bottom-up mediation in the rural areas had proved that this process would work where those exerting an influence on the area had been persuaded into acceptance. No formal plan along these lines was ever put to me but it was an idea sketched out in numerous informal private meetings with my Greek Cypriot and Turkish Cypriot contacts. TMT, while maintaining a general wish for total separation, seemed prepared to settle for what was probably the best they could hope for at this point if Ankara was to be dissuaded by the UK and US from military intervention.

An evolutionary solution of this sort was not going to emerge from the high-level liaison committees that sat in Nicosia. It needed to be tried and tested by gradual process of adjustment at ground level, and then presented for political approval only when it was functioning satisfactorily. For this there needed to be an effective field mediating entity at the heart of the communal interface. That entity needed to merit the absolute trust of both communities and to be seen as an extension of their own persona.

It was clear to me that the participation of competent and committed Greek and Turkish Officers was likely to be needed to make the process possible, together with the personal mandate from President Makarios and Vice-President Kutchuk that the joint patrols had always carried. The role of catalyst and co-ordinator would need an undivided commitment to the good of Cyprus. An initiative along these lines would surely be viable if supported by Washington and London.

As the date approached for the United Nations' takeover, I became increasingly disturbed at reports that the participation of Greek and Turkish officers in the patrol organisation was to be terminated. At a chance meeting that I had with General Young, who had reverted to his former post as Commander of the British bases, he told me to watch out for attempts to undermine the patrols' authority and suggested these were likely to be motivated by professional jealousy.

It was a problem in these circumstances that I could not be entirely open about what was being achieved. I was acting wholly within the format that General Young had approved, but to a large degree on my own initiative and independently of JFHQ. At no time had General Carver asked me to explain to him the real thrust of our operations, and I had thought it prudent not to volunteer to do so. The Greek Cypriot leadership was deeply distrustful of the British and convinced that programmes for re-engagement would, if publicised, be sabotaged by them. I was becoming involved in plans which had been drawn up by government leaders and district administrators for a number of schemes aimed to subsidise the Turkish Cypriots through a programme of developments in mixed and all-Turkish Cypriot areas. Makarios was now aware that any further erosion of Turkish Cypriot belief in a unitary state would calamitously undercut his efforts and that it was vital to lay foundations on which a genuine re-engagement could be based. The schemes were designed to create jobs for the Turkish Cypriots and to generate a substantial flow of funding to them, in such a way that the process could not be used by either community for propaganda purposes. Even TMT leaders had told me they believed that most Turkish Cypriot villagers who had not yet moved would, in spite of their insecurities, react positively to a programme of this sort.

I obtained strong support from both Makarios and Kutchuk for the continuation of the patrols in their current format, suggesting that designated

Greek and Turkish officers could be engaged under contract, even if their countries were not to be participants in UNFICYP. I pointed out to UNFICYP commanders who had arrived in advance of the transfer-date that the patrols had an exceptional record of success in the mediating field and that we had established a basis of inter-communal and Greek-Turkish trust from which we were now moving on to the securing of a significant island-wide re-engagement.

None of this pleading was to much avail. My arguments apparently were over-ruled by high-level British advice to the UN secretariat. I was told that patrols would continue, but with the use of Greek and Turkish army officers terminated: instead, civilian Greek and Turkish interpreters would be brought in from New York.

At the special request of Makarios and Kutchuk I was to continue as patrol commander for Nicosia Zone, with Major Burgess continuing as my assistant: all other patrol commanders were to be replaced by specialised UN mediators.

Tripartite patrols as constituted by General Young on 7 January came to an end on 27 March. They were just beginning to realise their full potential. The interpreters sent by the UN from New York would have not the slightest chance of matching the influence that was wielded by Greek and Turkish officers who, over the course of three harrowing months, had developed a deep knowledge of Cypriot affairs and a surprising commitment to the process of active mediation. Successful mediation that had evolved from the dispute itself and become genuinely representative of the Cypriot people was not seen as a priority by external authorities. From here on, under the UN concept, mediation was to be externally motivated and the province of outsiders, rather than a process of Cypriot self-help.

A March 1964 editorial in the *Guardian*, which examined the tasks facing the new UNFICYP, commented on the tripartite patrols:

> "The exhausting and dangerous work of mediation, village by village, pioneered since Christmas by the British Army, will have to be continued by the international force. It may never be possible to calculate the number of lives that have been saved by intrepid teams of British, Greek and Turkish officers preaching common sense and reason to villagers tortured by fear of their neighbours. The careful quenching of each individual flicker of hatred is a job that must go on."

44. UNFICYP GETS UNDERWAY.
MARCH/APRIL 1964

"....to act in the interest of preserving international peace and security, to use its best efforts to prevent a recurrence of fighting and, as necessary, to contribute to the maintenance and restoration of law and order and a return to normal conditions."

(Security Council Resolution 186 of 4 March 1964, published in UN security document S/5575, which established UNFICYP.)

I had long been a devotee of the United Nations, my youthful interest having been engaged when I was taken in 1946 to the organisation's inaugural session of the General Assembly in London. I therefore anticipated the coming of the UN to Cyprus with enthusiasm, assuming that it would introduce to the situation an ethical dimension which would enhance the potential for pro-active mediation, replacing British policies and attitudes which were inevitably dictated by self-interest.

On 27 March, in common with those others who were to continue in their posts, I removed my traditional headgear and replaced it with a blue beret. I was now answerable to the United Nations.

I was told that I was now authorised to draw three hundred cigarettes each day as an aid to mediation. Nobody explained whether my principal loyalties were supposed in future to lie with the British element of the peacekeeping force, with the UN Secretary General or his representative in Nicosia, or with the Cypriot people to the mediating of whose problems I had been mandated by General Young.

Having been told that my original mission was to continue, and given the hiatus that attended the UN take-over, I decided for myself upon the latter option.

It quickly became clear that things were going to get worse rather than better. I had already appreciated that the loss of my Greek and Turkish officers was sure to have very damaging effects. Now I realised that rather than coming in with new attitudes, the UN was likely to carry forward the fundamental thesis of the British peace-keeping approach from February onwards: the commitment was still to be a freezing of separated hostility, rather than to the introduction of a wholehearted drive for communal re-engagement.[1]

Under the UN structure, there would be a representative of the Secretary General, initially Finnish diplomat Sakari Tuomioja, then the former President of Ecuador, Senor Galo Plaza, responsible for political control and high-level negotiations, with a secretariat headed by Natalie Thomas. There would be an overall military commander of the peacekeeping force, initially the Indian General Gyani, with General Carver acting as his deputy. There would be a team of professional political mediators (referred to generically as 'The 38th Floor') headed by Kurt Janssen. There would be a number of national contingents, each with its own command structure, answerable to UNFICYP HQ.

Additionally, field mediation was to be continued through the Joint Patrol Organisation (JPO), composed of mediating officers and interpreters, whose mission was defined by UNFICYP HQ to be:

> 'Preventing armed clashes; restoring confidence; collecting information on the general situation throughout the island; collecting information to assist the Relief Organisation.'

The narrowness of this definition was bad enough, but significantly it meant that it was planned for patrols to report to military HQ rather than to the UN mediating body: in other words, the JPO was conceived essentially as an information-gathering adjunct of the status-quo-dedicated peacekeeping process, rather than as a front-line extension of the mediating effort under Kurt Jansson and Galo Plaza.

It took me time to realise the significance of this distinction which, with my Nelsonian blind eye towards the signal, I then decided to be applicable to the new patrol officers rather than to myself. While rendering to the military arm of UNFICYP such formal reports as would meet its requirements, I continued to build privately on the friendships and associations which had evolved over the past three months: in this I was encouraged through an informal linkage with Kurt Janssen and Natalie Thomas, who in turn had the ear of the Secretary General's representative.

Among the strengths of the tripartite patrols had been that they intimately represented both the people of Cyprus and their 'parental' patrons, that they had developed roots inside both communities to such extent that they had come themselves to compose a critical component of the re-engagement process, and that they acted with the direct private authority and support of President Makarios and Vice-President Kutchuk. They were now to be replaced by units composed of competent international bureaucrats, aided by outside interpreters, who had no roots whatever within the problem or the community and no direct linkage to communal or deep-state leaderships.

Nor were the new units to find that they had whole-hearted support from UNFICYP. Most incoming UN army contingents quickly showed a resentment of any independent field mediating operation, believing that they should have sole authority within the district for which they were responsible. Mediating units often found themselves operating in a climate of UNFICYP hostility, running from thinly-veiled to explicit, rather than of enthusiastic military support.

Furthermore, the UN was for some time to be mainly dependant on British infrastructure and advice. Most importantly, this meant a reliance on British intelligence assessments, whose bias in favour of separatism had always worried me. This, together with the fact that General Carver's strength of personality and experience would enable him to dominate the top-level decision-taking process, meant an effective British control of UNFICYP during the vital first period, when the template for future operations was being established.

The allocation of responsibility for each zone of Cyprus to a different national contingent led to new fiefdoms being established. A patchwork of interlocking bureaucracies quickly evolved, each with institutional sensitivities that would inhibit much of the broad-brush work that the tripartite patrols had pursued.

Most contingents quickly acquired their own prejudices, for or against the Greek Cypriots, the Turkish Cypriots or the British. By listening to their Greek Cypriot or Turkish Cypriot contacts, many of them soon became convinced that whatever the British army had done in the past three months had been a failure, which was palpably untrue. The most quickly prejudiced were the Canadians and Swedes, the most even-handed were the Finns, and the easiest to work with were the Irish, whose laid-back attitude and natural scepticism quickly endeared them equally to Greek Cypriots and Turkish Cypriots.

I hoped that these were mainly teething problems. In any event I had for the moment still to work mostly with British army units, since Britain would continue in the short term as the main provider of troops for UN peacekeeping operations in Nicosia Zone.

In the interregnum between the ending on 27 March of the British peacekeeping mandate and the moment when new UN patrol arrangements became effective, I debated with Tassos Papadopoulos and with Doctor Kutchuk how momentum could be maintained in the absence of the authority formerly conferred by my Turkish and Greek officers. We agreed that we could at least preserve some of the old tripartite persona of my patrol if there were a semi-formal secondment to it of a representative of each community. Mr Phyllactou was nominated for the Greek Cypriots and Nihat Bey for the Turkish Cypriots, both of them having until Christmas been respected members of the district administration. I then cleared their names with the 'Secret Army' and with TMT. I received from Georgadjis a general *passe-partout* (which was to prove invariably effective) that allowed Nihat to travel with me without risk of search or stoppage* and from Kutchuk and TMT a confirmation that Phyllactou could travel with me freely in Turkish Cypriot-controlled areas.

Our major problem now was not with the Cypriots in Nicosia Zone, by whom we were invariably made welcome, but with the new UN contingents, which made clear their opposition to any encroachment onto their territory by an independent mediating unit, except when specifically requested by them. I repeatedly was approached by communal leaders, or received calls from villages, asking that we help to resolve some problem of which we had

---

* See Appendix F.

an intimate knowledge, only to have UNFICYP HQ decline authorisation for such a visit.

That situation did gradually improve. We diplomatically promoted the service that we could offer and instances arose where UNFICYP contingents found that they could not cope with complex inter-communal problems. But our freedom of action as a general catalyst for the restoration of inter-communal relations in the villages was never restored and only grudgingly was it ceded in respect of new island-wide initiatives, such as those covering grain-storage and harvesting and public-works projects.

While the military changeover was in progress, I received an urgent request to try to deal with fighting that had started in Famagusta.

I helicoptered in to be greeted by a relaxed major of the newly disembarked Southern Irish Regiment. He told me: "Nothing at all to be bothered about. Just a little local excitement."

It transpired that the JF unit waiting to be relieved in Famagusta was a Northern Ireland regiment of the British army, The Royal Inniskillings. The incoming UN troops were Southern Irish. Having disembarked, they were marching through the town when they were jeered at by the northerners and then pelted by them with eggs and oranges. A series of fistfights broke out.

The watching Greek Cypriot crowd took this to be an attack by the British on the United Nations and set upon the British northerners, at which the southerners joined with the northerners to attack the Greek Cypriots. There had been a number of superficial injuries, but the incident had now given way to some amicable drinking.

Explaining to me the matter of Irish military politics, the major said: "You see, a lot of my boys are deserters from the north. Usually they've pushed off because of an affair with a woman. In the same way quite a lot of men in the northern regiment are deserters from the south, for the same reason. Each of these regiments has had a good few of their women stolen, so today there was a bit of a settling of scores. Of course the locals had no right to join in, and we taught them a thing or two, but we'll all be friends in the future."

On 30 March, there was a potentially more damaging confrontation. Major Burgess and I were in Kythrea with the gendarmerie discussing problems of the local irrigation system, when we realised that the Greek Cypriots were unusually restless. The Ayios Amvrosios bus had halted in the village and its passengers appeared to be more than ordinarily excited, but our enquiries as to what was afoot were met with expansive shrugs. We moved on to the Turkish Cypriot village of Bey Keuy and found its people all out in the streets in a state of jubilation. The local TMT leader invited us to walk with him to the edge of the village to see a heart-warming sight. United Nations forces, he said, were attacking the Greek Cypriot camp at Halefka.

The villagers described to us how a United Nations foot patrol had moved through Kalyvakia and on up into the foothills to the north and how soon afterwards they had heard the sounds of battle. They assumed that this was a punitive expedition by UNFICYP to put an end to the Greek Cypriot habit of shooting from Halefka at Turkish Cypriot shepherds. The TMT leader told me he was assembling a force to go and support the United Nations. Only with great reluctance did he accept our advice not to go through with this plan.

From outside Bey Keuy we could hear the sound of heavy automatic fire and exploding grenades. I radioed HQ with an explanation of what was happening and a request for aerial reconnaissance, and we drove at high speed back through Kythrea and up the winding mountain road to Halefka. There we found a sixty-strong force of the 'Secret Army' (in this case already calling itself the National Guard, although that title was not to become official until June) engaged in a firefight. They told us that they were under heavy attack by Turkish troops. They had beaten off the first attack, they said, but the enemy were still concealed in gullies to the south. They believed that the attackers were part of the Turkish national contingent, since they were all wearing identical blue helmets.

We stopped the firing and soon afterwards heard from the spotter plane that it had sighted a UN patrol moving from the area back towards Kalyvakia. The Greek Cypriot soldiers told us that their officers were all away at a conference in Nicosia. They refused to believe that they had made a mistake and excitedly regaled each other with stories of near-escapes and heroism.

When we moved on to Kalyvakia, two miles as the crow flies but fifteen by road, we were told by a UN patrol, from 1st Foresters, that they had been on a routine patrol when they had come under heavy fire, and that they had been forced to return fire in order to effect a withdrawal.

The Turkish Cypriots in Kalyvakia were all complaining that their sheep had been lost in the foothills, the shepherds having fled when the firing began. John Burgess volunteered to go with them to help with the recovery, while I returned to Halefka to make sure they were not shot at while doing so.

I found that Halefka had been reinforced by a large detachment of armed and uniformed gendarmerie and that the 'Secret Army' officers had returned from Nicosia. I was told that the UN was at fault for failing to inform the Greek Cypriots that patrols were to be mounted in this area. UNFICYP later received a similar complaint, together with apologies, from the Greek Cypriot authorities in Nicosia.

Within three days of the UN taking over from the British, far more rounds had been loosed off by peacekeeping troops than in the whole of the previous three months. The use of firepower by UNFICYP troops was in general to become fairly frequent.

The Greek Cypriot complaint about lack of warning was a valid one, given that all along the Kyrenia Range there were heavily armed Greek Cypriot and Turkish Cypriot positions waiting in expectation of attack and that the UN patrol had moved up under cover from the direction of a Turkish Cypriot village.

In writing up my report of the incident I suggested that, unless the UN had it in mind to forcibly disarm the whole of Cyprus, it would seem logical for communal authorities to be kept advised of intended UN troop movements, except in cases where there was special reason for them to be kept secret. This recommendation was rejected by UNFICYP HQ.

General Gyani, earlier in Cyprus as UN representative, took over in March as the overall military commander of UNFICYP. He is here with Brigadier Roly Gibbs.

Canadian troops landing in Cyprus, March 1964.

March 1964, British soldier replaces Union Jack with UN transfer on armoured car.

Major Burgess and I, having swapped our traditional headgear for UN blue berets. The core mediating team, from March, was completed by Nihat Bey, left.

TMT leader and Vingt-deux officer.

45. TILLYRIA. 3-7 APRIL 1964

Tillyria, the mountainous section of the north-west coastal hinterland that lies between Pomos and Xeros, had frequently since Christmas seemed likely to be the scene of armed clashes.

For several reasons this was the worst area of rural Cyprus for inter-village frictions. The main road that follows the north-west coast here alternated between sections under Greek Cypriot and Turkish Cypriot control: Greek Cypriot from Polis to Pakhy Ammos, Turkish Cypriot from Kokkina to Mansoura, Greek Cypriot around Kato Pyrgos, Turkish Cypriot again in the Petra tou Limniti region and finally Greek Cypriot on to Xeros. The route was an important one and both communities felt tempted at times of stress between them to use their sections to exert pressure, either by blocking the road or by capturing traffic.

Kokkina to Mansoura was the only stretch of coastline wholly under Turkish Cypriot control. It had in the past and was currently being used as the main clandestine landing-point for weapons and men being smuggled in from Turkey. (Galinoporni, in the north-east, being the other site most commonly used). From Mansoura, the weapons were normally transported along a network of tracks and back-roads that the Turkish Cypriots felt to be safe; occasionally they were smuggled to Nicosia by British or Swedish members of the peacekeeping forces, whose sympathies the Turkish Cypriots had managed to engage or whose services they had purchased; much less often, because of the near-certainty of a rigorous search by the police, they were moved down the main road concealed in Turkish Cypriot vehicles.[1]

Greek Cypriot leaders were well aware, from interrogations and informers, of what was going on. They thought the best way to put a stop to it was either to take full control of the Mansoura coastline or to put a stranglehold around it.

The situation was complicated by several other factors. First, the region was split between two 'Secret Army' command zones, with poor communications and co-ordination between them. Second, within these two zones the local leadership was distinctly independent, so that central control was tenuous: George Raftis,* who dictated affairs in the western sector, was a flamboyant nationalist whose appetite for heroic action was feared almost as much by the Greek Cypriot hierarchy in Nicosia as it was by the local Turkish Cypriots. Third, Mospilem was now the only Greek Cypriot village entirely surrounded by areas under Turkish Cypriot control, which made it an easy

---

* I was told that his surname derived from an admiration of George Raft, a famous Hollywood portrayer of gangsters.

target for the Turkish Cypriots whenever a need was felt to counter Greek Cypriot pressure against Turkish Cypriot villages elsewhere. Fourth, the whole region was an impoverished one and its villagers, whether Greek Cypriot or Turkish Cypriot, had the reputation of being particularly tough, fractious and addicted to fighting and vendettas.

The Makarios-Kutchuk island-wide cease-fire and disengagement agreements of late December and early January had made little impact on this region. What stability there was here had been built mainly on agreements negotiated by Major Greenwood's patrol. There had been a series of preliminary verbal understandings followed by several written concords, of which the most important were those dated 14 and 18 February, the first covering the opening of the coastal road and the second the terms for a comprehensive cease-fire.

Despite these agreements, there had been a succession of shooting incidents, mainly in two areas of particular contention: across the valley where the Greek Cypriots in Piyenia looked down onto the Turkish Cypriot defences around Ayios Theodhoros, and between the Turkish Cypriot Kokkina and the Greek Cypriot Pakhy Ammos, where whoever held Kaliphoudes Ridge could dominate the other village. Control of Kaliphoudes Ridge had become the most critical of all paramilitary issues in Tillyria.

The terms negotiated by Major Greenwood had stipulated that Kaliphoudes was not to be occupied by either community, but this provision was regularly disregarded. On 11 March, Major McIntyre's patrol found that the Turkish Cypriots were again entrenched on the disputed hill and a new agreement was made for its evacuation. Two weeks later the same patrol reported a much improved atmosphere throughout Tillyria and that the coastal road was open from Polis to Xeros.

With the arrival of the United Nations and the termination of Major McIntyre's tripartite patrol, the situation began rapidly to deteriorate. On 29 March a Turkish Cypriot car was ambushed by Greek Cypriots near Vroisha: the Turkish Cypriots at Limnitis took hostages in retaliation, but later in the day were persuaded to release them. On 1 April, Greek Cypriots ambushed a group of Turkish Cypriots near Selemani and barriers were afterwards re-erected at many points along the main road. On 2 April, there was repeated sniping into Selemani from Greek Cypriots hidden in the surrounding hills. On 3 April, heavy firing started between Piyenia and Ayios Theodhoros: a UN patrol trying to evacuate a wounded Turkish Cypriot from the latter village came under direct and extensive fire from Greek Cypriot paramilitaries; a British officer who arrived at Piyenia to try and restrain the Greek Cypriots there reported that he was met with extreme hostility.

Early on 4 April, I was instructed by UNFICYP HQ to try to stabilise the situation in Tillyria.

My patrol went first by helicopter to Piyenia and we were in the coffee-house there, amicably reviewing the position with the local Greek Cypriot leadership, when a message was received that serious fighting had broken out between Kokkina and Pakhy Ammos.

We landed at Pakhy Ammos at 1030, to find that heavy exchanges of fire were taking place all along the coastal belt and in the broken foothills. We were told that Greek Cypriot paramilitaries had just reoccupied Kaliphoudes Ridge.

This was another instance of the patrol coming into an unfamiliar region with whose leaders I had had no previous personal contact and in which there was a complex history of local antagonisms. Inevitably it was a slow and laborious process to reach an understanding of the intricacies of local relationships and animosities.

It appeared that the situation was fairly evenly balanced and that neither community felt any urgent disposition to stop the fighting. The position was further complicated for us because neither the Greek Cypriot or Turkish Cypriot overall commanders had direct communication with their forward positions: instead, verbal messages were being despatched by runner, with the natural risk (as with the charge of the British Light Brigade at Balaclava) that misunderstandings would occur.

The patrol therefore resolved to visit all front-line control-posts to get a better idea of the situation and to try and formulate mutually acceptable terms for a cease-fire. However, having set off down the road to Pakhy Ammos in the company of some Greek Cypriot gendarmerie officers, we came under heavy and accurate Turkish Cypriot machine gun fire.*

My discussion with the gendarmerie was continued as we crouched in the ditch, under constant and energetic fire from the Turkish Cypriots, until a UN armoured vehicle arrived to extract us. We were then delivered beyond Pakhy Ammos to the foot of a large conical hill which had been explained to us as forming the pivotal point of the Greek Cypriot defences: here we disembarked and crawled up, under renewed Turkish Cypriot fire, to reach the forward Greek Cypriot trenches. The 'Secret Army' soldiers there clearly had an enthusiastic appetite for further fighting and we had difficulty convincing them that a cease-fire was needed, but eventually they agreed that they would not shoot again unless under close attack. Major Aarnio, a Finnish officer who was temporarily attached to my patrol before taking over his own mediating area, was left behind by me to monitor this agreement.

Major Burgess and I then set off to seek a similar arrangement with the Turkish Cypriots. Our passage attracted a hail of fire, first from one side, then the other, from positions that we had not yet visited.

We contacted the Turkish Cypriot commander in Kokkina just as a runner arrived with news that his forces had recaptured Kaliphoudes. This produced a burst of celebration in the village, with armed men embracing each other and a firing of celebratory shots.

We gradually coaxed the Turkish Cypriots out of their euphoria and convinced them that it was time for a general cease-fire. Runners were despatched to convey this instruction to outlying positions.

Burgess and I moved on to Pakhy Ammos. Our arrival coincided with that of a Greek Cypriot armoured vehicle, sent up from Polis by George Raftis,

---

* I was impressed when one round hit the heel of Major Burgess' boot, without causing him any injury. He paused in the middle of the road, tapped his leg with his swagger-stick, uttered a mild imprecation and declined to join me in the ditch.

which immediately moved into an attack on Turkish Cypriot positions. This re-ignited the general firing that we had just managed to quench.

The Greek Cypriots were now in a state of high excitement and very reluctant to be restrained. Finally they were prevailed upon to call a temporary halt to hostilities, so that we could try and negotiate a new demilitarisation of Kaliphoudes. Major Burgess then stood alone in the centre of the road, in the hope that his physical presence would deter any forward movement by the Greek Cypriot armoured vehicle (a position made even less comfortable by the fact that the Turkish Cypriots were still directing accurate fire at it), while I went back through the crossfire to Kokkina.

Negotiations with the Turkish Cypriots dragged on. I was told on the radio link that more Greek Cypriot armoured vehicles had arrived and that Burgess had already been warned three times that he would be shot if he did not immediately remove himself from the road.

By 1600, I was edging the Turkish Cypriots towards acceptance of terms for their withdrawal from Kaliphoudes. However, the position of Major Burgess had become untenable (besides which he had urgent need of a toilet) and, with some misgivings, the local UNFICYP command decided to interpose its own armoured cars to prevent a Greek Cypriot advance. This action provoked a storm of protest from the Greek Cypriots and a renewed outburst of firing.

At 1715, the Turkish Cypriots agreed provisional terms for a general cease-fire and started to move their forces back from their forward positions on the lower slopes.

The Greek Cypriots, however, were deeply aggravated: not only had they been driven back off a key ridge but they had lost some of their weapons in the process. Claiming that some of his wounded might still be on the hill, the Greek Cypriot commander insisted on our going with him for a thorough search of the area. When we failed to find any of the missing weapons he worked himself into a towering rage.*

There was now a very ugly and resentful feeling among the Greek Cypriot paramilitaries, who placed the blame on the British for the day's reverses. Major Burgess, while going forward to locate the most advanced Turkish Cypriot positions, so that they could be handed over to UN control under the terms of the cease-fire, was fired on from behind by Greek Cypriots: the Turkish Cypriots took this to indicate a trap and resumed heavy firing against the village of Pakhy Ammos. This fire was returned by Greek Cypriot armoured vehicles.

Heavy incoming Bren gun fire led me to take hasty cover inside a nearby cottage. There I found six Greek Cypriot irregulars already sheltering: they were in a state of such intense anger, at what they took to be a British-sponsored defeat in the fighting in the hills, that they stuck a Sten gun in my stomach and told me to say my last prayers. Their attention was providentially diverted when the window behind them was shot out by a

---

* Later, the missing arms were located by British troops and handed over to the Greek Cypriot police.

burst of LMG fire and a party of international journalists simultaneously dived in through the front door seeking for cover.

After further exhortations, Burgess and I managed to persuade both sides to hold their fire. The stoppage allowed UN troops from 9 Para Field Squadron to take over the disputed entrenchments on Kaliphoudes Ridge. The road between Kokkina and Pakhy Ammos was then more effectively blocked with UN vehicles and leaders on both sides were told that any advance in this area on their part would be taken as an attack on the UN and met with force. There was no more firing that day.

I was late getting back to Nicosia that night, but had still to deliver a report to Dr Kutchuk and to discuss the day's events with Tassos Papadopoulos. Each had received a widely different, and extremely inaccurate, account from his own people in the field.

On 5 April, I was back in the area by mid-day. There had been dramatic developments. Under cover of darkness, the Greek Cypriots had launched a successful night attack from the east onto the commanding heights above Mansoura. Having captured all the Turkish Cypriot hilltop positions, fire was directed into Mansoura itself, where it seriously endangered the British UN force that was deployed there. Eventually, the Greek Cypriot fire was returned by two British armoured cars, causing casualties and obliging the Greek Cypriots to retire from the forward positions that they had just captured. I was told, but never had it confirmed, that the 'Secret Army' force-commander was killed during this firefight, but that the news of his death was being suppressed. Whether or not that was true, the incident caused further intense anti-British feeling and increased the likelihood of a general attack in Tillyria against the Turkish Cypriots.

Throughout the morning of the 5th there was scattered firing in the Piyenia – Ayios Theodhoros region. On my arrival, the Greek Cypriots made a token withdrawal from their advanced positions above Mansoura, which enabled me to obtain from the Turkish Cypriots an agreement to the salient points for a long-term cease-fire.

I arranged for an afternoon rendezvous with George Raftis in Pakhy Ammos, but he failed to appear and I was told by one of his lieutenants that he was leading a Greek Cypriot detachment into the hills. The details I was given suggested that a dawn attack from the south towards Kokkina was intended.

Throughout the day there was a build-up of Greek Cypriot forces, with reinforcements arriving in Kato Pyrgos by sea from Xeros and Morphou and moving up the road from Polis towards Pakhy Ammos. In Pakhy Ammos the newcomers were extremely militant, and particularly vituperative towards the British. John Burgess and I felt a distinct unease as we moved to and fro between the opposing positions. It looked as though the Greek Cypriots were preparing to shoot it out with the UN roadblock. News arrived that Greek Cypriot paramilitaries had taken British hostages in Kato Pyrgos and were demanding that in future UNFICYP should only allow Canadians troops into the Tillyria region.

A request from the local 'Secret Army' commander for a meeting, which I took to be for the furtherance of cease-fire negotiations, turned out to be for the presentation of a complaint that UN troops were causing damage to Greek Cypriot property. We went with an elderly villager to inspect his vegetable plot, where a team of UN paratroopers with grenade-launchers were sitting on his potato plants. I signed an undertaking that the United Nations (or, failing them, the British Government) would pay appropriate compensation for any damage done, and this produced a slight raising of spirits. In the meantime, the Greek Cypriot commander had had a good look at an impressive display of UN weaponry.

That night in Nicosia, I discussed the position with Tassos Papadopoulos and other leaders of 'The Organisation'. They said they had investigated my earlier private report on how the fighting had begun and accepted that it had been instigated from the Greek Cypriot side without their authority. They said that it was proving extremely difficult to exercise an effective control over Raftis: communication with him was patchy and their own reporting from the area was often unreliable.

They then told me that a command decision had already been taken that if the current cease-fire did not hold – and they did not expect it to – then a full-scale attack would be launched in order to re-impose government control throughout the whole of western Tillyria. To this end very large forces were being moved up secretly from the south and assembled in the mountains around Vroisha. They said that their final decision would be based purely on the situation on the ground and on the opinion of their military commander there, and that high-level political negotiations being conducted in Nicosia under UN auspices were only for window-dressing.

I showed them an outline cease-fire agreement, drawn up by me on the back of an envelope* and they said that its terms would be acceptable if they could be fully imposed. The terms applied only to the ending of hostilities: they carried a rider that they would be continued until superseded by a comprehensive arrangement, which would cover freedom of movement on the main road.

On the morning of 6 April, I was shown a warning issued by TMT the previous evening that the main road bridge between Kokkina and Pakhy Ammos was to be blown, as they had no confidence that the UN would continue to block Greek Cypriot armoured vehicles from breaking through and attacking the Turkish Cypriot village. Such a move would have isolated British UN troops to the west of the bridge: these had therefore been withdrawn from the main road and from Kaliphoudes Ridge by 2200 on the night of the 5th. Predictably, Greek Cypriot units had then re-occupied the positions evacuated by the UN. At dawn on 6 April, the situation was thus back to where it had been on the morning of the 4th. The Greek Cypriots now resumed firing into Kokkina.

The Turkish Cypriots responded by mounting a new attack against Kaliphoudes and by 0700 the ridge was again in their hands. This in turn triggered an attack by the Greek Cypriots, supported by armoured vehicles,

---

* See Appendix E.

along the road towards Kokkina. An attempt by TMT to dynamite the road-bridge did only limited damage to the main structure.

At this point my patrol was flown in by helicopter. I sent Burgess to try to restrain the Turkish Cypriots. He arrived at their front line on the ridge just in time to see them using rocket launchers to drive off a Greek Cypriot attack, one armoured bulldozer being hit and abandoned.

In Pakhy Ammos, the 'Secret Army' commander acknowledged to me that he had received new instructions from Nicosia and gave me a general undertaking that he would hold back his troops during the day to give a further chance for mediation.

At 1020 a more successful explosion blew out the main span of the bridge, which was left passable only to pedestrians. This produced a flurry of firing, but relative calm had resumed by the time that General Gyani, the UN Force Commander, flew in to visit Kokkina. Meanwhile, Greek Cypriot reinforcements were continuing to move into Pakhy Ammos.

Having obtained a general picture of the situation and spoken with those leaders that I could locate, I helicoptered back to Nicosia and there met a senior contact in the 'Secret Army'. I reported on my own reading of events and was told that a totally different picture, which he accepted as probably inaccurate, was being relayed from his local sources. He said that Raftis was responsible for the continuation of the fighting: he and the Greek Cypriot leadership, much to their annoyance, now found themselves manoeuvred by Raftis and the press into a position where they felt that they could not do other than authorise a general attack, which they accepted might trigger an attack by the Turkish air force. However, since promises given to me had clearly been broken I was being offered one last chance. If the patrol could that same day obtain a settlement subscribed to by all units in the area, including Raftis, then the attack, scheduled for dawn on the 7th would be cancelled. The deadline was that all key leaders must have reported their acceptance to Nicosia, over their own lines, by nightfall.

I returned immediately by helicopter to Pakhy Ammos and eventually was able to contact Raftis. He was very chastened, clearly having been admonished from Nicosia. Fortunately, he appeared not to ascribe any of the blame for this to me. After a long, amicable and surprisingly cogent review of the problems of Cyprus and the needs of the local area, and my usual sermonising that without Turkish Cypriot trust and acquiescence from Ankara no happy outcome for Cyprus would be possible, he agreed to sign up to all points of the agreement.

However, by now there was general firing again between Kokkina, Alevga and Pakhy Ammos, and the same laborious process as in the past was needed to get all the outlying positions under control.

By 1700, all firing had ceased and it had been agreed that Burgess and I would bring the Turkish Cypriot and Greek Cypriot commanders to a joint meeting at the blown bridge. Raftis and I were to come in a UN armoured vehicle.

In Pakhy Ammos, George Raftis, despite the urgency of other matters, was keen to show me a newly arrived armoured car which he said had been built to his own specifications. Not wishing to alienate him at this key moment, I accepted his invitation to inspect the inside of the vehicle, at which moment he set off down the road, telling me that he preferred to go to the meeting by his own means. The car had a machine-gun mounted in a half-turret: Raftis, in a state of exhilaration, shouted down to me that he was going to give it a try-out.

Major Burgess and the Turkish Cypriot commander and a bevy of international pressmen had formally assembled in the middle of the road to await the Greek Cypriot party. En masse they dived into the ditch when, instead of a peace-delegation, they were confronted by an armoured car, with its machine gun firing, rounding the corner towards them.

The UN armoured car which had been sent to bring me to the meeting was in close pursuit. Nearby Turkish Cypriots, taking this to be part of a new Greek Cypriot attack, opened up a heavy but ineffectual fire against the two vehicles. As Major Burgess sallied forth from the ditch, to try to restore the situation, a bullet tore through the UN flag he was waving. Firing now recommenced from the surrounding hills.

Burgess and I started again from square one, using the incident as an anecdote to produce a general good humour in both camps. By 1830, all firing had stopped, a UN patrol was moving back by mutual agreement to take over all disputed positions on Kaliphoudes Ridge, and Raftis and the Turkish Cypriot leaders had agreed ceasefire terms and confirmed to me that they had so informed Nicosia.

In the gathering dusk, Major Burgess, preceded by his driver carrying a UN flag and followed by the key Turkish Cypriot leaders, walked out from Kokkina. At the same time, also preceded by a UN flag, I set off on foot from Pakhy Ammos accompanied by George Raftis and other Greek Cypriot unit commanders. When we met by the bridge, there were general salutations and embraces, as though this were the ending of a close-fought football match. The cease-fire was then deemed to be effective.

That night in Nicosia, I was told that the planned Greek Cypriot attack had been cancelled and that all out-of-area troops would be withdrawn the next day. As the night progressed, reports came into UNFICYP HQ that front-line positions in western Tillyria were being stood down and that there were no remaining signs of tension.

Throughout the course of this fighting, the Greek Cypriot press had devoted itself to attacking the role of the British in UNFICYP with unprecedented venom, particularly citing the firing at Mansoura and the halting of Greek Cypriot armoured reinforcements moving up from Polis. So distorted was the picture given to Greek readers that UNFICYP HQ thought it unlikely that British troops could again be used effectively by the UN in north-west Cyprus.

Nor was the picture presented with any greater accuracy in the mainline British press: on 6 April, the Daily Mirror opined that any Englishman trying to visit Kato Pyrgos or Pakhy Ammos in the coming days would be torn to pieces by enraged Greek Cypriot villagers.

I spent 7 April visiting villages in the region, starting with Kato Pyrgos, Mospilem and Pakhy Ammos. John Burgess and I were everywhere given a deeply moving reception. In Pakhy Ammos I had heaped upon me an embarrassment of gifts: I knew that the villagers could ill-afford them, but that they would have been hurt by any rejection. Both there and in Kokkina we were inducted as honorary villagers and asked to return whenever we could.[2]

We had arrived in Kato Pyrgos with personal introductions from the President. We discussed events with the villagers for over an hour and were heartened by their response. They said this was the first time that real issues had been talked through with them and that no-one before had put it to them that their own security and their own ambitions depended on an effective re-engagement with the Turkish Cypriots.

The fighting in Tillyria carried various lessons. It probably would not have started if an effective tripartite patrol operation had been active in the area in the days leading up to 3 April, but Major McIntyre's unit had been disbanded on 27 March and mine had no prior experience of the area or contacts in it and was only called in after hostilities had begun. It certainly could have been stopped by me very much sooner and more easily (given the will to this effect in Nicosia) if Greek and Turkish officers had still been with me, but the patrol had been deprived by the UN of this basic element of its operations.

The huge gulf between events on the ground and associated local decision-taking on the one side and deliberations and negotiations in Nicosia on the other, confirmed the inadequacy of communal command structures in situations of crisis, hardly surprising in such a young and untested state. On this score I was left to wonder to what degree past fighting in other districts of Cyprus, Ktima and Limassol for example, might have been avoided if command structures and communications had been adequate and if mediating mechanisms had existed there which genuinely related to local realities and to local power structures.

This particular incident also reinforced my view that it was better to seek agreement in principle at local level and take that to the top for approval or fine-tuning rather than seek to deliver into the local battle situation a solution arbitrarily negotiated in Nicosia.

A ceasefire in Tillyria was produced not because of the intervention of UN forces, but because agreement was available from both communities once an effective mediating mechanism had been supplied to them. The only real animosities that I saw in Tillyria were those generated by extremist propaganda. For most of the men involved, battle had seemed to be a sort of sport, from which they desisted with some regret, rather than an attempt to eliminate their neighbours, whom they greeted with apparent affection once the shooting had stopped. Nobody could reasonably suggest that this fighting had any genocidal content. The only real hatred on display had been that sometimes shown by the Greek Cypriots towards the British.

To my belief that the Tillyria fighting could have been avoided was added another: that had the Greek Cypriots pressed home their main attack it almost certainly would have succeeded. But that could have had dangerous consequences.

A quick Greek Cypriot assumption of control over the coastal area would have shut off the major route for the delivery by Turkey of weapons and clandestine personnel. But it very probably would have led to Turkish military intervention, as did the subsequent August attack by the Greek Cypriots, directed by General Grivas, in precisely the same area.[3]

Almost certainly any result other than a negotiated settlement would have set back the process of communal re-engagement, as did the fighting in August. The Makarios government clearly feared the repercussions if Ankara were further provoked and accepted that re-engagement was now more than ever critical to the preservation of a unitary state.

Turkish Cypriot paramilitaries on Kaliphoudes Ridge, overlooking Kokkina.

UNFICYP officers inspecting the main road bridge at Kokkina after TMT had blown it up to prevent an advance by Greek Cypriot armoured vehicles.

General Gyani listening to a local Turkish Cypriot leader in Kokkina.

46. Kyrenia Range East (Pentadaktylos). 11 April Onwards 1964

TMT planning for the areas to the north of Nicosia was explained to me as being for a slow encroachment outwards from St Hilarion along the Kyrenia range. To the west this was to end at the point from which it would be possible to bring the Myrtou-Kyrenia road under Turkish Cypriot control: to the east the objective was for an eventual link-up with the Chatos enclave.

The progress of these encroachments was to be matched by the build-up of civilian population within the Photta-Mandres district, anchored on the Turkish army contingent and the airstrip* that was being constructed for it to the north of Geunyely. The outcome was intended to be a single, compact enclave resting on the north of Nicosia and stretching from Myrtou to Lefkoniko, with direct access to the Karpas peninsula through Artemi and Ayios Iakovos and with the ability to isolate Kyrenia at will. This ambitious scheme was to be pursued, in the face of overwhelmingly greater Greek Cypriot strengths, upon the assumption that support would eventually be provided from Turkey. Since the plan was known to the Greek Cypriots, by way of the many Turkish Cypriot informers whose reports were collated by Georgadjis, it gave them solid reason to accuse the Turkish Cypriots of a separatist insurrection which justified suppression by force. But, faced by the more powerful PR mechanisms of Britain and Turkey, the Greek Cypriot authorities failed to impress on the international community a convincing presentation in this light.

Greek Cypriot planning staff usually over-estimated Turkish Cypriot capacity for concerted military action, but they were accurate in their assessment of this TMT strategy.

A detailed Greek Cypriot plan to recapture the whole of the Kyrenia Pass area, based on an attack through the Karmi Forest from the west, had been in existence from early February and units had since then been training on similar terrain around Makheras Monastery for specific tasks in the assault. Urgency was now added by Greek Cypriot alarm at TMT's plan to extend its control along the Pentadaktylos ridge and by the steady trickle of Turkish Cypriots who were relocating into the Chatos and Photta enclaves from the south.

On the night of 10 April, the Greek Cypriots moved a force of about three hundred men through Pano Dhikomo and by the morning of the 11th they were established in strength astride the ridge above. The Turkish Cypriots

---

* See photograph p. 273

took this holding operation on the peaks around Trypa Vouno as a main assault and diverted a disproportionate part of their defensive strength to meet it. The line thus established, across the summit of the Pentadaktylos, was explained to me in detail by both Greek and Turkish Cypriots when I was asked by UNFICYP on 11 April to find out what was the position. It was to remain entirely static in the months to come. Occasional shooting between the opposing peaks, designated by UNFICYP HQ as 'Whiskey' and 'Gin', had no operational significance and I was never called back to this area.

One offshoot of the readjustments on the ridge had more significance for my patrol. During the night of 12 April, Turkish Cypriot fighters moved eastwards from Aghirda and occupied a hill that commanded the approaches from Pano Dhikomo to the Kyrenia road. This hill, soon to be christened 'Small Beer' by UNFICYP, also commanded the DEKO Cement Works, a large Greek Cypriot co-operative farm at Onishia and a considerable expanse of farmland owned by Greek Cypriots at Pano and Kato Dhikomo. Firing soon became general across the area between Aghirda and Pano Dhikomo, and the Greek Cypriots assembled a well-trained and heavily armed unit of three hundred men for an attack westwards.

While I was in Nicosia, seeking guidance on Greek Cypriot, Turkish Cypriot and UN intentions, Major Burgess sought to hold in check the situation on the ground. He persuaded the Greek Cypriots to pull back from an attack that they were just starting; managed, under desultory Turkish Cypriot fire, to shepherd the farm workers from Onishia back to safety in Dhikomo; then contacted the Turkish Cypriot fighters on 'Small Beer' and induced them to stop firing. Both the cement factory and the farm were then declared to be UN posts.

The willingness of UNFICYP to designate all epicentres of friction as UN posts, and station UN troops there and run up a UN ensign, was a significant change from JFHQ practice. Had this been used as an adjunct of an active mediating process, it could have provided major benefit: instead it became part of a process by which a series of mini-Green-Lines was established across Cyprus, to the general benefit of TMT, and then jealously defended by one or other of the UNFICYP contingents.

I joined Major Burgess at midday and we managed to persuade the military commanders on the two sides to refrain from further armed action while political discussions went forward over the transfer of 'Small Beer' from Turkish Cypriot to UN control. In the evening, Umit Suleiman arrived at the scene as representative of Kutchuk, with empowerment to authorise the hand-over. The TMT commander took no part in the subsequent discussion, but Superintendent Ali Assad, the senior Turkish Cypriot police officer in the area, took violent exception to the decision.

At 1500 Kutchuk's office informed UNFICYP HQ that Turkish Cypriot fighting units had refused to accept the proposal for evacuation of the hill and that the earlier agreement must therefore be considered void.

Subsequent attempts by UNFICYP to sponsor a mediated settlement for the area got nowhere and it remained a constant irritation – a fixed front across which shepherds and farmers were frequently sniped at and in which bored Greek Cypriot paramilitaries took long-range pot-shots at Turkish

Cypriot vehicles on the Kyrenia road. Privately I was told by TMT and 'Secret Army' leaders of an arrangement that would be acceptable to them for a partial disengagement and UN interposition. When I delivered this plan to UNFICYP HQ I was told not to pursue it, as an initiative by me might upset the Canadian unit which had UN responsibility for the area and which was jealous of any infringement of its bailiwick.

The unfortunate outcome of the 'Small Beer' affair for the patrol was that it made a temporary enemy of Ali Assad, the Turkish Cypriot regional police commander. He had become convinced that we were responsible for the decision of Umit Suleiman to authorise the transfer of the hill to the UN. He took this to show partiality towards, or collaboration with, the Greek Cypriots, and confided this view to officers that he knew in the Canadian Regiment (1 R22eR, normally referred to as the 'Vingt-Deux' or the 'Vingt-Douze'), who in turn used it as an excuse for not using the mediating patrol in the Kyrenia area.[1]

Worried that the patrol's influence with the Turkish Cypriots in general would be damaged, I raised the matter privately with senior TMT contacts and with Doctor Kutchuk. I was told by both that they were well aware of the real facts and that Ali Assad was suffering stress symptoms and likely to be moved shortly. Not long afterwards they let me know that the Superintendent was back in Nicosia 'for reasons of ill health'.

47. KYRENIA RANGE WEST (ST HILARION). 24 APRIL ONWARDS 1964

An outline of the Greek Cypriot plan to attack along the Kyrenia ridge towards Saint Hilarion Castle was given to me two weeks before the event. Planning for this had been going on for several weeks. It was now felt to be justified by the imminence of completion of the Turkish airstrip below Aghirda and by the continuing TMT threat against Karmi.

During the night of 24 April a small force of Greek Cypriot paramilitaries scaled the rocks above Karmi and established an ambush point about a thousand yards to the west of Saint Hilarion Castle. Their position overlooked the road that runs close to the crest of the range from the castle by way of Kornos Peak to Vasilia: this road was used by the Turkish Cypriots to reinforce and re-supply their outposts in the western sector of the range. The Turkish Cypriot defence system in this area relied on a small number of fixed emplacements, each with a screen of unarmed shepherds who were supposed to give warning of attack, and a heavily armed mobile reserve.

Near dawn on 25 April, the Greek Cypriots launched their main attack through the Karmi Forest area from the direction of Lapithos towards the castle, using a total of about four hundred men. They caught the westerly Turkish Cypriot shepherd lookout asleep and killed him, surrounded the first outpost and made rapid progress eastwards.

Turkish Cypriot command reacted by sending forward their mobile reserve along the mountain road from the castle in six vehicles, hoping to stem the Greek Cypriot advance. The two Land Rovers leading this sortie ran into heavy fire from the ambush party and suffered severe casualties. But the ambush attack had been slightly mistimed and the remainder of the Turkish Cypriot force was able to deploy, leaving the road blocked by damaged vehicles.

This now became the front line. The main Greek Cypriot force joined up here with the ambush party in mid-morning. They could now fire directly into Saint Hilarion Castle and also into the Turkish Cypriot villages in the southern foothills of the range – Pileri, Krini, Keumurju and Aghirda.

The Greek Cypriot assault had been so rapid that UNFICYP had no idea it had taken place until Kutchuk phoned to ask for urgent help. Major Burgess was then sent to assess the position. He continued until nightfall to report on the military build-up and the attitudes of the two sides.

At midday the morale of the Turkish Cypriot defenders was extremely low, and it is likely that if the Greek Cypriots had pressed home their attack they would have captured St. Hilarion Castle that afternoon without serious losses. However the rather inflexible 'Secret Army' battle-plan, as approved by the leaders of 'The Organisation', had specified that the first attack must stop short of an actual assault on the castle: this stipulation gave the Turkish Cypriots time to move reinforcements up to the pass and to establish a new defence-line facing the Greek Cypriots on the castle's western approaches.

Greek Cypriot 'Secret Army' unit with captured ensign after assault on the strategic western end of Kyrenia range.

Although Greek Cypriot leaders never claimed to me that it was so designed, the stoppage may in fact have been providential. Turkish Cypriot fighters were preparing that afternoon to pull back from all of their positions on the Kyrenia Range on either side of St. Hilarion Pass, in the hope that they could establish a new sustainable line of defence which rested on the encampment of the Turkish contingent. As an adjunct to this pull-back, TMT was proposing to launch one of its 'doomsday schemes'. This was to involve island-wide attacks and ambushes against Greek Cypriots with the specific aim of provoking civil conflict of such dimensions that Ankara would be forced into full-scale intervention. My TMT contact gave me to understand that this plan had been co-ordinated with the Turkish army.[1]

The area was generally quiet on 26 April, but on the 27th 'Secret Army' troops mortared the area of the castle all through the morning, narrowly missing my patrol on two occasions. At midday a white flag was hoisted over the castle and the Greek Cypriots delivered an ultimatum. The Turkish Cypriots were then allowed time to seek a decision from Nicosia.

The reply authorised TMT to act as it thought best. The commander at St Hilarion announced that he would fight on. The 'Secret Army' then mounted attacks from the west and north and made a probing sortie up the hillside from Kyrenia, which captured a critical peak between the castle and the pass.

At the same time there was very heavy, and apparently indiscriminate, firing by Greek Cypriots from the Kyrenia Range down into the Turkish Cypriot villages to the south. Many of the villagers moved towards Geunyely for shelter. My patrol visited the area to assess the danger to those who were still trapped in their homes. In Keumurju, Major Burgess had to rescue a Red Cross team which was pinned down under heavy fire.

Abruptly, in mid-afternoon, the Greek Cypriot forces received an order from Nicosia that the attacks were to be stopped. Firing into the southern Turkish Cypriot villages ceased. Assault teams on the ridge, which were progressing towards the castle, were halted and then withdrawn to their former lines.

There were to be no more major attacks, although the final action of the 'campaign' did not take place until the night of 29 April, when a Turkish Cypriot fighting patrol probing to locate Greek Cypriot forward headquarters was shot up and badly mauled. Next day Major Burgess investigated the action and located the bodies of the Turkish Cypriots who had been killed.

Shortly afterwards, UNFICYP established posts with the forward positions of the Greek Cypriots and Turkish Cypriots on the ridge, and the area reverted to a state of uneasy stasis. A huge and frequent expenditure of ammunition in fruitless exchanges of fire produced no benefit at all to either side.

My main concern was now the vulnerability to bombardment from the heights above of the Turkish Cypriot villages south of the Kyrenia Range. Occasional sniping at the villages had resumed. John Burgess and I were shot at daily during the next week as we moved on foot between the villages.

There was a huge difference between accounts being submitted by the villagers to Kutchuk's office, and thence to UNFICYP HQ, and those submitted by UNFICYP patrols, which suggested that the Turkish Cypriots were grossly exaggerating the threat. The fact, we quickly realised, was that Greek Cypriot snipers were careful to stop firing as soon as a UN vehicle entered the area.

On our recommendation, a UN post was established in each village: the incidence of firing then rapidly dropped (although the occasional shot remained a natural hazard of the area) and we were able to persuade most of the women and children who had fled southwards to return to their own homes.

Plans for a new attack on the Kyrenia Pass were several times discussed by the Greek Cypriot command and each time rejected. With UN observer posts in place and Turkish Cypriot defences strengthened, a renewal of the assault would have been difficult, although certainly not impossible.

Tassos Papadopoulos told me that the attack had been stopped because of intense international pressure. He said that Makarios and other ministers had been surprised and deeply disturbed at the way pressure was applied by the UN, the US and the UK, and at the general world outcry, when it had seemed that St Hilarion Castle was about to fall. They had genuinely believed that the coming of UNFICYP was going to result in progress towards democratic rule by the majority and towards an ending of the Turkish Cypriot insurrection: instead they were faced with a new drawing of 'Green Lines' and a further inhibiting of their freedom of action.

Furthermore, since Christmas they had frequently been told that if there had to be fighting, why not have it in the hills, away from the women and children? Now a logical, low-key action in the hills to restore governmental control over a key part of the national road system had provoked a world-wide storm of outrage. The palpable bias in this was assumed by the Greek Cypriots to be British-led.

Greek Cypriot leaders equated their actions against TMT with those of the British in the suppression of insurrection in Malaysia. Their attempts to extend government control in Tillyria and on the Kyrenia Pass assumed that they had both moral and legal justification. In their conversations with me, they seemed not to give serious weight to the likelihood that UNFICYP decisions were largely dictated by the US and the UK and that decisions in Washington and London would rest upon the thesis that Ankara must in no circumstances be seriously alienated.

St Hilarion Castle, overlooking the north coast of Cyprus and Kyrenia town.

TMT fighters and Turkish volunteers on St Hilarion. March 1964.

TMT hoisting equipment up the rocks to St Hilarion. March 1964.

Greek Cypriots on Kyrenia range, looking down on Turkish airstrip (still under construction) and Aghirda village, during battle around St Hilarion Castle. April 1964.

48. CHANGING OF THE GUARD.
NICOSIA ZONE.
27 MARCH - 12 JUNE 1964

There was a sharp escalation in incidents of violence as the British peacekeeping mission ended and that of the UN began. The changeover, with the flawed perceptions that each community had of the significance of United Nations involvement in the island's affairs, was clearly a major factor in this.

There was no fundamental difference between the methodology of peacekeeping as applied by the UN and by the British. Policies on escorts and the positioning of observer posts were to vary and prejudices and favouritism would be differently directed, but the underlying principle of both forces was that the answer to inter-communal friction lay in a militarily safeguarded separation linked to top-down central negotiation. This policy rewarded Turkish Cypriot extremists, just as the UN's designation of the Greek Cypriot administration as the sole government of Cyprus, rather than seeking a wording that recognised the old partnership formula, militated against a Greek Cypriot inclination for compromise.[1]

Much greater difference lay in the process of active mediation. Under the British initiative, a tripartite patrol organisation had been created by General Young, given near-total independence and proved that it could act as a real catalyst for communal re-engagement. This was achieved despite the absence of an effective central mediating mechanism in Nicosia.[2]

The incoming UN, on the one hand created a much stronger central mediating presence in Nicosia but on the other axed the tripartite medium, which had covered the rural areas, provided access to paramilitary units and offered private conduits between various leadership sections of the two communities.

I thought, confusedly then but subsequently very clearly, that had the old tripartite organisation (with its links through the Greek and Turkish armies to Athens and Ankara) been retained and enlarged and placed under the direct control of Kurt Janssen[3] there would have been real hope for an early solution in Cyprus. Instead the most volatile areas of communal interface were left without a channel through which, in their own language and to somebody they trusted, the key individuals could unburden themselves of their ambitions, complexes, fears and frustrations. That absence was one obvious factor in the heightened inter-communal antagonisms and outbursts of violence that Cyprus suffered at the end of March and in April.

My own direct contacts with the villages were now restricted. I repeatedly received requests from villagers to visit them, but could not do so for fear of causing offence to prickly UN contingents. The old routine of a frequent regular visit, at least once weekly, to every problem village in Nicosia Zone was ended: from here on I normally was directed to go by the UN only when there were problems that UNFICYP contingents felt unable to handle.

Cyprus, with its governmental processes still in their infancy, was in a situation where unelected figures exercised a disproportionate influence. Within the Greek Cypriot community, individual strong-men, like the barons in medieval England, wielded their own armed strength and pursued their own concept of the destiny of Cyprus. They were, however, usually prepared to be swayed towards one course of action or another by forceful personal argument: in the past this had mostly been received from Greek army officers who were passionate believers in *enosis*, but since January they had been responsive to approaches by the tripartite patrols. Among Turkish Cypriots the vital contacts were with local leaders of TMT.

With the dismantling of the patrols, a critical linkage with key parastatal leaders and a powerful means of identifying extremist trends and exerting influence on them was lost.

Such visits as I continued to make to the rural areas were mostly now linked to the advancement of major island-wide schemes and national harvesting arrangements, rather than to the promotion of inter-communal liaison at village level. However, even if involvement with village communities was lost, the projects themselves made a strong contribution to the relaxation of tension in mixed areas, exploiting foundations laid by the tripartite patrols since January.

One measure of how far we had come in three months was the lessening impact that outside events had on the villages. The Turkish Cypriots were depressed for a while by the defeat of their fighters on the western ranges of the Kyrenia hills, but the event had far less impact on inter-communal relations than it would have a short while previously.

The Economist, usually one of the more sober and thoughtful commentators on Cypriot affairs, wrote on 25 April, after the fighting in Tillyria, of the danger that the island would lapse into something on the lines of the Spanish civil war. On 2 May, after the fighting around St Hilarion, the same periodical described the attacks as "insane" and quoted UN Secretary General U Thant's condemnation of them as "senseless acts of violence." These comments, which mirrored British thinking in UNFICYP, were at odds with reality and disregarded the very reasonable Greek supposition that statal authority should be exercised over the national infrastructure, including key elements of the road system. In this context, the Turkish Cypriot seizure of St Hilarion, a famous Cypriot landmark, could be seen as a highly symbolic move in a process of imposed partition. Furthermore, St Hilarion was critical to any realistic plan for defence against foreign invasion.

Despite the prevalence of arms, of fortified villages and of occasional communal confrontations, I had no sense whatever of being involved in a situation of civil war. It felt, rather, like an awkward, inconsistent, family rough-house, or a shotgun marriage unravelling, with the Greek Cypriots wanting to enforce their patriarchal rights and the Turkish Cypriots to pursue their ideas of personal fulfilment, with two sets of relatives shouting their own advice.

Solutions were available, but being disregarded in the brawling. Forms of closer association with Greece could have been found that were acceptable to Ankara. Demographic readjustment could have come without destroying the unity of Cyprus, through a gradual, negotiated process: instead it was being imposed through haphazard violence springing from unreasoned nationalisms. It was a mixture of foreign meddling, impatience, the absence of a mature centrist leadership and the lack of appropriate mediating mechanisms that destroyed the opportunity for Cypriots to work out for themselves in the 1960s a suitable future for their common home.

The major preoccupation in Cyprus throughout April and May was the harvest. Remembrance of the battles of Tillyria and St. Hilarion faded rapidly, as both rural communities applied themselves to the most critical of their traditional trades.

49. HARVEST-TIME. APRIL/MAY 1964

In the UN Secretary General's report to the Security Council of 15 June, he described the scheme which had allowed both communities in Cyprus to gather in their crops without any serious trouble as the major success-story of the United Nations' presence in Cyprus. This programme derived from my discussions with Kutchuk and Papadopoulos and it was negotiated and implemented by the joint patrols. It was one instance in which, for the most part, we had excellent support from the various UNFICYP contingents. It was always designed to have consequences more far-reaching and significant than those related solely to the harvest itself.

During late March and early April, I had become increasingly aware of the problems likely to be posed by the harvesting of crops that were in abandoned areas or in regions where armed paramilitaries faced each other across intervening farmland. I had assumed that planning to cover these matters was in hand in Nicosia, but discovered that such discussions as were proceeding, under the aegis of UN political negotiators who had only just arrived in Cyprus, were lacking in urgency and in understanding of realities on the ground. A decision was then taken in UNFICYP that gave me responsibility for drafting and implementing a comprehensive island-wide arrangement.

The matter fell into three parts. In those areas of the island where all land was the property of the community which now exercised control over it, there was no problem for the Greek Cypriots; for the Turkish Cypriots the problems were simply those of organisation and administration, including arrangements for the transfer of harvesting machinery between different areas.

In mixed areas and along inter-communal boundaries, the requirement was to ensure that each community could gather its harvest without fear or interference.

In areas which had been abandoned, there were numerous difficulties: it was not known what crops were still standing; it was uncertain which Greek Cypriot communities would countenance the return of their former neighbours, particularly in areas considered strategically sensitive, or which Turkish Cypriots would be prepared to come back to work their fields; no survey had yet been carried out to determine where Turkish Cypriot evacuees were now living; few of those who had left had any transport available to them; and the actual process of arranging for Turkish Cypriot villagers to harvest under UN protection was obviously going to be very complex.

The peacekeeping forces, Cypriot leaders and the foreign press had for some time been forecasting that the period of the harvest would be very dangerous, since there would be a renewal of inter-communal contacts in areas evacuated by the Turkish Cypriots because of harassment or violence, and because many Turkish Cypriots would for the first time be faced with the damage that had been done to their property since their departure.

In fact, the harvesting programme was to throw up no major inter-communal incident.*

I sounded out Dr Kutchuk and TMT and some of the Turkish Cypriot *mukhtars* and had lengthy meetings with Tassos Papadopoulos, who was then, in addition to his two other ministerships, Acting Minister of Agriculture. He produced and delivered to me privately a first draft proposal for Greek Cypriot measures to facilitate the harvesting. I cleared with him a number of suggested amendments and then presented the revised formula to the Turkish Cypriots as a UN proposal. The Turkish Cypriots produced their own set of suggested amendments. After repeating this process a second time we had a set of measures that appeared to be acceptable to all sides.

The finished document was then published separately, each party to the agreement giving it his own introduction: the Greek Cypriots announced the scheme as being the government's measures to cover harvesting arrangements; the Turkish Cypriots used a different preamble and described the measures as those agreed between themselves and the UN; and the UN simply stated that they were measures to be followed under its supervision. This somewhat ponderous formula allowed the Greek Cypriots to refer to the scheme as a government measure and the Turkish Cypriots to side-step any reference to 'the government'. In fact, Greek Cypriot adherence to the scheme was an act of genuine moderation, which was followed by a strict observance of its terms.

The basic provisions of the agreement were: first, that both communities would do all in their power to facilitate harvesting arrangements (a vital clause since it was agreed to over-ride previous communal prohibitions: for instance the Greek Cypriots thereby accepted that Turkish Cypriots could travel in UN vehicles if this contributed to the harvesting); second, that all harvesting in areas to which both communities had access, covering border areas, should be done exclusively under UN protection; third, that Turkish Cypriots who had abandoned their villages should be allowed freely to return to inspect the state of their crops; fourth, that harvesting in abandoned areas should be done by whatever means was determined by the local UN commander to be best, either by the Turkish Cypriots returning under UN protection to harvest, or by the Greek Cypriots harvesting the Turkish Cypriot crops in the presence of Turkish Cypriot and UN observers and transferring the value of the crops, less expenses, to the Turkish Cypriot owners; fifth, that local rates owed by individual Turkish Cypriot farmers at the time of their evacuation would be recovered solely from the government's grain subsidy; and sixth, that neither community would have any right to

---

* A parallel could be drawn with the 2003 opening of the Green line crossings. The international community had forecast incidents and friction; instead, there was a rapid re-establishments of friendly inter-communal contact at village level, without any serious incident.

distrain on these crops or on income deriving from them for the recovery of private debts.

The point on which no agreement was reached was that of compensation for Turkish Cypriot crops which had been destroyed by the Greek Cypriots and vice versa, but a clause allowed for the consideration of this point later. In fact, a considerable proportion of Turkish Cypriot crops had already been destroyed, during the period when the gendarmerie was denying any responsibility for the protection of Turkish Cypriot property, but from the moment that the agreement was approved firm steps were taken by both communities to prevent any further damage.*

One further clause in the agreement specified that its implementation by the Greek Cypriots was conditional on the return, prior to the 1964 collection, of all 1963 grain still held in stores under Turkish Cypriot control or on a cash settlement for any shortfall that might be discovered.

All dealings in cereals in Cyprus were confined to the national Grain Commission, which alone had the right to buy, sell, import or export grain. Normal procedure was that, starting from a published collection-date, grain was purchased from the farmers by the village branches of the Greek or Turkish Cypriot co-operative societies, acting as agents for the Grain Commission. From the moment that grain was moved into the local co-operative store-house, it became the property of the Grain Commission: it was then moved into the Commission's central stores according to an overall programme that continued until the next grain collection.

At Christmas, when the troubles exploded, hardly any of the 1963 harvest had so far been collected into central storage. From then until now, in May, there had been no contact between the Greek and Turkish Cypriot members of the Grain Commission and no dealings in grain between the two communities. Where necessary, local co-operatives had re-opened their storehouses and distributed grain back to the villagers, usually on credit.

Working partly in private and partly through joint meetings, I got agreement from Greek Cypriot representatives on the Grain Commission, the heads of the Turkish Cypriot Banking Organisation and of the Turkish Cypriot Co-operative Society and other Turkish Cypriot leaders. I then drafted proposals for Mr Sefrna, of the UN political staff, under whose responsibility this subject fell, and these were translated into an island-wide plan. This was issued by UNFICYP and its implementation overseen by joint patrol teams.

Our initial survey involved not only an enquiry into the grain quantities still being held by each Turkish Cypriot village co-operative in Cyprus but also the production of complete statistics on grain expenditure over the past six months, the ratio of cash-sales to credit-sales and a summary of delivery problems. From this survey one could also deduce what Turkish Cypriot grain-transporters were still serviceable and what was the proximate financial state of every Turkish Cypriot community in the island.

---

* See Appendix H.

The survey was pushed through in about a week of intensive visiting. We discovered, to our surprise, that about two thirds of the 1963 grain stock in Turkish Cypriot-controlled areas was still under storage and intact. Detailed plans were instituted by us for the transportation of this grain, under UN escort, to the Commission's central stores, all of which were under Greek Cypriot control.

Delivery began on 25 May, when a start was made on transferring the one thousand tons of grain held in Mora to central storage near Palouriotissa. Initial difficulties came from a Greek Cypriot police insistence on searching every vehicle on every trip, ostensibly in case there was a TMT plot to sabotage the grain stores, but this was ended after representations by my patrol. Thereafter the procedure worked smoothly.

At the same time, negotiations went forward over questions relating to the collection of 1964 crops: in this the main difficulty sprang from the refusal of the Grain Commission to appoint the Turkish Cypriot Co-operative Society as its agent or to guarantee payments made by the co-operatives. Urging the Greek Cypriots to show flexibility on this point, I left its remaining negotiation in the hands of Mr Sefrna.

While harvesting was being started satisfactorily in all-Greek Cypriot and all-Turkish Cypriot areas, the Turkish Cypriots were persuaded to nominate area committees, whose job would be to co-ordinate arrangements for pre-defined regions, in particular planning for the most economical co-operative use of available machinery and manpower. I produced an overall plan for the protection of harvesters in border areas of Nicosia Zone, giving a detailed breakdown of requirements for the provision of UN escorts.

Greek and Turkish Cypriot members of the District Administration were then brought into the running of the scheme and local UN commanders worked out plans for its implementation within their own districts. As soon as the programme was properly underway, its day-to-day management, and liaison between Greek and Turkish Cypriot officials, were handed over to an officer in zone headquarters, Lieutenant Paxton, who had worked with my patrol on the scheme since its inception.

Arrangements made by local UN commanders were usually excellent, so that hardly any difficulties occurred in the harvesting of border areas. Paxton had bigger problems with UN sensitivities than he did with those of the Greek or Turkish Cypriots. Two potentially explosive districts, between Photta and Skylloura and between Mandres and Vouno, were both divided by contingent boundaries between Canadian and YKSP (Finnish) detachments, who took great offence if other UN troops entered their administrative area without due warning.

Another border region where difficulty had been expected was that between Aghirda and Pano Dhikomo, which was still virtually a battle area. As with other critical spots, my own patrol supervised the start of the harvesting operation here. In this case a crisis was narrowly averted. Major Burgess' report for 22 May noted:

"All of this was within range of GC and TC defensive positions. Before allowing the GC combine-harvesters to start work I visited all TC posts to ensure that they had been warned that the GC were to commence harvesting: it was evident that they had.

I then allowed the harvesting to begin. When it had been in full swing for about thirty minutes a group of heavily armed GC National Guardsmen began to infiltrate through the cornfields towards the TC posts, some of them even attempting to climb aboard the combine-harvesters. After great difficulty I found their commander and ordered their immediate withdrawal before the TC became aware of their presence. The GC officer stated that his men had come to protect the farmers, as they did not trust the UN troops. Some of the men themselves joined in the discussion and their attitude became increasingly abusive. With the arrival of a large group of GC reporters and photographers it began to appear as if this were a deliberate attempt to create an incident.

I threatened to withdraw the UN troops and to inform the TC of the reason for my action. The GC commander eventually withdrew his men to the edge of the field and, after more argument, I managed to get them to return to Dhikomo. There I complained most forcibly to the GC overall commander who apologised and stated that it had all been a mistake and that his orders had been misunderstood."

Complaint over this incident was later also made to the Greek Cypriot administrator of the scheme and there were no further such occurrences.

The harvest was from average to very good in border areas and both Greek and Turkish Cypriot committees said they had been delighted with the arrangements.

Meanwhile, with harvesting progressing smoothly in border regions, my patrol shifted its main concentration to the joint inspection of crops in abandoned areas. Except at Neokhorio and in the Dhali-Ayios Sozomenos region, where local UN units handled the surveys, I personally arranged and accompanied all of the visits in Nicosia Zone, so that I could see how villagers of the two communities reacted to the first return since evacuation. Forewarning of the visit would be passed by the Greek Cypriot harvesting contact to the police and *mukhtar* of the village concerned. Two or three Turkish Cypriots from the village would then be taken there by us in patrol vehicles under a guarantee of safety.

The process of inspection varied from village to village. In some areas, the inspection would be accompanied on the part of the Greek Cypriots only by a member of the local police; in others the rural constable also attended; where the local 'Secret Army' commander was available, he usually walked round with me. In several villages no Greek Cypriot would agree to accompany us.

In some districts it was quickly clear that all crops had been destroyed; in some it was easy to make a spot-estimate of percentages remaining; but in the majority of areas it was necessary to examine every single field. In no instance were the results of the survey ever queried by the Greek Cypriot authorities.

The resultant picture showed very wide and sometimes unexpected variations. In Palekythro and Chumlekji, as we had expected, there was very little damage, whereas in neighbouring Neokhorio and Naysan Chiflik the crops had been totally destroyed. In the Pyroi - Ayios Sozomenos – Dhali – Nisou - Mathiati region, damage averaged from twenty-five to forty percent. In Aredhiou the destruction was complete, but in the adjoining villages of Kato Dheftera and Pano Lakatamia, the crops were virtually unharmed. Crops at Eliophotes and Orounda were mostly intact, but down the road in the very large Turkish Cypriot-owned farmlands around Akaki, Dhenia and Peristerona everything had been destroyed or stolen. At Ayia Marina there was fifty percent damage, at Ayios Vasilios thirty percent and, most unexpectedly, at Skylloura the damage was negligible.

Almost all the damage that we saw had been done by Greek Cypriot shepherds grazing their flocks on abandoned Turkish Cypriot fields. Cultivation in Cyprus was still on the medieval strip pattern, with enclosures very rare, and shepherds were the traditional foes of the crop-farmers of both communities: in the absence of supervision by the Rural Constables or the gendarmerie the shepherds had grabbed an opportunity for easy pasturing. Only in Peristerona, Dhiorios and Ayios Vasilios had there been any theft of crops on a significant scale and since the official collection had not yet begun, it was possible in these cases to start legal recovery proceedings.

By walking mile after mile peering closely at half-chewed cornfields, John Burgess and I became experts in the assessment of crop-damage: this expertise was essential because in each case it was necessary to determine to what degree the crop would have been sub-standard even if there had been no grazing upon it (up to the level where harvesting would not in any event have been justified).

In general the process of inspection was distressful. It is not easy to spend the day with men who are slowly discovering, field by field, that their whole fortune has been lost. We had to do this time after time.

The thoroughness of the destruction in those villages where nothing had been left standing was remarkable. The team would come to a vast expanse of magnificent wheat and the Turkish Cypriot farmer, reassured, would point out that his field was out in the middle: we would then wade out through the wheat, admiring its quality, only to discover a section, its edges precisely straight, which had been grazed to the ground. The only logical explanation would seem to be that Greek Cypriot shepherds had carried their sheep out to these isolated areas and then controlled their grazing to the nearest stalk.

Questioned about their feelings, most Turkish Cypriot farmers who had suffered serious losses said that this was what they had expected and that the time for vengeance was yet to come. Those whose losses were minimal were full of praise for their former neighbours.

Often, more interesting than the state of the crops, however, were the varying reactions of Greek Cypriot villagers, police and army personnel, when the Turkish Cypriots were brought back among them and of the Turkish Cypriots when presented with their former neighbours. Most striking was the frequent demonstration of real cordiality between the Turkish Cypriot farmers and the regular local Greek Cypriot police. Speaking to me afterwards, the Turkish Cypriots said that these "weren't such bad people": their fear and dislike was reserved for what they called "EOKA people", particularly for those who had been inducted at Christmas as police specials.

From the moment that government acceptance of the harvesting plan was announced, the most co-operative Greek Cypriots in any region were almost invariably the senior members of the local 'Secret Army' leadership. Thus in Skylloura there was a great deal of bitter opposition from the Greek Cypriot villagers when the proposal was presented to them that the Turkish Cypriots would return for the harvest, the attitude being that the Turkish Cypriots should come back to stay or not at all: the local 'Secret Army' commander, on the other hand, provided me with an honest assessment of the situation and undertook that if necessary his own men would defend the Turkish Cypriots against any attempt by the Greek Cypriot villagers to interfere with or intimidate them.

The attitudes of Greek Cypriot villagers were predictably mixed, in line with the local history of inter-communal relations. In those villages where the events of Christmas had been most violent, Neokhorio, Mathiati, Skylloura and Ayios Vasilios, the reception was openly hostile: these also were the villages where Turkish Cypriot homes had mostly been destroyed.

The second grouping, of which Peristerona, Dhiorios, Ayia Marina and Aredhiou were typical, were villages where the Turkish Cypriots had been pressurised by the Greek Cypriots into evacuation and where most of the Turkish Cypriot houses had subsequently been looted and Turkish Cypriot crops destroyed. Here the reception was mixed, with very little display of friendship: there were frequent suggestions that the Turkish Cypriots ought to return, but these mostly sounded insincere and were probably the result of political urging: the underlying impression was that the last thing they wanted was to have their former neighbours back.

In Peristerona, the regional 'Secret Army' commander took the opportunity to assemble the Greek Cypriot villagers in the main square and, in the presence of the Turkish Cypriots on the inspection team, deliver to them a powerful lecture on the need for reconciliation and the understanding and sacrifices that this would entail. Among his statements was a guarantee that the 'Secret Army' would protect the Turkish Cypriots if they decided to return. He said that justice for the Turkish Cypriots would be public: if any Greek Cypriot were to be reported for an offence against a Turkish Cypriot, he would be tried summarily in this very square by the military and if found guilty he would be summarily punished in public.

The speech was excellent, but when the Turkish Cypriot *mukhtar* spoke to me afterwards he said: "He is a good man and I believe him but there is nothing that anyone can do or say now that would persuade me ever to live among those Greek villagers again. I don't care what guarantees I might have or how safe I might be. This sort of antagonism that we now have goes on forever."

In the third group of villages, of which Akaki, Palekythro and Dhenia were typical, the Greek Cypriots were clearly undecided how to react. These were villages which the Turkish Cypriots had abandoned on instructions from TMT, without having been subjected to any serious pressure from the Greek

Cypriots. At first the Greek Cypriots had looked after the abandoned property extremely well, but petty looting and minor damage had then been allowed to occur; most of the crops had been destroyed, except at Palekythro where they were entirely intact. It is probable that the Greek Cypriots would have accepted a Turkish Cypriot return to these villages without serious complaint if urged to do so by their political leaders.

Cyprus army, 1 April parade in Nicosia.

Finally there were some villages, of which Kato Dheftera and Orounda were examples, where the Turkish Cypriots were welcomed back with great enthusiasm and obvious sincerity. In these villages all Turkish Cypriot property had been preserved in perfect condition and in those few cases where there had been some minor damage to the crops, the Greek Cypriots immediately offered to pay compensation. Dheftera and Orounda were obviously a good starting point for a reintegration programme. Both were relatively affluent villages in which the Turkish Cypriots had formed a small minority and had had an economic level considerably lower than that of the Greek Cypriots.

Harvesting arrangements for the abandoned areas were split by us into two categories. In those areas where the main body of evacuees had resettled close to their old villages, it was relatively simple to arrange for them to be brought in on a daily basis to carry out the work. However the Turkish Cypriots from villages like Orounda, Eliophotes and Kato Dheftera had evacuated to a quite different region: for them we arranged, with 'Secret Army' support, with approval from 'The Organisation' and with TMT acceptance that they return, privately and without any press report, to their own homes for the period of the harvesting. This trial was based substantially on the trust that the villagers had for my patrol: when we were ordered out of Cyprus in early June it was immediately aborted.

In Nicosia Zone, the areas abandoned by Greek Cypriot farmers to Turkish Cypriot control were limited to a few fields close to Kambyli, Mora, Margi and Epikho, which had mostly remained unharmed, and to a considerable area on both sides of the Kyrenia road to the south of Aghirda. Major Burgess supervised the inspections in these areas under an arrangement that so long as he was with them the Greek Cypriots could move without restriction. To the west of the Kyrenia road sixty percent of the crops had been grazed down and one Greek Cypriot farmer found, to his dismay that an airstrip had been laid across his land: to the east of the Kyrenia road the crops were all unharmed. The Turkish Cypriots gave top priority to the harvesting of these crops on behalf of the Greek Cypriots and provided an unreserved promise of full compensation for whatever crops had been destroyed: it was taken by us that this wholly helpful attitude was designed to strengthen the Turkish Cypriot bargaining position when final discussions started on general reparations for crop-damage.

The general influence on inter-communal relations in the rural areas of the successful progress of the harvesting programme was very marked, particularly where damage was found to be less than expected. Rather than provoke rising tensions, as British observers had forecast, the human contacts that were re-established by the programme had an almost wholly beneficial effect. A foundation for communal re-engagement was thus laid that could have been steadily built on if the means of its furtherance had been left in place.

50. Projects. April - June 1964

The success of the harvesting programme in the lowering of rural tensions was mirrored by that of a new UN escorts policy.

All through the period of British peacekeeping, tripartite patrol officers had argued that safety of movement on the roads was essential to any process of communal re-engagement and that to get this started a comprehensive escort programme was needed. This contention was initially rejected by Makarios and invariably opposed by the police, who saw it as insulting and an incursion on their area of responsibility. Makarios reversed his position in February, but JFHQ remained adamant in its refusal to countenance such a programme.

That Turkish Cypriots in the villages travelled hardly at all during January and February (and that little mostly due to the efforts of the tripartite patrols), and had thereby become more and more alienated from the Greek Cypriots, was partly due to TMT discouragement, partly to the very real dangers that faced them on the roads and partly to the fact that many of their cars and buses had been impounded by the Greek Cypriot police.

Whatever may have been the logic of a Greek Cypriot policy designed to crush the strength of TMT, the prevalence of ambushes and hostage-taking on the roads in early 1964 seriously undermined the chances of future unity in Cyprus. The fact that police officers were often involved in these acts gave ammunition to proponents of communal separation. The failure of the gendarmerie during the first two months of 1964 to comply with Makarios' undertakings on freedom of movement meant that the Turkish Cypriots could validly complain of statal oppression.

General Young decided in January that he lacked the manpower to mount effective general escort arrangements but he made no objection when tripartite or regular patrols escorted on an ad hoc basis. Under General Carver, however, JFHQ refused permission to escort "as a matter of principle", although I never managed to get an explanation of what this principle was. Regular army patrols, aware of the dangers, sometimes overlooked this order, or regarded themselves as 'accompanying' Turkish Cypriot vehicles rather than escorting them: tripartite and joint patrols provided unobtrusive escort whenever a special need arose.

Under General Gyani this JFHQ policy was reversed in May, on a trial basis. I was invited to work with UNFICYP HQ staff in formulating an escort timetable for Nicosia Zone. In fact the gendarmerie was by now disciplined and co-operative: if it had not been for the wave of abductions that followed the killing of Constable K. M. Pantelides (the son of Chief Superintendent Pantelides) and two Greek officers from ELDYK, in the Turkish Cypriot held old town of Famagusta[1], I would have said that the roads for the most part were safe. What was more relevant was that the Turkish Cypriots did not yet believe them to be safe. They were still burdened by traumatic memories of December and January and encouraged in alarm by the media and by TMT. What was needed was a short-term process that would restore their confidence.

The implementation of the escorts programme had a profound effect. At a stroke the Turkish Cypriot rural community felt that the underpinnings of normality had been restored. Suddenly they again had access to work, to hospitals and other centralised services, and to the means of their traditional commerce.

Escorted vehicles were normally subjected to rigorous search by the Greek Cypriot police. Escort arrangements therefore provided no benefit to TMT, which continued to move its weapons and key personnel cross-country rather than by road and which saw its authority in the villages weakened by the relaxation of isolationary pressures.

22 May 1964. Police conducting search at a road block outside Nicosia. In this case the search, under the observation of UNFICYP, accords with agreed procedures.

The new circumstances were accompanied by a radical change in my routine. A large measure of confidence and optimism had been restored to rural communities by a combination of the escort programme and agreement on harvesting arrangements. Joint committees established by us in mixed areas were continuing to function well. In most villages inter-communal relationships had improved to a point where local mediation was no longer needed. At the same time the antagonism of some UN contingents and the need to advance new privately agreed bi-communal projects were combining to shift the focus of my work away from mediation in individual villages. An increasing amount of my time was spent in Nicosia.

President Makarios was now prepared to accept the need for a positive tilt towards the Turkish Cypriots. Some bi-communal public work projects had already been unobtrusively started; Tassos Papadopoulos now advanced arrangements for a series of further measures, for which I was to provide the private conduit to Vice President Kutchuk. This was preferred to official UN channels partly because of the experience of rural affairs that I now had: partly also because of the need to avoid any publicity until the projects were well enough established to withstand the basilisk gaze of a ferociously jingoistic press, the objections of those who believed that separation or conquest rather than re-engagement was the right way forward, and the sidelining that might come through the internal workings of the UNFICYP bureaucracy.

Various of the more unobtrusive initiatives involved re-establishing central administrative links. Many civil servants in Nicosia had worked in offices to which they were now denied access because of the Green Line: since Christmas they had been cut off from their documents and files and personal gear. At the instigation of Tassos Papadopoulos and Kutchuk, I acted as go-between in a steady, private, two-way exchange of material of this sort. Success in this field was in total contrast to the difficulty encountered in trying to arrange for the restitution of civil property through formal channels, and particularly in the recovery of property that was under Greek Cypriot police control.

Some documents needed to be shared between Greek and Turkish Cypriot administrators and for these I would act as office-boy in acquiring the necessary signatures. For instance the payment from an already-approved budget for 1963 Crop-Loss Insurance settlements required explanations to be conveyed to and approvals obtained from various departmental heads of whom some were Greek Cypriot and some Turkish Cypriot. All the necessary paperwork was completed and due payments were made without any publicity or problem.

Similarly, my patrol provided an intermediary service for the Passport Office. I would sometimes take with me to Turkish Cypriot and mixed villages a sheaf of passport application forms and a photographer: completed applications would then be delivered to a Turkish Cypriot official, (operating in what was formerly the National Passport Office), where they would be reviewed and in due course countersigned by a Turkish Cypriot assistant District Officer. On two mornings a week my patrol would collect the signed applications, transfer them to the central Passport Office and there pick up those passports that were ready for issue, for later delivery to the Turkish Cypriot applicants.

The patrol also established an administrative link between Kutchuk's office and outlying Turkish Cypriot villages under an arrangement approved by Tassos Papadopoulos and the President. Once a week, Mr Nihat would accompany me on a programme of district-wide visits during which he distributed pay-packets to Turkish Cypriot Rural Constables[2], delivered passports and other documentation, exchanged information with local Development Boards and generally organised the running of the lower levels of the District Administration. This process represented a degree of devolution and of inter-communal tolerance that was in total contradiction to foreign trumpetings of irreconcilability.

Freedom of travel allowed a resumption of Turkish Cypriot earnings from employment in Nicosia and the SBAs, but neither this, nor harvesting nor the restoration of administrative processes would have been adequate if Turkish Cypriot impoverishment was not more generally addressed. Tassos Papadopoulos therefore piloted through programmes for new major public works which were designed to provide direct financial benefit to the Turkish Cypriots by way of local employment, albeit unobtrusively. These involved road-construction, road-repair and land-conservation schemes for mixed and all-Turkish Cypriot areas of Nicosia Zone and irrigation or domestic water projects for the Pyroi/Ayia/Avdhellero area and for Ayia Irini, Epikho and other villages. These projects were all to be financed through the diversion of funds from budgets already approved for other sectors. In some schemes, as at Ayia Irini, the Turkish Cypriots would be working jointly with the Greek Cypriots, usually under Greek Cypriot foremen, while in others the work was to be in wholly Turkish Cypriot areas and without any Greek Cypriot participation. Besides the provision of work and cash to Turkish Cypriots who had been deprived of income for the past three months, the scheme had a specific aim of encouraging inter-communal re-engagement within the labour sector.

It would hardly have been possible to get these projects going without a detailed knowledge of local pitfalls, personalities, relationships and requirements, together with the private linkage with Kutchuk's office and with TMT that I had established. Nor were they likely to have succeeded if they had become the object of media attention. When I was removed from Cyprus in June, some of the programmes (such as that for harvesting) were sufficiently entrenched to be carried forward by UN political negotiators: others were to die for lack of the intermediary glue that had made them viable.

Despite the intransigence shown in formal inter-communal Liaison Committee meetings in Nicosia, the continuing expression of extremist national sentiment in public political announcements and the occasional recurrence of armed confrontations, the underlying movement to which I was exposed during April and May was towards a compromise understanding that would have left the Turkish Cypriots with a large degree of devolved power within readjusted zonal boundaries and with a genuine and internationally guaranteed security.

Sadly, neither communal leadership yet felt in sufficient control of its extremists to drive this process through by way of public debate, and the fact that I no longer had Greek and Turkish officers working directly with me meant that the critical conduits to Athens and Ankara were missing. On the other hand, I was sufficiently encouraged by Kurt Janssen and Natalie Thomas to feel assured of UN political backing. I felt that these developments would provide assurance to Washington and London, and to Athens and Ankara, that the Cypriots were capable of putting their own affairs into order. Of the Acheson/Ball Plan I was at that moment still unaware.

51. 'CRYSTAL PALACE'. APRIL 1964

The beginning of the UN's peacekeeping stewardship had been marked by mutual misunderstandings, the Greek Cypriots expecting to be supported in the island-wide re-imposition of central government control, the Turkish Cypriots expecting that they were to be more forcefully protected than before, and the UN unaware of Cypriot complexities or of the degree to which most of the policies they were inheriting from the British were unsupportive of communal re-engagement. The outcome of these misunderstandings was a general heightening of tensions, a series of clashes, and then the onset of disillusionment.

UN command became effective on 27 March. Immediately afterwards, Greek Cypriot pressure in Tillyria was ratcheted up. On 1 April there was a fatal shooting in Selemani. On 2 April there was a renewal of heavy firing across the Green Line in Nicosia. On 3 April serious fighting began in Tillyria, with a Greek Cypriot intention that their control over the Kokkina-Mansoura coastline be re-established.* On 5 April a Greek Cypriot policeman named Stokkos was killed: this was followed the next day by a botched attempt at vengeance when four Turkish Cypriots were seized and two of them killed. An officer in the 'Secret Army' was arrested as being responsible: he showed no regret and stated that, since he was Stokkos' closest relative, he had had no choice in the matter. A further series of shooting incidents followed in Nicosia. On 11 April the first major Greek Cypriot attack was launched on the Kyrenia range.† Both communities saw the situation as moving towards a climax. Rumour had it, as I was told by Major Macey and others, that a general showdown would start on 19 April.

Makarios left Cyprus on the morning of 18 April for a visit to Athens. One of his ministers told me that before departing he had told his cabinet that he would be "upset" if the situation was to turn to violence while he was away.

Later that day I was contacted by a friend in the Greek Cypriot police. He warned me that the police intelligence unit was claiming to have intercepted a TMT message which instructed that all Greek Cypriot hostages held by TMT units were to be executed at midnight. He believed the message was a forgery designed to provoke a violent reaction against the Turkish Cypriots and thus provide the touch-paper for a general armed confrontation.

Very dangerously, the Greek Cypriot administration had allowed the myth to be continued that all thirty-two Greek Cypriots unaccounted for since 22 December were still alive and being held by the Turkish Cypriots as hostages.

---

* See chapter 45
† See chapter 47

There had been frequent distressing demonstrations by their relatives. These were a catalyst for popular anger: they had been played up in the media, which had kept the issue in the forefront of public attention. In private, however, Greek Cypriot policemen told me that the force had firm information from its informers that at least twenty-eight, and probably all, of the missing thirty-two were already dead.

In the past it had been a normal pattern that the inflaming of passions over an emotive issue was the prelude to acts of violence, which the communal leadership then claimed to be beyond its control, followed by a Greek Cypriot paramilitary response which was declared to be a restitution of law and order. Major Macey assured me, and it fitted the pattern of past events, that the myth of the thirty-two hostages was being kept alive by extremists to provide, at an appropriate moment, the trigger for a major attack against Turkish Cypriot armed resistance.

Early in the evening of 18 April, I received an urgent request from Tassos Papadopoulos to join him at the Chanteclair nightclub. I found him with a group which included (as they were described to me) the executive head of the 'Secret Army', the Deputy Minister of the Interior, one of the heads of the Greek Cypriot intelligence organisation and two other ministers.

As soon as I arrived I was shown a copy of what was claimed to be a translation of an intelligence intercept. I noted that it had a header-designation: 'Crystal Palace'.* It stated precisely what I had already been told by my contact in the police.

I quickly assumed that Papadopoulos and all those at the table recognised the intercept as a forgery, wished to have it so proved, but also wished to avoid an open rift with those of their colleagues who were seeking to use it as justification for general and forceful action against the Turkish Cypriots. I took it that the group at the table was strongly opposed to any such action and that an exit-route was needed.

The subject was discussed. I was told that it was difficult for them to cast doubt on the provenance of the intercept.

There was a good deal of dramatic declamation as the clock moved towards midnight. Tassos Papadopoulos told me that, in the absence of Makarios, it was the ministers at the table who must decide for or against moderation.

I asked how they thought events were likely to unfold if the text of the intercept was released without refutation. I was reminded of the Stokkos incident, told that tension was already high, and that widespread retaliation would be inevitable. I asked why no-one was broadcasting an appeal for restraint. I was told that under the circumstances such an appeal was "politically impossible."

---

* From whatever Turkish equivalent the 'Crystal Palace' title was supposedly translated, its similarity to the 'Krystal Nacht' title of the Nazis notorious first attack on the Jews was obvious. The coincidence suggested the possibility of a foreign involvement in the creation of this piece of disinformation.

I said that I thought the 'Crystal Palace' message was completely bogus. I asked to be allowed to seek confirmation and this was agreed. I was taken to a telephone by the intelligence leader, who dialled the number that I gave him before disappearing into another office.

My call was to Major Macey by way of the RAF Nicosia switchboard, a line that Macey previously had told me was being tapped by the Greek Cypriot intelligence service. I explained the position to Macey. He told me he had irrefutable proof that this was a set-up and that exactly the same plan had been prepared on a previous occasion and then aborted. He gave me a list of those involved and suggested that Georgadjis was likely to be the minister responsible.

The Intelligence officer got back to the table a few minutes after I did. There was some urgent whispering and one minister then departed for a lengthy round of telephoning. That night the story was killed in the Greek press. I was told that all 'Secret Army' units were being told to regard the story of the intercept as false.

Curiously the whole fake story did appear in *I Makhi* the following Monday but by then the general tension was down, there was no corroboration from other sources and the account had no apparent impact.

The President returned to Nicosia and on 22 April made a unilateral offer to the Turkish Cypriots of amnesty and resettlement, conditional on agreement to a joint demilitarisation. As expected by Greek Cypriot ministers, the offer was rejected.

On 25 April, the Greek Cypriots launched their major attack from the west towards St Hilarion Castle and TMT came close to the triggering of its doomsday plan.

After more dithering in the Greek Cypriot leadership, the St Hilarion action was finally terminated on 29 April. An attack planned for the 30th against Temblos was similarly called off. A five-week chapter of flirtation with extraordinary danger for Cyprus ended at that point. Both communal leaderships now came to recognise that the advent of UNFICYP had provided no sudden answer to their hopes.

The climactic events that unfolded in Nicosia and on the Kyrenia and Tillyria hills seemed curiously distanced from the general course of rural affairs in other areas of Nicosia Zone. In these the harvesting and other normalisation programmes promoted by Tassos Papadopoulos and Kutchuk rolled forward through April and May with strong support from both communities. As Turkish Cypriots went with me to visit their abandoned villages and linkages with their former neighbours were restored a conviction grew that a general re-engagement in the rural areas would soon follow.

52. TRIKOMO - LEFKONIKO AREA.
APRIL/MAY 1964

The foundations laid here by my patrol held together well. The Irish UN contingent, which had taken over responsibility for Famagusta Zone, proved to be an extremely effective peacekeeper, with a genial, laid-back attitude and a general sympathy for the complexities of the conflict, probably bred from their own national history.

The Irish were the least interventionist of United Nations' units. In one instance, when I was called to a firefight that had developed on the fringe of their sector over a farming dispute between a Greek Cypriot and a Turkish Cypriot village, I was surprised to find the Irish unconcernedly drinking imported Guinness in their encampment a mile away. Any other national contingent would have been hovering on the edge of the fight, seeking to contribute to a cease-fire, but the Irish commanding officer said: "Let the laddies bash away at each other for a while. They'll get tired and finish sooner without an audience. Nobody's likely to get hurt and they'll feel better afterwards and then they'll be more amenable to sitting down quietly with us and sorting things out."

After the abductions and murder of Turkish Cypriots that followed the killing of Pantelides and two Greek army officers in Famagusta on 11 May, the Irish asked me back to take soundings of Turkish Cypriot attitudes across the region. It was reassuring to find that, although a new wave of fear had temporarily washed through the area and despite the proximity to Famagusta, there apparently had not been any general worsening of relationships, or of working arrangements, between the two communities.

On one other occasion I returned to the Lefkoniko region much against my will, when I was ordered by General Carver to investigate the disappearance of an English tobacco salesman, Mr Gibbins. The removal of the joint patrol from its work on Cypriot projects and its allocation to this task, which could have been better handled by professional police investigators, struck me as a misuse of our time and a provocation to the Cypriots. The incident weakened the patrol's contention that its sole commitment was to the Cypriot good, and I found objectionable the implication that a British life was of more significance than a Cypriot one.

Predictably, the very large effort devoted to this case, at British urging, by UNFICYP created ill-feeling within both communities and an extreme cynicism as to the nature of the peacekeeping role: this was directed mainly at the British, who by now were generally assumed to have hi-jacked the management of UNFICYP affairs.

Most Cypriots believed that Gibbins had been acting for the British in an intelligence-gathering role. I was given no evidence for this, and in the end it was taken by the UN that he had been murdered during an attempted robbery rather than for political motives. After a couple of days of complaining to UNFICYP that they should be working through the local gendarmerie or through Major Macey, rather than through me, I was allowed to dissociate myself from the case without having contributed in any way to its solution.[1]

53. Mora - Ayia Area. April/May 1964

Here, too, no serious incidents were reported to me and it was apparent that inter-communal liaison arrangements were continuing to work well. Even Ayia, which had always been one of the most isolated villages in Nicosia Zone, began to relax under the influence of the harvesting and escort programmes. Difficulties over local harvesting arrangements between Mora and Palekythro were resolved in an atmosphere of mutual goodwill and this contributed to an area-wide tranquillity. The fact that the Greek Cypriots in Palekythro, under the watchful eye of a now-conciliatory gendarmerie, were now doing everything possible to protect abandoned Turkish Cypriot property in the village had a similar effect. Turkish Cypriots returning to harvest their fields were able to see that this was so and that houses that they had supposed to be destroyed were still in good repair. Most importantly, the harvest was a particularly good one and it was all gathered without incident.

Encouraged by this, the Turkish Cypriot leadership in Mora began to plan ahead on the basis of continuing normality. I received a request from the *mukhtar* to join him for the opening of the next hunting season, the invitation concluding with a note that shotguns would be provided by my hosts.

54. Epikho - Kythrea Area.
April/May 1964

On 12 April, Greek Cypriot newspapers carried an item saying that, as a result of the United Nations presence, the road from Kythrea to Lefkoniko was now fully open to Greek Cypriot traffic. The report derived from an UNFICYP hand-out which was distributed after a UN unit, new to the area, had passed down the road and failed to spot any Turkish Cypriot roadblocks or defences.

Nobody had consulted the local Turkish Cypriot leaders or asked for confirmation from my patrol. In fact, Turkish Cypriot paramilitaries maintained a close control over the stretch of road from Bey Keuy to Psilatos. They would have allowed unarmed Greek Cypriot civilians to use the road, but only if they were prepared to submit to search, mirroring the process imposed elsewhere on the Turkish Cypriots. This would have been unacceptable to the Greek Cypriots. Any attempt at passage by armed Greek Cypriots or by the police would have been opposed by force. In any event, I knew of no Greek Cypriot who was prepared to attempt the journey.

Relations between the Turkish Cypriot villagers in Epikho and Bey Keuy and the Greek Cypriots in the villages to the west, Kythrea, Neokhorio and Voni, continued to be frigid, but each side was now held under adequate political control and no violent incidents were reported.

The pillaging of abandoned Turkish Cypriot property at Neokhorio and Naysan Chiflik was still the greatest source of bitterness, with virtually all of the Turkish Cypriot houses now destroyed. When joint inspection was arranged it was found that all abandoned Turkish Cypriot crops had been damaged, by the deliberate pasturing on them of Greek Cypriot flocks, to such a degree that harvesting was nowhere justified. In retaliation, despite genuine efforts by local Turkish Cypriot leaders to prevent it, all Greek Cypriot property within the boundaries of Bey Keuy had been destroyed. Such property was mostly comprised of olive groves and citrus orchards, from which the Turkish Cypriots might have gathered a profitable return in future, had they not been vandalised.

Harvesting arrangements elsewhere proved satisfactory, but a local agreement between Epikho and Exometokhi covering the payment of compensation for damaged crops was revoked by the Greek Cypriots as soon as they had completed the harvesting of those of their own fields that were under Turkish Cypriot control. Since the Turkish Cypriots had guarded these Greek Cypriot fields so meticulously that there was no single instance of damage, the Epikho villagers were provoked to extremes of wrath. Insult was added to injury when, on the evening of 24 May, the same day that the Greek Cypriots announced the refusal to honour their commitments, Epikho was shot up from the south, apparently by members of a 'Secret Army' unit returning from a training weekend at Halefka.

The Epikho Turkish Cypriots prepared for a retaliatory sortie against Exometokhi, but I managed to persuade them against it, arguing that to be provoked into such action would merely play into the hands of Greek Cypriot extremists. Instead, they embarked on a thorough burning of all of their post-harvest stubble, which traditionally had been used for grazing by Greek Cypriot shepherds from Exometokhi, and this had the desired effect of aggravating the Greek Cypriots.

I arranged a joint meeting which was attended by Greek Cypriot representatives of the Ministry of Agriculture and of the District Administration. This ended with the Nicosia officials finding in favour of the Epikho Turkish Cypriots and publicly berating the Exometokhi Greeks, to the astonishment of both communities. Experience over the past five months and their own communal propaganda had convinced the Turkish Cypriots that they could never hope for impartiality from a Greek Cypriot administration: what happened at this meeting had a significance and an impact that went far beyond the local area.

Local irrigation problems led to further joint meetings at Palekythro, with a similar result. In this case, the Greek Cypriot officials from the central water authority arrived with a conviction that right would lie with the Greek Cypriot villagers and gradually were persuaded that it was rather the Turkish Cypriot villagers who had justification. Their ruling to this effect sent out a powerful message which the surrounding areas had not previously heard, that impartiality and co-operation were feasible, despite the political divide.

Unfortunately there was not yet an end to isolated acts of lawlessness. The Turkish Cypriot *mukhtar* of Epikho was suspected (probably wrongly) by the Greek Cypriots of heading the local TMT organisation and it took some courage on his part when he accompanied me to meetings in neighbouring Greek Cypriot villages. We were returning together from one such encounter when I pulled off the road to wait for the District Officer's car to catch up with us. The *mukhtar* and I left my Land Rover to look for shade. We were standing close together in conversation when a bullet passed between us, ripping the fabric of my jacket.

I contacted the local gendarmerie sergeant and asked that he convey my displeasure to whomever had done the shooting. Three days afterwards I was told that the villagers of Exometokhi wished to see me so that they could convey their apologies and reassure me that I had not been the intended target.

I collected the bullet that had been fired at me. Like many others I had seen, it was a home-made construction of soft lead. It was a practice to tamp these into the end of a hunting cartridge and fire them from a shotgun. The chance of accuracy was near zero and the range limited, and it was remarkable that they had got so close to hitting their intended target.

55. SKYLLOURA - PHOTTA - MANDRES AREA. APRIL/MAY 1964

This area, hinged on the Turkish Regiment's barracks on the northern outskirts of Nicosia and running up to the southern foothills of the Kyrenia range, contained the most critical of all Turkish Cypriot enclaves. Inside it, under orders from TURDYK, Turkish Cypriots were finalising their construction of a military airstrip. TMT leaders had told me that this area was to be the core of a Turkish Cypriot state of northern Cyprus. However it was overlooked by high ground under Greek Cypriot control and it had no natural defence-line: its survival in any armed confrontation clearly would depend wholly upon the intervention, or threat of intervention, of the Turkish army and air force. Greek Cypriot leaders believed that could only happen if Britain and America allowed it.

The sensitivity of the area meant a continuing tension along its borders, which were speckled with paramilitary emplacements. I expected this to lead to some difficulties in the implementation of the harvesting programme and was not surprised at incidents that occurred during the first couple of days. In a few areas, as at Pano Dhikomo, either the Greek or Turkish Cypriots tried to move armed units forward to back up the UN in defence of their farming parties, and the programme had to be halted while we prevailed upon these troops to retire behind their usual defence-lines; similarly it took us some time to convince Greek Cypriot unit commanders on the Kyrenia ridge and around Pano Dhikomo that there must be no further sniping whatsoever by their troops at Turkish Cypriot harvesting parties.

However by the third day of the programme, these teething troubles had all been resolved and harvesting in this area then proceeded under UNFICYP supervision with complete success.

That a UN soldier was killed during this period emphasised how complex was the environment within which the harvesting went forward. The Finnish contingent (YKSP) was administering the programme around Kanli. After dusk on the second day of harvesting they sent out a party to recover one of their vehicles which had broken down in the fields during the day. They came under fire from a Turkish Cypriot strongpoint, suffered one fatality, and returned the fire.

Talking to me about the incident next day the responsible Turkish Cypriot commander (whose HQ was not particularly close to Kanli) explained that the Finnish troops had been moving in the half-light from the direction of a Greek Cypriot village towards his own outpost without any prior warning or display of identification. When the first shots were fired, the UN had brought up reinforcements accompanied by members of the Greek Cypriot police, which had further confused his men. The UN had then brought out a Turkish Cypriot politician who did not know the area and who had no knowledge of local TMT structures and no power over local paramilitary units. During all this time, he said, nobody had tried to contact either him or his headquarters. Nor had they tried to speak to my patrol, which could immediately have provided them with the right contacts.

At the time of the Greek Cypriot attack through the Karmi Forest towards St Hilarion Castle, on 24/25 April, a number of large flocks of sheep owned by Turkish Cypriots in Photta, Pileri and Krini were being grazed on the southern uplands of the Kyrenia Range. These were abandoned when their shepherds took to their heels at the start of the fighting and later they were rounded up by the Greek Cypriots. I was asked for help by the *mukhtar* of Photta, who told me that the loss was very serious for his people, but that the local UN contingent had said there was nothing they could do.

I explained the position to Tassos Papadopoulos, saying that if a return of the sheep was possible, it would have a very positive effect on local inter-communal relations, which had further need of some such tranquilliser. The next day, the minister told me that he had arranged for what remained of the flocks to be driven to Skylloura and that I could take delivery of them there later in the day. He reminded me, however, that this was the season of the Orthodox Easter, when it was traditional to roast lambs on the spit.

"We have a lot of troops at that western end of the ridge" he said, "and I wouldn't count on too many of the lambs having survived."

I contacted the *mukhtar* of Photta, who declined to believe that any significant part of the flocks would be returned. He said that, in any event, none of his shepherds was brave enough to go with me to Skylloura. I therefore set off with the sole accompaniment of my Land Rover crews.

When I arrived in Skylloura, I was taken immediately to the local 'Secret Army' commander, an exceedingly tough-looking ex-EOKA fighter. He thrust into my face a hand from which the ends of most fingers were missing and said "That's what your countrymen did to me."

I feared that I was to be spat at or kicked in the balls or worse but instead he embraced me very warmly. He said: "Even though they tortured me I always had a respect for the British army. That was the sort of war we were fighting. It's your politicians that I can't stand."

I was told that the Turkish Cypriots should think themselves lucky because they were going to get almost all their sheep back. "A few more days", he said, "and it would have been a very different story."

No Greek Cypriot shepherd was prepared to venture out with me on the five-mile track to Photta. Eventually, one of the shepherds who had herded the flock down from the hills advised me what to do. "Put the smallest lamb in the flock over your shoulder and hurry in front. The mother will follow you, bleating, and the rest of the flock will follow her. You have some very old rams with you so the Land Rover should come at the back and pick up any of them that can't keep up with you."

Preparing to lead a mixed herd of sheep and goats from Skylloura back to Photta. Greek Cypriot shepherd from Skylloura on the left and me on the right.

The lamb that led the way.....

.....and elderly ram bringing up the rear. Too tired to walk the whole journey, he ended up riding in the Land Rover.

With the lamb slung over my shoulder, I was cheered on my way by the various paramilitary outposts that I passed on the two hour trek, first Greek Cypriot and then Turkish Cypriot. When we reached the outskirts of Photta, we were greeted by the entire population, who acted as though I were a prophet coming in from the desert with the holy grail[1].

Less encouraging was our involvement in a macabre spin-off of the fighting around St Hilarion. On 26 April, a woman in Aghirda asked us if we could recover for her the bodies of her husband and her son, who had both been killed in the fighting on the Kyrenia Ridge the day before. Kutchuk seconded the request, asking that I do it "as a personal favour."

I consulted Sergeant Makrides, who had led the initial assault, and he told me that those Turkish Cypriots killed in the attack had been buried in shallow graves at the scene of the fighting and that the 'Secret Army' units would have no objection to returning the bodies, which he said could easily be re-located. However, in Nicosia Tassos Papadopoulos told me that the matter needed to be properly negotiated at top level and he put me in touch with the Attorney General, Mr. Criton Tornaritis.

Discussions then dragged on, with extraordinary dithering among the authorities. The bodies were twice exhumed and twice re-buried in the same spot following a last-minute Greek Cypriot change of mind. As in other cases where the government knew the whereabouts of the bodies of Turkish Cypriots killed in the fighting or after abduction, the decisive consideration seemed to be the propaganda that the Turkish Cypriots would have made out of their return.

When he eventually handed me his final ruling, the Attorney General apologised for not having been able to find a more recent precedent on which to rest his decision. The ruling that he gave me, that the bodies should not be moved, was based on what King Priam had resolved in similar circumstances during the first Trojan War.

Later I was asked by Kutchuk to try and stop the continued occasional shooting from the Kyrenia Range at Turkish Cypriots in the villages of Pileri and Keumurju. I spoke to the Greek and Turkish Cypriot paramilitary commanders in the region and identified with them a mutually acceptable arrangement that would have dealt with any further breaches of the cease-fire. Nothing came of this because of a demand from the Canadian contingent in the area that they alone should be responsible for such matters.

56. Kyrenia Area. April/May 1964

Within the disarmed Turkish Cypriot communities of Kyrenia and Kazaphani the atmosphere was now mournful and depressing, with the people acting with unctuous humility towards the UN peacekeeping forces and with veiled bitterness towards the Greek Cypriots. Since the Canadian contingent that was responsible for Kyrenia asked for the visit of a mediating team only at moments of crisis, I was seldom in the area. When I did go, I would be deluged with complaints about the actions and attitudes of UN troops, with the Turkish Cypriots insistent about their continuing sense of insecurity.

For reasons beyond my understanding, UNFICYP had selected Kazaphani for demonstration to visiting VIPs of the ability of the two communities to live together in harmony. There were many villages that did offer genuine proof of this thesis, but Kazaphani was not one of them.

It was not that actual incidents of inter-communal strife since the disarming of the village in March were significant - one Turkish Cypriot mysteriously abducted, threats against Turkish Cypriot shepherds, outlying Turkish Cypriot property looted - but that the Turkish Cypriots felt wholly disenfranchised. In reality they were staying on only because of the presence in the village of a permanent UN garrison, of a wish not to abandon their homes and of a Turkish Cypriot political decision in Nicosia. Beneath their circus smiles they were the epitome of a traumatised, oppressed and fearful minority: they had no say in their own administration, their activities were subject to control by the Greek Cypriots, their rights were ignored by the Greek Cypriot police, they had no access to any process of law and order that they trusted, and they felt that they were hostages to an uncertain future. Deprived of the mediation previously supplied by the tripartite organisation, real inter-communal engagement had withered towards zero since the end of March: Turkish Cypriot villagers continued to exchange the formalities of friendship with their Greek Cypriot neighbours, but they now regarded the Greek Cypriots in general with fear and loathing. Lacking a common language with their UN protectors, they had no way to unburden themselves of their resentments. They detested being used as a UN showpiece for inter-communal harmony: the same would have been true even in those villages where a genuine harmony existed. It was an indictment of the UN presence that many of its units failed to display any sympathy for the underlying realities of the situation. To this the Irish contingent was a notable exception.

The Greek Cypriot villagers, on the other hand, were prepared to display a willingness for co-existence so long as it was on their own terms, although they would have preferred that the Turkish Cypriots were gone, leaving them free to get on with their own lives without complication. They did not lack friendship for the Turkish Cypriots in their own village, but their sympathies did not extend to any deep understanding of general Turkish Cypriot insecurities. They shared the common Greek Cypriot view of the Turkish Cypriots in general as Turks rather than Cypriots, and in this they feared and disliked them as being an extension of the reach of Ankara and as an impediment to their own profound wish for *enosis*.

Neither Kyrenia or Kazaphani drew much benefit from the normalisation programmes that I was delivering to other areas, largely because the Canadian contingent lacked any enthusiasm for involvement in the schemes and because there was as yet no sign that local Greek Cypriot authorities other than the 'Secret Army' were responding to the government's aim for a positive tilt towards Turkish Cypriot communities. Even from these dysfunctional beginnings, an equal and inclusive society might eventually have emerged, as was the aim, but in neither Kyrenia nor Kazaphani was there now any framework to help it happen.

An even more negative picture was presented by Klepini, a small mountain village of 300 Greek Cypriots and 25 Turkish Cypriots. During January, the Turkish Cypriots here had been earnestly pressed by TMT and by their communal leadership in Kyrenia to evacuate to a Turkish Cypriot region. Counter-pressure from the Greek Cypriots had been even more persuasive and, after receiving guarantees from the Greek Cypriot village leaders that they would be protected against all danger, they had eventually resolved to stay.

The Turkish Cypriots continued to live peaceably and in genuine harmony with their Greek Cypriot neighbours until 21 April. On that day a party of armed Greek Cypriot civilians arrived in the village and seized Nyazi Huseyin and his three sons, who were working together in the fields. The Greek Cypriot *mukhtar*, who was working in the same area, protested strongly at the seizure and tried to protect Huseyin but was told not to interfere and that the Turkish Cypriots were required for questioning and would not be away for long. When the *mukhtar* insisted on a better explanation, the outsiders said that suspicions had been aroused because a Turkish Cypriot woman from the village had visited Mandres (which she later explained to me had been merely to see her pregnant daughter). They declined to say who they were or where the Turkish Cypriots were to be taken.

Before he was led away, Nyazi Huseyin shook hands with the Greek Cypriot *mukhtar*, said that he had done nothing wrong and asked that his wife be told what had happened. His three sons, arrested with him, were all too frightened to speak.

That night, Nyazi's wife went to the police in Kyrenia, described what had occurred and asked for news of her family. The police said they knew nothing of the incident but that they would hunt for the missing men and keep her informed. Next day a police sergeant came to Klepini and told her not to worry, that her husband and sons would be found and that if they were not back by the next day, they definitely would be by Friday. On Friday, Mrs Nyazi went back to the police and was told that she must be patient.

That Friday night, the Turkish Cypriots had all gathered fearfully in Nyazi's house when the door was kicked open and a group of armed Greek Cypriots demanded that they be given Nyazi's shotgun. This was handed over.

Then the Turkish Cypriot men were called outside one by one, while the women begged for them to be spared. "They will be all right" they were told by the Greek Cypriot leader, "so long as their records are clean." They were then driven away. There was now no Turkish Cypriot man between fifteen and seventy left in the village.

Rumours of what had happened reached UNFICYP two days later. A unit from the local Canadian contingent visited the village, was told by the Greek Cypriots that everything was in order (none of the Turkish Cypriots still there spoke any English) and reported to HQ that there was no problem. There were further Turkish Cypriot requests for action, including that a joint patrol should visit Klepini, but these were all rejected by the Canadians, who re-affirmed that they were "on top of the situation" and that everything was in order.

Eventually, Kutchuk insisted to the UN that I should go to Klepini to investigate and I did so with Mr Nihat.

The Turkish Cypriots unburdened themselves to us. The Greek Cypriot *mukhtar* then confirmed to me in private that their story was entirely true and told me that 'EOKA' was responsible. He said that he had not told the UN unit what had happened because he was scared of repercussions from "local EOKA people."

I contacted Tassos Papadopoulos with the details that the *mukhtar* had given me. Within a few hours he let me know that he had managed to locate the missing Turkish Cypriots, who were being held in Vouno, and to arrange for their transfer to police custody. Later I was told by the police that some or all of the men would probably have been executed if their discovery had been any longer delayed.

The Turkish Cypriots were held by the Greek Cypriot police in prison until 18 May, but their treatment, which had been very rough while they were in Vouno, was now good. The police claimed that their continued detention was to allow investigation of the circumstances of their seizure and of a suspicion that they had been implicated in a Turkish plot to capture Buffavento Castle. This plan was said to have involved the participation of a secretly-landed force of Turkish soldiers*.

The more probable explanation for the abduction was that some Greek Cypriots had thought it expedient to have a few hostages in hand in case of any Greek Cypriot losses during the attack along the Kyrenia range.

The Greek Cypriots in Klepini were deeply upset by what had happened. They said to me with apparent sincerity that they had a real affection for the Turkish Cypriots in the village; that they had given their guarantee of protection in the belief that their own feelings and influence would ensure that no harm came to their neighbours; and that when the Turkish Cypriots were seized they had been very shocked and had made representations to the local authorities to try and secure their release.

---

* It was claimed that these were to be carried up to the castle in British ambulances.

"They were not guilty of anything at all" the Greek Cypriot *mukhtar* said. "We wanted to defend them, but what could we do? Could we take up our shotguns against the forces of our own side?"

The story had a postscript that also was symptomatic of the times. When the Turkish Cypriots were finally released, they were interviewed privately by my patrol. The three men who had been worst treated while they were at Vouno decided not to return to Klepini, opting instead to stay on in Nicosia: the others, somewhat surprisingly, all decided to return home and were then escorted by me back to the village, where they were received with great joy by both communities.

However when I next visited Klepini, a couple of weeks later, the Turkish Cypriots whispered to me that they were now under pressure from their Greek Cypriot neighbours, who were demanding that the other three of their men also return. When I talked to the Greek Cypriots, they said they were suspicious and unhappy because the other three villagers had not come back and that they had decided to restrict the 'privileges' of the other Turkish Cypriots so that they would force their relatives to rejoin them. Inevitably, the actual effect of this pressure was to persuade the remaining Turkish Cypriots into plans for evacuation.

The one remaining Turkish Cypriot village in Kyrenia district, Temblos, remained a source of friction and unrest. During early April, there were frequent exchanges of fire between its garrison and the gendarmerie or 'Secret Army' units that were surrounding it. In this the only casualty was a Turkish Cypriot who blew himself up while trying to dismantle an unexploded mortar round.

Following Greek Cypriot threats to impose their own police authority on the village, the cordon around it was tightened on 12 April, two days after fighting began in the Pentadaktylos, to the east of the Kyrenia Pass: however, no assault was launched nor, more curiously, was any real attempt made to close the village's direct supply line to St Hilarion Castle.

On 27 April, with the fighting around St Hilarion three days old and a clear likelihood that an attack on Temblos was imminent, UNFICYP established a permanent post in the village. The next day all the Turkish Cypriot fighters in Temblos were pulled out as reinforcement for the main Turkish Cypriot groups astride the pass. A message was then passed by TMT to UNFICYP saying that Temblos "must now be considered an undefended village under UN protection" and that any attempt at incursion by the Greek Cypriot police would result in an immediate evacuation of the whole population.

On 29 April, when the Greek Cypriot leadership in Nicosia ordered an end to paramilitary action against St Hilarion Castle and the Kyrenia Pass, they also cancelled an attack against Temblos, which had been scheduled for the 30th. That same day a Turkish Cypriot shepherd, convinced that the UN presence meant greater security, set out with his sheep from Temblos and was shot dead by a Greek Cypriot patrol.

I was asked by Captain Augustis to try and establish who was responsible for this act. Major Burgess then took it upon himself to conduct a somewhat unprofessional autopsy. The bullet which he extracted was turned over, together with a full report, to the police in Kyrenia, who promised an urgent analysis and full investigation. Nothing more was heard from them on the matter. In the meantime we returned the body to Temblos, together with the man's sheep. The villagers professed themselves too frightened to go out to the local cemetery, even under UN escort, and the shepherd was buried in his own back garden.

While en route to a follow-up visit to Temblos I was asked by the Kyrenia police to deal with an incident nearby. A villager had been knocked down and killed by a Canadian armoured car in the fields between Karmi and Temblos. John Burgess and I arrived to find the armoured car still in the field, going round and round in small circles. Its crew-members appeared to be totally drunk. Feeling that this was one investigation that it was better to keep well clear of, we radioed a report to Canadian HQ and departed on other business as soon as we saw a military police Land Rover approaching.

In early June, when there were renewed rumours that Ankara was preparing to intervene, Turkish Cypriot fighters were moved from St Hilarion back into Temblos. Until then, all through May, spirits in the village were at a very low ebb. On a clear day the Turkish coastline was visible from the village, looking much closer than its actual forty miles. When I walked into the village one day with Mr Nihat it was to find the men-folk all sitting in front of their coffee-house, gazing to the north and nervously fingering their worry-beads.

I asked what was the meaning of their steady murmuring. Mr Nihat told me that they were all saying: "Why don't they come?"

57. KAMBYLI - DHIORIOS - AYIA IRINI AREA.
APRIL/MAY 1964

The fact that gendarmerie officers at Myrtou were no longer acting aggressively towards the Turkish Cypriots, even if not yet safeguarding their rights or trusted by them, meant that the mood in the Turkish Cypriot village of Kambyli, which was home to most of the refugees from Dhiorios, had changed from belligerence to resigned discontent.

Resentment was repeatedly fuelled by reports on the destruction of their property in Dhiorios and by the messages sent them by the Greek Cypriots of that village, even though those were usually well-intended. A periodic re-surfacing of bad feeling between the Kambyli Turkish Cypriots and the Maronites of Asomatos added to the sense of persecution, as did the occasional harassment of their shepherds when they were grazing their flocks close to Greek Cypriot-controlled areas.

Until the end of March, Turkish Cypriot fighters on the Kyrenia Range had held positions as far west as Ayios Pavlos (SE of Vasilia), even though their strength was greatly over-extended by doing so. Their proximity had given a wholly unjustified encouragement to Turkish Cypriot villagers in the Kormakiti peninsula and had infuriated the Greek Cypriots, who assumed the strength of the Turkish Cypriot mountain outpost to be much greater than it really was. The Turkish Cypriots here acted as did the Greek Cypriots at Halefka, casually and harmlessly shooting at shepherds who too closely approached their mountain post, and sometimes using a Greek Cypriot goat for target practice.

On the day that UNFICYP assumed control of the area, a report was received by them of Greek Cypriot casualties in a shooting incident near Ayios Pavlos. Major Burgess was detached by me to investigate, taking with him a Greek Cypriot gendarme as interpreter.

Outside Lapithos they were introduced by the local police to a young Greek Cypriot shepherd, who described how he and his father had been scything hay on the mountain-side when they were fired at: he said that his father had been killed and that he had run back to give the alarm.

Major Burgess set out to climb to the spot, near Ayios Pavlos, which had been described. On the way he encountered an old man scrambling down the rocks, who gave a dramatic report of how he and his son had been fired at by the Turks and his son killed.

Re-united with his son at a coffee-house in Lapithos, the shepherd and the remainder of the coffee-house's clientele were lectured by the gendarme, who had been aggravated by the unwished-for mountain climb. He said that if they insisted on cutting grass so close to a Turkish Cypriot outpost, they must expect to be shot at.

The advice was apparently ignored by local Greek Cypriot shepherds and there were further similar incidents up to 25 April, when the Greek Cypriot attack on St. Hilarion cleared the western end of the Kyrenia Range of Turkish Cypriot strong-points.

British UN soldier talking to Greek Cypriot shepherd and policeman.

Around Kambyli itself there was only one shooting incident. At the beginning of May an out-of-area police Land Rover taking reinforcements to a station in the Lapithos region mistook the road and drove up to Kambyli. A surprised Turkish Cypriot sentry fired at the vehicle, which stopped, was unable to reverse and was quickly abandoned by its occupants. The Turkish Cypriots then collected the Land Rover and drove it into the centre of the village.

Later that day a local British UNFICYP unit persuaded the Turkish Cypriots to release the vehicle and returned it to the Greek Cypriot police. The gendarmerie at Myrtou continued in a very black mood for several days, during which I felt it best to postpone joint meetings that had been planned to discuss harvesting arrangements.

The Turkish Cypriots in Kambyli always professed to a contempt for the Maronites at Asomatos but they did little to provoke them and in general took good care of Maronite property that lay within their boundaries. The extent of that property was considerable, as many of the Asomatos Maronites had once lived in Kambyli, and in the centre of the Turkish Cypriot village there was a fine Maronite church. In January, when the influx of refugees from Dhiorios suddenly doubled the population of Kambyli, the Turkish Cypriots started to use the Maronite church as a food store, having carefully stacked all of the church furniture in the crypt.

British UN soldiers making friends with the children in Kambyli.

This infuriated the Maronites. When I offered to return the furniture they greeted the suggestion with scorn, saying that there would be nothing left intact. I then arranged for everything in the church to be transferred to Asomatos. The Maronites found to their astonishment that everything was in perfect condition, and appeared much put out at having nothing to criticise.

The Maronites were similarly ungrateful when it was found, during the joint inspection that I organised, that the crops on fields that they owned within the boundaries of Kambyli had been well cared for by the Turkish Cypriots and were virtually undamaged. Rather than be thankful for this good fortune, they looked diligently for some other cause for complaint. When they discovered that a small olive tree belonging to them had been felled by the Turkish Cypriots, in the construction of village defence-works, they assailed me with irritating grumbling, as though all of their fortune had been lost.

It was as well that they had not suffered the depredations inflicted on Turkish Cypriot property in Dhiorios. The Turkish Cypriots of that village had been among the richest farmers in northern Cyprus, with large acreages of excellent crop-lands, which in 1963 had given a yield of barley, beans and fodder worth over £50,000. In 1964 these crops had been entirely destroyed or stolen by Greek Cypriots.

The extent of the loss was discovered when I took a party of Turkish Cypriot farmers back to inspect their fields. In all the hours of that careful survey, with nothing but loss revealed, there was no complaint or abuse from the Turkish Cypriots, and the uniformed Greek Cypriot policeman who was with us as a witness was treated with the utmost courtesy. In the course of the afternoon, we encountered a party of Greek Cypriot villagers. "Why don't you come back?" they asked the Turkish Cypriots. The Turkish Cypriots, all of whose homes had been looted and stripped down to their bare shells, said: "We've been thinking about it, but for the moment our women don't want to."

Out of earshot of the Turkish Cypriot farmers I asked the Greek Cypriots why they had stolen the Turkish Cypriot crops. Somebody answered that they had needed to recover debts owed to them by the Turkish Cypriots. I said "But those debts totalled only about £500 and the Turks had sent word to you that they were willing to pay any debts in cash." Another man said: "So long as the Turkish villagers stay away from here they have no rights. Let them come back and then we shall forget the past."

In Ayia Irini, with the Turkish Cypriots fortified by their surmounting of past difficulties and reassured by the presence of a permanent UNFICYP post and with inter-communal relations working well, both through the formal liaison committee and through the resumption of private friendships, the period passed in relative calm. There was a further considerable increase in 'Secret Army' training exercises in the wooded area between the village and Dhiorios and a continuing high level of activity in the construction of coastal defences: as a result there were more frequent confrontations between Turkish Cypriot shepherds and Greek Cypriot patrols and more frequent thefts of Turkish Cypriot sheep from outlying byres. However, the 'Secret Army' had matured rapidly: it was now much more disciplined and its attitude towards the Turkish Cypriots in this area had become one of good-natured tolerance.

The Greek Cypriot police at Morphou, on the other hand, continued to regard the Ayia Irini Turkish Cypriots with a particularly jaundiced eye. They probably were justified in their suspicions that the Turkish Cypriots had been tampering with local antiquities, trespassing on government lands and poaching in conservation areas. But they also suspected them of two other more serious offences, the looting of a nearby RAF meteorological station and the running of an illicit timber business, using wood stolen from government forests. Captain Augustis told me that in fact the Greek Cypriots in Ayia Irini were the culprits in both these latter cases and that they had cooked up evidence to throw suspicion on the Turkish Cypriots.

None of these events produced particular anxiety in the village, but the change-over of local UN responsibility from a British to a YKSP (Finnish) unit led to the last occasion on which I was summoned urgently to Ayia Irini to argue against a threatened Turkish Cypriot evacuation. Both Greek and Turkish Cypriots professed themselves to be frightened of their new guardians, unable to communicate with them and incapable of fathoming their intentions. We suggested that they be patient. Within two weeks the Finns were on excellent terms with both communities and the Turkish Cypriots never again suggested to me that they were thinking of departure.

The police at Myrtou were less happy, for they found that the Finns treated them more firmly than had the British and that they were less able to elicit sympathy from UNFICYP HQ when they felt slighted. They also disliked the Finnish habit of patrolling on bicycles, the silence of which meant that they did not have the customary early warning when a detachment was approaching.

Following up one of the normalisation projects that were being introduced by Tassos Papadopoulos, on 20 April I convened in Ayia Irini a very successful joint meeting. This was the result of lengthy preparation for an unobtrusive channelling to the Turkish Cypriots in this area of government spending through a scheme that would provide them with long-term employment. Present at the meeting were Greek and Turkish Cypriot members of the District Administration, members of the Water Board, Superintendent Vassiliou from Kyrenia and the leaders of the Greek and Turkish Cypriot communities in Ayia Irini.

Before starting any discussion of the project, it was agreed that there would be no publicity of any sort. The meeting then proceeded on an entirely workmanlike and positive note, without any histrionics or arrogance or innuendo, and ended in complete agreement. Even though the project was not of any great size it was, so far as I was aware, the first new bi-communal construction project to be launched in Nicosia Zone since December. I was told afterwards that the co-operation and cross-communal harmony evidenced at the meeting would previously have been thought impossible, even in the years of independence up to Christmas 1963.

This was not some startling breaking of a mould, but it did show what could be achieved, despite all the violence and polarisation of the past four months, if political and paramilitary sympathies had been adequately secured, and where the process of inter-communal re-engagement could be shielded from outside interference. It was the more striking that this could happen in such proximity to the armed confrontation that was developing along the Kyrenia Range. It was as if Cypriots were a dysfunctional family, some of whose members arbitrarily shifted from acrimonious argument to caring closeness and back again, while others got on with a stable life.

Harvesting around Ayia Irini went forward smoothly. Normality of economic life for the Turkish Cypriots was further restored in May when new UNFICYP policies led to the provision of escorts for a regular weekly bus programme, so that villagers could resume their travel and the delivery of their produce to Nicosia.

Early in May, however, the Turkish Cypriots in Ayia Irini discovered that, while gaining benefit from the public-works programme, they were to be deprived of one of their traditional, albeit questionable, sources of income. For many years it had been their habit to plant considerable crops in government forests or on *hali*-lands. These encroachments had annually been the source of government complaint and penalty, but there was no history of any forceful action against those responsible.

The delivery of warnings from the gendarmerie at Morphou to the Ayia Irini Turkish Cypriots had seemed this year to fall into the usual pattern. The villagers went ahead with the planting of barley. The police issued a demand for the payment of the usual fines and the villagers agreed to pay.

Harvesting of the crops began satisfactorily, but was then stopped on orders from the police. The Turkish Cypriots asked for a conference with the UN and one of their own leaders. I was unable to be present, but the British UN officer who did attend passed on to UNFICYP HQ an optimistic report suggesting that the matter had been resolved.

Two weeks later, Turkish Cypriot farmers going to harvest fields within the Morphou *hali*-lands were turned back by a unit of the 'Secret Army' and told that they were no longer to be allowed to gather crops from any land belonging to the government. When this was reported to the local UN commander, he contacted the 'Secret Army' leader for the area and put it to him that, in the interest of inter-communal calm, no changes should be made to the policy that had applied to these lands over the past few years. The Greek Cypriot commander undertook to support this proposal with his superiors and two days later he reported back that his suggestion had been agreed to and that the Turkish Cypriots could continue with their harvesting. All of the crops from these fields were then gathered without incident.

On 27 May, I was at Myrtou at Greek Cypriot request to attend a meeting with local Greek Cypriot leaders, including Captain Augustis and Superintendent Vassiliou and representatives from the Lands and Forestry Department. I had been told that the objective was to assess local crop damage, but as soon as proceedings started there was an announcement that the government had decided that its own appointees would harvest all crops still standing on government-owned and common lands in the region and that any attempt by the Turkish Cypriots to interfere would be met with force. They wished the UN to be associated with this move and proposed an immediate delineation of the areas in question.

Having had a lengthy struggle to understand the intricacies of the *hali*-lands question, I had some sympathy for the view that the situation needed to be regularised. However, with the harvesting programme providing the key to communal re-engagement, this seemed an inopportune moment to force a change in existing practice. I said that I did not know enough about the question to speak with any authority but that, whatever rights the government had, I felt the problem must not be dissociated from four other considerations: first, the matter of inter-communal relations and general stability within the area as a whole; second, that I was under the impression that a local agreement had already been reached under UN auspices, which should not be altered; third, that there should be no bias in application between Greek and Turkish Cypriot encroachments; and fourth, that a Turkish Cypriot representative should participate in any process of delineation. The Ministry representatives said that they were unaware of any local agreements and suggested that they investigate these and seek for a ruling from their minister before discussions were continued.

To my surprise, Superintendent Vassiliou reacted to my remarks with an embarrassing apoplexy, reverting to the most extreme and intransigent of police attitudes. He said that only one consideration applied, and that was the rights of the government. He said the Turkish Cypriots had forfeited all their rights through their act of rebellion; that no local UN agreement had any validity if the police were not specifically a party to it; and that I had no business to be suggesting that a Turkish Cypriot representative should participate in the proposed discussion. The declaration turned into a near-hysterical diatribe against the Turkish Cypriots and the British, with Vassiliou unburdening himself of a load of prejudices that must have been festering for several years.

I was tired, and already exasperated by the frequency with which elements of the police had damaged the chances of communal reconciliation, and I lost my temper. I pointed out to Superintendent Vassiliou that over the past months he personally had been a party to numerous agreements and policies that he was now forswearing. An angry exchange followed, during which he denied his own past undertakings and denounced the process of re-engagement with the Turkish Cypriots.

When the exchange had blown itself out, Captain Augustis gave a conciliatory summary of the earlier discussion. Since the Greek Cypriots were convinced that the villagers would fire the crops if they got wind of what was intended, I undertook not to discuss the matter in Ayia Irini until a final decision had been reached. The ministry officials undertook that no action would be taken pending a further meeting. Vassiliou announced that nothing on earth would stop him from placing guards forthwith on whatever crops remained on the *hali*-lands.

Captain Augustis had invited me to lunch with him that day and afterwards to spend the afternoon with him searching for snakes and wild honey. As we left Myrtou together, he said that the argument had been "unfortunate." "Vassiliou was wrong, of course, but his nerves have almost gone again and he's only just hanging on. He's about to be retired and he's terrified that there may be some disgrace about it and that he's going to lose his pension. Now he's going to be in an even worse state than he was before."

Augustis had arranged that we should lunch that day with the Turkish Cypriots in Ayia Irini. Without having tempered his commitment to *enosis*, he was a genuine believer in the need for communal re-engagement and the provision of complete security and equality to the Turkish Cypriots. He also was rare among Greek Cypriot leaders of that moment in his willingness to accept the faults of his own community and to face the realities that communal re-engagement would bring, and to do so publicly in front of both communities.

The Turkish Cypriots, sadly, treated his efforts with cynicism: the pressures against them since Christmas had left them with an assumption that people like Superintendent Vassiliou were the real representatives of Greek Cypriot feeling. Our lunch that day, paid for by Augustis, passed off with great good humour, but whenever Augustis spoke of reconciliation those Turkish Cypriots who were out of his line of sight winked broadly at me and at each other.

Next day I learned that Vassiliou had been complaining about me to his contacts in the Canadian contingent, who had embellished his remarks and passed them on to UNFICYP HQ. In fact, with Captain Augustis' support, I had covered my position with other contacts in the police and with Tassos Papadopoulos and Tasos Panayides, had apologised for the intemperance of my own outburst, and had made my peace with Vassiliou. In response I had received from President Makarios a message of his complete confidence in me.

On 31 May I was asked by Kutchuk to see him on a matter of urgency. He told me that the leaders of the Turkish Cypriot community in Ayia Irini had come to Nicosia to report that contractors acting for the government had begun to harvest the remaining crops that Turkish Cypriot villagers had planted on the *hali*-lands and in minor-forest areas; that they were working under the protection of large paramilitary forces; and that the Turkish Cypriot *mukhtar* doubted if he could prevent his people from trying to fire those crops that were still standing.

Having discussed the matter several times with Tassos Papadopoulos, in his capacity as Acting Minister of Agriculture, I knew now that the government would not budge over the harvesting of illegally planted crops. In response to my plea that there be no hazarding of the process of communal re-engagement that was otherwise proceeding so well in this area, the minister said that any tilt towards the Turks had to be through processes that had a legal basis, not through the ceding of constitutional rights. I gathered that the illegal use of *hali*-lands was an issue on which progress had been blocked by Turkish Cypriot intransigence prior to December 1963 and on which the opportunity for resolution was not now to be missed.

What was given was an assurance that for 1964 there would be a full-value payment of compensation for the all crops harvested from the *hali*-lands by the government. Armed with this and supported by Kutchuk's blessing, Mr Nihat and I persuaded the Turkish Cypriots against further thoughts of retaliation. In this, the local Finnish contingent provided a calming influence. On the other hand, those Greek Cypriots who were keen to provoke the Ayia Irini Turkish Cypriots into conflict and evacuation felt they had missed another opportunity to do so.

When I left Cyprus in June the Turkish Cypriot community was, against the odds, still securely ensconced in Ayia Irini.

58.   Louroujina ~ Kochati Area. April/May 1964

Throughout April, Louroujina continued in its militant isolation, determined to retaliate in kind to every action against it and regarded with trepidation by the Greek Cypriots, who viewed it as a bastion of Turkish Cypriot insurrection.

Greek Cypriot hostages had been held here in the past, but the last of those originally seized had been released on 31 March: none was remaining on 18 April, the date set by the Greek Cypriot police Intelligence unit for publication of forged evidence that there were still prisoners at Louroujina and that they were all to be executed by TMT at midnight.*

Although the planned Greek Cypriot provocation had been aborted, I was concerned in case any attempts at kidnap or assassination were mounted against Turkish Cypriots in the Louroujina area, and I arranged for my patrol to rendezvous there at midday on 19 April so that we could counsel the Turkish Cypriots on potential dangers and urge restraint on them.

Major Burgess reached the village first. His later report read:

> *"After explaining to the TC leaders why I had come, I asked to be allowed to visit the cells in the police station, since we knew that hostages had been held there on previous occasions. The TC agreed that I could go anywhere in the village I wished to search and took me on a guided tour, including inspection of the school and most of the large houses, but not of the police station.*
>
> *I was then taken to the coffee-house and there it was explained to me that they did in fact have one hostage in the police cells: he was a Greek who had driven up to the village early that morning, apparently having lost his way.*
>
> *I suggested to the TC that, in view of the press reports that were to be expected that day and the fake execution-signal intercept, it would be wise of them to hand over the hostage to me as proof of the fact that they were not holding anyone in the village. After considerable discussion they agreed to do so. I was then taken to the police station and Markos Ioannou was released into my custody and his car was given back to him. Afterwards I was allowed to see the other cells and to satisfy myself that no other persons were held.*

---

* See Chapter 51 re the 'Crystal Palace' intercept:

Markos Ioannou, who had suffered no physical violence, was so shaken by his experience that his first act on being released was to enter his car, engage the wrong gear and reverse into my Land Rover.

I handed Ioannou and his car over to Perakhorio gendarmerie post at about 1600. He was greeted by the police with absolute disbelief."

Towards the end of April, coincident with the fighting on the Kyrenia range, there were a number of minor and haphazard shooting incidents in the fields around Louroujina. Typically, Turkish Cypriot shepherds told me of two occasions on which, while they were in fields towards Potamia, they were approached by a group of Greek Cypriots. Instead of the expected attack, they had found themselves being offered cigarettes, given the President's line on reconciliation and told about the benefits they would have from communal re-engagement.

From their forward positions, Turkish Cypriot paramilitaries of the Louroujina garrison saw that their shepherds had been approached by the Greek Cypriots assumed that an arrest was being attempted and opened fire. Greek Cypriot defensive positions forward of Potamia fired back in response. The shepherds and their intending benefactors dashed off at their best speed in opposite directions.

During April, with escorting still banned by UNFICYP HQ, travel between Louroujina and Nicosia was minimal, perhaps one trip every week or ten days. The Turkish Cypriots who made the journey did so in a state of constant fear. The trips were monitored by my patrol as a yardstick to gauge the general safety of travel.

On 2 May, all travel halted after the Louroujina bus was shot up while returning from Nicosia, with one of its passengers, an old man, killed and the others severely traumatised. The whole incident was witnessed by two UN officers who, after the bus had escaped back to Louroujina, spoke with the Greek Cypriots who had done the shooting. In their later report to Headquarters the UN officers described the killers as 'a group of young hoodlums'.

The Turkish Cypriots in Louroujina requested that a doctor be sent from Nicosia so that a proper death certificate could be signed before the man was buried. Because of the incident, no Turkish Cypriot doctor would make the drive on his own and an escort was asked for by Kutchuk's office. Echoing former British practice this request was refused by UNFICYP as contrary to current policy.

Two days later, on 4 May, almost every Turkish Cypriot in Louroujina participated in a bitter demonstration against the United Nations, claiming that the peacekeeping force had failed to bring them the security that they had a right to expect. On 6 May, the Turkish Cypriots began to advance their forward positions to the south and east, towards the Larnaca road, claiming that they were doing so to protect their harvesters. The Greek Cypriots did the same to the south-west, using the same excuse. Firing between these positions soon became general, with the addition of some indiscriminate shooting by the Greek Cypriots directly into Louroujina.

Mr Nihat and I visited Louroujina on the afternoon of 4 May, after the anti-UN demonstrations. The atmosphere was very aggressive and we had some difficulty in gaining access to the TMT leaders, whom we found to be planning retaliatory ambushes on the Larnaca road. I persuaded them against this only by promising that I would either secure from UNFICYP an agreement for escorts or else that Major Burgess or I would personally travel with the bus once weekly.

On 9 May, I worked with the local British UN contingent, the 1st Foresters, to negotiate a regional cease-fire from the shooting that had started on the 6th, and later that day a UN post was established in Louroujina. On the evening of that same day, as had happened on previous occasions, police headquarters in Nicosia rejected the terms that had been agreed by the local Greek Cypriot commanders. Sporadic firing was resumed and a new round of negotiations, in which I was not involved, dragged on for six days before an agreement was reached that in no significant way differed from the original one. On 15 May UN, troops took over the advanced positions on both sides and during the week that followed all major defensive emplacements were dismantled, with agreement that no new ones would be constructed so long as the UN maintained a permanent presence in Louroujina.

Two incidents in mid-May were symptomatic of the pressures placed on many rural Turkish Cypriot families. In the first case, an elderly Turkish Cypriot couple who had stayed on in Dhali told me that they wanted to encourage their daughter, who had fled to Louroujina at the time of the major evacuation, to come home. I was assured by the Greek Cypriot *mukhtar* of Dhali, by the local commander of the 'Secret Army' and by the gendarmerie that she would be entirely safe if she did return.

In Louroujina the TMT leaders at first refused me permission to consult the girl as to her real wishes, but eventually allowed Mr Nihat and me to speak with her privately in her own home, on condition that they could reconsider their position if she opted to go. The girl said that at present she did not wish to move back to Dhali, but that she would think about it again if the situation changed. When informed of this the Greek Cypriots, and her parents, refused to believe that she was genuinely unwilling to come. I therefore arranged for a meeting to be held midway between the two villages.

The reunion, conducted in the presence of armed men from each community, in case either half of the family should try by force to persuade the other half to join it, was fraught with extraordinary pathos. In the end it was the parents who were almost persuaded to join their daughter in Louroujina. Before parting, the father handed over to the girl all of his savings: through having continued to live with the Greek Cypriots in Dhali, he still had some income: she, through staying isolated with her own community in Louroujina, had none.

The second case was that of an unhappy and impoverished Turkish Cypriot in Louroujina who had agreed with his wife that he would try to escape to a Greek Cypriot area and that she and their two children would try to join him if he managed to do so. Having let it be known that he was going out to gather wood, he made off to Dhali, where he told the Greek Cypriots of how difficult life had been in Louroujina and of how the people there were suffering "under a TMT dictatorship."

The man's wife failed to get away and eventually I was asked by the Greek Cypriots to try and arrange for her to join her husband. I went and discussed the position with Erol Huseyin and other TMT leaders in Louroujina. When she was called into the meeting, the woman said her husband had deserted her and that she had no wish to go. Later, however, when I talked to her in private, she told me that she was desperate to rejoin her husband but that she was very frightened. She believed she would be badly beaten if her real feelings became known in the village. I therefore let it be known that she had not yet made up her mind.

A week later, when I judged that feelings would have simmered down, I returned to Louroujina and persuaded the TMT leaders that it was a poor advertisement for their cause if they could only hang onto their people by force or threat. They then agreed that she could go if she declared to them that she wished to do so. With great trepidation she joined me and told the meeting that she had no complaints against Louroujina, but that she and her children did want to be back with her husband.

At this point, the woman's parents appeared and announced that under no circumstances would they let her go. They were illiterate and very rough and neither my arguments nor those of Mr Nihat seemed to move them at all. Eventually the TMT leaders called a halt, saying that they would not force the woman to go against the wish of her parents.

Rather apologetically, they afterwards advanced to me the argument that, however hard it might seem, this was a struggle that could only be won though the unity of the people. The will of the majority was to resist, and it was the task of the leadership to reinforce that resistance. They gave me an absolute promise that no harm would come to the woman or her children and said that Nihat and I could visit them whenever I wanted. Later I explained the position to Kutchuk and asked that he give backing to an effort by Mr Nihat to get the family reunited.

Meanwhile, the situation in Kochati and Margi had deteriorated. Even more isolated than Louroujina, travel from these villages had stopped in February and their economic situation had been declining ever since. By the end of April, both villages were approaching a state of total destitution, with their stocks of food almost at an end, those of coffee and cigarettes totally exhausted and no money left. The large numbers of refugees from Mathiati, a disruptive influence since December, had created pressure for revenge attacks against neighbouring Greek Cypriot villages. On 27 April, there was an ineffectual attempt to mount an ambush on the Limassol road, followed by other similarly unproductive forays and by some shooting incidents around Margi and Mathiati.

The situation for these villages was transformed through a local works programme (like that at Ayia Irini), the resumption of payments to local officials, such as Rural Constables and school staff, and the institution in the last week of May of an escorted convoy programme, which allowed local Turkish Cypriot products from the area to be delivered to the market in Nicosia for the first time since December.

After the initial friction between Louroujina and Limbia, harvesting arrangements for the whole Louroujina-Dhali-Kochati region, outstandingly well organised by a British UN unit of 1st Foresters, went forward with complete success. The start of an escorts programme, local agreements on the removal of fortifications, the end of fighting on the Kyrenia range, improved discipline in the 'Secret Army', a less belligerent stance by the gendarmerie and the quiet beginning of the programme of public works combined to produce a startling ebbing of tension in the rural areas and an optimism that normality was returning.

At the beginning of June, discussions started, initiated jointly by communal leaders in Louroujina and Dhali, for the reopening to Greek Cypriots of the road through Louroujina, an idea that would have been unthinkable only a few weeks before.

59.   ENDINGS.   JUNE 1964

International press comment continued to be in striking variance from what I was seeing on the ground, and unhelpful to any process of communal re-engagement. The Greek Cypriot attack along the Kyrenia range in April, which had endangered no civilian lives and which appeared in no substantial way to differ from various past British actions against insurgency in its colonies, was excoriated in the foreign press. The Economist labelled this an attempt by the Greek Cypriots to "impose their will by force of arms in flagrant defiance of the United Nations" (Economist, 24/4/64 and 2/5/64).

The Turkish Cypriots, now regarded by the British press as plucky underdogs, were described by the same press as "reinvigorated" from the increasing flow of arms smuggled through Mansoura and by renewed assurances of backing from Ankara. Foreign correspondents claimed they were being told by the Turkish Cypriots that their aim now was to achieve 'communal separation' as a position from which to negotiate a federation in which the northern 38 per cent of the island would be under their control.

The international press reported Makarios as ready to accept the presence of an international police force, but wholly refusing to discuss with the UN Secretary General's representative any movement towards a federal solution. Greek Cypriot ministers were reported as insisting that *enosis* was still a primary aim of their community.

In general, foreign correspondents, particularly after the Pantelides killing in Famagusta and the reactive Greek Cypriot seizure of hostages, depicted a Cyprus still principally characterised by the anarchy of December and January, with neither communal leadership in effective control of its armed irregulars and no signs of compromise.

The reality in rural areas of Cyprus was very different. Central political control had been re-established and I was reporting an emergent and effective dialogue and inter-communal re-engagement, a sense that separation had gone far enough, and a belief that a return to the normality of a working partnership (albeit adjusted from the 1960 model) was not far distant. In parallel the back-channel through me between Makarios and Kutchuk was being used to develop areas of practical co-operation and to assess how mutual trust could be recreated and new formulae for co-existence found.

One further major step was needed, to add to the works, harvesting and escort programmes that were combining to restore Turkish Cypriot confidence: a return by Turkish Cypriot evacuees to their abandoned homes in villages where it was jointly agreed between communal leaders and myself that it would be both sensible and safe to do so. No one supposed that this would currently be possible on an island-wide scale, but even a small start clearly would have profound implications for the general course of inter-communal relations.

I saw this as the opening of a new period of opportunity. Local and central authorities and paramilitary commands from both communities were prepared to allow the trial to go ahead. Local groundwork had been completed. There was now an apparent readiness for secret political compromises.

TMT leaders explained to me that this degree of re-engagement was acceptable to them because their interim targets for ethnic reorganisation had been met, through the limited population movements that had already taken place and through Green Line' separations that had placed key areas under UN supervision, and because armed intervention from Turkey no longer seemed to be an early likelihood. In any event, the villages to which a return was planned would not greatly have altered the picture of a semi-cantonal layout in Nicosia Zone.

Turkish Cypriot villagers who saw that their homes were still intact and their former Greek Cypriot neighbours welcoming, and who believed that the works programme, the escort arrangements and the presence of UN police would afford them adequate security, were desperate to get back. Even the evacuees from Omorphita, who were surveyed in considerable numbers by my patrol, mostly said they would be willing to return if the UN assumed joint responsibility for the policing of their area. TMT appeared to accept that the suffering imposed on Turkish Cypriot rural communities had reached a level that must not be exceeded.

I took it that TMT saw this as a temporary concession, as a breathing space in a long-term process of ethnic separation, which could be reversed if or when they felt a further round in the struggle was needed. Similarly I took it that the concessions over UN escort and policing arrangements, to which Makarios had belatedly agreed, despite continuing objections from the heads of his police forces, would do no more than provide a breathing-space during which more permanent arrangements must be made.

Nor had I any illusions about the difficulties of achieving a general and sustainable solution for Cyprus. I did not believe, as General Carver was later to charge, that by solving the problems of the villages one solved the whole problem of Cyprus.[1] I realised that inter-communal re-engagement in the rural areas, even if they included over seventy per cent of the island's population, would be no more than one key building-block in the edifice of an overall settlement.

What I did very strongly believe was that fostering and protecting areas of successful inter-communal co-operation, wherever those might occur, was at present the only route available through which a general mutual trust could be generated, and that without that trust no equitable construction of a new inter-communal partnership would be possible.

I also believed that in areas where an appropriate re-engagement of the two communities had been achieved and where that was being fostered by the UN and by moderate Cypriot opinion, it would in future be hard for outsiders or extremists to resurrect the enmities and fears of January, so long as effective mechanisms for ground-level mediation remained in place.

My optimism had been increased by news that specials inducted into the police forces since Christmas, whom I had seen as the main destabilisers of the reconciliation process, were being transferred into the 'Secret Army' (soon to be renamed the National Guard), where discipline was more effective and where leadership was in the hands of officers who openly supported the Makarios' line. At the same time, the police and gendarmerie were being combined into a single force.

It was not a question of rebuilding a satisfactory past. During the years of independence, irrespective of personal friendships, there had been no real trust between the communities. Since the first outbreak of serious inter-communal violence in 1958, each community had been fearful of the other. There needed now to be a bottom-up building of new foundations. The history of tripartite mediation had showed that was possible.

By the beginning of June I knew, from conversations with them, that hard-liners in both communities were prepared to go along with a trial process of further limited re-engagement. Since the UN's cancellation on 27 March of Greek and Turkish participation in the mediating process, I had had no formal contact with the Greek and Turkish military, but my experience with Major Sepici and Colonel Akova and the Greek officers who had served with me in the early months of the year led me to suppose that they would hold views broadly similar to those of TMT and of the 'Secret Army'.

The remarks made to me by George Ball in February should have taught me to be less optimistic. I still knew nothing of the Acheson Plan and it had not occurred to me that the Foreign Office and State Department would actually oppose an inter-communal re-engagement if that were demonstrated to be a workable proposition. I had been directly encouraged in my concepts by Galo Plaza's views, as relayed to me by Natalie Thomas and Kurt Janssen, and by support given me by a contact in the High Commission. I was under the impression that the UN would be wholly supportive of the re-engagement process.

On 7 June, Ted Macey and his driver, Corporal Platt, disappeared while on an assignment in north-eastern Cyprus. Macey and I had talked the previous evening and I had told him that I had been given new and very clear warning by contacts in the 'Secret Army' that there were likely to be assassination attempts against both him and General Carver. As with previous warnings from me, he had laughed this off, said that he could take care of himself and told me not to be concerned.

Greek Cypriot passions, and press vituperation, against the British were particularly inflamed, following the arrest a few days earlier of LAC Marley, who was caught by Greek Cypriot police in the act of smuggling weapons for the Turkish Cypriots inside a British UN vehicle.

Duncan Sandys, the British minister responsible for Commonwealth affairs, had responded to comments from Makarios by concurring that the usefulness of British participation in the peacekeeping process in Cyprus might be coming to an end.

I was told by UNFICYP HQ to seek news of Macey. Such an instruction, like the earlier order to seek for a missing British tobacco salesman, Mr Gibbons, clearly conflicted with a mediating role, but I undertook to pass on whatever advice my contacts were prepared to convey.[2] By the Greek Cypriots I was told that Macey and Platt were both dead, and why, and was advised not to let myself be involved in further investigation.[3]

On 9 June, two days after Macey's disappearance, I delivered to UNFICYP HQ the details of the impending movement of Turkish Cypriot villagers back to Orounda and Eliophotes, with a note that submissions would later be made covering a similar return to Akaki, Kato Dheftera and Palekythro.

I noted that these moves were in accordance with UN mediating policy, were fully supported by President Makarios and Vice-President Kutchuk and their advisers and had the active backing of all local paramilitary and village leaders. I included a standard request that the escort programme be extended to take in these villages (which provision had already been okayed by the local UNFICYP contingent), that UN troops should temporarily be stationed in the near vicinity and that there should be UN participation in the villages' policing (which had been agreed with the local gendarmerie). The return was due to start on 11 June.

UNFICYP HQ was controller of the peacekeeping process, entailing the provision of UN-controlled military force for the maintenance of law and order. But it was not a participant in mediating operations, for which Galo Plaza, Tuomioja and Janssen were now answerable directly to the UN Secretary General, other than through the JPO. Properly, it should have been standard procedure for UNFICYP to provide support for a plan which carried the approval of the UN mediating section.

Four hours after presenting the plan, I was summoned to a meeting with General Carver. He first of all told me that he had decided to cancel the entire escort programme forthwith. He justified this by saying that he personally believed that there was no longer any serious threat on the roads and that the Turkish Cypriots should be obliged to travel unescorted so as to learn this fact for themselves.

I was dumbfounded at a decision which I knew would undermine the entire process of inter-communal re-engagement in the rural areas. I tried to explain this, but General Carver, very differently from General Young, was unreceptive to argument from junior officers and apparently unwilling to accept that Turkish Cypriot actions were still affected by the psychological traumata that they had suffered at Christmas and in the first months that followed. That such a decision had been taken without any reference to those who were responsible in the field or to senior UN mediating staff seemed to confirm that communal re-engagement was not now a target of British policy.

General Carver then told me that he had decided to terminate my service in Cyprus and to close down my patrol. He said he was doing this in light of the disappearance of Major Macey and because he considered that my life might be in danger.[4]

I tried to say that it was ludicrous to compare my position, as a mediator between the two communities strongly supported by both leaderships, with that of Macey, who was an intelligence operative working with the Turkish Cypriots and generally supposed by the Greek Cypriots to be advising TMT on the advancement of its plans for partition. I explained how critical was the point now reached in the process of communal re-engagement. I said that the job had always been assumed to entail some risk and that this I was fully prepared to accept.

None of my pleading had the slightest effect. Carver was clearly not going to reverse his decision.

Carver said that, for my safety, I was to remain in my quarters with Major Burgess and consider myself under protective arrest until he could arrange for me to be flown out of Cyprus. This instruction I disregarded, believing that Kurt Janssen was the proper source of my authority and that there were matters of greater importance than the general's view of my personal safety.

I first contacted Tassos Papadopoulos and Kutchuk, the architects of the plan for communal re-engagement, to whom I felt that I was directly answerable. Kutchuk said that he would ask for my expulsion to be reversed; Tassos Papadopoulos said he would seek a similar initiative from the President. I then spoke to Kurt Janssen, who said that technically the British Government had administrative responsibility for me but that the UN would seek for my continuation or return. He went on to suggest that I consider asking for a permanent transfer to his section of the UN Secretariat, as a professional mediator, which would place me under full and direct UN authority.

My next target was to try to locate Harald Folke, who had taken over from me the mediating responsibility for the western section of Nicosia Zone. I aimed to hand on to him the projects for which I was responsible, since he was the only man that I felt might be able to carry them forward.

Folke was a colonel in the Swedish army with an impressive record as a mediator. He had fought with a Finnish regiment first against the Russians and then against the Germans, and had subsequently become assistant to Count Bernadotte, the Swedish diplomat who acted as an intermediary between the allies and Nazi Germany in the closing stages of the 1939-45 war. In 1945, on Bernadotte's behalf, Folke had sought out Himmler and through him secured the saving from execution and release of large numbers of concentration camp inmates. More recently he had acted for the UN under Dag Hammarskjold in the Congo.

I had for him a very high respect, although I doubted that he shared my commitment to an 18-hour working day in the cause of Cyprus. Unfortunately, I learned that he was absent in Tillyria.

I next spoke to Natalie Thomas, so that she could seek intervention on my behalf from Galo Plaza. She asked if she could join me in a farewell tour that I told her I had arranged and we set off in my Land Rover, first to say goodbye to the Turkish Cypriot leaders in Louroujina and the Greek Cypriot leaders in Dhali and Potamia. From there we drove via Myrtou and Lapithos to Kyrenia, where there was an emotional parting from Sergeant Makrides and Captain Augustis.

We then continued up to St. Hilarion Castle, where the commander of the Turkish Cypriot fighters had insisted that I go for a farewell drink. We arrived to find General Carver at the castle gates, obviously irritated. He was being barred from entry by Turkish sentries who, to my somewhat embarrassment, immediately waved me forward. I was warmly embraced by the Turkish commander and led by him into the castle to share a bottle of raki. I asked, as I had all my other contacts, that he transfer his trust to Harald Folke.

Back in Nicosia, I paid my respects to Doctor Kutchuk and gave my thanks to Mr Nihat, who since the beginning of April had played a key part in my patrol as the Vice-President's emissary. Then I went on to a sad late-night party with George and Harry Fessas and their sister Vera and their mother and Tassos Papadopoulos and Nicos Sampson.

Next day I was contacted by Tasos Panayides with a message from Makarios of regret at my going. Late in the morning, Colonel Folke got back from Tillyria: I did my best to brief him on the more urgent of the projects that were under way, but time was too short for anything but a cursory explanation. In any event I doubted how much he would be able, or allowed, to resuscitate.[5] Already messages were coming in that key villages were reacting with disbelief and outrage to Carver's cancellation of the escort programme, and that barricades were going up again.

A village conference, May 1964: Colonel Harald Folke, in sunglasses, second from right of UNFICYP group and me on the left of the group.

That afternoon, on orders from UNFICYP HQ, I reported with my bags to Nicosia Airport. No one asked me where I wanted to go. I was directed to board an unmarked American C-47 transport, apparently provided by the CIA. I found that a single seat had been bolted for me in the middle of the cargo area. Seated in this I was removed from Cyprus. Two hours later I was deposited at the US Air Force base at Hellenikon, on the outskirts of Athens.

Next day, I was told from Cyprus that plans for Turkish Cypriots to move back to abandoned villages had been aborted.

60. DEBRIEFINGS. JUNE 1964

Severed from Cyprus at precisely the moment when a long-sought target had seemed to be attainable, it was some time before I could readjust my brain from the intense focus of five months of total involvement. I felt like a runner unjustifiably disqualified when leading in the last fifty yards of an Olympic marathon. People meeting me commented that I was fixated and zombie-like.

On 13 June, I met Stavros Kostopoulos, the Greek Foreign Minister in the then government of George Papandreou, at his request. He questioned me at length about my experiences of the past five months, my view of leading Cypriot figures and my assessment of the degree to which Cypriot paramilitaries and extremists were under effective control. Kostopoulos spoke as though wholly unaware of the activities in Cyprus of the Greek intelligence agency.¹

Neither of us made mention of there being major Greek forces clandestinely in Cyprus. I was to discover that most leading figures in Athens were paranoically determined to try to conceal this fact, although every detail was already well known to British and American intelligence agencies.²

Kostopoulos ended the meeting by asking that I meet and keep in touch with a John Sossidis, whom he described as a former Greek ambassador to Nicosia who now had special responsibility for advising the Greek government on Cypriot affairs.

The following day, 14 June, the British embassy in Athens learned of my whereabouts. I had meetings there with the Counsellor and the Ambassador, Sir Ralph Murray, who were both very pessimistic about the chances of any early resolution in Cyprus. Later that day I was phoned from the embassy with an urgent summons to London for a meeting with Duncan Sandys.

In signalling to London the details of my arrival the ambassador added a plea that I be given a break before returning to my duties in Malta. He wrote: "I saw Packard yesterday and have the impression that he is totally exhausted after a very demanding period of duty. I recommend that he be given time in Athens to recover. His presence here will also be useful to us for the advice he can give on Cypriot affairs."

I flew from Athens to London on 15 June. The termination of my Nicosia posting had been widely reported in the British press.*

I had become accustomed to the sun-dappled streets of Cypriot villages, with seats spilling over the sidewalks from the local coffee-house and a crowd of grizzled, moustachioed Cypriot men, fiercely flicking their worry-beads, waiting to engage me in intense political conversation. London seemed an

---

* See Appendix M for centre page in the *Guardian* of 12 June, 1964.

alien city when I arrived there, still feeling immensely weary. I reported first to the Admiralty and then went on to Duncan Sandys' office, where the depth of its carpets and the comfort of its furnishings produced in me an immediate sense of extreme somnolence.

The Minister greeted me warmly, with a generous speech in which he said he had wanted to express the government's thanks to me for my efforts in Cyprus. We talked about the realities of power in Nicosia, who was pulling what strings and what were the chances of a genuine re-engagement between the two communities. Sandys commented that I was much more knowledgeable and much more complimentary about both Makarios and Kutchuk than any of his other informants. He said that my account tallied with the picture given him by General Young, but was at total variance with the reports that had been presented by the Foreign Office and the Joint Intelligence Committee (JIC)[3] both of which were reporting that communal re-engagement was not a viable option.

I tried to say how strongly I felt that I had left unfinished a mission that was achievable and how much I wanted to get back to continue it. Sandys said that Cyril Pickard (the Commonwealth Relations Office high-flyer who at Christmas had taken over Sir Arthur Clark's job of High Commissioner in Cyprus on a temporary basis) had specially commended my efforts. General Carver, he said, had also been complimentary but felt it would be unsafe for me to continue in a mediating role.

Still shell-shocked from the manner in which I had been blasted out of Cyprus, I argued my case badly. Duncan Sandys was benignly avuncular. I left his office with the sense of dissatisfaction I once had felt at my prep school when leaving the headmaster's study after failing to convince him that I did not merit a beating.

After a couple of days in London I returned to Athens to complete my leave entitlement. There I was kept informed of developments in Cyprus by meetings at the embassy and with Greek politicians, by long discussion with Costas Kalligas, and by occasional phone-calls from Natalie Thomas and other friends in Nicosia. I continued to hope that my banishment from Cyprus would soon be ended.

I met with John Sossidis, as Kostopoulos had asked, and found him interesting but hawkish in his views. He had an encyclopaedic knowledge of Cypriot affairs, but was scathing in his comments on Greek Cypriot political leaders and their inability to keep control of their extremists.

While in Athens I received notice from Malta that the Admiralty had approved a request from Cyril Pickard for me to be seconded temporarily to the CRO.

Like General Carver, Pickard* was a man of impressive intellect and competence, with an incisive mind and a driving personality. He was viewed as the rising star of his department. Unlike Carver, he was approachable and sympathetically patient with those less talented than himself. He was despatched to Nicosia after the events of Christmas 1963, directed to deliver a

---

* See note 29/2

clear, tough line of British policy, in replacement of ambiguities engendered by Sir Arthur Clark. He had served in Nicosia for almost the same period as I had. I was not in any way answerable to the High Commission nor did I ever get drawn into the Nicosia cocktail party circuit in which it was an energetic participant, so it happened that we had never talked together while I was there.

I worked for him in London for three months and ended with a high respect for him, although his views on Cyprus, like those of John Sossidis in Athens, were initially much less tolerant and much more acerbic than my own.[4] In our early association, he gave no credit to the youth and inexperience of Greek Cypriot leaders or to the extraordinary diversity of pressures under which they had found themselves; he rejected my comparisons with the emergence of democratic governance in Britain, when administrations had been surrounded by independent-thinking barons, scheming prelates and an awakening clamour from the populace for civil rights; he declined to give much significance to the divisive thrust of TMT and of the Turkish intelligence services: so far as he was initially concerned the problems of Cyprus rested firmly on the failure of the Greek Cypriot leaders to keep their militant extremists under control. That those militants were, like TMT, in large measure being prompted by NATO intelligence agencies had not previously occurred to him.

Over the subsequent time of my knowing him his negative attitude to Makarios and other Greek Cypriot ministers was gradually transformed to a degree of real sympathy and he began in private to acknowledge the harm that Cyprus had suffered from British involvement, both before and after independence.

My appointment to his office entailed the production of an account of field mediating operations in Cyprus during my time there. To work on this, John Burgess and I holed ourselves up in a garret in Knightsbridge and used whatever notes we had kept to produce a voluminous report. I had occasional sessions with Pickard in which we would rake over events as seen from two very different viewpoints: his from the refined isolation of the High Commissioner's office in Nicosia; mine from the rough-and-tumble hotspots of conflict and of Cypriot village coffee-houses.

A typed copy of the 250-page report was delivered by me to Pickard in October and I received from him a warm and enthusiastic letter commending the work.* The report must then have been circulated to other senior members of the CRO or Foreign Office, as a number of their comments on it have been located in recently released archives. The report then disappeared.

Burgess and I were visited in our garret by gentlemen from an unidentified agency of the British government, told that the document was to be given a security classification and instructed to hand over all our copies and raw material. Cyril Pickard, who had commissioned it, told me he had handed over his copy to the Foreign Office upon the understanding it was to be printed by HMSO (the government's printing office) and then returned to him, but that

---

* See Appendix O.

he had then seen no further sign of it, despite requests for its return. The United Nations, under whose aegis I had latterly been working and for whom the study would have provided an important case history, heard about it, applied to the British government for a copy and were told that it could not be located. On a visit to the Foreign Office in 2000, I was told by the archivist for papers concerning Cyprus that records showed it had been sent to HMSO for printing in 1964 and then "lost."

The comments on the report which have survived show that I was considered by the mandarins in London to have been a dangerous loose cannon and to have exceeded what they felt should have been my authority. The general tenor of comment was that mine was an intriguing story, but that it clearly was unacceptable that I should have presumed to play a mediating role, particularly one outside any direct British governmental control.

While in London I renewed an acquaintance with Francis Noel-Baker[5] whom I had met in Nicosia and with Michael Wall, who had been the *Guardian*'s correspondent in Cyprus for most of my time there.[6] Peter Preston, later to be Managing Editor of the Guardian Group, took over in Cyprus from Wall and he too was to become a staunch friend. These friendships evolved into an informal alliance, between Michael Wall, Francis Noel-Baker and myself, which aimed to provide a channel through which valid Cypriot views could reach key figures in London.

Leading Greek commentator on Cyprus. Costas Kalligas. President Makarios told him that proposals for constitutional change were fully supported by the UK.

Leading British commentator, Peter Preston was correspondent for the *Guardian* in Cyprus in Spring 1964. Subsequent managing editor of the Guardian Group

In November, I returned to Athens to take some further leave that was due to me. John Sossidis told me that the Greek government was growing increasingly impatient with Makarios: despite the support that they were offering him he still was failing to impose adequate authority on Greek Cypriot extremists, so that a constant danger remained that inter-communal incidents in Cyprus would entangle Greece and Turkey in a major confrontation, from which Greece would be likely to emerge the loser. At the same time Athens felt uncomfortable with Makarios' links with the left and with his attempts to obtain leverage from the Soviet Union and the Non-Aligned group of nations.

When I was due to return to my duties in Malta I arranged to fly commercially to Cyprus and from there take a free seat in an RAF transport flight from Akrotiri to Luqa. This arrangement had been authorised by the CRO and was the cheapest route available.

I then contacted Tassos Papadopoulos. I told him that I would be in Cyprus for one night and that it would be a pleasure to have a drink with him and other old friends if that was convenient. Papadopoulos asked that I be his guest for the evening and suggested that I stay at his home for the night, rather than use accommodation at Akrotiri. He also told me that Makarios had said he very much wanted to see me. He said that he would check whether a meeting could be fitted into the President's schedule.

Before I could depart from Athens, I was approached by two proverbial spooks from the British embassy. My memory has it that they wore identical belted raincoats. I was told by them that I had been declared persona non grata in Cyprus.

Two explanations for this message later reached me. The British claimed that the edict came from the Cyprus government and was due to my having tried to force myself on Tassos Papadopoulos for the evening of the proposed visit, an action which they said had caused grave embarrassment to all concerned. This allegation was later repeated in a communication to my admiral in Malta, giving me an opportunity to inform the British authorities that the story they were circulating was wholly false and an unwarranted slander.

The story from Tassos Papadopoulos, confirmed later in writing, was somewhat different. He said that when Makarios was told of the fleeting visit, he said that he definitely wished to see me. He told his secretary to cancel any previous engagements, which happened to include his attendance at a reception being given by the British High Commission. Papadopoulos said he was asked by a UN officer why the President would not after all be at the reception and inadvertently mentioned my visit. In his words this news, when delivered to the High Commission, "caused all hell to break loose."

Unaware of this arcane background and assuming, from what I had been told by the British spooks in Athens, that I had inadvertently offended Greek Cypriots whom I held in high regard, I despatched to Papadopoulos a letter of apology. He replied that far from having taken any offence Makarios in fact had had in mind to name a street in Nicosia after me.

The degree to which British officialdom in Cyprus was determined to keep me distanced from the island's affairs was underlined after I returned to my staff job in Malta. To help me present to C-in-C Mediterranean (Admiral Sir John Hamilton) the weekly report on Cypriot affairs that was expected of me, my office asked the High Commission in Nicosia if it could be sent on a regular basis its standard digest of Cypriot press reports. This request was refused on the grounds that the British authorities in Cyprus did not consider that Lieutenant Commander Packard should be given this assistance.*

---

* I arranged for a copy of the digest to be sent from London instead.

Tassos Papadopoulos came to Athens to meet me. First he wanted to be certain that I was assured that the debacle of my attempted visit to Nicosia was not of Cypriot making. The President, he said, wanted me to know that I would always be welcome in Cyprus, however much the British might declare me to be persona non grata there. The President had commented that, if necessary, he could always arrange to have me smuggled into the island.

Then he talked about the current situation. As always, he was vigorously optimistic. Despite all the setbacks and difficulties he was confident that the Greek Cypriot cause would in the end prevail. He believed that the tide of world politics had turned inexorably towards the right of former colonies to achieve genuine self-determination, and that an overwhelming wish for it of the Greek Cypriot population made certain that *enosis* would eventually become possible. He added: "But will we still want it when it's on offer? I and everyone else will have to decide then whether we'd rather be little fish in someone else's big pond or big fish in our own little pond." He suggested that the romance of the struggle had been more alluring than the outcome might be.

Papadopoulos said: "We shot ourselves in the foot by letting the Turkish Cypriots provoke us into a violent confrontation. It needn't have been so, but now our future is going to hang on how the wind blows in Ankara. We should have realised from the beginning that we needed to keep the trust of the majority of the Turkish Cypriots. We should have been patient. Even Makarios kept running behind events rather than controlling them."

He went on to say how much the present situation was complicated by misrepresentation. Ankara and London and Washington all wanted to see Cyprus under NATO control and Athens, whatever it was saying in public, now went along with that view. They all claimed that the Makarios government was unable to control Greek Cypriot extremists and ignored the fact that the motivating of those extremists came almost entirely from foreign intelligence services. Ankara, Athens, London and Washington all wanted to work out a future for the Cypriots, as they had tried to do before, without Cypriots taking part in the discussion.

The President was particularly worried, he said, that since my departure there had been no route through which a sympathetic, or realistic, picture could be delivered to London. Official Cypriot representatives tried to do so, but their views were sidelined or given no serious consideration. Makarios saw the British High Commission as deeply biased and had not the slightest confidence that it would convey a balanced picture. Papadopoulos ended with a query. Makarios wanted to know whether I could help to provide a back-channel to London through which his real views could be injected into the governmental debate there. If so he would arrange for me to receive a regular confidential briefing.

I said that I could try to help informally through the links with Michael Wall and Francis Noel-Baker, but that those would only lead into political and media circles. For something more formal I would need to get clearance from my boss in Malta, Admiral Hamilton, and from the Royal Navy representative on the JIC, Ken Farnhill, who formerly had had my job in Malta and now was Chief of Naval Intelligence. If they both accepted the logic of the approach there was no reason that a regular analysis of Cypriot affairs should not be sent to London by Hamilton, along with other special reports on Mediterranean affairs originated by the admiral's staff, and placed by Farnhill onto the JIC agenda. Since the JIC was the ultimate co-ordinator of analysis and option-papers for the British government, any paper or views transmitted by it would at least receive ministerial attention.

To both John Hamilton and Ken Farnhill I said that, as they well knew, I had an exceptional range of senior governmental contacts in Greece and Cyprus: at the same time my job in Malta involved the reading of confidential British government reporting from Athens and Nicosia, much of which I believed to present a biased, establishmentarian view that ignored the realities. It seemed to me that in consequence British interests were being damaged and the residue of deep affection and respect in which Britain had been held in the eastern Mediterranean was being lost, without any parallel advantage.

I suggested that options were being ignored that could lead to the preservation of a unitary Cyprus in a format that would be acceptable to Ankara and that simultaneously would enhance British status in the area. I thought that Britain had been led by Washington into the playing of a subversive covert agenda when an overt ethical policy was available that could pay much greater dividends. I said that at the very least there surely was nothing to be lost by putting up alternative viewpoints for policy-makers to scrutinise.

John Hamilton and Ken Farnhill both agreed. I received a critique from Tassos Papadopoulos and submitted my first report. Almost instantly, as I was informed by Ken Farnhill, there was an explosion of wrath from the Foreign Office. Apparently it was wholly unacceptable to them that views in contradiction to their own should be put on the table. Farnhill told me that, to his regret, it would be impossible to get any analysis originated by me onto the record in London. He asked me to continue to keep him privately and personally informed and said he would do his best to exert informal influence.[7]

Before leaving Athens in December 1964 I had another long session with John Sossidis on the 6th. At the end of that meeting, to be sure that I had properly understood him, I wrote down the key points that he had made to me, read them back to him and received his verification that they were accurate.

The gist of the message, which Sossidis said came directly from the prime minister, George Papandreou, was that the Greek government continued to believe that Makarios was failing to keep control of extremist elements and that in consequence he was putting Greek national interests at risk; that it therefore was necessary that Makarios be removed from power; that the Greek government now had over twelve thousand troops in Cyprus and believed that it could execute a *coup* without difficulty and thereafter control the course of events; and that it had 'indications' that a suitable deal could then be done with the Turkish government.

Sossidis said that the Greek government already had a green light from Washington for the ousting of Makarios; to proceed, it now needed to receive a similar secret confirmation of approval from the British government, and it would not act without that approval. However, he said, it was not felt appropriate to handle this through normal diplomatic channels. He was therefore asking me to establish a reliable private conduit to London.

This was not a role that I had any wish to play, but nor did I wish to lose the confidences of Sossidis. I suggested that Noel-Baker would be the best man to handle it and passed on to him an account of the conversation: in doing so I took it that the Labour Party would be highly unlikely to support a *coup* attempt against Makarios. I also provided Ken Farnhill with a summary of the proposal, as an indication of what was brewing behind the scenes.

Shortly after this, I was told by Admiral Hamilton that the Foreign Office was again complaining vociferously about my continuing involvement in political affairs. He suggested, paternally, that if I was to stay in the Navy, I must cease to play any role that aggravated the Foreign Office, although he said he was happy that I continue to keep him and Ken Farnhill informed of my views.

I took it as likely that the Foreign Office's knowledge that I was aware of the Sossidis proposal would kill it dead for them.

From early 1965, therefore, I was removed from the loop. I told Tassos Papadopoulos, with regret, that there probably was no further help that I could usefully give.

Nicos Sampson flew to Athens and sought out my wife, who was a trainee psychologist. He quickly was confiding in her as though she were his analyst. He took her all through his earlier life and repeated to her the stories about how, as a youth, he had committed himself to the cause of *enosis*. He then told her that he had for a long time recognised in himself the weakness that he needed invariably to lean on someone else. He said that since he had known me in Cyprus he had seen me as a friend on whom he could depend for sensible advice. Now that I was gone he was having again to find his support from Greek officers whose motives and character he now distrusted, but without whose encouragement he found himself 'immobilised'. He told her, as an example, that they had persuaded him to be involved with them in forging documents with which they aimed to undermine George Papandreou.[8] My wife thought that he was profoundly insecure. She counselled him to break with the plotting and to try to act honourably, so that his conscience was clear. Echoing an earlier comment to me, he said: "If I had had friends like you and Martin in the past, the history of Cyprus would have been different."

I continued to write my regular analysis for Admiral Hamilton, none of my friendships faltered, and the pain of separation from Cyprus gradually faded.

Sait Sepici, the Turkish army major who had been such a tower of strength in the tripartite mediating process, wrote to me very movingly to say that the assignment had been the high-point of his life, an extraordinary opportunity to be engaged in an undertaking that he had seen to be committed wholly to justice and human good.

Encouraged by Natalie Thomas and Kurt Janssen, I let the Admiralty know that I was interested to seek a permanent transfer to the United Nations staff in New York, and the Admiralty, probably keen to be rid of my upsetting of the Foreign Office, accepted this approach with equanimity and appointed me to a university course in Arabic, which language the UN had suggested would be useful to them.

In the meantime, from visits to Athens and from the comments of friends there and of Tassos Papadopoulos, I had become increasingly concerned at the gathering storm-clouds in Greece and at the conviction that a military seizure of power was being prepared with the blessing of the American intelligence community. The scenario appeared to be interwoven with NATO concerns over Cyprus. I began quietly and privately to lobby for an awareness that a US-supported military dictatorship in Greece could prove a catastrophe for the eastern wing of NATO, rather than provide the advantages that other analysts were suggesting. For the years to come, the focus of my commitment shifted towards Greece.

61.   AFTERTHOUGHTS

"We have no eternal allies and we have no perpetual enemies. Our interests
are eternal and perpetual, and those interests it is our duty to follow."
Lord Palmerston: 1 March 1848

"British imperialism has been second to none in projecting itself as benign,
wise and essentially truthful. That the opposite is true may shock some people."
Mark Curtis: 'Web of Deceit'

In 1994 Mark Higson, a senior desk officer at the Foreign Office during the
1980s, was asked at a public enquiry to comment on his former service: he
described Britain's foreign policy establishment as "a culture of lying".
Whether or not this comment has general validity, my experience suggests
that it certainly did apply in the case of Cyprus. In all of my association with
Cypriot affairs since 1964 I have come up against the promulgation from
London of a picture that is deeply at odds with the facts as I knew them. The
demonisation of President Makarios, and of other later Cypriot leaders who
failed to find favour in Whitehall, was one symptom of this: another was the
repeated espousing of measures that were essentially divisive, while claiming
a benign interest in the promotion of communal unity.

In the 1950s and early 1960s British intelligence assessments were that
Volkan, or later TMT, presented a greater threat to Cypriot internal security
than did EOKA. And yet *Volkan* and TMT were cultivated as allies by the
British intelligence services. Similarly, extremists in both Cypriot
communities were cultivated, and covertly armed, by UK/US agencies as allies
against the left.

The pursuit by foreigners of their supposed national interests has
bedevilled Cyprus, a small country made important by its geographic position
and made intensely vulnerable to foreign manipulation by the make-up of its
population.

Sadly, there is nothing in my experience to contradict a contention that
Britain, the supposed bastion of democratic principle, has been a consistent
betrayer of that principle in Cyprus, provoking ethnic separatism, sabotaging
inter-communal re-engagement and tolerating, or encouraging, Turkish
intervention when it was contended that those policies would provide
advantage in the retention of British bases and regional influence. In the mid-
1950s a genuine independence was seen by the Foreign Office as the worst of
all possible options for Cyprus. The idea of a potential British support for

partition may first have been suggested at that time by the Foreign Office in order to frighten the Greek Cypriots, but it was a genie that could not afterwards be easily re-bottled. Britain urged on NATO and the US the view that their interests would be threatened if Cyprus were left to the governance of the Cypriots.

Over the course of the last fifty years, foreigners have jockeyed the country progressively closer to partition, with local extremism the ally in this process.

Cyprus has many genuine friends in Britain. Those British policies that proved so destructive to Cyprus were not the will of parliament. Sir Anthony Eden, Sir Alec Douglas Home and others may have believed that partition was the proper answer for the island, but this was never translated into official policy. Rather, those in the Foreign Office and the intelligence services who believed in the continuance of an imperial role for Britain in the eastern Mediterranean and those who gave pre-eminence to relations with Turkey prevailed over those who believed that an ethical policy in the region would in the end pay greater dividends.

The clash in 1963/4 between the thinking in London of the Foreign Office and the CRO was symptomatic of this division. So, too, was the fate of Sir Arthur Clark, whose belief in the necessity for constitutional reform and efforts to help that be achieved ran foul of Foreign Office strategies.

Sir Arthur Clark and General Young were both sympathetic to the need for the Turkish Cypriots to be provided with real security and for Cyprus to achieve a workable constitution. They appreciated that for this to be achieved the island would need shielding against foreign interference and that political leadership would need help in bringing armed extremism in both communities under control. In his conversations with me, General Young, perhaps naively, never suggested an awareness that such a view ran counter to Foreign Office policy. He thought that British support for effective mediation, and impetus towards regional convergence, would make an equitable solution achievable and would eventually deliver major benefit to Turkey. He believed that competent British diplomacy could have facilitated an appropriate adjustment of the constitution and that the minor population movements needed to reduce inter-communal friction could have been achieved quietly and unobtrusively. But no consensus towards this route ever emerged in London. The opportunity was finally closed down when General Carver dismantled key elements of the mechanism through which re-engagement was being carried forward. In 'The Cyprus Conspiracy', by Brendan O' Malley and Ian Craig, it is claimed that this was done because of fears in Ankara that the success of the re-engagement initiative was threatening the Turkish push for partition.

Cyril Pickard arrived in Cyprus with a 'Foreign Office stance' on the island's affairs and, by his own admission to me, a bias against the Greek Cypriots. His views underwent a sea change over the course of the years that I knew him. It presumably was in recognition of our having reached a mutuality of view that he directed, just before he died, that his private 1964 correspondence with Duncan Sandy's should be delivered to me.

The correspondence confirmed that Pickard had received from Georgadjis the same gruesome story about a massacre of Turkish Cypriots in Nicosia

General Hospital, a story that I had later come to see as a pivotal piece of disinformation designed to provoke communal separation. That, and other horror stories which now appear to have been deliberate distortions, had helped convince George Ball that a 'NATO solution' ought to be imposed on Cyprus.

The correspondence between Pickard and Sandys acknowledged how serious were the implications of Arthur Clark's involvement with efforts to amend the constitution. It was agreed that the British government must deny any responsibility. It suggested that it might be necessary, if Nicosia was found to have evidence of the part played by Clark, to say that illness had led to his mental impairment.

My experiences, and what I learned from the key players of the 1964 period, have direct bearing on questions that are central to all of modern Cypriot history. They chime with an interlocking series of contentions: that core elements of State Department and Foreign Office thinking were that a genuine independence in Cyprus would be inimical to US and British interests and that US/UK relationships with Turkey took precedence over other regional considerations; that NATO policy-makers, similarly persuaded, considered that the strength of the left in Cyprus and the leaning of Makarios towards non-aligned policies justified the imposition of external controls on the island's governance; that the tentacles of NATO's 'Stay-behind' organisation, with elements of the extreme right covertly armed in opposition to the left, provided a ready mechanism for the exercise of manipulation; that the encouragement by Britain of Turkey's involvement in Cypriot affairs allowed the Turkish army to develop a determination to be a decider of the island's future; that TMT, established to project the Turkish army's power into Cyprus and a constant proponent of partition, was a committed underminer of inter-communal cohesion; that Greek determination on *enosis* and Turkish opposition to it provided a ready material for conflagration; that the failure of Greek Cypriot police forces in December 1963 and early 1964 to apply their efforts primarily to a defence of legality and human rights handed the initiative to separatist extremists; that the passions of extremists in Cyprus and Turkey and Greece made them blind to the damage that was being inflicted on their own national interests; and that Britain made no serious effort to shield Cyprus against subversion or to create a genuine inter-communal unity.

Watching the imposition in Greece of a right wing military dictatorship, the Greek *coup d'etat* against Makarios, the Turkish invasion that followed, and the various outsider efforts to engineer a compromise between British and Turkish strategic objectives on one side and Cypriot democratic rights on the other, my sympathy for the Cypriots has steadily increased. Turkish Cypriots and Greek Cypriots alike continue to pay the price of foreigners' ambitions.

A country in which concepts of separate communality had been encouraged by foreigners over many years, specifically formulated in the municipalities proposals, and then taken forward in a divisive, externally-constructed, constitution, found itself faced in 1963 with an appalling dilemma, when each community realised that it was threatened by armed parastatal conspiracy sponsored from abroad. Within each community the agenda was dictated by tough, foreign-linked extremists rather than by democratic process. A resolution to this should have been found through pro-active mediation, but the British antipathy for independence in Cyprus meant that none was available. Instead there was NATO involvement with the conspirators.

All of my experience in Cyprus showed that Greek Cypriots and Turkish Cypriots could work out effective solutions when provided with an appropriate mechanism through which to do so and with an accurate appraisal of the problems that confronted them. That was so in the numerous local disputes to which the tripartite mediating process was applied. It could have worked equally if the process had been extended to the roots of inter-communal misunderstanding. In each respect, the crucial factor was that the mediating process must be answerable to communal leaderships rather than to an outside power. Such a concept was hardly likely to be attractive to Washington or London or Ankara. The comment by Mark Curtis (in 'Web of Deceit') that 'British and US policy generally rejects action genuinely based on multi-lateral legal and ethical standards to cover all nations equally', would here seem particularly apposite.

Ultimately, everyone has lost from Britain's pursuit of its own narrow interests in Cyprus and its encouragement of Turkish involvement there. Cyprus has been a prime cause for regional division, when it might have been a catalyst for convergence between Turkey and Greece, with vast economic and social benefit for both countries and for all Cypriots. The EU could have inherited a cohesive association of eastern Mediterranean states. Turkey could have found its route towards EU accession less littered with impediments.

A genuine independence for Cyprus, within a formula that provided real protection for each community against extremism, that satisfied Turkey's valid strategic concerns and that left London with a staunch regional ally, could have been achieved. Britain should have taken a lead towards that end but signally failed to do so.

This book has described a mediating process that was palpably successful in proving the ability of Cypriots to resolve their own problems.

That the process was prevented from realising its potential redounds to the deep discredit of those who were unwilling to tolerate Cypriot independence.

*   *   *

There was a day in February 1964 when I struggled for some hours to bring to an end a sharp burst of fighting in Tillyria. After a ceasefire was achieved, my Greek and Turkish officers went ahead by Land Rover for a coffee in the nearest Greek Cypriot village. I said that I would come on foot to join them and that I would be an hour or so getting there. It was a very tranquil evening, with clear skies and slight traces of mist in the valleys.

I was crossing an area of open pastureland, ruminating on the fact that such likeable people in such an idyllic setting should be struggling against each other for the sake of artificial, imported passions, when there was a burst of Sten gun fire and I heard some bullets skittering past me.

I retreated to the edge of the field and took a circuitous route through a grove of olive trees towards the source of the shooting. There, standing benignly under a carob tree, I found an elderly Greek Cypriot priest, white-bearded, his cassock fading and tattered at the edges. I greeted him with the usual formalised exchange of Greek pleasantries and he told me that he was well in health and that things were going fine.

I said: "Have you perhaps seen anyone around here with a gun? Somebody was shooting at me."

He replied: "I'm very sorry to hear that. I haven't seen anyone else here."

I took him by the arm and asked him to walk with me to the village so that we could talk and have a coffee together. After one awkward pace a Sten gun fell from under his cassock.

I said: "Why were you shooting at me, father?"

He said: "I'm very sorry, my child. I thought you were the barbarians. Unfortunately my eyesight isn't so good these days."

"But why should you want to shoot at the Turkish Cypriots, who are your neighbours?"

He seemed shocked. "I wasn't shooting at my neighbours. I should be very unhappy to think it was them. I thought they were foreigners. The Turks in the villages here are good people."

We walked together companionably to the village, chatting about the beauties of Tillyria and about world events. He was continually amazed that I could speak his language and that I knew Greece so well. He carried the Sten gun as though it was an umbrella, and I was happy when he deposited it in the first house we came to.

At the coffee-shop we joined Major Sepici and Captain Michos. They had collected the Turkish Cypriot *hodja* and *mukhtar* from Ayios Theodhoros, to seal the ceasefire, and the four of them were sitting smoking and drinking coffee with the village's Greek Cypriot *mukhtar*.

Wine and *mezzedes* were delivered to us regularly. Argument about who should pay was settled when the owner of the coffee-house refused to accept money from any of us. There was a great sense of friendship between us all, and a common feeling of how beautiful was the place, looking out across Kato Pyrgos to the sea and beyond to the distant hilltops of Anatolia, and that it was a privilege to be together on such an evening.

At one point the *hodja* said: "This has always been my home. All my history is here. My neighbours are good people. I don't understand what the politicians are shouting about."

I told them, in a kindly way, the story of the priest shooting at me and the reason he had given. The *hodja* leant across and patted the priest on the hand. "Papa Antoni", he said, "for so many months we've been telling you to get new glasses."

LIST OF ACRONYMS

COMEDSOUEAST	Commander, Mediterranean, South East
CRO	Commonwealth Relations Office
CYTA	Cyprus Telecommunication Authority
EAM	Left & Centre Greek resistance against German occupation
EDES	Right-wing & royalist resistance against German occupation.
ELDYK	Greek Contingent
EOKA	National Organisation of Cypriot Fighters
EU	European Union
FCO	Foreign and Commonwealth Office
GSO	General Staff Officer
HQ	Head Quarters
KKE	Communist Party Greece
KYP (Cyprus)	Cyprus Intelligence Service
KYP (Greece)	Central Intelligence Service (Greece)
LMG	Light Machine Gun
JF	Joint Force
JIC	Joint Intelligence Committee
JLC	Joint Liaison Committee
JPO	Joint Patrol Organisation
MI	Military Intelligence
MILO	Military Intelligence Liaison Officer
NATO	North Atlantic Treaty Organisation
RHA	Royal Horseguards Artillery
SBA	Sovereign Base Area
SWD	Special Warfare Department
TMT	Turkish Resistance Organisation
TPO	Tripartite Patrol Organisation
TURDYK	Turkish Contingent
UN	United Nations
UNFICYP	United Nations Forces in Cyprus
YKSP	Finnish Contingent

APPENDICES

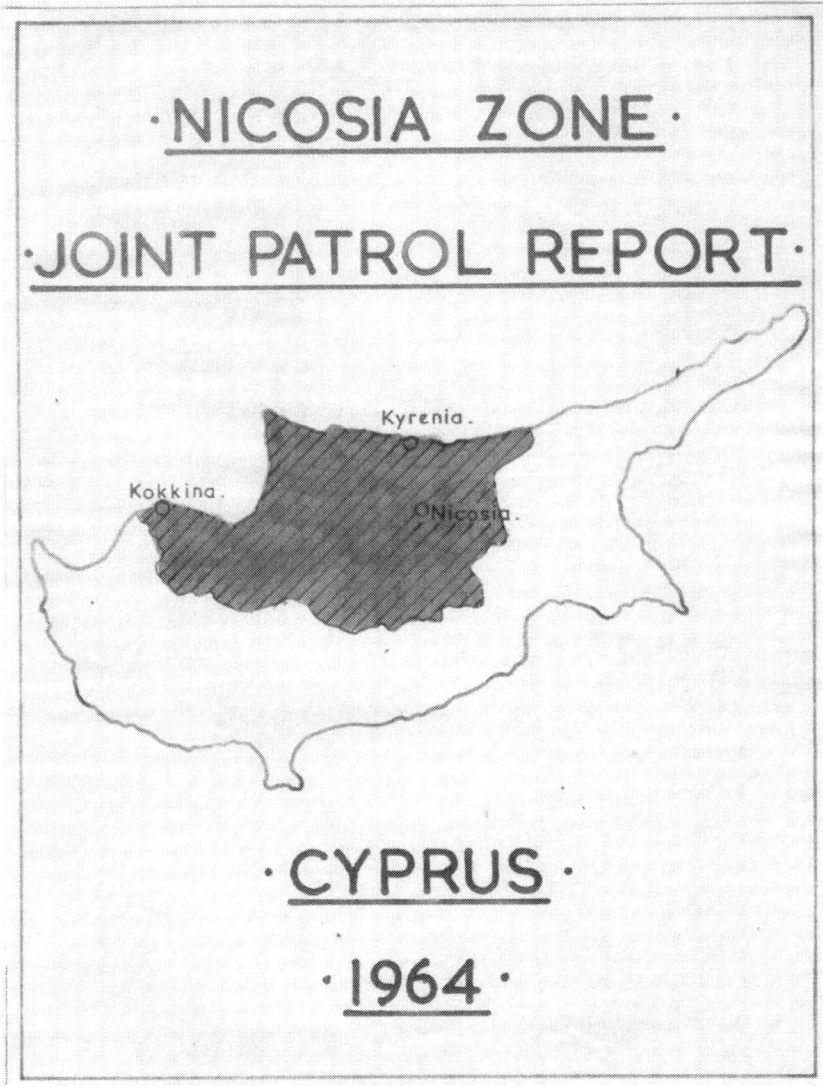

Cover for the Joint Patrol report which was delivered by Cyril Pickard to the Foreign Office in late 1964 and then described as 'lost'.

APPENDIX A

Green Line Agreement

1. At a time to be fixed by the Joint Force Commander (General Young) all such Greek Cypriot and Turkish Cypriot posts in the vicinity of the green line from point X to point Y as he may designate shall be evacuated; and he will occupy such evacuated posts as he may consider necessary (subject to the provisions of paragraphs 3 and 4 below).

2. At the same time as the action described in paragraph 1 above all Greek and Turkish posts in the vicinity of the green line between point Y and point Z, which may be designated by the Force Commander, will be evacuated.

3. Before the posts on either side of the green line between points A and B are evacuated, the Force Commander will set up such posts as he may consider necessary with the object of creating conditions of security in the blue shaded area (BYCA) to enable the population to return to their homes. As soon as this action has been taken by the Force Commander, all Greek and Turkish posts in the vicinity of the green line between points A and B which may be designated by the Force Commander will be evacuated.

4. For the avoidance of doubt, the positions to be occupied by the Force Commander will include the flour mill, the cold storage plant, the Roccas bastion and the CYTA building; and the positions to be evacuated but not occupied, will include the Mula, Barbaro and Loredano bastions.

5. As soon as the Force Commander begins to take over Greek and Turkish posts he will be entitled, in so far as he considers it necessary, to send patrols at any time without further consultation anywhere in Nicosia and the surrounding area.

Dated 28 December 1963, this is the original text taken from the archives of General Young.

APPENDIX A (ADDENDUM) GREEN LINE, NICOSIA

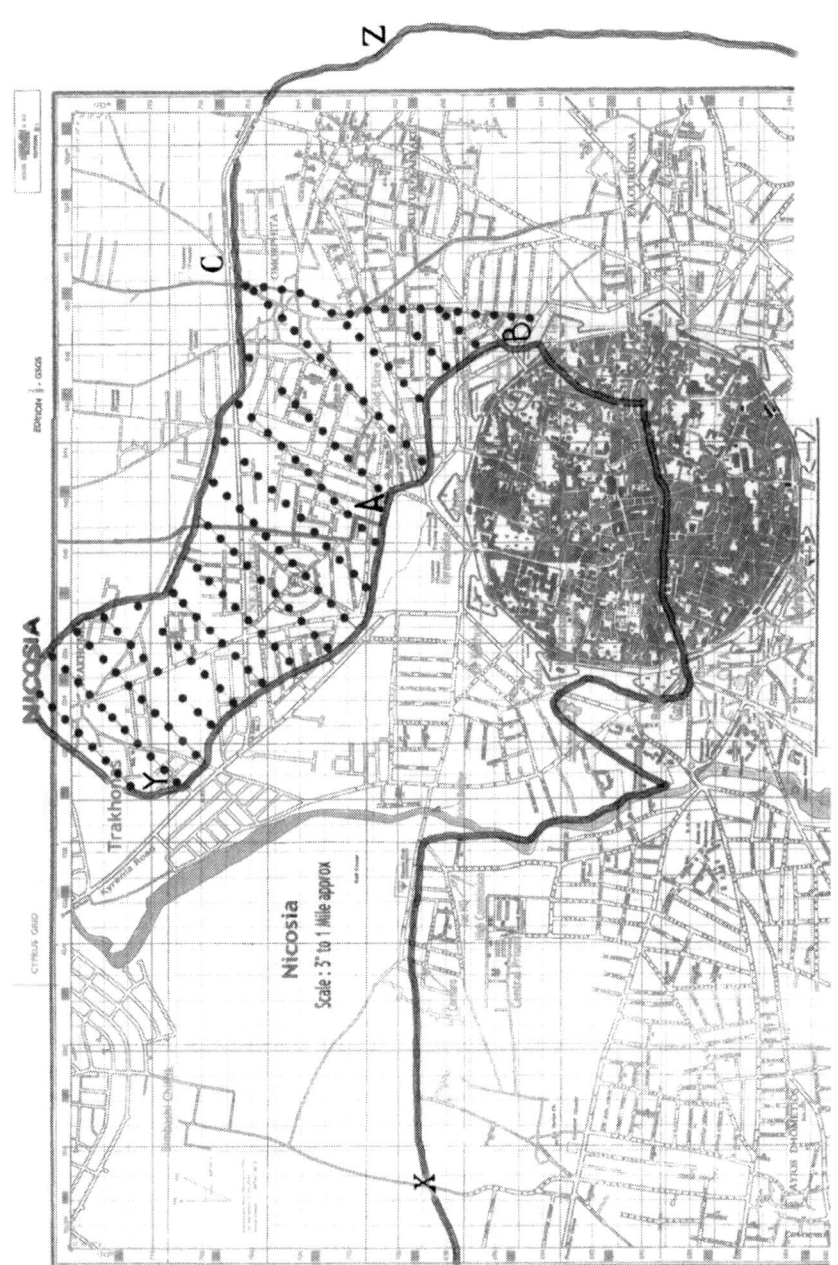

The Green Line, as defined in the agreement of 28 December 1964, with blue shaded area marked out in dots.

ＡＰＰＥＮＤＩＸ Ｂ

Arrangements between Cypriot Police and British Troops

<u>Relationship between Cypriot Police
and British Troops</u>

1. The following agreement has been made with the Greek Cypriot side:

    a. Only Police will search and arrest. All such action will be under military supervision to ensure impartiality and fairness,

    b. If troops wish to arrest and search, they will request the police to carry this out under military supervision.

    c. If the military commander has any complaints against a policeman, he will charge him in writing to the Station Superintendant. If satisfactory action is not taken , refer the matter to this HQ.

    d. The closest liaison to ensure impartiality and fairness is to be maintained between local Military Commanders and Police Superintendants

2 It is most important that this agreement is faithfully observed on the British side throughout the island.

3. There there are properly constituted uniformed Turkish Police and Gendarmerie we will work in the same way with them.

This agreement between JF and the police was reached with difficulty on 7 January 1964. That it was quickly disregarded by the Greek Cypriots was symptomatic of the deterioration in relations between them and British forces.

Ayios Sozomenos Poem

CYPRUS HEROES   Ayios Sozomenos: Feb 1964.

Ask why Ali Huseyn died.
(He was hit by seventeen sten-gun bullets
And the eleventh mixed his one good eye with his brain.)
He was sixty-eight and had been used to sit in the sunlight
And he died in pain.

Ali Huseyn died defending his village
With an unpronounceable name, with a shotgun,
Against a company-strength assault
Nor did he learn by what error this battle started
Or whose the fault.

Ali Huseyn was sixty-eight and was hit
By seventeen sten-gun bullets and never did fire
His shotgun. And the battle was a mistake
Though this was the sort of inevitable error that
Leaders sometimes make.

Ali Huseyn lies on the floor of the mosque
Twisted into a grotesque shape to accentuate
His sixty-eighth year's dying and his eyeless head.
And his propaganda value has become considerable
Being thus dead.

Ali Huseyn, dead, has his picture
On the front page of Halkin Sesi
And is now well-known, although not by name:
From the mess he is in, from his years, from the way of his dying
Finding fame.

           + + + + + + + + + + + +

Andros Cotsellis is considered a hero
Having shot one Huseyn, who was a rebel,
During the course of his company's attack
Kicked open the door like in a Western and shot a rebel
In the back.

Andros Cotsellis was sick afterwards
Not having killed before, but just for a moment:
Now he is well enough to receive his proper acclaim.
He will go into the new history books, heroically,
By name.

Andros Cotsellis is sixteen and fights for his people,
For a dream, for a way of life that is threatened
And because rebellion cannot be tolerated. What's more
He is now a hero and likes this better than the quiet life he led
Before.

See chapter 28 for the fighting at Ayios Sozomenos on 8 February 1964. This poem was
written by me a few days later.

The Organisation

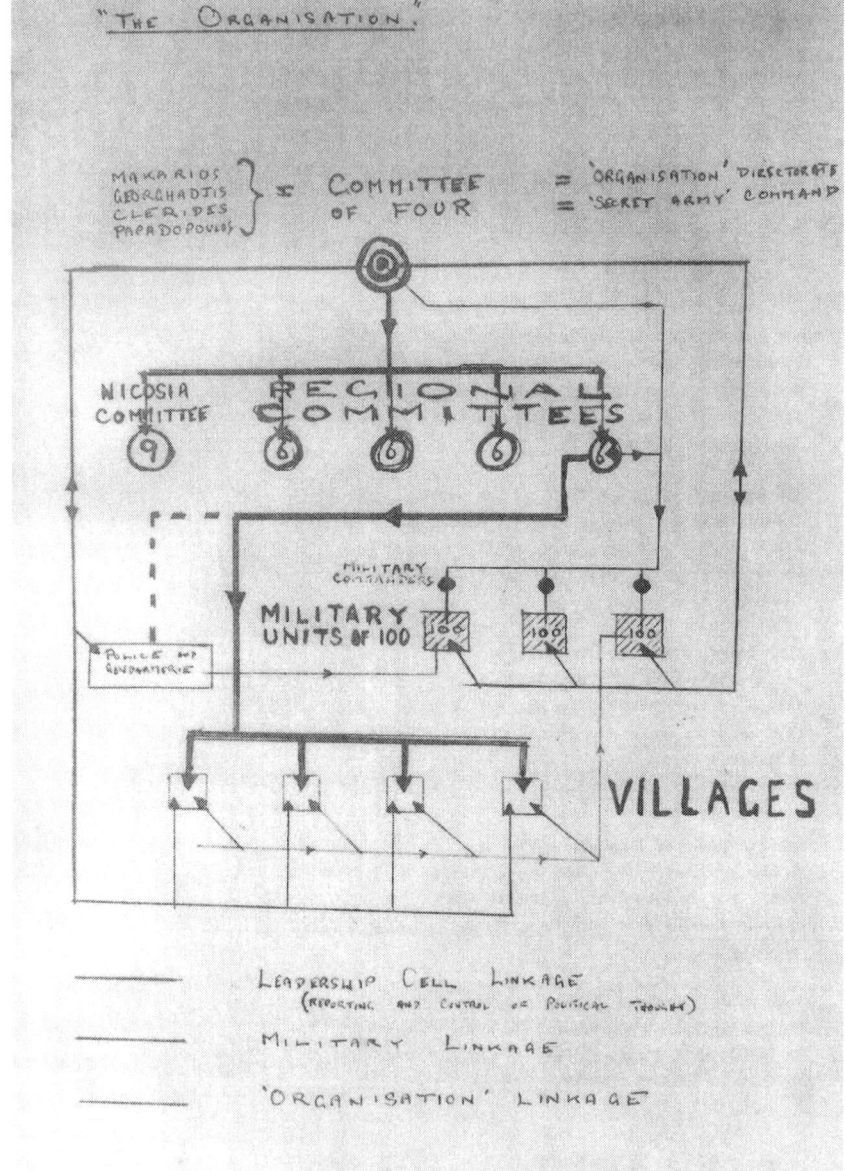

This is the schematic drawn by me immediately after a meeting with Organisation leaders in February 1964, precisely representing details that they gave me.

Tillyria Cease Fire Agreement

These were the terms of the Tillyria agreement as accepted by local paramilitary commanders on 5 April, and noted by me on the back of an envelope, before I took them to Nicosia for ratification by communal leaders there.

Passe-Partout

ΥΠΟΥΡΓΕΙΟΝ ΕΣΩΤΕΡΙΚΩΝ
ΓΡΑΦΕΙΟΝ ΥΠΟΥΡΓΟΥ

"Ἅπαντα τά μέλη τῆς Ἀστυνομίας, τῆς Χωροφυλακῆς, τῆς Ἐθνικῆς Φρουρᾶς, τοῦ Στρατοῦ ἐντέλλονται διά τοῦ παρόντος ὅπως ἐπιτρέπουν τήν ἐλευθέραν καί ἀπρόσκοπτον διέλευσιν καί ἐπικοινωνίαν τοῦ κ. Δ. Νιχάτ, ὑπαλλήλου τῆς Ἐπαρχιακῆς Διοικήσεως Λευκωσίας, εἰς ὅλα καί ἀπό ὅλα τά χωριά, κωμοπόλεις καί πόλεις τῆς Ἐπαρχίας Λευκωσίας διασφαλιζομένης τῆς ἐλευθέρας κινήσεως τούτου ἄνευ συλλήψεως, κρατήσεως, ἐρεύνης ἤ ἀνακρίσεως ἤ περιορισμοῦ τῶν κινήσεων τούτου καθ'οἱονδήποτε τρόπον διά περίοδον δύο μηνῶν ἀπό τῆς 12/4/1964.

Αἱ ὡς ἄνω διευθετήσεις εἶναι ἀναγκαῖαι διά τήν ἐπίσκευσιν τῆς ἐκτελέσεως διαφόρων χωριτικῶν ἔργων καί ἄλλων ἔργων κοινοτικῆς ἀναπτύξεως.

(Πολύκαρπος Γεωργάτζης)
'Υπουργός Ἐσωτερικῶν.

Λευκωσία
Τῇ 11η. Ἀπριλίου, 1964.

Ministry of Interior Affairs
Office of the Minister

    All members of the Police, the Gendarmerie, the National Guard, the Army are ordered at this presentation to allow for the free and smooth passage and crossing of Mr. D. Nihat, employee of Nicosia District Administration, to all and from all the villages, townships and towns of Nicosia District securing his freedom of movement without arrest, detention, search or interrogation or limit to his movements by any means for the period of two months from 12/4/1964.

    The above arrangement is necessary for the prompt execution of various district works and other community development works.

(Polycarpos Georgadjis)
Minister of Interior.

Nicosia
11 April 1964

Re-Engagement Process

From Commander Packard

1. Vaccniation: possible arrangements for the team (list already given) to visit villages and carry out the job.

2. Public assistance to villages as well as old age pension. Enquiries from the Ministry of Labour for outstanding payments.

3. Road safety for the villages to travel to and from Nicosia to their villages safely.

This reminder addressed by me in early May 1964 to GSO 2 (OPS), HQ Nicosia Zone, provides an example of the process by which bi-communal administrative arrangements were being quietly restored to Turkish Cypriots in the rural areas. Approved arrangements were executed by the JPO on behalf of Tassos Papadopoulos and Faisal Kutchuk, within the general framework of an island-wide re-engagement process.

Crop Protection Memo. 12 May 1964

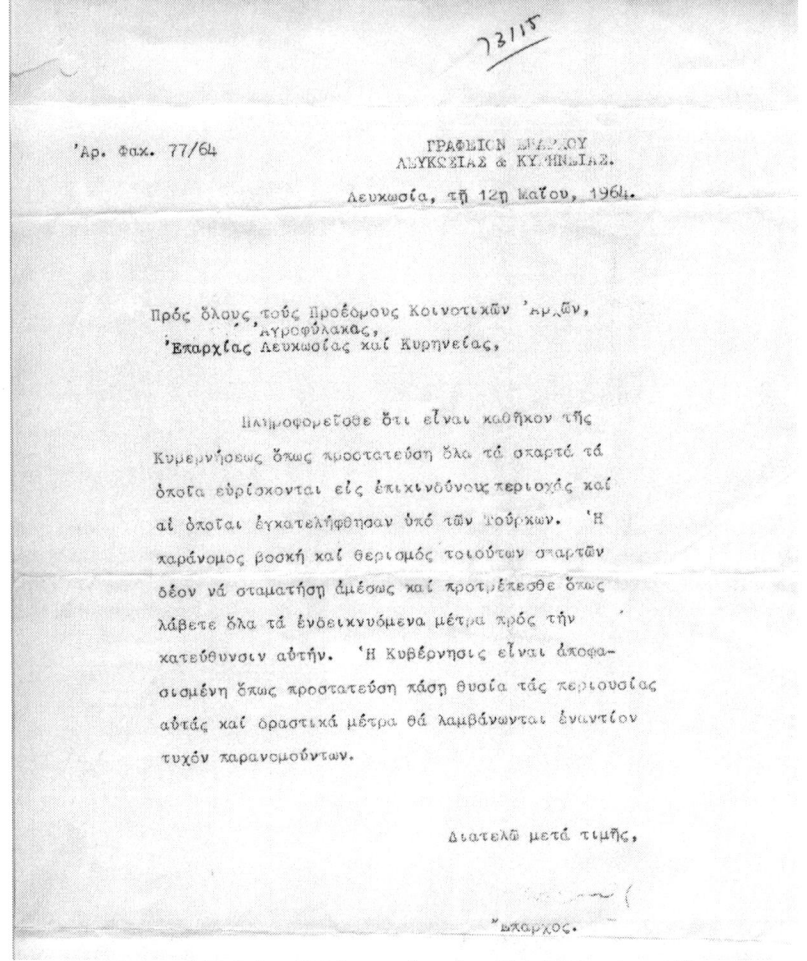

Fax no: 77/64 dated 12 May 1964 sent by the Chief District Officer from the Office of the Administrator of Nicosia and Kyrenia Districts and addressed to all Council Leaders and Field Constables of the districts of Nicosia and Kyrenia:

You are hereby informed that it is the duty of the Government to protect all crops located in dangerous areas which have been abandoned by the Turks. The unlawful grazing and harvesting of these crops must stop immediately and you are urged to undertake all necessary action towards this course. The Government is determined to protect these properties by all means and effective measures will be taken against any persons breaking the law.

This memo attests to the Greek Cypriot commitment to protect Turkish Cypriot rights in the agricultural sector, in support of general arrangements between the two communities. There was complete compliance with this directive.

Harvesting Escort Form. May 1964
Linked to Appendix H. 12 May 1964

HQ NZ 5276-1

HEADQUARTERS NICOSIA ZONE

HARVESTING ESCORT REQUEST

1. Requesting Community:-GK/TK_____.

2. Village concerned:-_____.

3. MUKHTAR or Representative:-_____.

4. Area of HARVEST:-_____.

5. Type of CROP:-_____.

6. Date of Commencement:-_____.

7. Estimated time for completion:-_____.

8. Harvesting team a. Combines:-_____.

                    b. Lorries :-_____.

                    c. Men   :-_____.

9. Rendevous for Escort and Harvestors:-_____.

10. Time of RV:-_____.

11. REMARKS:-_____

_____

_____

_____

_____.

Signature:.....................

12. Remarks by HQ NIC ZONE:-_____

_____

_____

_____

_____.

13. Unit Notified:-_____. DATE COMPLETED_____.

Signature:........................

This form covers the provision of support for 1964 harvesting in disputed and abandoned areas. The arrangements, implemented under JPO supervision, were everywhere effective.

Freedom of Movement Agreement. 15 May 1964

UN SECRET

M E M O R A N D U M

HQ NZ 2390-2

HQ NICOSIA ZONE
CYPRUS, 16 May 64

Freedom of Movement
NICOSIA ZONE

1.   For a number of reasons travel by TK CYPS into and out of NICOSIA on roads under the control of GK CYP security forces has now virtually ceased. It must be accepted that under the present circumstances TK CYPS will NOT resume travelling merely through force of verbal persuasion. It is also apparent that this lack of movement is, in certain areas:

    a.   considerably heightening tension and increasing the risk of outbreaks of local violence;

    b.   creating major local problems of an economic and social nature.

2.   As a purely temporary measure, UN patrols will at certain fixed times each week accompany those wishing to travel between NICOSIA and certain outlying areas.

3.   All escorts will be of section strength comd by an offr mounted in a minimum of two vehs. The schedule at Annex A details timings, villages and the unit responsible for escort.

4.   TK CYP civilians ONLY will be permitted to travel under these arrangements. Prior to travel each village will be briefed by Cdr PACKARD who will ensure the following points are clearly understood:

    a.   NO one known to be on the GK CYP GOV list of wanted persons should travel;

    b.   NO weapons, ammunition or illegal matter or documents of any sort are to be carried;

    c.   prior to departure all those travelling agree to submit to properly authorized searches under UN observation;

    d.   all vehicles and persons are to be legally documented.

5.   Agreement has been received from the GK CYPs on the following points:

    a.   there will be one search only on each trip; on the occasion of the search a certificate will be issued which will provide inviolability to further searches on that journey;

    b.   searches by GK CYP police will be carried out at fixed points under the observation of UN police.

6.   UN patrols will treat any attack upon persons or vehicles being accompanied under these arrangements as an attack upon themselves.

(ADM Matheson) Maj
GSO 2 (OPS)
HQ NICOSIA ZONE

Not to be confused with the agreement of 6 January, these measures had long been sought by patrol officers but were only instituted by UNFICYP after Famagusta abductions in May 1964. Escort arrangements were organised and administered by the JPO and had immediate major effect. (See pp. 286-287)

APPENDIX K

Escort Programme. 16 May 1964
Linked to May 1964 Freedom of Movement Agreement. See Appendix J.

ANNEX A
TO HQ NZ 2390-2
Dated 16 May 64

ESCORT OF TK CYP

All trips will depart first named village at 0800B.
All return trips will leave KYRENIA GATE NOT later than 1600B.

Serial	Unit Responsible	Day of Week	Villages	Comment
1.	26 MED REGT	MON and FRI	KOCHATI and LOUROUJINA	PETROPHANI may join if required. Escort to pick up bus at 0715B at KYRENIA GATE, and go to KOCHATI via NISOU. LO at Dr KUCHUK Residence to provide veh reg no and dvr's name direct to 26 MED REGT.
2.	1 FORESTERS (DANISH CONT wef date to be advised)	TUE and SAT	MORA	AYIA KEBIR, APHANIA to RV at CHUMLEKJI CHIFLIK.
3.	1 FORESTERS (DANISH CONT wef date to be advised)	MON and FRI	BEY KEUY	EPIKHO, PETRA TOU DHIYENI, KOUKOU MONASTIR, KALYVAKIA to RV at BEY KEUY.
4.	YKSP 1	TUE and SAT	AYIA IRINI and KAMBYLI	Escort will pick up vehs from KYRENIA GATE at 0700B. LO at Dr KUCHUK to provide veh reg nos and dvr's name direct to YKSP 1.
5.	1 R22eR	As required	KAZAPHANI TEMBLOS KYRENIA	To be arranged by CO 1 R22eR with village concerned. Minimum requirement one trip weekly.

This is one element of the regional Escort Programme organised by me in May 1964, which made a profound impact on the rural areas. It was terminated by General Carver on 9 June 1964 with very adverse effect. (See pp. 324-326)

Poster circulated after the disappearance of Major Macey and driver Platt. 8 June 1964.
(See pp. 323-325)

Guardian Article. 12 June 1964

Cyprus trouble-shooters by Peter Preston

TODAY two British United Nations officers, Lieutenant - Commander Martin Packard and Major John Burgess, will leave Cyprus and their work as liaison officers because of fears for their safety after the disappearance of Major Edward Macey. In Cyprus "Packard's Patrol" is already something of a legend; but a legend that has received little attention.

Martin Packard is a slight, dark, quiet man who first came to Cyprus six months ago from a naval intelligence post in Malta. He speaks Greek fluently, has a Greek wife, and knows the Greek way of thinking. He passed out from Dartmouth, and his father is vicar of a small village—Sandford St Martin—deep in the green of Oxfordshire, but Packard has served in Korea and seen the world; traditional attitudes are buried far below the surface.

John Burgess seems his complete antithesis—short, rotund, florid, open—the bluff kind of Briton who crops up on travel posters behind a side of roast beef. He was working with the territorial side of his regiment, the Queen's Royal Surreys, in Guildford, when he was whipped out to Cyprus almost overnight.

Together they made a perfect and formidable team. Packard plumbing the obscure depths of Greek Cypriot reasoning, Burgess exuding common sense and stalwart dependability for Turkish Cypriot consumption. While they were embroiled in the intricacies of Cyprus, it was difficult to write about their rôle. Too much excitement in the British press soon sparks the virulent, baseless sort of Cypriot newspaper campaign which has surrounded Major Macey's tragic disappearance.

It is ironical that fears for their safety should have brought the decision that they should leave Cyprus, for they have both lived on the razor-edge of disaster ever since first setting foot on the island. The poky bungalow they shared was plumb in the middle of the Nicosia "Green line" between Turkish and Greek positions. Most mornings breakfast began with coffee, toast, and Bren gun fire screaming overhead. It was a dull week if they missed being shot at.

Packard's original tripartite patrol—with a Greek and a Turkish army officer—was one of four set up in January during the early, bloody days of the crisis. They had a simple brief: go out, meet the people, stop fighting starting and, if this fails, negotiate.

Blinkered

Packard knew little of Cyprus, but he learned very quickly, and he learned as his patrol drove into mixed villages, to understand the complete, blinkered subjectivity of both sides. His Greek officer could seldom conceive that Greek Cypriot villagers were responsible for any trouble; his Turkish officer merely talked to the Turkish Cypriots and swallowed what he was told whole.

He learned how patchwork truces—like the many he erected at Kazaphani, near Kyrenia—could collapse time and again at the clap of an antique shotgun; how trust could evaporate at the scream of a newspaper headline. He learned rapidly to spot the early signs of violence—wrangles over water rights, rising anger because Turkish sheep had grazed Greek grass, puffing pride in some backwater of a village which felt that it, too, should be allowed to fight and win eternal glory.

People learned from him as well. Packard met many high officials in the Greek and Turkish administrations — the men who in theory controlled events, who in practice often seemed swept along by them. None of these ruling cliques would venture beyond Nicosia; they relied purely on what their men in the field told them, which was usually garbled beyond belief. Packard, however, had been to villages that Ministers had never heard of and uncovered root grievances and crimes that they sometimes refused to credit. It was significant that Greek Cypriot chains of information appeared suddenly to be shaken into some kind of order.

When the United Nations took over, the tripartite patrols had to be stopped. Packard, however, now joined by Major Burgess, was allowed to carry on. They led a hectic and hair-raising existence, one day chugging from village to village, chatting with the mukhtar, arranging food convoys for Lefka or a school bus to Epikho, the next in the firing line.

At Pakhyammos, a tiny Greek village in the north-west hills, Burgess stood alone for hours on a bridge waving a big UN flag while Greeks revved an armoured bulldozer a few feet away, howling threats, and Martin Packard toiled to restrain the Turks. The Pakhyammos effort did not work immediately. "More bullets flew around up here than they did in any hour I can remember in Korea," said Burgess. A lot flew at the peace patrol, which had to escape up a mountain gully which, their ancient guide assured them, was quite safe because "all shots go at least six inches over the top of your heads."

The next day, though, they achieved something. Burgess persuaded the Turkish mukhtar to come with them and talk together into the open and into another flurry of bullets, repaired that fiasco; a tenuous truce was built around Kokkina and Pakhyammos, which still holds today, many weeks later.

Two stories summed up the whole business. Once Packard entered a Greek Cypriot village and met bitter hostility; then he began to speak and understand how no one could understand the Greek cause who did not feel it in his heart. It was a fine harangue and afterwards an old man came up with tears in his eyes and said: "Ah, Commander, you are the only one who understands us."

Potato patch

It was different after Pakhyammos. As, finally, the last round of negotiations was sealed and the hamlet saved from attack, a shrivelled Greek elbowed through a maze of sten guns and shook his fist in Packard's face. "British scum," he bayed. "You have trampled all over my potato patch."

Packard and Burgess were like one of those juggling teams who spin dozens of plates on a long table. They will be replaced, but nobody can replace their contacts and experience. Some of the plates will fall and shatter. And Cyprus without Major Macey and Packard's patrol must lurch on; an island where even the peacemakers are murdered.

Order for the Cessation of my Liaison Activities.

```
ROUTINE.        1107182.

FROM            CBFC

TO              CINCMED

INFO            UNNICYP (BNNLO).


CONFIDENTIAL.    RTT 533.

1.  FOLLOWING RECEIVED FROM COMBRITCON UNCICYP

        " IN VIEW DISAPPEARANCE MACEY HAVE DECIDED CANNOT LET
        LIEUT. COMMANDER PACKARD CONTINUE FACE SIMILAR RISKS.
        HAVE THEREFORE MOST RELUCTANTLY ORDERED HIM TO CEASE
        HIS MOST VALUABLE LIAISON ACTIVITIES".

2.  LT. CDR. PACKARD HAS DONE AN EXCELLENT JOB IN CYPRUS AND AM SORRY
TO SEE HIM GO.

3.  INTEND PACKARD RETURN MALTA MEDAIR 19 JUN.

        1107182.

CONFIDENTIAL.
```

Recommendation for Leave.

```
PRIORITY        1517302

FM              NAVAL ATTACHE ATHENS

TO              C IN C MED

INFO            MOD NAVY.


CONFIDENTIAL

I HAVE JUST SEEN LIEUTENANT COMMANDER PACKARD, RECENTLY FROM
CYPRUS, WHO SAYS HE IS SUPPOSED TO REPORT BACK TO MALTA ON THURSDAY

2.  THE CHARGE D'AFFAIRES AND I BOTH GOT THE IMPRESSION THAT HE IS
EXTREMELY TIRED AND OVERWROUGHT AND BADLY IN NEED OF A REST.  HE HAS
OF COURSE, BEEN WORKING CONTINUOUSLY IN THE MOST TRYING CIRCUMSTANCES
FOR OVER FIVE MONTHS, WITHOUT LEAVE.


3.  WHILE I UNDERSTAND FROM HIM THAT HIS FUTURE IS UNDER
CONSIDERATION, I STRONGLY RECOMMEND THAT HE BE GIVEN SOME
LEAVE IN ORDER TO RECOVER.

        1517302

        CONFIDENTIAL
```

2-MED.14/128/1

Commonwealth Relations Office,
Downing Street,
London, S.W.1.

23rd November 1964.

Dear Packard,

I hope this will reach you before you leave for Malta.

All I really have to say is "thank you". I hope that I have in fact already said this adequately, but I thought I ought to put on record my gratitude, and that of my colleagues, for the admirable report you have made of your work in Cyprus. It is a fascinating story of a unique operation, and will be of great value, for a long time to come.

As you know, we shall shortly be submitting the report to the Ministry of Defence on your, and John Burgess's, behalf.

I have also written a letter of thanks to Burgess.

Yours sincerely,

(C.S. PICKARD)

Lt.-Cdr. M.H. Packard, R.N.,
The Vicarage,
Sandford St. Martin,
Nr. Oxford.

Immediately after Pickard had written this letter to me all copies of the report 'disappeared'.

M. SAIT SEPICI   İZMİR

My Dear Commander Packard

I received recently your 18th December dated letter after Two months through Cyprus.

I am not in Cyprus now. Last year, the end of October I came back to Turkey. Now I am supply officer (S-4) for 70th infantry battle group at İzmir.

Believe me I have never forgotten you. So you know our friendshipness came out from troubles in Cyprus. The job as a liaison officer was really hardest one. It is impossible to forget our common memories.

You were brave and brilliant officer in your complicated duty. When I was with you always I trusted you. You had done your best as a man for humanity.

You are absolutely right. Still did not come out any good solutions for Cyprus. As you know the other side never accepted any negotiation. If they wish to talk ar negotiate on every subject with sincerly I hope we will get a miracle result. This will be happen in near future. Maybe this is my illusion.

I should very much like to keep in touch with you.

With every good wish for the future and Warmest regards

Letter to me from Major Sait Sepici, of the Turkish army, written after he left Cyprus. He had been highly effective as a mediating officer within my unit.

NOTES

INTRODUCTION

1. The so-called Acheson Plan of 1964, like the later Annan Plan (See note 10 below), was developed through a number of stages. Its authors, US Secretary of State Dean Acheson and Under Secretary of State George Ball, proposed a NATO solution for Cyprus. Ball's memoirs note: "The issues were clear enough. Cyprus was a strategically important piece of real estate at issue between two NATO partners: Greece and Turkey. We needed to keep it under NATO control."

    The plan went through various distinct versions. The nub of the proposal was that a substantial area of the Karpas peninsula be granted to Turkey for use as a military base; that the remainder of Cyprus be united with Greece, after the island's division into eight cantons, of which two would be administered by the Turkish Cypriots; and that Greece would cede to Turkey the island of Kastellorizo.

    The first version of the plan was accepted by Turkey as a basis for negotiation, but rejected by Makarios as being partitional and by Greece on the grounds that no ceding of Greek territory to Turkey would be accepted by parliament.

    The final version, which proposed that any territory granted to the Turkish army be by way of a 25-year lease, was accepted in principle by Greece but eventually rejected by Ankara, on the grounds that nothing less than full Turkish sovereignty over the proposed base in the Karpas peninsula would be acceptable. Rejection was confirmed by the Turkish Foreign Minister, Feridun Erkin, in a letter to Dean Acheson: the date of this letter, 28 August 1964, marks the rejection of compromise by Turkey and the ending of the 'Acheson process'. Subsequent mythology has represented non-acceptance by Makarios of the Acheson formula as an opportunity missed by him, whereas in fact the ultimate rejection of the plan came from Ankara.

2. TMT (*Turk Mukavemet Teskilati* - Turkish Resistance Organisation). From 1943 (a time when Ankara was indifferent to Cyprus) a political organisation, KATAK, was, according to Turkish Cypriot historians, encouraged by the British as a balance against Greek Cypriot agitation for *enosis*. An armed adjunct of the Turkish Cypriot leadership (*Volkan*) was formed in 1945, reportedly also with occasional British support. This was replaced in January 1958 by a secret paramilitary organisation, TMT, founded by the Turkish army, with the approval of the Ankara government and in co-operation with Rauf Denktash. TMT also was originally conceived as a counterweight to EOKA, a safeguard against any move towards *enosis* and a promoter of *taksim* (partition) as the proper alternative to British colonial rule. It became a medium for the projection of Turkish military strength into Cyprus. The original target was for the arming of a force of 10,000 men, many of whom were expected to be former

members of the British army or of the special police units formed by the British in the battle against EOKA. The initial development of TMT was tolerated by the British army, which saw it as a potential ally: only in 1958 was it proscribed, after violent inter-communal clashes. Its continuing activity after Cypriot independence was seen by the Greek Cypriots as a threat to the cohesion of Cyprus and a barrier to the popular wish for *enosis*. In the period after 1960 TMT built up a broader organisation, The Turkish Fighters, to act as an armed reserve (See note 9 below and note 31/1 for British support of TMT).

3. *Enosis* (union) was the concept of Cyprus uniting with Greece. Considered by its proponents as a natural progression from the earlier incorporation into Greece of other areas with a large Greek-speaking majority (i.e. Crete in 1913 and the Dodecanese Islands in 1947), there were at least three occasions (in 1907, 1914 and 1940) when Britain appeared ready to adopt this option.

   Enosis was particularly supported by the Greek Orthodox Church and by right wing activists. In a 1950 census 96 per cent of Greek Cypriots (who composed 80 per cent of the population of Cyprus) professed themselves to be *enosis* supporters.

   'Double-*enosis*' was the concept of a simultaneous union of part of the island with Greece and part with Turkey.

   Enosis was one element of the *megali idea* (See note 7/2).

4. See Noam Chomsky 'Failed States', pp. 143-4, with references there to original sources.

5. Sheepskin/SWD - The 'Stay-behind' network. During the Cold War, a major element of NATO contingency planning against the perceived threat of Soviet expansionism involved the establishment across Europe by US/UK intelligence agencies of a network of sleeper cells, or 'Stay-behind' units. These were financed, armed and trained in covert resistance activities, including assassination, political provocation and disinformation. They were supposed to be activated only in the event of Soviet invasion or serious internal threat from elements sympathetic to Moscow, but tended to become self-motivated and then to pursue local right-wing objectives. Knowledge of their existence was concealed from all but an inner circle of the intelligence community. The network as a whole is often referred to as 'Gladio', which was the Italian branch of the organisation. Local members were selected on the basis of their anti-leftist credentials. This led to alliance with former Nazis in Germany, with former members of 'X' or *tagma asphaleias* in Greece (where the organisation was known as 'Sheepskin'), and with Grey Wolves in Turkey (where the network came under the SWD - the Special War Department).Still cloaked in secrecy to the present day, the first public glimpse into this organisation came when terrorist activities in Italy in 1972 were ascribed to a Gladio cell, acting on local initiative (See p. 5 footnote). In Cyprus it appears that units were established within the Greek Cypriot community as an adjunct of Sheepskin and within the Turkish Cypriot community as an adjunct of the SWD and that they fell under the remit of Polycarpos Georgadjis and Rauf Denktash respectively. Both

would have been directed against the strong leftist presence in Cyprus, which was regarded by UK/US intelligence agencies as a particular threat to NATO interests.

Daniele Ganser, in "NATO's Secret Armies: Operation Gladio and Terrorism in Western Europe". Frank Cass: 2005, likens the Stay-behind operation in Western Europe with the Brezhnev Doctrine in Eastern Europe, with each embodying a hidden strategy to manipulate and limit the sovereignty of friendly states. He writes: *"The strategic rationale to protect NATO from within cannot be brushed aside lightly. But the manipulation of the democracies of Western Europe by Washington and London on a level which many in the European Union still today find difficult to believe clearly violated the rule of law.../...Tragically the secret warriors linked up with right-wing terrorists, a combination that led – in some countries including at least Belgium, Italy, France, Portugal, Spain, Greece and Turkey – to massacres, torture, coups d'etat or other violent acts. Most of these state-sponsored terrorist operations, as the subsequent cover-ups and fake trials suggest, enjoyed the encouragement and protection of selected highly placed governmental and military officials in Europe and in the United States."*

6.   Tassos Papadopoulos, a lawyer by profession, was elected President of Cyprus in 2003. An EOKA leader during the Greek Cypriot struggle for independence, he was a delegate at the London Conference in 1959, when he and the AKEL delegate cast the only votes against signing the London and Zurich Agreements. Highly regarded by Archbishop Makarios, he was appointed at the age of 26 to be Minister of Labour and Social Security in the first post-independence government. During my time in Cyprus he also held the posts of Minister of Health and acting Minister of Agriculture.

7.   EOKA (*Ethniki Organosis Kyprion Agoniston* - National Organisation of Cypriot Fighters) was a Greek Cypriot armed resistance movement, formed in 1955 under the leadership of Colonel George Grivas (See note 1/6) following declarations by the British government that independence for Cyprus was to be barred in perpetuity. The declared objectives of EOKA were for the ending of British rule and the achievement of *enosis*. Over the four years of the EOKA insurgency six hundred people were killed (including 156 British servicemen) and over twelve hundred injured, most of them Greek Cypriots.

8.   Radio *Bayrak* broadcast from the Turkish Cypriot sector of Nicosia, starting at Christmas 1963. It became the main disseminator of news to the Turkish Cypriot community and an essential part of the push for communal separation. Surprisingly, TMT seems previously to have had no suitable equipment and the initial transmitter was assembled in part from components hastily collected from the public.

9.   There is considerable evidence of interface between TMT and UK intelligence agencies during the 1950s. In 1963 regular Turkish army officers arrived clandestinely in Cyprus to take command of Turkish Cypriot paramilitaries, a move that the Greek army paralleled in January 1964. A BBC Radio 4 programme in January 2006 offered first-time testimony that in 1963/4 there

was direct British involvement in the smuggling of Turkish weapons and personnel into Cyprus and in the delivery of support to TMT, including the provision of weapons, training, covert transportation and tactical advice (See note 31/1).

10. The UN's so-called Annan Plan, for resolution of the Cyprus problem, evolved through five different texts. Up to Annan III the proposal was subject to negotiations with the Cypriots: it was generally acceptable to the Greek Cypriots but rejected by Denktash and his army supporters in Turkey. The final proposal, Annan V, radically changed to satisfy the wishes of the Turkish army, was not made subject to Greek Cypriot or Turkish Cypriot negotiation. Its apparent objective was to secure a deal, of any sort, in advance of Cypriot accession to the EU, in such formula as would help to decriminalise Turkey's position in Cyprus and ease Turkey's path to EU accession.

Clare Palley was a legal advisor to the UN process. It has been written that no one reading her exhaustive documentation of events and statements relating to Annan V could fail to be convinced "that the rush to force a settlement on the Greek and Turkish Cypriots in 2004 was motivated and executed with deceit, stupidity and flagrant disregard for the sovereignty and freedom of peoples."

11. Christopher Hitchens in 'Hostage to History', p 164.

CHAPTER 1

1. The Sovereign Bases (SBAs) were ceded to Britain under the terms of the 1960 constitution, comprising a total area, principally at Akrotiri and Dhekelia, of 99 square miles. Additionally, Britain acquired special rights covering freedom of movement and of armed response if British lives or property were deemed to be under threat. The arrangement was a compromise, British military and intelligence leaders having insisted up to 1959 that the execution of their assigned mission would require that the whole of Cyprus remain under British control.

2. Stavros Kostopoulos, the brother of my father-in-law's best man, was Foreign Minister in the centrist 1963 government of George Papandreou and a family friend. Admiral Toumbas, Deputy Minister of Defence in that same government, was another close family acquaintance.

3. Janissaries were elite members of the Turkish infantry. They often were specially recruited Greek Christians, trained by the Ottomans to provide a personal guard for the sultans.

4. The Ottoman Millet administrative system defined the two communities on the basis of religion, with taxation and administrative matters handled through religious channels and each group treated as a distinct entity. The Ottoman occupiers restored the Orthodox Church of Cyprus with this system in mind. This separation of Greek Cypriots and Turkish Cypriots cemented ethnic identities. The system was modified, but not wholly abolished, under British rule.

5. See Spiros Vryonis' The Mechanism of Catastrophe. 'The Turkish Pogrom of September 6-7, 1955 and the Destruction of the Greek Community in Istanbul.' which on pp 27-98 documents the connection between Turkish domestic politics, Cyprus and the pogrom.

6. George Grivas was a Cypriot-born officer in the regular Greek army. Always a royalist, from early in his career he became a ferociously committed anti-communist. During the German occupation of Greece, from 1940-1944, he was active in the underground resistance. He came to believe that left-wing resistance organisations would in the long term pose a greater threat to his concept of Hellenism than did the Germans: he therefore became prominent in the formation of the extreme right-wing 'X' organisation, which was prepared to co-operate with the occupying forces to secure the defeat of the left-wing resistance organisation, EAM, and its adherents.

    Grivas returned again to Cyprus in June 1964 (See p. 229). Published US accounts say that this was with the support of the CIA, which saw value in him as a wholly committed anti-leftist and as a counterweight to President Makarios. Thereafter he was central to the formation of 'EOKA B', an anti-Makarios movement devoted to the achievement of *enosis*, whose primary linkage was to the Greek intelligence service and to irredentist right-wing groups in Greece.

    Grivas distrusted the leaders of the 1967 military *coup d'etat* in Greece, seeing them as inept, divisive and anti-monarchist. Nevertheless, he was working with them, in preparing for a *coup d'etat* against Makarios, when he died in January 1974.

7. The Macmillan Plan was offered in June 1958 after violent clashes and population-movements in Cyprus, demonstrations in Istanbul and a Turkish government demand for partition. The plan aimed to safeguard the British position in Cyprus but allowed for internal self-government with 'functional partition', with each community having autonomy over its own affairs. It was delivered with a threat that a failure to accept it could result in an offer of self-determination to each community separately: at the same time Greece was privately warned that rejection might lead Britain to call in Turkey to take over the northern areas of the island. The plan was initially rejected by Turkey, as failing to provide immediate partition, but then accepted in a modified format in the belief that its proposed partnership would soon collapse and partition follow. The Greek Cypriots rejected the plan, recognising that it would preclude the development of a unitary state. Background manoeuvring over the plan heralded an increased US involvement in the island's affairs.

8. Makarios drafted 13 points on which he considered the constitution needed to be amended for the effective operating of the state. Although Dr Kutchuk, the Turkish Cypriot leader and Vice President, was prepared to discuss these, they were summarily rejected by Ankara. At the end of December 1963, Makarios suggested to Duncan Sandys that a unilateral imposition of these amendments might be necessary. Sandys advised that such a move would put the Greek

Cypriots in the wrong, whereas if the Turkish Cypriots withdrew unilaterally from government, as in fact they did, it would be they who were acting illegally.

9. Documents recently released by the FCO show that this was indeed the case, and that the British High Commissioner had even helped with drafting the proposals. This is well covered by Diana Markides in 'Cyprus 1957-1963 From Colonial Conflict to Constitutional Crisis.'

10. Archive material amplifies this position. At a critical meeting at the CRO in London on 27 September 1963, Sir Arthur Clark is quoted as saying, with reference to Turkey; "It would suit them if the archbishop did attempt to change the constitution unilaterally. The resulting clash would help them to carry out their plan for partition of the island. In these circumstances it is vital that we should dissuade the Greek Cypriots from taking unilateral action; we must also persuade the Turkish Cypriots to negotiate. If we fail, one side or the other would take precipitate action and bloodshed would follow. We should suffer as a result of this since the use of our bases would be jeopardised and, if the matter was taken to the United Nations, we might well be blamed." At the same meeting D.S.L. Dodson of the Foreign Office said that the British government should: "...persuade the Turks that some modifications in the constitution were essential. We might then be able to go on to persuade the Greek Cypriots to put forward reasonable proposals for modifications of the more troublesome provisions of the constitution. The British government might perhaps be in a good position to suggest modifications as a disinterested party. There might be a better chance of achieving settlement if we could fill the role of 'honest broker'."

CHAPTER 2

1. The trigger for armed confrontation was an incident on the night of 21 December. Greek Cypriot suspicions that armed action was planned by TMT led to the searching of Turkish Cypriot cars in Nicosia, aimed at hampering the movement of weapons. TMT ordered that such searches should be resisted. The stopping of a car in the red light district led to an angry response from bystanders, police shots and two deaths.

   General Carver's memoirs "Out of Step" note his belief that confrontation at Christmas 1963 was deliberately provoked by TMT to pre-empt an intention of Makarios to bring about an enforced amendment of the constitution in mid-1964.

2. Polycarpos Georgadjis was Minister of the Interior in the first government after independence: he thereby had control of the police, the gendarmerie and Cypriot intelligence mechanisms. A former EOKA leader under General Grivas, with a record of arrest and imprisonment by the British army, he had a very strong following among the EOKA rank and file. With advice from Greek army and intelligence officers, Georgadjis was primary author of the Akritas Plan: supposed to be a blueprint for the achievement of *enosis*, sections of this

document that dealt with the defeat of armed Turkish Cypriot resistance were construed by some commentators as genocidal. He also was executive head of 'The Organisation' (See note 7/3). He had contacts with, and received funding from, US/UK intelligence organisations, which regarded him as a major anti-communist asset.

3. ELDYK; TURDYK. Under the 1960 constitution, Greece and Turkey were entitled to maintain small military contingents in Cyprus. The Greek army contingent, ELDYK, had a strength of 900 men and that of Turkey, TURDYK, 650 men.

4. The contention of ELDYK involvement in the fighting in Omorphita has been attested to me by some eye witnesses but is rejected in official accounts. Greek Cypriot paramilitary leaders apparently argued for such intervention, as did members of KYP, the Greek intelligence service. General Young told me that part of the Greek contingent moved out of its barracks on 24 December, but then returned on 26 December at his request. It is possible that there was limited involvement on 24-25 December by a number of Greek soldiers, perhaps acting without official sanction.

5. I was later told by Makarios' secretary, Tasos Panayides (who subsequently had appointments as High Commissioner in London and Head of the Foreign Office), that Makarios had come bitterly to regret this lost opportunity and to see it as a moment of crucial error.

6. In his book 'From the East', Costas Yennaris claims to have compelling Turkish testimony that the murderer was in fact a temporarily deranged Turk, and not a Greek Cypriot. A British intelligence assessment at the time was that the killings were arranged by TMT in order to provoke an involvement of TURDYK or to provide Ankara with an excuse for intervention. Whatever the truth, the corpses were used by Turkey and TMT, as in other incidents later, to generate international condemnation of the Greek Cypriots.

7. Nicos Sampson, a fervent former member of EOKA, who was credited by the British with numerous assassinations during the 1950s emergency, and Vassos Lyssarides, Archbishop Makarios' personal physician, organised 'private' paramilitary groups. It is probable that Makarios saw these as a potential counter-balance to the power of the Minister of the Interior, Polycarpos Georgadjis (See note 2 above), who was the main organiser of secret Greek Cypriot paramilitary forces, under the umbrella of 'The Organisation' and the Akritas Plan, and who commanded the loyalty of most ex-EOKA militants.

8. The island was delineated by peacekeeping forces into three zones: Western, Nicosia and Eastern. These were sometimes referred to as Paphos, Nicosia and Larnaca Zones. The largest, Nicosia Zone, ran from Pomos Point to the eastern Karpas peninsula and from Kyrenia to Famagusta. For operational purposes Nicosia Zone was sometimes further subdivided, with the Famagusta area considered as a sub-zone. TMT and 'The Organisation' each had its own zonal boundaries.

CHAPTER 3

1. Rauf Denktash, deputy to Turkish Cypriot leader Fazil Kutchuk and reputedly political leader of TMT, was generally regarded as the strong-man of his community, as the key proponent of partition and as the counterpart of Georgadjis. I next met him thirty-six years later. He claimed to remember our first meeting well and said I would recall that in 1964 his real target was for a federal solution, not for partition, although the threat of partition was the bludgeon. But there was no way, he said, then or now, that he was going to discuss a federal settlement until his people had real security and an equality of negotiating status, and the form of any federation would depend on the degree to which mutual trust had been re-established. This claim sits curiously with Denktash's long term involvement with the "Cyprus is Turkish" association and is belied by most of his public statements. Greek Cypriots, for their part, say that Denktash is a wily negotiator and a classic mover of goalposts, and decline to believe that his targets ever lay anywhere but with partition.
2. Sadly, however, the Freedom of Movement Agreement of 6 January 1964 was soon being disregarded by paramilitaries in both communities. The Turkish Cypriots, according to General Young, were the initial culprits. They made no move to open the Kyrenia road, and JF, after an initial demand on 7 January 1964 that they do so, which was ignored, made no serious effort to oblige them to comply. The Greek Cypriots used this as one explanation for their imposition of roadblocks elsewhere and for their conviction as to British bias.

CHAPTER 4

1. Spyros Kyprianou. I did not meet the Kyprianou family again that year. Later I was told that after my visit to his relatives Cavadias had spread word in Athens that I was *philotourkos* (a friend of the Turks).
2. It was never made clear to me what the 'principle' was that caused JFHQ to reject the concept of an escort programme to cover areas where there was a clear danger on the roads. Makarios was initially reluctant to accept the proposal, on the grounds that it was opposed by his police advisers and was an infringement of Cypriot sovereignty, but did so when it became apparent that hostage-taking was continuing in defiance of his orders. (See note 17/1).
3. The media. Reporting in most of the Cypriot press tended to be lurid, alarmist and subjective. *I Makhi* (The Battle) was a rightist paper owned by Nicos Sampson.

CHAPTER 5

1. Maronites are Syrian Christians by origin. Together with the Armenians they constituted about 2 per cent of the Cypriot population. For the most part they were concentrated in a few villages, or sectors of villages, in northwest Cyprus.

2. Subsequently 21 bodies were exhumed from a site near Ayios Vasilios but it transpired that most of these were from other areas (See also story re General Hospital p 194). The story of the killings in Ayios Vasilios itself, as later relayed to me, was that the Turkish Cypriot villagers had mostly evacuated during the night of 24 December following abuse, threats and some shooting by armed Greek Cypriots. One large family refused to leave. Their house, which was assumed by the Greek Cypriots to contain arms, was surrounded, but its occupants refused to come out and surrender. In the darkness, the Greek Cypriots heard footsteps approaching, assumed it was an attack and opened fire, only to find that they had killed a grandmother and child who were trying to return to their home. Panicking, and hoping to cover up what had happened, they then threw grenades into the house and killed all of its occupants. Official documents note a total of thirteen Turkish Cypriots 'missing' in Ayios Vasilios on 24 December, of whom one was a visitor from Ayia Moni.

3. Major Ted Macey. For additional on Ted Macey see chapter 59.

Chapter 7

1. KYP (*Kentriki Yperisia Plyrophorion* – Central Intelligence Agency).

    KYP (*Kypriaki Yperisia Plyrophorion* – Cypriot Intelligence Agency).

    Confusingly for this narrative, the intelligence agencies of Greece and Cyprus had the same acronym, KYP (although the 'K' stands for Central in one case and Cypriot in the other). The two agencies had no direct connection or interface. KYP in Greece had been organised by the CIA and in 1964 was still under CIA oversight.

    When he came to Power in late 1963, Greek Prime Minister George Papandreou, according to his close circle, discovered that his own intelligence agency, KYP, was in fact reporting directly to the CIA and that he himself was only receiving reports that had first been vetted by US intelligence advisers. The issue became a prime element in friction between Papandreou and the palace, which had aligned itself closely with US policy. This friction led to Papandreou's ousting by the king, under US advice, and the subsequent political instability which culminated in the April 1967 overthrow of democratic government in Greece, in a *coup d'etat* led by members of the Greek intelligence community.

2. The *megali idea* (the Great Concept) represented the dream of Greek irredentists to recover into a single Hellenic entity all of the territories where there was a Greek-speaking majority or where Athens had once held sway. In their view, the latter provision covered both Constantinople and much of Anatolia. In reality, Cyprus was the only predominantly Greek-speaking region that they could hope to see achieving *enosis*. It was the constitutional barriers, and Turkish and Turkish Cypriot opposition, that Greek Cypriot *enotists* sought to overturn.

Proponents of the *megali idea* were few in number and mostly to be found in the Greek army, the Greek Orthodox Church and extreme right-wing groupings in Greece and Cyprus, but their continued use of the phrase was claimed by Turks to justify a hostility to Greece. *Megali Idea* had its parallels in Turkey with the irredentists and Pan-Turkism and 'Cyprus-is-Turkish' movements.

3.   The Organisation'. (See Appendix D for structure). In 1963 each community forecast that a paramilitary attack against it would be launched within a year. The same conclusion was reached in British intelligence assessments, which originally expected a clash to come in mid-1964. The Turkish Cypriots already had a strong paramilitary structure in TMT and the associated 'Turkish Fighters'. EOKA, on the other hand, had not survived as an organised force, although many of its former members had been enrolled in 'private' paramilitary groups, which were known about and tolerated by the Greek Cypriot political leadership. Fear of Turkish intentions and determination to keep open the option of *enosis* led on the one hand to the drafting of the Akritas Plan and on the other to a decision to create an island-wide, centrally-controlled, wholly Greek Cypriot structure, 'The Organisation', which would provide an effective sub-surface mechanism and oversee the formation of a co-ordinated armed Greek Cypriot force (See note 4 below).

4.   The co-ordinated Greek Cypriot paramilitary force, formed under the aegis of 'The Organisation', was generally referred to by JF as The 'Secret Army', and that term is used throughout this narrative. In June 1964, it would be transformed into the National Guard. (In the meantime it was sometimes also referred to as 'The Organisation' or as the 'Akritas Army'.) From January 1964 it absorbed the major 'private' paramilitary groups and Greek Cypriot appointees to the Cyprus Army, the completion of whose formation had been blocked by disagreement between Makarios and Kutchuk. A number of army officers arrived clandestinely from Greece in January 1964 to take command positions. Initially weapons were made available from stocks secretly stored under the President's control, or passed on by ELDYK or smuggled in from Greece. An island-wide training network was established.

CHAPTER 8

1.   Hostage-taking. During the first half of 1964, paramilitaries in both communities continued, despite a prohibition in the agreement of 28 December, occasionally to seize hostages. By far the greater number seized were Turkish Cypriots, usually under a claim that they were suspected of TMT connections. Greek Cypriot authorities for some time kept alive the myth that about thirty Greek Cypriots, missing since the December fighting, were still alive and being held by Turkish Cypriots as hostages, although the police had learned through informers that most or all were dead. (p. 291.) This was sometimes used as justification for the continued holding of a larger number of Turkish Cypriots. Following the Turkish Cypriot seizure of Greek Cypriot

police officers in the Chappas building there was an exchange of hostages on 7 March which saw the release of most of those centrally held. Thereafter there were some further instances, usually related to local frictions, but in most cases those seized were soon released.

CHAPTER 10

1. Police structures. Until re-organised later in 1964, the overall policing structure had a three way split. The police were responsible for city and municipal areas; the gendarmerie had overall responsibility for rural areas; and special village constables, operating within the District Officer structure, were responsible for the functioning of the water system and the observance of grazing boundaries. The 1960 constitution specified that manning of the police and gendarmerie should be on a 70:30 ratio between Greek Cypriots and Turkish Cypriots. From Christmas 1963 Turkish Cypriot officers ceased to participate in the national police and gendarmerie forces: from then on the *de facto* position was of two wholly separate forces, with those of the Greek Cypriots seeking to implement an island-wide control and those of the Turkish Cypriots operational only in areas to which Greek Cypriot units had no access. There was no similar splitting of the village constable element: as part of the re-engagement package, organised by Tassos Papadopoulos, central funds were distributed by my patrol to Turkish Cypriot rural constables.

2. Text of the Akritas Plan is quoted in full in 'My Testimony' by Glafcos Clerides. Its existence and contents were explained in some detail to me by Greek Cypriot leaders soon after the start of the mediating process, with the claim that its drafting was initiated when it became apparent that the 1960 constitution was likely to prove unworkable. I was told that it was a 'defensive' measure in response to the threat of an insurgency that was being planned by TMT, with the cognisance of both Kutchuk and Denktash, as well as a potential blueprint for the achievement of a majority-sought *enosis* in the event of armed opposition from TMT.

   I was told that Georgadjis was principal author of the plan, assisted by Greek army and intelligence officers, but that it had been approved by President Makarios and the other main 'Organisation' leaders, Glafcos Clerides and Tassos Papadopoulos.

   The Akritas Plan was matched by a similarly militant TMT master-plan (the text of which also is quoted in the memoirs of both Clerides and Souliotou), whose aim was to defend the Turkish Cypriot community, while initiating a process of ethnic separation and creating circumstances which would demand intervention by the Turkish army. Each plan assumed that the initial phase would require an armed response to attack by the other community.

3. Georgadjis - Gladio. It is now generally believed that Georgadjis oversaw arrangements and control of the local Sheepskin network (See note I/5). For this he would have qualified by convincing US/UK intelligence agencies of his

anti-communist credentials. This would have put him indirectly into a NATO line-of-command, with Denktash similarly placed within the Turkish Cypriot community through his linkage with Ankara's Special War Department.

4. Some of these divisions were later to be reflected in the schism between pro-Makarios loyalists and EOKA B, the anti-Makarios organisation formed by Grivas and Greek army officers in order to pursue the aim of *enosis*. EOKA B's attempted *coup* against Makarios in 1974 provided Ankara with an excuse for the Turkish army to seize control of large areas of sovereign Cypriot territory.

CHAPTER 17

1. JFHQ policy had evolved from meetings of Duncan Sandys with Makarios and Kutchuk in late December. It was supposed to deliver an even-handed provision of peacekeeping support to the Cypriot population. JFHQ (and later UNFICYP HQ) continued to embargo the provision of escorts until May. Tripartite and Joint Patrol Officers considered that the absence of an escorts programme was extremely damaging to their efforts to achieve communal re-engagement. The general policy quickly came to be reviled in both communities: by the Turkish Cypriots because British forces provided them with no real protection from attack (as was proved at Ayios Sozomenos in February) and by the Greek Cypriots because the Green Lines created and patrolled by the British army provided a shield behind which TMT could pursue its separatist targets.

CHAPTER 19

1. This invasion scare coincided with the breakdown of the 15-24 January London Conference, which had been arranged by the British government as a follow-up to the agreement brokered by Duncan Sandys on 28 December. It was slightly out of synch with press and JFHQ reports of a major invasion threat on 28/29 January.

CHAPTER 20

1. Wherever may have been directed their subsequent sympathies, both Augustis and Makrides, with whom I had a friendly and productive association, appeared at this time to be strongly supportive of Makarios' policies for communal re-integration and prepared to clash openly with those Greek Cypriot extremists who opposed them.

CHAPTER 25

1. See also note 1/7 re Macmillan Plan.

2. For background on Arthur Clark's support for Makarios' efforts to amend the constitution see Diana Markides' 'Cyprus 1957-63 - Form Colonial Conflict to Constitutional Crisis ' and William Mallinson's 'A Modern History of Cyprus'. p 35 & 108 and note 13. Further verification of this support, and the British government's efforts to deny it, was provided for me by Cyril Pickard's private 1964 correspondence with Duncan Sandys.

3. Crete. In 1821 47% of the Cretan population were Muslims, although many of these were Greek-speaking converts. By 1900 the percentage was down to 11%. After enforced population changes resulting from the 1927 Treaty of Lausanne, by 1928 there were no Muslims left in the island.

4. 'Secret Army". See notes 7/3 and 7/4.

CHAPTER 26

1. See pp. 194-195 concerning events at the General Hospital.

2. In this they had little success, as almost all TMT fighting strength had concentrated in the cities. Most of the Turkish Cypriots who were seized had only a tenuous link with TMT, if any.

CHAPTER 28

1. Reminiscing later about this incident, it occurred to me that Major Sepici must have over-ruled the 'Sancaktar', the army officer secretly infiltrated from Turkey as regional commander in its covert organisational structure. He was known to the Turkish Cypriots only by this *nom de guerre*. Overall command was held by a general, as 'Bayraktar'. I had been told that the Nicosia Zone *Sancaktar* had arrived in early 1963, with deep cover as an Ishrak Bank employee.

CHAPTER 29

1. For comment on this event see 'Spycatcher' by Peter Wright: Viking Penguin Inc NY; 1987; pp 368-377.

2. Cyril Pickard was Assistant Under Secretary of State at the CRO from 1962 1966 and regarded there as destined for high position in the Foreign Service. He was temporarily seconded to be Acting High Commissioner in Cyprus for the early months of 1964. He subsequently served as High Commissioner in Pakistan from 1966 to 1971. He died in 1992.

CHAPTER 30

1. Force Alpha was a helicopter-borne rapid-deployment unit constituted by General Carver for application to situations of crisis. Lacking interpreters, it was not particularly relevant to events in Cyprus, which required an increased

mediating input rather than a more dynamic application of British military force.

CHAPTER 31

1. One British serviceman, LAC Marley, was arrested by the Greek Cypriot police while acting for TMT in the delivery of weapons which had been landed clandestinely from Turkey on the Tillyria coast. Handed over to the British authorities, he was court-martialled in the UK and given a long prison sentence but then quickly released. Archive material shows that other UK personnel were identified by the British authorities as involved in similar activities: they were quickly removed from Cyprus and the matter hushed up. Some light was shed on these activities when a BBC Radio 4 programme on 27 January 2006 revealed that in 1963 and 1964 TMT had been provided by elements of the British military and intelligence services with direct and significant support, in the form of weapons, training and tactical advice.
2. Geunyeli Incident. In a notorious incident, on 12 June 1958 at the height of inter-communal friction ahead of the Macmillan Plan and following a TMT escalation of sectarian violence, British troops punished 35 unarmed Greek Cypriot civilians by obliging them to walk home cross-country past the Turkish Cypriot village of Geunyeli. There they were set upon by Turkish Cypriots; eight of them were murdered and five seriously injured.
3. Brigadier Dimitrios Ioannides was US-trained and regarded by the CIA as a prime asset. He was later to become the 'hard man' in the military junta which seized power in Greece in 1967. In November 1973 he led the ousting of the other *coup* leaders (Papadopoulos, Pattakos and Makarezos) and then proceeded with final planning for the *coup d'etat* against Makarios, for which he claimed to have specific US backing. The CIA head of station in Athens is claimed to have boasted that he used Ioannides to orchestrate events in Cyprus.
4. One such later plot by precisely this group was the 21 April 1967 overthrow of democratic government in Greece.
5. This remark was to be curiously echoed in 1967 when King Constantine of Greece, talking to me in Rome after the failure of his attempted counter-*coup*, expressed his bitterness with the British and Americans. "I only ever did what they asked me to do, and look how they betrayed me."

CHAPTER 33

1. There were two subsequent occasions when the movement of TMT leaders in British ambulances came to my notice. At the time I assumed the missions were legitimate.

CHAPTER 34

1. A reference by me to the original Georgadjis story was included by the *Guardian* in a story 'Hope that Britain Destroyed' carried in its 2 April 1988 issue. This was picked up by Ankara and used as the basis for a Turkish *demarche* to the UN Secretary General, claiming that it provided evidence of Greek Cypriots' true intentions. When I learned soon afterwards that the story was almost wholly untrue, I wrote immediately to the Secretary General asking that my refutation be given the same circulation and publicity as had Ankara's submission.

2. One such officer was Colonel, later General, George Karoussos, whom I came to know many years later. He arrived in Cyprus clandestinely from Athens on 6 January and took command of various Greek Cypriot paramilitary groups. Later he returned to Cyprus as Athens-nominated deputy-commander of EOKA B. He assumed command on the death of Grivas in January 1974 but was then arrested by the Greek military junta for refusing to authorise finalisation of planning for the intended *coup* against Makarios.

CHAPTER 39

1. Before I had received a reply from Tassos Papadopoulos the facts emerged of another, more serious, incident in the area (See pp. 224-225 re killings at Liveras).

2. Similar difficulty was faced in other states, such as Algeria, where independence, or liberation from foreign occupation or dictatorship, followed an armed struggle and where post-independence leadership, needing to implement centrist policies, found itself in conflict with former militants who felt their struggle had been betrayed.

3. Alternatively the story given me could have been designed to put a more flattering spin on a *fait accompli*, in which a return of Grivas had been imposed by Athens, with CIA encouragement.

CHAPTER 44

1. With hindsight, one could see this as another window of opportunity quickly closed. Instead of exploiting a critical chance for change, Cyprus was to be preserved in limbo, to the harm of both communities, until some external event would move the situation closer to a solution acceptable to Whitehall and Washington, perhaps akin to that formulated by Acheson/Ball.

CHAPTER 45

1. See note I/9 and note 31/1 for British complicity in the illegal transport of arms and personnel for TMT.

2. The Swedish UN contingent which became responsible for the area refused to give permission for my patrol to accept the invitation.

3. Turkey responded to the 6 August attack by launching its air force against Greek Cypriot positions in northern Tillyria on 8-9 August, with considerable loss of life, and by sinking a Greek Cypriot gunboat off the Tillyria coastline.

CHAPTER 46

1. The 'Vingt Deux' consisted for the most part of French-speaking Quebecois. It quickly came to be regarded as belligerently anti-British and pro-Greek Cypriot, whereas other Canadian units were taken to be pro-Turkish Cypriot.

CHAPTER 47

2. As explained to me, TMT's 'Doomsday Plan' involved the instigation of armed action throughout Cyprus, in the expectation that this would trigger massive Greek Cypriot retaliation, leading to military intervention from Turkey.

CHAPTER 48

1. *Vide* UN security Council Resolution 186 of 4 March 1964.

2. The British High Commission in Nicosia had little success in trying to play this role single-handedly, since British intentions were wholly distrusted by the Greek Cypriots, who viewed the UK as unqualified to act as honest broker. No attempt was made to establish in Nicosia an effective tri-partite mediating entity, on the lines that had proved so successful in the rural areas.

3. Kurt Janssen was a talented and effective head of the UN Mediating Mission. He reported to the Secretary General's special representative in Cyprus, who at this point was Senor Galo Plaza, a former president of Ecuador.

CHAPTER 50

1. Pantelides and the two Greek officers from ELDYK were killed in Famagusta on 11 May having, probably inadvertently, entered the Turkish Cypriot held Old City. 32 Turkish Cypriots were subsequently abducted from the roads of Famagusta Zone and never seen again. The claim in General Carver's memoirs that the total of those abducted was twelve is inaccurate.

2. Rural Constables (See note 10/1) were part of the rural administrative structure and not part of the police or gendarmerie forces.

CHAPTER 52

1. Recently released reports from Turkish Cypriots claim that Gibbons was killed by TMT, on suspicion of intelligence-gathering.

CHAPTER 55

1. In the BBC Radio 4 programme of 27 January 2006 (See note I/9) a villager in Photta, who said that he had been local Turkish Cypriot paramilitary commander in 1964, had clear recollection of the incident. Asked what would have happened if the sheep had not been returned, he said: "We would have seized twice as many Greek sheep."

CHAPTER 59

1. Interview of Field Marshal Lord Carver with Peter Murtagh, quoted in article by him in the *Guardian* dated 2 April 1988.
2. Much later General Karoussos (See note 34/2) told me that he had reached the area just after the killings.
3. The explanation given was that Macey was known to be actively assisting TMT in its efforts to promote partition.
4. Later, when interviewed by Peter Murtagh, then researching for his book 'The Rape of Greece', Carver advanced various alternative contentions as to why he had me removed, one being that I had seduced the affections of Galo Plaza's girlfriend. (The lady concerned described this allegation as grotesque.)
5. Colonel Folke told me that his subsequent mediating initiatives were consistently undermined by UN peacekeeping contingents. After one such incident he was removed from Cyprus after a trumped-up allegation of having been drunk on duty. He told me that he was successful in a consequential legal action in the Swedish courts against the commander of Sweden's UNFICYP contingent.

CHAPTER 60

1. Greek intelligence officers were prime covert movers in Cypriot affairs in the 1960s. The Greek army, on the other hand, had from the beginning of January appeared a consistent opponent of extremism in Cyprus and a supporter of the restitution of central political control; the same went for those individual Turkish army officers who worked with me.
2. A close friend in the Greek navy was commanding a patrol-boat that had been privately donated to the Greek Cypriots. When the boat was sunk by the Turkish air-force off Mansoura during the August attack he was severely wounded. When I tried to get in touch with him, without any thought but a wish to help, he was told by his naval command that he must avoid any contact with me. Apparently it was believed in Athens that I might be part of a devious British plan to deliver him to the United Nations as evidence of a duplicitous Greek involvement in Cyprus.
3. The JIC has ultimate responsibility to the British government for the gathering, collation, analysis and assessment of intelligence and for the formulation of contingency plans.

4. For Pickard see note 29/2.
5. Francis Noel-Baker was a Labour MP with substantial land holdings in Greece. He was his party's expert on Greek and Cypriot affairs.
6. Peter Preston occasionally accompanied me on patrol. He amazed me by the speed with which he fathomed the most abstruse and devious elements in Cypriot affairs.
7. To my surprise it appears that some of my subsequent missives to Farnhill did get into official files. A Greek newspaper (*Eleftherotypia*) published in 2000 an analysis of archive material recently released by the British Foreign Office covering correspondence between Whitehall and the British embassy in Athens. The paper commented that nowhere in all this correspondence was there any sign of a real understanding of the situation in Greece in advance of the 1967 military *coup*, apart from one single item. That was a private report by a Lieutenant Commander Packard. The paper noted that a copy of the report had been sent by the Foreign Office to the British ambassador for his comment, and that its observations had been peremptorily rejected by him. This was the same ambassador who in 1967 responded to my vehement rejection of his allegation that my wife and her family were communist (they were actually pro-British Venizelist centrists) by saying: "Well, they may not actually be communists but they are anti-monarchists, and as far as we are concerned that's the same thing."
8. This was the so-called '*Aspida* Plan', in which documents delivered to Greece appeared to prove that the Prime Minister's son, Andreas Papandreou, had been involved in attempts to create a left-wing cell within the Greek army.

BIBLIOGRAPHY

There exists a huge variety of books, reports and articles which relate to the history and problems of Cyprus. The list that follows covers some of my own reading. Those interested in a more comprehensive bibliography should refer to the World Bibliographical Series of Clio Press (Oxford & Santa Barbara): its 28th volume covers Cyprus in an original (1982) and a revised (1995) edition, compiled by Paschalis Kitromilides and Marios Evriviades.

Acheson, Dean. 'Cyprus: The Anatomy of the Problem.' *Chicago Bar Record*, vol. 46, No 8: May 1965.

Alasya, Halil Fikret. *The Republic of Cyprus and the Events that have come to Pass*, Ankara: Ayyildiz Matbaasi, 1969.

Attalides, Michael. *Cyprus. Nationalism and International Politics*, Q Press, 1979.

Bahceli, Tozun. *Greek-Turkish Relations since 1955*, Westview Press, London, 1985.

Ball, George. *The Past Has Another Pattern*, W. W. Norton & Co. London, New York, 1982.

Beckingham, C.F. 'Islam and Turkish Nationalism in Cyprus'. *Die Welt des Islams. N.s.* vol. 5, No. 1-2. 1957.

Birand, M.A. *30 Hot Days*, Rustem, Istanbul, 1985.

_____ *The General's Coup in Turkey: An Inside Story of 12 September 1980*, Brassey's Defence, London, 1987.

Carver, Gen. Michael. *Out of Step*, Hutchinson, London, 1989.

Chomsky, Noam. *Failed States. The Abuse of Power and the Assault on Democracy*, Hamish Hamilton; Penguin Books, London, 2006.

Clerides, Glaucos. *Cyprus: My Deposition*, Volumes 1 & 2, "Alithia", Nicosia, 1989.

Cook, Steven. *Ruling but not Governing: The Military and Political development in Egypt Algeria and Turkey*. John Hopkins University Press, Baltimore 2007.

Coufoudakis, Van. 'US Policy and the Cyprus Question: An Interpretation.' *Millennium: Journal of International Studies*. vol. 5, No. 3. 1976.

_____ 'Cyprus. A Contemporary Problem in Historical Perspective.'

Crawshaw, Nancy. 'Cyprus: a failure in Western diplomacy.' *The World Today*: vol. 40, No. 2. Feb 1984.

_____ *The Cyprus Revolt: An Account of the Struggle for Union with Greece*, George Allen & Unwin, London. 1978.

Curtis, Mark. *Web of Deceit: Britain's Real Role in the World*, Vintage, 2003

Denktash, Rauf. *The Cyprus Triangle*, Rustem, London, 1988 rev. ed.

_____ 'The Problem of Cyprus.' *Review of International Affairs*. vol. 22, No 544. 1972.

Drousiotis, Makarios. *EOKA B and the CIA*, Alphadi, Nicosia, 2002.

_____ *Eoka: The Dark Side*, Staxy, Athens, 1988.

Durrell, Laurence. *Bitter Lemons*.

Eden, Anthony. *Full Circle*, Houghton Miflin, Boston, 1960.

Ertogun, Necat. *The Cyprus Dispute*, Rustem, Nicosia, 1984.

Evriviades, Marios. The US and Cyprus: The Politics of Manipulation in the 1985 U.N. Cyprus High Level Meeting, Panteion University, Athens, 1992.

_____ 'Greek Policy and Cyprus: an interpretation.' *Journal of the Hellenic Diaspora*, vol. XIV, 1987.

_____ 'The Problem of Cyprus.' *Current History*, vol. 70, No. 412, 1976.

Faltas, Sami and Jansen, Sander, Editors, *Governance and the Military: Perspectives for Change in Turkey*. Centre of European Security Studies (CESS) Groningen, 2006.

Feroz, Ahmad. *The Making of Modern Turkey*, Rutledge, London, 1993

Foley, Charles. *The Struggle for Cyprus*, Hoover Initiative Press, 1975.

_____ *The Memoirs of George Grivas*, Fr. Praeger, NY, 1965.

Foot, Hugh. *A Start in Freedom*, Hodder & Stoughton, London, 1964.

Foot, Michael. *Quietly Men 1957: Suez + Cyprus*, Rinehart & Co, 1957.

Foot, Paul. *Who Framed Colin Wallace?*, Pan Books, 1990.

Galo Plaza. 'Report of the UN Mediator on Cyprus to the Secretary General.' *UN Security Council Official Records*, Supplement. Doc. S/6253, 1965.

Ganser, Daniels. *NATO's Secret Armies. Operation Gladio and Terrorism in Western Europe*, Frank Cass, London, 2005.

Hale, William. Turkish Politics and the Military. Routledge, London 1994.

Hitchens, Christopher. *Hostage to History*, Noonday Press, New York, 1989.

_____ 'Détente and Destabilisation: Report from Cyprus.' *New Left Review*, 1975.

Holland, Robert. *European Decolonisation, 1918-1981: An Introductory Survey.* Macmillan, London, 1985.

_____ *Britain and the Revolt in Cyprus 1954-1959.* Clarendon Press, Oxford, 1998.

_____ 'Greek - Turkish Relations, Istanbul and British Rule in Cyprus, 1954-59: Some Excerpts from the British Public Archive'. *Bulletin of the Centre for Asia Minor Studies vol. 10, 1993-1994*

_____ 'Never, Never Land: British Colonial Policy and the Roots of Violence in Cyprus 1950-54'. In *Emergencies and Disorder in the European Empires after 1945*, edited by Robert Holland. London, Frank Cass, 1994

Hughes, James. 'The Cypriot Labyrinth.' *New Left Review No 29*, 1965.

James, Alan. *'Keeping the Peace in the Cyprus Crisis of 1963-64.'* Palgrave 2001

Karpat, Kemal H. *Turkey's Foreign Policy in Transition 1950-1974*, E.J.Brill, Leyden. 1975.

Kyriakides, Klearchos A. 'Cyprus after the Suez Campaign: The Perceived Strategic Significance of the island and its Military Bases to Britain, 1956-1960'. M.Phil. diss. University of Cambridge, 1992.

Lanitis, N.C. *'Our Destiny.'* Nicosia, 1963.

Macmillan, Harold. *Riding the Storm, 1956-1959.* Macmillan, London, 1971.

Mallinson, William. *A Modern History of Cyprus*, I B Taurus, London, 2005.

Markides, Diana. *Cyprus 1957-196: From Colonial Conflict to Constitutional Crisis*, Minnesota, 2001.

Markides, Diana & Holland, Robert. *The British and the Hellenes*, Oxford University Press, 2006.

Mayes, Stanley. *Makarios: a biography*, St Martin's Press, New York, 1981.

Murtagh, Peter. *The Rape of Greece*, Simon & Schuster, London, 1994.

O'Malley, Brendan and Craig, Ian. *The Cyprus Conspiracy. America, Espionage and the Turkish Invasion*, I B Taurus, London, 1999.

Ozbudun, Ergun. *The Role of the Military in Recent Turkish Politics*, Cambridge 1966

Palley, Claire. *An International Relations Debacle: The UN Secretary General's Mission of Good Offices in Cyprus 1999-2004*, Hart Publishing, Oxford & Portland, Oregon, 2005.

Polyviou, Polyvios G. *Cyprus: Conflict and Negotiation 1960-1980*, Duckworth, London, 1980.

Reddaway, John. *Burdened with Cyprus: The British Connection*, Weidenfeld & Nicolson, London, 1986

Richter, Heinze A. *Geschichte der Insel Zypern*, Volume I, 1878-1949, Bibliopolis Möhnesce, 2004. Volume II, 1950-1959 Bibliopolis Möhnesce, 2006. Volume III 1959-1965, Rutzen Verlag, Ruhpolding, 2007

Souliotou, Stella. *Fettered Independence: Cyprus, 1878-1964*, Volumes 1 & 2, Minnesota, 2006

Stegenga, James A. *The United Nations Force in Cyprus*, Ohio State University Press, 1968.

Stephens, Robert. Cyprus, a Place of Arms: Power, Politics and Ethnic Conflict in the Eastern Mediterranean, Pall Mall, London, 1966.

Stern, Laurence. 'Bitter Lessons: How We Failed in Cyprus.' *Foreign Policy*, No. 19, 1975

_____*The Wrong Horse: The Politics of Intervention and the Failure of American Diplomacy*, Times Books, New York, 1977.

US House of Representatives. 'U.S. Intelligence Agencies and Activities. Hearings and proceedings: parts 1-6', *Select Committee on Intelligence*', US Government Printing Office, 1975-76.

Venizelos, Ignatiou, Meletis. Annan Plan: The Secret Auction. The 129 Days that Rocked Hellenism, Livani, Athens, 2005.

Vryonis, Spiros. The Mechanism of Catastrophe. The Turkish Pogrom of September 6-7, 1955 and the Destruction of the Greek Community in Istanbul, Greek Works, 2005

Weintal, Edward and Bartlett, Charles. *Facing the Brink*, Charles Scribner's Sons, NY, 1967

Windsor, Philip. 'NATO and the Cyprus Crisis.' Institute for Strategic Studies, London, 1964.

Yennaris, Costas. *From The East. Conflict and partition in Cyprus*. Elliot & Thompson, London, 2000.

INDEX

ABOUT THE AUTHOR

Martin Packard, the son of a country parson, joined the Royal Navy at the age of fourteen as a Dartmouth cadet. In 1950 he served on anti-opium patrols from Hong Kong and then in Korea for the first year of the war there. Later he trained in America as a Fleet Air Arm pilot and, after front-line carrier service, qualified as flying instructor. In 1956 he married Kiki Tsatsoulis, whom he had met in Greece while on a Navy assignment. In 1963 he was appointed to the NATO staff in Malta as an intelligence analyst, a title that led the uninformed to the mistaken supposition that he was part of the British Intelligence Service. From Malta he was seconded, as a Greek interpreter, to the staff of General Peter Young in Cyprus. The ensuing months provide the material for this book.

After a proposal for his permanent transfer to the UN he read Arabic at Durham University, but the seizure of power by the army in Greece led to his involvement, in support of his family and friends there, in their struggle against dictatorship. Demands by the Foreign Office that he be court-martialled, for interference in politics, were rejected by the Admiralty, which instead approved his retirement at the age of 36.

Joining the textile business of his wife's family in Greece, he took the agency for Levi Strauss, for which he set up a factory in Kalamata. In 1975 he was asked by Karamanlis to help counter a CIA demand for an enhanced presence in Greece. This led to his categorisation as a CIA target and a period of extreme harassment.

A family introduction led to friendship with Dom Mintoff, at whose request he set up a Levi's factory in Malta and assessed possibilities for the establishment there of a new University of the Mediterranean. He again ran foul of the CIA when asked for advice in the face of foreign efforts to destabilise the Mintoff government. In the meantime his Malta factory had become a major supplier of jeans-wear to the Soviet Union.

When USSR buying was cut in 1986 because of a hard-currency shortage, he was told in Moscow of the changes to come in five years and asked, under sponsorship of the USSR Olympic Committee, to assess and develop opportunities for linkage between Russian and EU companies. The outcome was a $2 billion per year trade proposal to run through Malta. This led to him being approached by a bevy of US agents, told he was damaging Washington's plans for a comprehensive destruction of the Soviet economy and asked to terminate the proposal.

Packard's history is one of principled motivation running into the buffers of virulent opposition from those who wanted to manipulate events for their own interests.

Lightning Source UK Ltd.
Milton Keynes UK
UKOW03f0016021014

239466UK00004B/136/P